5th Linguistic Annotation Workshop 2011

(LAW V)

Held at ACL HTL 2011

Portland, Oregon, USA
23-24 June 2011

ISBN: 978-1-61839-240-4

Printed from e-media with permission by:

Curran Associates, Inc.
57 Morehouse Lane
Red Hook, NY 12571

CURRAN ASSOCIATES INC. proceedings.com

Some format issues inherent in the e-media version may also appear in this print version.

Printed by Curran Associates, Inc. (2011)

Association for Computational Linguistics
209 N. Eighth Street
Stroudsburg, Pennsylvania 18360

Phone: 1-570-476-8006
Fax: 1-570-476-0860

acl@aclweb.org

Additional copies of this publication are available from:

Curran Associates, Inc.
57 Morehouse Lane
Red Hook, NY 12571 USA
Phone: 845-758-0400
Fax: 845-758-2634
Email: curran@proceedings.com
Web: www.proceedings.com

Introduction

The Linguistic Annotation Workshop (The LAW) provides a forum to facilitate the exchange and propagation of research results concerned with the annotation, manipulation, and exploitation of corpora; work towards the harmonization and interoperability from the perspective of the increasingly large number of tools and frameworks for annotated language resources; and work towards a consensus on all issues crucial to the advancement of the field of corpus annotation. Although this year's LAW is officially the fifth edition, LAW itself is the convergence of several previous workshops-including NLPXML, FLAC, LINC, and Frontiers in Corpus Annotation-dating back to the first NLPXML in 2001. This series of workshops attests to the rapid developments in the creation and use of annotated data in both language technology and empirical approaches to linguistic studies over the past 10 years.

We received a sizeable number of papers this year. A total of 37 submissions were received. After careful review, the program committee accepted 10 papers and 11 posters. One of the papers selected for oral presentation was withdrawn later, leaving the total of full papers to 9. Selection of the papers was not an easy task, as the papers cover the full range of linguistic facts and their corresponding annotation frameworks, from predicate-argument to discourse structure, speech to social networks, and learner corpus to CVs. The papers also deal with a range of annotation levels, from the macro perspective on infrastructure for international collaboration and interoperability, to the micro perspective on tools to deal with inter-annotator inconsistencies. It is this richness of the topics that attest to the growing maturity of field. This year we tried a slightly different approach where we allowed the posters to be full length papers and have a ten minute talk associated with each.

We would like to thank SIGANN for its continuing endorsement of the LAW workshops. We would also like to thank the the ACL workshop co-chairs John Carroll and Hal Daume III and the publication chair Guodong Zhou for their support and help in producing the LAW V proceedings. Most of all, we would like to thank all our program committee members and reviewers for their dedication and helpful review comments. Without them, LAW V could not be implemented successfully.

Sameer Pradhan and Katrin Tomanek, Program Committee Co-chairs
Nancy Ide and Adam Meyers, Organizers

Workshop Organizers

Organizers:

Nancy Ide, Vassar College
Adam Meyers, New York University

Organizing Committee:

Sameer Pradhan (Program Co-chair), BBN Technologies
Katrin Tomanek (Program Co-chair), Friedrich-Schiller-Universität Jena
Chu-Ren Huang, The Hong Kong Polytechnic University
Antonio Pareja-Lora, Universidad Complutense de Madrid
Massimo Poesio, University of Trento
Manfred Stede, Universitat Potsdam
Nianwen Xue, Brandeis University

Program Committee:

Collin Baker	ICSI/University of California, Berkeley
Pushpak Bhattacharyya	IIT Bombay
Nicoletta Calzolari	ILC/CNR
Richard Eckart de Castilho	Technische Universitt Darmstadt
Mona Diab	Columbia University
Tomaz Erjavec	Josef Stefan Institute
Alex Chengyu Fang	City University of Hong Kong
Christiane Fellbaum	Princeton University
Charles Fillmore	ICSI/UC Berkeley
Eduard Hovy	USC/ISI
Chu-Ren Huang	Hong Kong Polytechnic
Nancy Ide	Vassar College
Richard Johansson	Lund University
Aravind Joshi	University of Pennsylvania
Edward Loper	BBN Technologies
Adam Meyers	New York University
Antonio Pareja-Lora	Universidad Complutense de Madrid
Martha Palmer	University of Colorado
Massimo Poesio	University of Trento
Rashmi Prasad	University of Pennsylvania
Vasin Punyakanok	BBN Technologies
James Pustejovsky	Brandeis University
Manfred Stede	Universitt Potsdam
Nianwen Xue	Brandeis University

Table of Contents

Conference Program

Thursday, June 23, 2011

Thursday, June 23, 2011 (continued)

Session II:

14:00–14:10 *A Collaborative Annotation between Human Annotators and a Statistical Parser*
Shun'ya Iwasawa, Hiroki Hanaoka, Takuya Matsuzaki, Yusuke Miyao and Jun'ichi Tsujii

14:10–14:20 *Reducing the Need for Double Annotation*
Dmitriy Dligach and Martha Palmer

14:20–14:30 *Crowdsourcing Word Sense Definition*
Anna Rumshisky

14:30–14:40 *A scaleable automated quality assurance technique for semantic representations and proposition banks*
K. Bretonnel Cohen, Lawrence Hunter and Martha Palmer

14:40–14:50 *Proposal for an Extension of Traditional Named Entities: From Guidelines to Evaluation, an Overview*
Cyril Grouin, Sophie Rosset, Pierre Zweigenbaum, Karën Fort, Olivier Galibert and Ludovic Quintard

14:50–15:00 *Assessing the practical usability of an automatically annotated corpus*
Md. Faisal Mahbub Chowdhury and Alberto Lavelli

15:00–15:10 *Subjectivity and Sentiment Annotation of Modern Standard Arabic Newswire*
Muhammad Abdul-Mageed and Mona Diab

15:10–15:20 *Creating an Annotated Tamil Corpus as a Discourse Resource*
Ravi Teja Rachakonda and Dipti Misra Sharma

15:30–16:00 Coffee Break

Thursday, June 23, 2011 (continued)

Session III:

16:00–16:10 *A Gold Standard Corpus of Early Modern German*
Silke Scheible, Richard J. Whitt, Martin Durrell and Paul Bennett

16:10–16:20 *MAE and MAI: Lightweight Annotation and Adjudication Tools*
Amber Stubbs

16:20–16:30 *Empty Categories in Hindi Dependency Treebank: Analysis and Recovery*
Chaitanya GSK, Samar Husain and Prashanth Mannem

16:30–17:00 SIGANN task announcement

17:00–17:30 SILT challange annoncement

Friday, June 24, 2011

8:45–9:00 Opening

Session IV:

9:00–10:30 Poster Session

10:30–11:00 Coffee Break

11:00–11:30 *Annotating Events, Temporal Expressions and Relations in Italian: the It-Timeml Experience for the Ita-TimeBank*
Tommaso Caselli, Valentina Bartalesi Lenzi, Rachele Sprugnoli, Emanuele Pianta and Irina Prodanof

11:30–12:00 *Increasing Informativeness in Temporal Annotation*
James Pustejovsky and Amber Stubbs

12:00–12:30 *Discourse-constrained Temporal Annotation*
Yuping Zhou and Nianwen Xue

On the Development of the RST Spanish Treebank

Iria da Cunha
Institute for Applied Linguistics (UPF), Spain
Instituto de Ingeniería (UNAM), Mexico
Laboratoire Informatique d'Avignon (UAPV), France
iria.dacunha@upf.edu

Juan-Manuel Torres-Moreno
Laboratoire Informatique d'Avignon (UAPV), France
Instituto de Ingeniería (UNAM), Mexico
École Polytechnique de Montréal, Canada
juan-manuel.torres@univ-avignon.fr

Gerardo Sierra
Instituto de Ingeniería (UNAM), Mexico
gsierram@iingen.unam.mx

Abstract

In this article we present the RST Spanish Treebank, the first corpus annotated with rhetorical relations for this language. We describe the characteristics of the corpus, the annotation criteria, the annotation procedure, the inter-annotator agreement, and other related aspects. Moreover, we show the interface that we have developed to carry out searches over the corpus' annotated texts.

1 Introduction

The Rhetorical Structure Theory (RST) (Mann and Thompson, 1988) is a language independent theory based on the idea that a text can be segmented into Elementary Discourse Units (EDUs) linked by means of nucleus-satellite or multinuclear rhetorical relations. In the first case, the satellite gives additional information about the other one, the nucleus, on which it depends (ex. Result, Condition, Elaboration or Concession). In the second case, several elements, all nuclei, are connected at the same level, that is, there are no elements dependent on others and they all have the same importance with regard to the intentions of the author of the text (ex. Contrast, List, Joint or Sequence). The rhetorical analysis of a text by means of RST includes 3 phases: segmentation, detection of relations and building of hierarchical rhetorical trees. For more information about RST we recommend the original article of Mann and Thompson (1988), the web site of RST[1] and the RST review by Taboada and Mann (2006a).

RST has been used to develop several applications, like automatic summarization, information extraction (IE), text generation, question-answering, automatic translation, etc. (Taboada and Mann, 2006b). Nevertheless, most of these works have been developed for English, German or Portuguese. This is due to the fact that at present corpora annotated with RST relations are available only for these languages (for English: Carlson et al., 2002, Taboada and Renkema, 2008; for German: Stede, 2004; for Portuguese: Pardo et al., 2008) and there are automatic RST parsers for two of them (for English: Marcu, 2000; for Portuguese: Pardo et al., 2008) or automatic RST segmenters (for English: Tofiloski et al., 2009). Scientific community working on RST applied to Spanish is very small. For example, Bouayad-Agha et al. (2006) apply RST to text generation in several languages, Spanish among them. Da Cunha et al. (2007) develop a summarization system for medical texts in Spanish based on RST. Da Cunha and Iruskieta (2010) perform a contrastive analysis of Spanish and Basque texts. Romera (2004) analyzes coherence relations by means of RST in spoken Spanish. Taboada (2004) applies RST to analyze the resources used by speakers to elaborate conversations in English and Spanish.

We consider that it is necessary to build a Spanish corpus annotated by means of RST. This corpus should be useful for the development of a rhetorical parser for this language and several other applications related to computational linguistics, like those developed for other languages

[1] http://www.sfu.ca/rst/index.html

Proceedings of the Fifth Law Workshop (LAW V), pages 1–10,
Portland, Oregon, 23-24 June 2011. ©2011 Association for Computational Linguistics

(automatic translation, automatic summarization, IE, etc.). And that is what we pretend to achieve with our work. We present the development of the RST Spanish Treebank, the first Spanish corpus annotated by means of RST.

In Section 2, we present the state of the art about RST annotated corpora. In Section 3, we explain the characteristics of the RST Spanish Treebank. In Section 4, we show the search interface we have developed. In Section 5, we establish some conclusions and future work.

2 State of the Art

The most known RST corpus is the RST Discourse Treebank, for English (Carlson et al., 2002a, 2002b). It includes 385 texts of the journalistic domain, extracted from the Penn Treebank (Marcus et al., 1993), such as cultural reviews, editorials, economy articles, etc. 347 texts are used as a learning corpus and 38 texts are used as a test corpus. It contains 176,389 words and 21,789 EDUs. 13.8% of the texts (that is, 53) were annotated by two people with a list of 78 relations. For annotation, the annotation tool RSTtool [2] (O'Donnell, 2000) was used, with some adaptations. The principal advantages of this corpus stand on the high number of annotated texts (for the moment it is the biggest RST corpus) and the clarity of the annotation method (specified in the annotation manual by Carlson and Marcu, 2001). However, some drawbacks remain. The corpus is not free, it is not on-line and it only includes texts of one domain (journalistic).

For English there is also the Discourse Relations Reference Corpus (Taboada and Renkema, 2008). This corpus includes 65 texts (each one tagged by one annotator) of several types and from several sources: 21 articles from the Wall Street Journal extracted from the RST Discourse Treebank, 30 movies and books' reviews extracted from the epinions.com website, and 14 diverse texts, including letters, webs, magazine articles, newspaper editorials, etc. The tool used for annotation was also the RSTtool. The advantages of this corpus are that it is free and on-line, and it includes texts of several types and domains. The disadvantages are that the amount of texts is not very high, the annotation methodology is not specified and it does not include texts annotated by several people.

Another well-known corpus is the Potsdam Commentary Corpus, for German (Stede, 2004; Reitter and Stede, 2003). This corpus includes 173 texts on politics from the on-line newspaper Märkische Allgemeine Zeitung. It contains 32,962 words and 2,195 sentences. It is annotated with several data: morphology, syntax, rhetorical structure, connectors, correference and informative structure. Nevertheless, only a part of this corpus (10 texts), which the authors name "core corpus", is annotated with all this information. The texts were annotated with the RSTtool. This corpus has several advantages: it is annotated at different levels (the annotation of connectors is especially interesting); all the texts were annotated by two people (with a previous RST training phase); it is free for research purposes, and there is a tool for searching over the corpus (although it is not available on-line). The disadvantages are: the genre and domain of all the texts are the same, the methodology of annotation was quite intuitive (without a manual or specific criteria) and the inter-annotator agreement is not given.

For Portuguese, there are 2 corpora, built in order to develop a rhetorical parser (Pardo et al., 2008). The first one, the CorpusTCC (Pardo et al., 2008), was used as learning corpus for detection of linguistic patterns indicating rhetorical relations. It contains 100 introduction sections of computer science theses (53,000 words and 1,350 sentences). To annotate the corpus a list of 32 rhetorical relations was used. The annotation manual by Carlson and Marcu (2001) was adapted to Portuguese. The annotation tool was the ISI RST Annotation Tool[3], an extension of the RSTtool. The advantages of this corpus are: it is free, it contains an acceptable number of texts and words and it follows a specific annotation methodology. The disadvantage is: it only includes texts of one genre and domain, only annotated by one person.

The second one, Rhetalho (Pardo and Seno, 2005), was used as reference corpus for the parser evaluation. It contains 50 texts: 20 introduction sections and 10 conclusion sections from computer science scientific articles, and 20 texts from the on-line newspaper Folha de São Paulo (7 from the Daily section, 7 from the World section and 6 from

[2] http://www.wagsoft.com/RSTTool/

[3] http://www.isi.edu/~marcu/discourse/

the Science section). It includes approximately 5,000 words. The relations and the annotation tool are the same as those used in the CorpusTCC. The advantages of this corpus are that it is free, it was annotated by 2 people (they both were RST experts and followed an annotation manual) and it contains texts of several genres and domains. The main disadvantage is the scarce amount of texts.

The Penn Discourse Treebank (Rashmi et al., 2008)f for English includes texts annotated with information related to discourse structure and semantics (without a specific theoretical approach). Its advantages are: its big size (it contains 40,600 annotated discourse relations) allows to apply machine learning, and the discourse annotations are aligned with the syntactic constituency annotations of the Penn Treebank. Its limitations are: dependencies across relations are not marked, it only includes texts of the journalistic domain, and it is not free. Although there are several corpora annotated with discourse relations, there is not a corpus of this type for Spanish.

3 The RST Spanish Treebank

As Sierra (2008) states, a corpus consists of a compilation of a set of written and/or spoken texts sharing some characteristics, created for certain investigation purposes. According to Hovy (2010), we use 7 core questions in corpus design, detailed in the next subsections.

3.1 Selecting a Corpus

For the RST Spanish Treebank, we wanted to include short texts (finally, the average is 197 words by text; the longest containing 1,051 words and the shortest, 25) in order to get a best on-line visualization of the RST trees. Moreover, in the first stage of the project, we preferred to select specialized texts of very different areas, although in the future we plan to include also non-specialized texts (ex. blogs, news, websites) in order to guarantee the representativity of the corpus. We did not find a pre-existing Spanish corpus with these characteristics, so we decided to build our own corpus. Following Cabré (1999), we consider that a text is specialized if it is written by a professional in a given domain. According to this work, specialized texts can be divided in three levels: high (both the author and the potential reader of the text are specialists), average (the author of the text is a specialist, and the potential reader of that text is a student or someone interested in or possessing some prior knowledge about the subject) and low (the author of the text is a specialist, and the potential reader is the general public). The RST Spanish Treebank includes specialized texts of the three mentioned levels: high (scientific articles, conference proceedings, doctoral theses, etc.), average (textbooks) and low (articles and reports from popular magazines, associations' websites, etc.). The texts have been divided in 9 domains (some of them including subdivisions): Astrophysics, Earthquake Engineering, Economy, Law, Linguistics (Applied Linguistics, Language Acquisition, PLN, Terminology), Mathematics (Primary Education, Secondary Education, Scientific Articles), Medicine (Administration of Health Services, Oncology, Orthopedy), Psychology and Sexuality (Clinical Perspective, Psychological Perspective).

The size of a corpus is also a polemic question. If the corpus is developed for machine learning, its size will be enough when the application we want to develop obtains acceptable percentages of precision and recall (in the context of that application). Nevertheless, if the corpus is built with descriptive purposes, it is difficult to determine the corpus size. In the case of a corpus annotated with rhetorical relations, it is even more difficult, because there are various factors involved: EDUs, SPANs (that is, a group of related EDUs), nuclearity and relations. In addition, relations are multiple (we use 28). As Hovy (2010: 13) mentions, one of the most difficult phenomena to annotate is the discourse structure. Our corpus contains 52,746 words and 267 texts. Table 1 includes RST Spanish Treebank statistics in terms of texts, words, sentences and EDUs.

	Texts	Words	Sentences	EDUs
Learning corpus	183	41,555	1,759	2,655
Test corpus	84	11,191	497	694
Total corpus	267	52,746	2,256	3,349

Table 1: RST Spanish Treebank statistics

To increase the linear performance of a statistical method, it is necessary that the training corpus size grows exponentially (Zhao et al., 2010). However, the RST Spanish Treebank is not designed only to use statistical methods; we think it will be useful to employ symbolic or hybrid algorithms (combining symbolic and statistical methods). Moreover, this corpus will be dynamic, so we expect to have a bigger corpus in the future, useful to apply machine learning methods.

If we measure the corpus size in terms of words or texts, we can take as a reference the other RST corpora. Nevertheless, as Sierra states (2008), it is "absurd" to try to build an exhaustive corpus covering all the aspects of a language. On the contrary, the linguist looks for the representativeness of the texts, that is, tries to create a sample of the studied language, selecting examples which represent the linguistic reality, in order to analyze them in a pertinent way. In this sense and in the frame of this work, we consider that the size will be adequate if the rhetorical trees of the corpus include a representative number of examples of rhetorical relations, at least 20 examples of each one (taking into account that the corpus contains 3115 relations, we consider that this quantity is acceptable; however, we expect to have even more examples when the corpus grows). Table 2 shows the number of examples of each relation currently included into the RST Spanish Treebank (N-S: nucleus-satellite relation; N-N: multinuclear relation). As it can be observed, it contains more than 20 examples of most of the relations. The exceptions are the nucleus-satellite relations of Enablement, Evaluation, Summary, Otherwise and Unless, and the multinuclear relations of Conjunction and Disjunction, because it is not so usual to find these rhetorical relations in the language, in comparison with others. Hovy (2010: 128) states that, given the lack of examples in the corpus, there are 2 possible strategies: a) to leave the corpus as it is, with few or no examples of some cases (but the problem will be the lack of training examples for machine learning systems), or b) to add low-frequency examples artificially to "enrich" the corpus (but the problem will be the distortion of the native frequency distribution and perhaps the confusion of machine learning systems). In the current state of our project, we have chosen the first option. We think that, including specialized texts in a second stage, we will get more examples of these less common relations. If we carry out a more granulated segmentation maybe we could obtain more examples; however, we wanted to employ the segmentation criteria used to develop the Spanish RST discourse segmenter (da Cunha et al., 2011).

Relation	**Type**	**Quantity**	
		N°	**%**
Elaboration	N-S	765	24.56
Preparation	N-S	475	15.25
Background	N-S	204	6.55
Result	N-S	193	6.20
Means	N-S	175	5.62
List	N-N	172	5.52
Joint	N-N	160	5.14
Circumstance	N-S	140	4.49
Purpose	N-S	122	3.92
Interpretation	N-S	88	2.83
Antithesis	N-S	80	2.57
Cause	N-S	77	2.47
Sequency	N-N	74	2.38
Evidence	N-S	59	1.89
Contrast	N-N	58	1.86
Condition	N-S	53	1.70
Concession	N-S	50	1.61
Justification	N-S	39	1.25
Solution	N-S	32	1.03
Motivation	N-S	28	0.90
Reformulation	N-S	22	0.71
Otherwise	N-S	3	0.10
Conjunction	N-N	11	0.35
Evaluation	N-S	11	0.35
Disjunction	N-N	9	0.29
Summary	N-S	8	0.26
Enablement	N-S	5	0.16
Unless	N-S	2	0.06

Table 2: Rhetorical relations in RST Spanish Treebank

3.2 Instantiating the Theory

Our segmentation and annotation criteria are very similar to the original ones used by Mann and Thompson (1988) for English, and by da Cunha and Iruskieta (2010) for Spanish. We also explore the annotation manual for English by Carlon and Marcu (2001). Though we use some of their postulates, we think that their analysis is too meticulous in some aspects. Because of this, we consider that it is not adjusted to our interest, which is the finding of the simplest and most objective annotation method, orientated to the future development of a rhetorical parser for Spanish. To sum up, our segmentation criteria are:

a) All the sentences of the text are segmented as EDUs (we consider that a sentence is a textual passage between a period and another period, a semicolon, a question mark or an exclamation point; texts' titles are also segmented). Exs.[4]

[Éstas son las razones fundamentales que motivaron este trabajo.]

[These are the fundamental reasons which motivated this work.]

[Estudio de caso único sobre violencia conyugal]

[Study of a case on conjugal violence]

b) Intra-sentence EDUs are segmented, using the following criteria:

b1) An intra-sentence EDU has to include a finite verb, an infinitive or a gerund. Ex.

[Siendo una variante de la eliminación Gaussiana,] [posee características didácticas ventajosas.]

[Being a variant of Gaussian elimination,] [it possesses didactic profitable characteristics.]

b2) Subject/object subordinate clauses or substantive sentences are not segmented. Ex.

[Se muestra que el modelo discreto en diferencias finitas es convergente y que su realización se reduce a resolver una sucesión de sistemas lineales tridiagonales.]

[It appears that the discreet model in finite differences is convergent and that its accomplishment is to solve a succession of tridiagonal linear systems.]

b3) Subordinate relative clauses are not segmented. Ex.

[Durante el proceso, que utiliza solo aritmética entera, se obtiene el determinante de la matriz de coeficientes del sistema, sin necesidad de cálculos adicionales.]

[During the process, which only uses entire arithmetic, the determinant of the system coefficient matrix is obtained, without additional calculations.]

b4) Elements in parentheses are only segmented if they follow the criterion b1. Ex.

[Este año se cumple el bicentenario del nacimiento de Niels (Nicolás, en nuestro idioma) Henrik Abel.]

[This year is the bicentenary of Niels's birth (Nicolás, in our language) Henrik Abel.]

b5) Embedded units are segmented by means of the non-relation Same-Unit proposed by Carlon and Marcu (2001). Figure 1 shows this structure.

[En décadas precedentes se ha puesto de manifiesto,] [y así lo han atestiguado muchos investigadores de la terminología científica serbia,] [una tendencia a importar préstamos del inglés.]

[In previous decades it has been shown,] [and it has been testified by many researchers of the scientific Serbian terminology,] [a trend to import loanwords from English.]

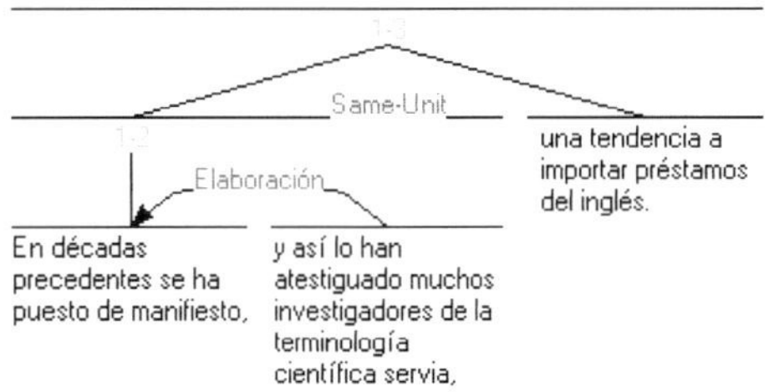

Figure 1: Example of the non-relation Same-Unit

3.3 Designing the Interface

The annotation tool used in this work is the RSTtool, since it is free and easy to use. Therefore, we preferred to use it instead of designing a new one. Nevertheless, we have designed an on-line interface to include the corpus and to carry out searches over it (see Section 4).

3.4 Selecting and Training the Annotators

With regard to the corpus annotators, we have a team of 10 people (last year Bachelor's degree students, Master's degree students and PhDs)[5]. Before the annotation, they took a RST course of 6 months (100 hours), where the segmentation and annotation methodology used for the development of the RST Spanish Treebank was explained.[6] We called this period "training phase". The course had a theoretical and a practical part. In the theoretical part, some criteria with regard to the 3 phases of rhetorical analysis (segmentation, detection of relations, and rhetorical trees building) were given to annotators. In the practical part, firstly, it was explained how to use the RSTtool. Secondly, annotators extracted several texts from the web, following their personal interests, as for example, music, video games, cookery or art webs. They segmented those texts, using the established segmentation criteria. Once segmented, all the doubts and problematic examples were discussed, and they tried to get an agreement on the most complicated cases. Thirdly, the relations were

[4] Spanish examples were extracted from the corpus. English translations are ours.

[5] We thank annotators (Adriana Valerio, Brenda Castro, Daniel Rodríguez, Ita Cruz, Jessica Méndez, Josué Careaga, Luis Cabrera, Marina Fomicheva and Paulina De La Vega) and interface developers (Luis Cabrera and Juan Rolland).

[6] This course was given in the framework of a last-year subject in the Spanish Linguistics Degree at UNAM (Mexico City).

analyzed (using a given relations list) and, once again, annotators discussed the difficult cases. After the discussion, texts were re-annotated to verify if the difficulties were solved. This process was doubly interesting, since it helped to create common criteria for the annotation of the final corpus and to define the annotation criteria more clearly and consensually, in order to include them in the RST Spanish Treebank annotation manual. Once annotators agreed on the most difficult cases, we consider that the training phase finished.

3.5 Designing and Managing the Annotation Procedure

We start from the following annotation definition:

> Annotation ('tagging') is the process of adding new information into source material by humans (annotators) or suitably trained machines. [...]. The addition process usually requires some sort of mental decision that depends both on the source material and on some theory or knowledge that the annotator has internalized earlier. (Hovy, 2010: 6)

Exactly, after our annotators internalized the theory and annotation criteria during the training phase, the "annotation phase" of the final texts included in the RST Spanish Treebank started. In this phase, the annotation tasks were assigned to annotators (the number of texts assigned to each annotator was different, depending on their availability). They were asked to carry out the annotation individually and without questions among them. We calculated that the average time to carry out the annotation of one text was between 15 minutes and 1 hour. This time difference is due to the fact that the corpus includes both short and long texts. The annotation process is the following: once a text is segmented, rhetorical relations between EDUs are annotated. First, EDUs inside the same sentence are annotated in a binary way. Second, sentences inside the same paragraph are linked. Finally, paragraphs are linked.

Hovy (2010) states that it is difficult to determine if, for the same money (we add "for the same time"), it is better to double-annotate less, or to single-annotate more. As he explains, Dligach et al. (2010) made an experiment with OntoNotes (Pradhan et al., 2007) verb sense annotation. The result was that, assuming the annotation is stable (that is, inter-annotator agreement is high), it is better to annotate more, even with only one annotator. The problem with RST annotation is that there are so many categories to annotate, that is very difficult to obtain a stable annotation. Therefore, we consider it is necessary to have at least some texts double-annotated (or even triple-annotated), in order to have an adequate discourse corpus. This is the reason why, following the RST Discourse Treebank methodology, we use some texts as learning corpus and some others (from the Mathematics, Psychology and Sexuality domains) as test corpus: 69% (183 texts) and 31% (84 texts), respectively. The texts of the learning corpus were annotated by 1 person, whereas the texts of the test corpus were annotated by 2 people.

3.6 Validating Results

Da Cunha and Iruskieta (2010) measure inter-annotator agreement by using the RST trees comparison methodology by Marcu (2000). This methodology evaluates the agreement on 4 elements (EDUs, SPANs, Nuclearity and Relations), by means of precision and recall measures (an annotation with regard to the other one). Following this methodology, we have measured inter-annotator agreement over the test corpus. We employ an on-line automatic tool for RST trees comparison, RSTeval (Mazeiro and Pardo, 2009), where Marcu's methodology has been implemented (for 4 languages: English, Portuguese, Spanish and Basque). We know that there are some other ways to measure agreement, such as Cohen's kappa (Cohen, 1960) or Fleiss's kappa (Fleiss, 1971), for example. Nevertheless, we consider that Marcu's methodology (2000) is suitable to compare adequately 2 annotations of the same original text, because it has been designed specifically for this task.

For each trees pair from the test corpus, precision and recall were measured separately. Afterwards, all those individual results were put together to obtain general results. Table 3 shows global results for the 4 categories. The category with more agreement was EDUs (recall: 91.04% / precision: 87.20%), that is, segmentation. This result was expected, since the segmentation criteria given to the annotators were quite precise and the possibility of mistake was low. The lowest agreement was obtained for the category Relations (recall: 78.48% / precision: 76.81%). This result is lower than the other, but we think it is acceptable. In the RST Discourse Treebank the trend was similar to the one detected in our corpus: the highest agreement is obtained at the segmentation level and the lowest at the relations level.

Category	Precision	Recall
EDUs	87.20%	91.04%
SPANs	86%	87.31%
Nuclearity	82.46%	84.66%
Relations	76.81%	78.48%

Table 3: Inter-annotator agreement

Precision and recall have not been calculated with respect to a gold standard because it does not exist for Spanish. Our future aim is to reach a consensus on the annotation of the test corpus (using an external "judge"), in order to establish a set of texts considered as a preliminary gold standard for this language. We consider that the annotations have quality at present, because inter-annotator agreement is quite high; however, this consensus could solve the typical annotation mistakes we have detected or some ambiguities.

We have analyzed the main discrepancy reasons between annotators. With regard to the segmentation, the main one was human mistake; ex. segmenting EDUs without a verb (one annotator segmented the following passage into 2 EDUs because she detected a Means relation, but the second EDU does not include any verb):

[Además estudiamos el desarrollo de criterios para determinar si un semigrupo dado tiene dicha propiedad] [mediante el estudio de desigualdades de curvatura-dimensión.]

[We also study the development of tests in order to determine if a given semi group has this property] [by means of curvature-dimension inequalities.]

The second reason was that in the manual some aspects were not explained in detail. For example, if a substantive sentence or a direct/object clause (which must not be segmented, according to the point b2) includes two coordinated clauses, these must not be segmented either. Thus, we found some erroneous segmentations. For example:

[Los hombres adultos tienen miedo de fracasar] [y no cumplir con el rol masculino de ser proveedores del hogar y de proteger a su familia.]

[Adult men are scared to fail] [and not to fulfill the masculine role of being the suppliers of the home and to protect their family.]

This kind of mistakes allowed us to refine our segmentation manual *a posteriori*. In the future, we will ask the test corpus annotators to make a new annotation of the texts, using the refined manual, in order to check if the agreement increases, in the same way as the RST Discourse Treebank.

With regard to rhetorical annotations, we detected 2 main reasons of inter-annotator disagreement. The first one was the ambiguity of some relations and their corresponding connectors; for example, Justification-Reason, Antithesis-Concession or Circumstance-Means relations, like in the following passage (in Spanish, "al" may indicate time or manner):

[Los niños aprenden matemáticas] [al resolver problemas.]

[Children learn mathematics] [when solving problems.]

The second one is due to differences between annotators when determining nuclearity. For example, in the following passage, one annotator marked Background and the other one Elaboration:

[Quedó un hueco en la pared de 60 x 1.20cm.]S_Background [Norma y Andrés quieren colocar en el hueco una pecera.]N_Background

[Quedó un hueco en la pared de 60 x 1.20cm.]N_Elaboration [Norma y Andrés quieren colocar en el hueco una pecera.]S_Elaboration

[A hole of 60 x 1.20 cm remained in the wall.] [Norma and Andrés want to place a fish tank in the hole.]

It is easier to solve segmentation disagreement than relations disagreement, since in this case annotator subjectivity is more evident; we must consider how to refine our manual in this sense.

3.7 Delivering and Maintaining the Product

Hovy (2010) mentions some technical issues regarding these points: licensing, distribution, maintenance and updates. With regard to licensing and distribution, the RST Spanish Treebank will be free for research purposes. We have a data manager responsible for maintenance and updates.

The description of the annotated corpus is also a very important issue (Ide and Pustejovsky, 2010). It is important to provide a high level description of the corpus, including the theoretical framework, the methodology (annotators, annotation manual and tool, agreement, etc.), the means for resource maintenance, the technical aspects, the project leader, the contact, the team, etc. The RST Spanish Treebank includes all this detailed information.

XML (with a DTD) has been used, in order the corpus can be reused for several aplications. In the future, we plan to use the standard XCES.

To know more about resources development, linguistic annotation or inter-annotator agreement, we recommend: Palmer et al. (on-line), Palmer and Xue (2010), and Artstein and Poesio (2008).

4 The Search Interface of the RST Spanish Treebank

The RST Spanish Treebank interface is freely available on-line[7]. It allows the visualization and downloading of all the texts in txt format, with their corresponding annotated trees in RSTtool format (rs3), as well as in image format (jpg). Each text includes its title, its reference, its web link (if it is an on-line text) and its number of words. The interface shows texts by areas and allows the user to select a subcorpus (including individual files or folders containing several files). The selected subcorpus can be saved on local disk (generating a xml file) for future analyses.

The interface includes a statistical tool which allows obtaining statistics of rhetorical relations in a subcorpus selected by the user. The RSTtool also offers this option but it can be only used for one text. We consider that it is more useful for the user to obtain statistics from various texts, in order to get significant statistical results. As the RSTtool, our tool allows to count the multinuclear relations in two ways: a) one unit for each detected multinuclear relation, and b) one unit for each detected nucleus. If we use b), the statistics of the multinuclear relations of Table 2 are higher: List (864), Joint (537), Sequence (289), Contrast (153), Conjunction (28) and Disjunction (24).

We are developing another tool, aimed to extract information from the annotated texts, which we will soon include into the interface. This tool will allow to the user to select a subcorpus and to extract from it the EDUs corresponding to the rhetorical relations selected, like a multidocument specialized summarizer guided by user's interests.

The RST Spanish Treebank interface also includes a screen which permits the users to send their own annotated texts. Our aim is for the RST Spanish Treebank to become a dynamic corpus, in constant evolution, being increased with texts annotated by users. This has a double advantage since, on the one hand, the corpus will grow and, on the other hand, users will profit from the interface's applications, using their own subcorpora. The only requirement is to use the relations and the segmentation and annotation criteria of our project. Once the texts are sent, the RST Spanish Treebank data manager will verify if the annotation corresponds to these criteria.

5 Conclusions and Future Work

We think that this work means an important step for the RST research in Spanish, and that the RST Spanish Treebank will be useful to carry out diverse researches about RST in this language, from a descriptive point of view (ex. analysis of texts from different domains or genres) and an applied point of view (development of discourse parsers and NLP applications, like automatic summarization, automatic translation, IE, etc.).

For the moment the corpus' size is acceptable and, though the percentage of double-annotated texts is not very high, we think that having 10 annotators (using the same annotation manual) avoids the bias of only one annotator. In addition, the corpus includes texts of diverse domains and genres, which provides us with a heterogeneous Spanish corpus. Moreover, the corpus interface that we have designed allows the user to select a subcorpus and to analyze it statistically. In addition, we think that it is essential to release a free corpus, on-line and dynamic, that is, in continuous growth. Nevertheless, we are conscious that our work still has certain limitations, which we will try to solve in the future. In the short term, we have 5 aims:

a) To add one more annotator for the test corpus and to measure inter-annotator agreement.
b) To use more agreement measures, like kappa.
c) To reach a consensus on the annotation of the test corpus, in order to establish a set of texts considered as a preliminary gold standard.
d) To finish and to evaluate the IE tool.
e) To analyze the corpus to extract linguistic patterns for the automatic relations detection.

In the long term, we consider other aims:

f) To increase the corpus, by adding non-specialized texts, and new domains and genres.
g) To annotate all the texts by 3 people, to get a representative gold-standard for Spanish (this aim will depend on the funding of the project).

[7] http://www.corpus.unam.mx/rst/

References

Ron Artstein, and Massimo Poesio. 2008. Survey Article: Inter-Coder Agreement for Computational Linguistics. Computational Linguistics, 34(4):555-596.

Nadjet Bouayad-Agha, Leo Wanner, and Daniel Nicklass. 2006. Discourse structuring of dynamic content. Procesamiento del lenguaje natural, 37:207-213.

M. Teresa Cabré (1999). La terminología: representación y comunicación. Barcelona: IULA-UPF.

Lynn Carlson and Daniel Marcu. 2001. Discourse Tagging Reference Manual. ISI Technical Report ISITR-545. Los Ángeles: University of Southern California.

Lynn Carlson, Daniel Marcu, and Mary Ellen Okurowski. 2002a. RST Discourse Treebank. Pennsylvania: Linguistic Data Consortium.

Lynn Carlson, Daniel Marcu, and Mary Ellen Okurowski. 2002b. Building a Discourse-Tagged Corpus in the Framework of Rhetorical Structure Theory. In Proceedings of the 2nd SIGDIAL Workshop on Discourse and Dialogue, Eurospeech 2001.

Jacob Cohen. 1960. A coefficient of agreement for nominal scales. Educational and Psychological Measurement, 20(1):37-46

Iria da Cunha, Eric SanJuan, Juan-Manuel Torres-Moreno, Marina Lloberes, and Irene Castellón. 2010. Discourse Segmentation for Spanish based on Shallow Parsing. Lecture Notes in Computer Science, 6437:13-23.

Iria da Cunha, and Mikel Iruskieta. 2010. Comparing rhetorical structures of different languages: The influence of translation strategies. Discourse Studies, 12(5):563-598.

Iria da Cunha, Leo Wanner, and M. Teresa Cabré. 2007. Summarization of specialized discourse: The case of medical articles in Spanish. Terminology, 13(2):249-286.

Dmitriy Dligach, Rodney D. Nielsen, and Martha Palmer. 2010. To Annotate More Accurately or to Annotate More. In Proceedings of the 4th Linguistic Annotation Workshop (LAW-IV). 48th Annual Meeting of the Association for Computational Linguistics.

Joseph L. Fleis. 1971. Measuring nominal scale agreement among many raters. Psychological Bulletin, 76(5):378-382.

Eduard Hovy. 2010. Annotation. A Tutorial. Presented at the 48th Annual Meeting of the Association for Computational Linguistics.

Nancy Ide and Pustejovsky, J. (2010). What Does Interoperability Mean, anyway? Toward an Operational Definition of Interoperability. In Proceedings of the Second International Conference on Global Interoperability for Language Resources (ICGL 2010).

William C. Mann, and Sandra A. Thompson. 1988. Rhetorical structure theory: Toward a functional theory of text organization. Text, 8(3):243-281.

Daniel Marcu. 2000. The Theory and Practice of Discourse Parsing Summarization. Massachusetts: Institute of Technology.

Mitchell P. Marcus, Beatrice Santorini, Mary A. Marcinkiewicz. 1993. Building a large annotated corpus of English: the Penn Treenbank. Computational Linguistics, 19(2):313-330.

Michael O'Donnell. 2000. RSTTOOL 2.4 – A markup tool for rhetorical structure theory. In Proceedings of the International Natural Language Generation Conference. 253-256.

Martha Palmer, and Nianwen Xue. 2010. Linguistic Annotation. Handbook of Computational Linguistics and Natural Language Processing.

Martha Palmer, Randee Tangi, Stephanie Strassel, Christiane Fellbaum, and Eduard Hovy (on-line). Historical Development and Future Directions in Data Resource Development. MINDS report. http://www-nlpir.nist.gov/MINDS/FINAL/data.web.pdf

Sameer Pradhan, Eduard Hovy, Mitch Marcus, Martha Palmer, Lance Ramshaw, Ralph Weischedel. 2007. OntoNotes: A Unified Relational Semantic Representation. In Proceedings of the First IEEE International Conference on Semantic Computing (ICSC-07).

Rashmi Prasad, Nikhil Dinesh, Alan Lee, Eleni Miltsakaki, Livio Robaldo, Aravind Joshi, and Bonnie Webber. 2008. The Penn Discourse Treebank 2.0. In Proceedings of the 6th International Conference on Language Resources and Evaluation (LREC 2008).

David Reitter, and Mandred Stede. 2003. Step by step: underspecified markup in incremental rhetorical analysis. In Proceedings of the 4th International

Workshop on Linguistically Interpreted Corpora (LINC-03).

Magdalena Romera. 2004. Discourse Functional Units: The Expression of Coherence Relations in Spoken Spanish. Munich: LINCOM.

Thiago Alexandre Salgueiro Pardo, and Lucia Helena Machado Rino. 2001. A summary planner based on a three-level discourse model. In Proceedings of Natural Language Processing Pacific Rim Symposium. 533-538.

Thiago Alexandre Salgueiro Pardo, Maria das Graças Volpe Nunes, and Lucia Helena Machado Rino. 2008. DiZer: An Automatic Discourse Analyzer for Brazilian Portuguese. Lecture Notes in Artificial Intelligence, 3171:224-234.

Thiago Alexandre Salgueiro Pardo, and Eloize Rossi Marques Seno. 2005. Rhetalho: um corpus de referência anotado retoricamente. In Anais do V Encontro de Corpora. São Carlos-SP, Brasil.

Gerardo Sierra. 2008. Diseño de corpus textuales para fines lingüísticos. In Proceedings of the IX Encuentro Internacional de Lingüística en el Noroeste 2. 445-462.

Manfred Stede. 2004. The Potsdam commentary corpus. In Proceedings of the Workshop on Discourse Annotation, 42nd Meeting of the Association for Computational Linguistics.

Maite Taboada. 2004. Building Coherence and Cohesion: Task-Oriented Dialogue in English and Spanish. Amsterdam/Philadelphia: John Benjamins.

Maite Taboada, and Jan Renkema. 2008. Discourse Relations Reference Corpus [Corpus]. Simon Fraser University and Tilburg University. http://www.sfu.ca/rst/06tools/discourse_relations_corpus.html.

Maite Taboada, and William C. Mann. 2006a. Rhetorical Structure Theory: Looking Back and Moving Ahead. Discourse Studies, 8(3):423-459.

Maite Taboada, and William C. Mann. 2006b. Applications of Rhetorical Structure Theory. Discourse Studies, 8(4):567-588.

Milan Tofiloski, Julian Brooke, and Maite Taboada. 2009. A Syntactic and Lexical-Based Discourse Segmenter. In Proceedings of the 47th Annual Meeting of the Association for Computational Linguistics.

Hai Zhao, Yan Song, and Chunyu Kit. 2010. How Large a Corpus Do We Need: Statistical Method Versus Rule-based Method. In Proceedings of the Seventh conference on International Language Resources and Evaluation (LREC'10).

OWL/DL formalization of the MULTEXT-East morphosyntactic specifications

Christian Chiarcos
University of Potsdam, Germany
chiarcos@uni-potsdam.de

Tomaž Erjavec
Jožef Stefan Institute, Slovenia
tomaz.erjavec@ijs.si

Abstract

This paper describes the modeling of the morphosyntactic annotations of the MULTEXT-East corpora and lexicons as an OWL/DL ontology. Formalizing annotation schemes in OWL/DL has the advantages of enabling formally specifying interrelationships between the various features and making logical inferences based on the relationships between them. We show that this approach provides us with a top-down perspective on a large set of morphosyntactic specifications for multiple languages, and that this perspective helps to identify and to resolve conceptual problems in the original specifications. Furthermore, the ontological modeling allows us to link the MULTEXT-East specifications with repositories of annotation terminology such as the General Ontology of Linguistics Descriptions or the ISO TC37/SC4 Data Category Registry.

1 Introduction

In the last 15 years, the heterogeneity of linguistic annotations has been identified as a key problem limiting the interoperability and reusability of NLP tools and linguistic data collections. The multitude of linguistic tagsets complicates the combination of NLP modules within a single pipeline; similar problems exist in language documentation, typology and corpus linguistics, where researchers are interested to access and query data collections on a homogeneous terminological basis.

One way to enhance the consistency of linguistic annotations is to provide explicit semantics for tags by grounding annotations in terminology repositories such as the General Ontology of Linguistics Descriptions (Farrar and Langendoen, 2003, GOLD) or the ISO TC37/SC4 Data Category Registry (Kemps-Snijders et al., 2009, ISOcat). Reference definitions provide an interlingua that allows the mapping of linguistic annotations from annotation scheme A to scheme B. This application requires linking annotation schemes with the terminological repository. This relation can be formalized within the Linked Data paradigm (Berners-Lee, 2006), which requires the use of uniform resource identifiers (URIs), the hypertext transfer protocol (HTTP), standard representation formats (such as RDF) and links to other URIs. Here, we propose a formalization of this linking in OWL/DL, a notational variant of the Description Logic $\mathcal{SHOIN}(\mathcal{D})$ that builds on RDF and Linked Data.

Another way to enhance the consistency of linguistic annotations is to make use of cross-linguistic meta schemes or annotation standards, such as EAGLES (Leech and Wilson, 1996). The problem is that these enforce the use of the same categories across multiple languages, and this may be inappropriate for historically and geographically unrelated languages. For specific linguistic and historical regions, the application of standardization approaches has, however, been performed with great success, e.g., for Western (Leech and Wilson, 1996) and Eastern Europe (Erjavec et al., 2003) or the Indian subcontinent (Baskaran et al., 2008).

Proceedings of the Fifth Law Workshop (LAW V), pages 11–20,
Portland, Oregon, 23-24 June 2011.

In this paper, we illustrate differences and commonalities of both approaches by creating an OWL/DL terminology repository from the MULTEXT-East (MTE) specifications (Erjavec et al., 2003; Erjavec, 2010), which define features for the morphosyntactic level of linguistic description, instantiate them for 16 languages and provide morphosyntactic tagsets for these languages. The specifications are a part of the MTE resources, which also include lexicons and an annotated parallel corpus that use these morphosyntactic tagsets.

The encoding of the MTE specifications follows the Text Encoding Initiative Guidelines, TEI P5 (TEI Consortium, 2007), and this paper concentrates on developing a semi-automatic procedure for converting them from TEI XML to OWL. While TEI is more appropriate for authoring the specifications and displaying them in a book-oriented format, the OWL encoding has the advantages of enabling formally specifying interrelationships between the various features (concepts, or classes) and making logical inferences based on the relationships between them, useful in mediating between different tagsets and tools (Chiarcos, 2008).

2 The MULTEXT-East (MTE) Morphosyntactic Specifications

The MTE morphosyntactic specifications define attributes and values used for word-level syntactic annotation, i.e., they provide a formal grammar for the morphosyntactic properties of the languages covered. The specifications also contain commentary, bibliography, notes, etc. Following the original MULTEXT proposal (Ide and Véronis, 1994), the specifications define 14 categories (parts of speech), and for each its attributes, their values, and the languages that every attribute-value pair is appropriate for. The morphosyntactic specifications also define the mapping between the feature structures and morphosyntactic descriptions (MSDs). MSDs are compact strings used as tags for corpus annotation and in the morphosyntactic lexicons. For example, the MSD Ncmsn is equivalent to the feature structure consisting of the attribute-value pairs Noun, Type=common, Gender=masculine, Number=singular, Case=nominative.

The specifications currently cover 16 languages, in particular: Bulgarian, Croatian, Czech, English, Estonian, Hungarian, Macedonian, Persian, Polish, Resian, Romanian, Russian, Serbian, Slovak, Slovene, and Ukrainian. For a number of these languages the specifications have become a de-facto standard and, for some, the MTE lexicons and corpora are still the only publicly available datasets for this level of linguistic description.[1]

Table 1 lists the defined categories and gives the number of distinct attributes, attribute-value pairs and the number of MTE languages which distinguish the category. The feature-set is quite large, as many of the languages covered have very rich inflection, are typologically different (inflectional, agglutinating), but also have independent traditions of linguistic description; this also leads to similar phenomena sometimes being expressed by different means (see Sect. 4.3).

Category	Code	Atts	Att-Vals	Langs
Noun	N	14	68	16
Verb	V	17	74	16
Adjective	A	17	79	16
Pronoun	P	19	97	16
Determiner	D	10	32	3
Article	T	6	23	3
Adverb	R	7	28	16
Adposition	S	4	12	16
Conjunction	C	7	21	16
Numeral	M	13	81	16
Particle	Q	3	17	12
Interjection	I	2	4	16
Abbreviation	Y	5	35	16
Residual	X	1	3	16

Table 1: MULTEXT categories with the number of MULTEXT-East defined attributes, attribute-value pairs and languages.

The specifications are encoded as a TEI document, consisting of an introductory part, the Common and the Language Specific Specifications, the latter two organized into tables by the

[1]The MTE specifications, as well as the other MTE resources, are available from the Web page of the project at `http://nl.ijs.si/ME/`.

```
<table n="msd.cat" xml:lang="en">
  <head>Common specifications for Noun</head>
  <row role="type">
    <cell role="position">0</cell>
    <cell role="name">CATEGORY</cell>
    <cell role="value">Noun</cell>
    <cell role="code">N</cell>
    <cell role="lang">en</cell>
    <cell role="lang">ro</cell>
    <cell role="lang">sl</cell>
    ...
  </row>
  <row role="attribute">
    <cell role="position">1</cell>
    <cell role="name">Type</cell>
    <cell>
      <table>
        <row role="value">
          <cell role="name">common</cell>
          <cell role="code">c</cell>
          <cell role="lang">en</cell>
          ...
```

Figure 1: Common table for Noun

14 defined categories.

Figure 1 gives the start of the Common table for Noun. It first gives the category, the languages that distinguish it, and then its attributes with their values; the meaning of a particular row or cell is given by its role attribute. As with the category, each attribute-value is also qualified by the languages that make use of the feature. Note that MTE is a positional tagset that specifies the position of the attribute in the MSD string, and the one-letter code of its value, so that Nc would correspond to Noun, Type=common.

The language-specific sections also contain tables for each category, which are similar to the common tables in that they repeat the attributes and their values, although only those appropriate for the language. The language-specific tables can also contain localization information, i.e., the names of the categories, attributes, their values and codes in the particular language, in addition to English. This enables expressing the feature structures and MSDs either in English or in the language in question. Furthermore, each language-specific section can also contain an index listing all valid MSDs. This index is augmented with frequency information and examples of usage drawn for a corpus.

In addition to the source TEI P5 XML, the MTE specifications are delivered in various derived formats, in particular HTML for reading and as tabular files, which map the MSD tagset into various feature decompositions.

3 Linking annotation schemes with terminology repositories

3.1 Linguistic terminology initiatives

There have been, by now, several approaches to develop terminology repositories and data category registries for language resources, systems for mapping between diverse (morphosyntactic) vocabularies and for integrating annotations from different tools and tagsets, ranging from early texts on annotation standards (Bakker et al., 1993; Leech and Wilson, 1996) over relational models and concept hierarchies (Bickel and Nichols, 2002; Rosen, 2010) to more formal specifications in OWL/RDF (or with OWL/RDF export), e.g., the already mentioned GOLD and ISOcat, OntoTag (Aguado de Cea et al., 2002) or the Typological Database System ontology (Saulwick et al., 2005).

Despite their common level of representation these efforts have not yet converged into a unified and generally accepted ontology of linguistic annotation terminology and there is still a considerable amount of disagreement between their definitions. As these repositories nevertheless play an important role in their respective communities, it is desirable to link the MTE specifications with the most representative of them, notably with GOLD and the morphosyntactic profile of ISOcat. As we argue below, different design decisions in the terminology repositories make it necessary to use a linking formalism that is capable of expressing both disjunctions and conjunctions of concepts. For this reason, we propose the application of OWL/DL.

By representing the MTE specifications, the repositories, and the linking between them as separate OWL/DL models, we follow the architectural concept of the OLiA architecture (Chiarcos, 2008), see Sect. 5.

3.2 Annotation mapping

The classic approach to link annotations with reference concepts is to specify rules that define a direct mapping (Zeman, 2008). It is, however, not always possible to find a 1:1 mapping.

One problem is **conceptual overlap**: A common noun may occur as a part of a proper name, e.g., German *Palais* 'baroque-style palace' in *Neues Palais* lit. 'new palace', a Prussian royal palace in Potsdam/Germany. *Palais* is thus *both* a proper noun (in its function), and a common noun (in its form). Such conceptual overlap is sometimes represented with a specialized tag, e.g., in the TIGER scheme (Brants and Hansen, 2002). ISOcat (like other terminological repositories) does currently not provide the corresponding hybrid category, so that *Palais* is to be linked to both `properNoun`/DC-1371 and `commonNoun`/DC-1256 if the information carried by the original annotation is to be preserved. **Contraction**s pose similar problems: English *gonna* combines *going* (PTB tag `VBG`, Marcus et al., 1994) and *to* (`TO`). If whitespace tokenization is applied, both tags need to be assigned to the same token.

A related problem is the representation of **ambiguity**: The SUSANNE (Sampson, 1995) tag `ICSt` applies to English *after* both as a preposition and as a subordinating conjunction. The corresponding ISOcat category is thus *either* `preposition`/DC-1366 or `subordinating Conjunction`/DC-1393. Without additional disambiguation, `ICSt` needs to be linked to both data categories.

Technically, such problems can be solved with a 1:n mapping between annotations and reference concepts. Yet, overlap/contraction and ambiguity differ in their meaning: While overlapping/contracted categories are in the intersection ($\sqcap$) of reference categories, ambiguous categories are in their join ($\sqcup$). This difference is relevant for subsequent processing, e.g., to decide whether disambiguation is necessary. A mapping approach, however, fails to distinguish $\sqcap$ and $\sqcup$.

The linking between reference categories and annotations requires a formalism that can distinguish intersection and join operators. A less expressive linking formalism that makes use of a 1:1 (or 1:n) mapping between annotation concepts and reference concepts can lead to inconsistencies when mapping annotation concepts from an annotation scheme A to an annotation scheme B if these use the same terms with slightly deviating definitions, as noted, for example, by Garabík et al. (2009) for MTE.

3.3 Annotation linking with OWL/DL

OWL/DL is a formalism that supports the necessary operators and flexibility. Reference concepts and annotation concepts are formalized as OWL classes and the linking between them can be represented by `rdfs:subClassOf` ($\sqsubseteq$). OWL/DL provides `owl:intersectionOf` ($\sqcap$), `owl:unionOf` ($\sqcup$) and `owl:complementOf` ($\neg$) operators and it allows the definition of properties and restrictions on the respective concepts. As an example, the MTE Definiteness=definite refers to either a clitic determiner or ($\sqcup$) to the 'definite conjunction' of Hungarian verbs. More precisely, it is in the intersection between these and ($\sqcap$) a category for ambiguous feature values (Sect. 4.3).

An OWL/DL-based formalization has the additional advantage that it can be linked with existing terminology repositories that are available in OWL or RDF, e.g., GOLD or ISOcat (Chiarcos, 2010). The linking to other terminology repositories will be subject of subsequent research. In this paper, we focus on the development of an OWL/DL representation of MTE morphosyntactic specifications that represents a necessary precondition for OWL/DL-based annotation linking.

4 Building the MTE ontology

We built the MTE ontology[2] in a three-step scenario: first, a preliminary OWL/DL model of the common MTE specifications was created (Sect. 4.1); we then built language-specific subontologies and linked them to the common ontology (Sect. 4.2); finally, the outcome of this process

[2]All MTE ontologies are available under `http://nl.ijs.si/ME/owl/` under a Creative Commons Attribution licence (CC BY 3.0).

was discussed with a group of experts and revised (Sect. 4.3).

4.1 Common specifications

Following the methodology described by Chiarcos (2008), the structure of the MTE ontology was derived from the original documentation. The initial ontology skeleton was created automatically (the organization of the specifications was exploited to develop an XSLT script that mapped TEI XML to OWL), but subsequently manually augmented with descriptions and examples found in the individual languages.

1. Two top-level concepts `MorphosyntacticCategory` and `MorphosyntacticFeature` represent root elements of the MTE ontology. An object property `hasFeature` maps a `MorphosyntacticCategory` onto one or multiple `MorphosyntacticFeature` values.

2. All MSD categories are subconcepts of `MorphosyntacticCategory`, e.g., `Noun`, `Verb`, `Adjective`, etc.

3. For every category, the MTE attribute Type was used to infer subcategories, e.g., the concept `ExclamativePronoun` ($\sqsubseteq$ `Pronoun`) for Pronoun/Type=exclamative.

4. From more specialized type attributes (e.g., Wh_Type, Coord_Type, Sub_Type, and Referent_Type), additional subcategories were induced at the next deeper level, e.g., `SimpleCoordinatingConjunction` ($\sqsubseteq$ `CoordinatingConjunction`) from Conjunction/Type=coordinating, Coord_Type=simple.

5. All remaining attributes are subconcepts of `MorphosyntacticFeature`, e.g., `Aspect`, `Case`, etc.

6. For every subconcept of `MorphosyntacticFeature` (e.g., `Aspect`) a corresponding `hasFeature` subproperty (e.g., `hasAspect`) was introduced, with the morphosyntactic feature as its range and the join of morphosyntactic categories it can cooccur with as its domain. An additional constraint restricts its cardinality to at most 1.

7. All attribute values are represented as subclasses of the corresponding attribute concept, e.g., `AbessiveCase` (for Case=abessive) as a subconcept of `Case`.[3]

8. Every concept was automatically augmented with a list of up to 10 examples for every language which were drawn from the language-specific MSD index.

4.2 Language-specific subontologies

Having represented the common MTE specifications in OWL, we decided to represent the annotation scheme for every language in a separate OWL model, and to make use of the OWL import mechanism to link it with the common specifications. The language-specific subontologies do not specify their own taxonomy, but rather inherit the concepts and properties of the common model. Unlike the common model, they include individuals that provide information about the tags (MSDs) used for this particular language.

Every individual corresponds to an MSD tag. We use data properties of the OLiA system ontology[4] to indicate its string realization (e.g., `system:hasTag 'Ncmsn'`) and the designator of its annotation layer (e.g., `system:hasTier 'pos'`). Additionally, `rdfs:comment` elements contain all examples of the original MSD specifications.

In accordance to the specified annotation values, every individual is defined as an instance of the corresponding `MorphosyntacticCategory` (e.g., `Noun`) and `MorphosyntacticFeature` (e.g., `SingularNumber`) from the common specifications. Additionally, for every `MorphosyntacticFeature` (e.g., `Number`, the superconcept of `SingularNumber`), it is assigned

[3]This ontology does not contain individuals. In our approach, individuals represent feature bundles in the language-specific subontologies, corresponding to the individual MSD tags. (or, in other application scenarios, the token that the tag is applied to).

[4]`http://nachhalt.sfb632.uni-potsdam.de/owl/system.owl`, prefix `system`

```
<mte:Noun rdf:ID="Ncmsn_sl">
  <system:hasTag>Ncmsn</system:hasTag>
  <system:hasTier>pos</system:hasTier>
  <rdf:type
    rdf:resource="...#CommonNoun"/>
  <rdf:type
    rdf:resource="...#MasculineGender"/>
  <rdf:type
    rdf:resource="...#SingularNumber"/>
  <rdf:type
    rdf:resource="...#NominativeCase"/>
  <mte:hasGender rdf:resource="#Ncmsg_sl"/>
  <mte:hasNumber rdf:resource="#Ncmsg_sl"/>
  <mte:hasCase rdf:resource="#Ncmsg_sl"/>
  <rdfs:comment>e.g., cas, svet, denar, ...
</mte:Noun>
```

Figure 2: MSD Ncmsn in the Slovene subontology

itself as target of the corresponding object property (e.g., `hasNumber`).

Figure 2 shows the subontology entry for the tag `Ncmsn` in the Slovene subontology. The individual could thus be retrieved with the following queries for "singular noun":

```
(1) Noun and hasNumber some
    SingularNumber
(2) Noun and SingularNumber
```

The language-specific subontologies were fully automatically created from the TEI XML using XSLT scripts. During the revision of the common specifications, these scripts were updated and reapplied.

4.3 Revision of the initial OWL model

After the automatic conversion from XML to OWL the resulting ontology skeleton of the common specifications was manually augmented with descriptions, explanations and selected examples from the language-specific MTE specifications. Furthermore, concept names with abbreviated or redundant names were adjusted, e.g., the concept `CorrelatCoordConjunction` (Coord_Type=correlat) was expanded to `CorrelativeCoordinatingConjunction`, and `DefiniteDefiniteness` (Definiteness=definite) was simplified to `Definite`. Finally, if one attribute value represents a specialization of another, the former was recast as a subconcept of the latter (e.g., `CliticProximalDeterminer` $\sqsubseteq$ `CliticDefiniteDeterminer`).

Moreover, a number of potential problems were identified. Some of them could be addressed by consulting MTE-related publications (Qasemizadeh and Rahimi, 2006; Dimitrova et al., 2009; Derzhanski and Kotsyba, 2009), but most were solved with the help of the original authors of the MTE specifications and an open discussion with these experts over a mailing list.

The problems fall in two general classes: (a) terminological problems, and (b) conceptual problems. By terminological problems we mean that a term required a more precise definition than provided in the MTE specifications; conceptual problems pertain to design decisions in a positional tagset (overload: the same annotation refers to two different phenomena in different languages) and to artifacts of the creation process of the MTE specifications (redundancies: the same phenomenon is represented in different ways for different languages). Figure 3 shows a fragment of the MTE ontology that showed all types of conceptual problems as described below.

Terminological problems include the use of non-standard or language-specific terminology (e.g., Clitic=burkinostka for conventional collocations in Polish, or Case=essive-formal for Hungarian), and the need to understand design decisions that were necessary for language-specific phenomena (e.g., Numeral/Class=definite34 for Czech and Polish quantifiers with the same patterns of agreement as the numerals 3 and 4).

In the course of the revision, most non-standard terms were replaced with conventional, language-independent concept names, and language-specific phenomena were documented by adding relevant excerpts from discussions or literature as `owl:versionInfo`.

For a few concepts, no language-independent characterization could be found. For example, Numeral/Form=m_form refers to numerals with the suffix *-ma* in Bulgarian (a special form of the numerals '2' to '7' for persons of masculine gender). In the ontology, the concept `MFormNumeral` is preserved, but it is constrained so that every instance matches the following OWL/DL expression:

```
(3) CardinalNumber and hasAnimacy some
    Animate and hasGender some Masculine
```

Attribute overload means that one attribute groups together unrelated phenomena from different languages. In a positional tagset, attribute overload is a natural strategy to achieve compact and yet expressive tags. As every attribute requires its own position in the tag, the length of MSD tags grows with the number of attributes. Overload thus reduces tag complexity. To an ontological model, however, these complexity considerations do not apply, whereas proper conceptual differentiations are strongly encouraged.

We thus decided to disentangle the various senses of overloaded attributes. For example, the `MorphosyntacticFeature Definiteness`, is split up in three subconcepts (cf. Fig. 3).

`CliticDeterminerType`: presence of a post-fixed article of Romanian, Bulgarian and Persian nouns and adjectives.

`ReductionFeature`: the difference between full and reduced adjectives in many Slavic languages.

`PersonOfObject`: the so-called 'definite conjugation' of Hungarian verbs.

Value overload has a similar meaning to attribute overload. Definiteness=definite, for example, can refer to a clitic definite determiner (a `CliticDeterminerType` in Romanian and Bulgarian), to a clitic determiner that expresses specificity (a `CliticDeterminerType` in Persian), or to a verb with a definite 3rd-person direct object (a `PersonOfObject` in Hungarian).

In the ontology, this is represented by defining `Definite` as a subconcept of the `owl:join` (⊔) of `CliticDefiniteDeterminer`, `CliticSpecificDeterminer` and `PersonOfObject`. Additional concepts, e.g., `AmbiguousDefinitenessFeature`, were created to anchor ambiguous concepts like `Definite` in the taxonomy (see Fig. 3).

Redundancy: For many languages, the MTE specifications were created in a bottom-up fashion, where existing NLP tools and lexicons were

Figure 3: Definiteness in the MTE ontology

integrated with a pre-existing taxonomy of annotation categories. Language-specific features were introduced when necessary, but sometimes in different ways for the same phenomenon in closely related languages. The MTE specifications thus comprise a certain degree of redundancy.

For example, the distinction between full and reduced adjectives in Slavic languages is expressed differently: For Czech, reduced adjectives are marked by Formation=nominal, but for Polish by Definiteness=short-art.

In the ontology, such redundancies are resolved by `owl:equivalentClass` statements, marked by ≡ in Fig. 3.

5 Summary and Discussion

We have described the semi-automatic creation of an ontological model of the MTE morphosyntactic specifications for 16 different languages. Such a model may be fruitfully applied in various ways, e.g., within an NLP pipeline that uses ontological specifications of annotations rather than their string representations (Buyko et al., 2008; Hellmann, 2010). The ontological modeling may serve also as a first step towards an ontology-based documentation of the annotations within a corpus query system (Rehm et al., 2007; Chiarcos et al., 2008), or even the ontological modeling of entire corpora (Burchardt et al., 2008; Hellmann et al., 2010) and lexicons (Martin et al., 2009). As an interesting side-effect of the OWL conversion of the entire body of MTE resources, they could be easily integrated with existing lexical-semantic resources as Linked Data, e.g., OWL/RDF versions of WordNet (Gangemi et al., 2003), which are currently being assembled by various initiatives, e.g., in the context of the LOD2 project (`http://lod2.eu`) and by the Open Linguistics Working Group at the OpenKnowledge Foundation (`http://linguistics.okfn.org`).

Another very important element is that the ontological modeling of the MTE annotations allows it to be interpreted in terms of existing repositories of annotation terminology such as ISOcat and GOLD. A bridge between these terminology repositories and the MTE ontology may be developed, for example, by integrating the ontology in an architecture of modular ontologies such as the Ontologies of Linguistic Annotations (Chiarcos, 2008, OLiA), where the linking between annotations and terminology repositories is mediated by a so-called 'Reference Model' that serves as an interface between different levels of representation.

The MTE ontology will be integrated in this model as an annotation model, i.e., its concepts will be defined as subconcepts of concepts of the OLiA Reference Model and thereby inherit the linking with GOLD (Chiarcos et al., 2008) and ISOcat (Chiarcos, 2010). The linking with these standard repositories increases the comparability of MTE annotations and it serves an important documentation function.

More important than merely *potential* applications of the MTE ontology, however, is that its creation provides us with a new, global perspective on the MTE specifications. A number of internal inconsistencies could be identified and strategies for their resolution (or formalization) were developed. Redundancies and overload were documented, and we further added expert definitions of controversial or non-standard concepts. When used as a documentation, these specifications may prevent misunderstandings with respect to the meaning of the actual annotations. For later versions of the MTE morphosyntactic specifications, they may even guide the refactoring of the annotation scheme.

The result of the development process described above is a prototype, that has to be augmented with definitions for non-controversial and well-understood concepts, which can be derived from the linking with OLiA, GOLD and ISOcat.

As for its language type, our strategy to resolve overload requires OWL/DL (`owl:join`). Without value overload and redundancy, the ontology would be OWL/Lite, as were the initial ontologies (Sect. 4.1 and Sect. 4.2). However, the current modeling is still sufficiently restricted to allow the application of reasoners, thereby opening up the possibility to use SemanticWeb technologies on MTE data, to connect it with other sources of information and to draw inferences from such Linked Data.

We would also like to point out that the conversion of the MTE specifications to OWL required relatively little effort. The total time required for conversion (without the revision phase) took approximately four days of work for a computational linguist familiar with OWL and part-of-speech tagsets in general (the most labor-intense part were discussions and literature consultation during the revision phase). Given the complexity of the MTE specifications (a highly elaborate set of morphosyntactic specifications for 16 typologically diverse languages and with more than thousand tags for many of the languages), this may be regarded an upper limit for the time necessary to create OWL models for annotation schemes.

We have thus not only shown that the ontological modeling of annotation schemes is possible and that it allows us to use our data in novel ways and to perform consistency control, but also that this was achievable with relatively low efforts in time and personnel.

Acknowledgements

The authors would like to thank the members of the mocky-l mailing list for their invaluable input; all errors in the paper remain our own. The research on linguistic ontologies described in this paper was partially funded by the German Research Foundation (DFG) in the context of the Collaborative Research Center (SFB) 632.

References

Guadalupe Aguado de Cea, Inmaculada Álvarez de Mon-Rego, Antonio Pareja-Lora, and Rosario Plaza-Arteche. 2002. OntoTag: A semantic web page linguistic annotation model. In *Proceedings of the ECAI 2002 Workshop on Semantic Authoring, Annotation and Knowledge Markup*, Lyon, France, July.

Dik Bakker, Osten Dahl, Martin Haspelmath, Maria Koptjevskaja-Tamm, Christian Lehmann, and Anna Siewierska. 1993. EUROTYP guidelines. Technical report, European Science Foundation Programme in Language Typology.

S. Kalika Bali Baskaran, Tanmoy Bhattacharya, Pushpak Bhattacharyya, Monojit Choudhury, Girish Nath Jha, S. Rajendran, K. Saravanan, L. Sobha, and KVS Subbarao. 2008. Designing a common POS-tagset framework for Indian languages. In *6th Workshop on Asian Language Resources*, pages 89–92, Hyderabad, India.

Tim Berners-Lee. 2006. Design issues: Linked data. `http://www.w3.org/DesignIssues/LinkedData.html` (May 11, 2011).

Balthasar Bickel and Johanna Nichols. 2002. Autotypologizing databases and their use in fieldwork. In *Proceedings of the LREC 2002 Workshop on Resources and Tools in Field Linguistics*, Las Palmas, Spain, May.

Sabine Brants and Silvia Hansen. 2002. Developments in the TIGER annotation scheme and their realization in the corpus. In *Proceedings of the 3rd International Conference on Language Resources and Evaluation (LREC 2002)*, pages 1643–1649, Las Palmas, Spain, May.

Aljoscha Burchardt, Sebastian Padó, Dennis Spohr, Anette Frank, and Ulrich Heid. 2008. Formalising Multi-layer Corpora in OWL/DL – Lexicon Modelling, Querying and Consistency Control. In *Proceedings of the 3rd International Joint Conference on NLP (IJCNLP 2008)*, Hyderabad, India, January.

Ekaterina Buyko, Christian Chiarcos, and Antonio Pareja-Lora. 2008. Ontology-based interface specifications for a NLP pipeline architecture. In *Proceedings of the 6th International Conference on Language Resources and Evaluation (LREC 2008)*, Marrakech, Morocco, May.

Christian Chiarcos, Stefanie Dipper, Michael Götze, Ulf Leser, Anke Lüdeling, Julia Ritz, and Manfred Stede. 2008. A flexible framework for integrating annotations from different tools and tag sets. *Traitement Automatique des Langues (TAL)*, 49(2).

Christian Chiarcos. 2008. An ontology of linguistic annotations. *LDV Forum*, 23(1):1–16. Foundations of Ontologies in Text Technology, Part II: Applications.

Christian Chiarcos. 2010. Grounding an ontology of linguistic annotations in the Data Category Registry. In *Proceedings of the LREC 2010 Workshop on Language Resource and Language Technology Standards (LR&LTS 2010)*, Valetta, Malta, May.

Ivan Derzhanski and Natalia Kotsyba. 2009. Towards a consistent morphological tagset for Slavic languages: Extending MULTEXT-East for Polish, Ukrainian and Belarusian. In *Mondilex Third Open Workshop*, pages 9–26, Bratislava, Slovakia, April.

Ludmila Dimitrova, Radovan Garabík, and Daniela Majchráková. 2009. Comparing Bulgarian and Slovak Multext-East morphology tagset. In *Mondilex Second Open Workshop: Organization and Development of Digital Lexical Resources*, pages 38–46, Kyiv, Ukraine, February.

Tomaž Erjavec, Cvetana Krstev, Vladimír Petkevič, Kiril Simov, Marko Tadić, and Duško Vitas. 2003. The MULTEXT-East Morphosyntactic Specifications for Slavic Languages. In *Proceedings of the EACL 2003 Workshop on Morphological Processing of Slavic Languages*, pages 25–32.

Tomaž Erjavec. 2010. MULTEXT-East Version 4: Multilingual Morphosyntactic Specifications, Lexicons and Corpora. In *Proceedings of the 7th International Conference on Language Resources and Evaluation (LREC 2010)*, Valetta, Malta, May.

Scott Farrar and D. Terence Langendoen. 2003. A linguistic ontology for the semantic web. *Glot International*, 7(3):97–100.

Aldo Gangemi, Roberto Navigli, and Paola Velardi. 2003. The OntoWordNet project: Extension and axiomatization of conceptual relations in WordNet. In R. Meersman and Z. Tari, editors, *Proceedings of On the Move to Meaningful Internet Systems (OTM 2003)*, pages 820–838, Catania, Italy, November.

Radovan Garabík, Daniela Majchráková, and Ludmila Dimitrova. 2009. Comparing Bulgarian and Slovak MULTEXT-East morphology tagset. In *Mondilex Second Open Workshop: Organization and Development of Digital Lexical Resources*, pages 38–46, Kyiv, Ukraine. Dovira Publishing House.

Sebastian Hellmann, Jörg Unbehauen, Christian Chiarcos, and Axel-Cyrille Ngonga Ngomo. 2010. The TIGER Corpus Navigator. In *Proceedings of the 9th International Workshop on Treebanks and Linguistic Theories (TLT 2010)*, pages 91–102, Tartu, Estonia, December.

Sebastian Hellmann. 2010. The semantic gap of formalized meaning. In *Proceedings of the 7th Extended Semantic Web Conference (ESWC 2010)*, Heraklion, Greece, May 30th – June 3rd.

Nancy Ide and Jean Véronis. 1994. MULTEXT (Multilingual Tools and Corpora). In *Proceedings of the 15th International Conference on Computational Linguistics (COLING 1994)*, pages 90–96, Kyoto.

Marc Kemps-Snijders, Menzo Windhouwer, Peter Wittenburg, and Sue Ellen Wright. 2009. ISOcat: remodelling metadata for language resources. *International Journal of Metadata, Semantics and Ontologies*, 4(4):261–276.

Geoffrey Leech and Andrew Wilson. 1996. Recommendations for the Morphosyntactic Annotation of Corpora. EAGLES Report EAG–TCWG–MAC/R, ILC, Pisa. `http://www.ilc.cnr.it/EAGLES96/annotate/` (May 11, 2011).

Mitchell P. Marcus, Beatrice Santorini, and Mary Ann Marcinkiewicz. 1994. Building a large annotated corpus of English: The Penn Treebank. *Computational Linguistics*, 19(2):313–330.

Fabienne Martin, Dennis Spohr, and Achim Stein. 2009. Representing a resource of formal lexical-semantic descriptions in the Web Ontology Language. *Journal for Language Technology and Computational Linguistics*, 21:1–22.

Behrang Qasemizadeh and Saeed Rahimi. 2006. Persian in MULTEXT-East framework. In Tapio Salakoski, Filip Ginter, Sampo Pyysalo, and Tapio Pahikkala, editors, *Advances in Natural Language Processing, Proceedings of the 5th International Conference on NLP (FinTAL 2006)*, pages 541–551, Turku, Finland, August.

Georg Rehm, Richard Eckart, and Christian Chiarcos. 2007. An OWL-and XQuery-based mechanism for the retrieval of linguistic patterns from XML-corpora. In *Proceedings of Recent Advances in Natural Language Processing (RANLP 2007)*, Borovets, Bulgaria, September.

Alexandr Rosen. 2010. Mediating between incompatible tagsets. In *Proceedings of the Workshop on Annotation and Exploitation of Parallel Corpora (AEPC)*, pages 53–62, Tartu, Estonia, December.

Geoffrey Sampson. 1995. *English for the computer: The SUSANNE corpus and analytic scheme*. Oxford University Press.

Adam Saulwick, Menzo Windhouwer, Alexis Dimitriadis, and Rob Goedemans. 2005. Distributed tasking in ontology mediated integration of typological databases for linguistic research. In *Proceedings of the 17th Conference on Advanced Information Systems Engineering (CAiSE 2005)*, Porto, Portugal, June.

TEI Consortium, editor. 2007. *TEI P5: Guidelines for Electronic Text Encoding and Interchange*. TEI Consortium.

Daniel Zeman. 2008. Reusable tagset conversion using tagset drivers. In *Proceedings of the 6th International Conference on Language Resources and Evaluation (LREC 2008)*, Marrakech, Morocco, May.

Analysis of the Hindi Proposition Bank using Dependency Structure

Ashwini Vaidya **Jinho D. Choi** **Martha Palmer** **Bhuvana Narasimhan**
Institute of Cognitive Science
University of Colorado at Boulder
{vaidyaa,choijd,mpalmer,narasimb}@colorado.edu

Abstract

This paper makes two contributions. First, we describe the Hindi Proposition Bank that contains annotations of predicate argument structures of verb predicates. Unlike PropBanks in most other languages, the Hind PropBank is annotated on top of dependency structure, the Hindi Dependency Treebank. We explore the similarities between dependency and predicate argument structures, so the PropBank annotation can be faster and more accurate. Second, we present a probabilistic rule-based system that maps syntactic dependents to semantic arguments. With simple rules, we classify about 47% of the entire PropBank arguments with over 90% confidence. These preliminary results are promising; they show how well these two frameworks are correlated. This can also be used to speed up our annotations.

1 Introduction

Proposition Bank (from now on, PropBank) is a corpus in which the arguments of each verb predicate are annotated with their semantic roles (Palmer et al., 2005). PropBank annotation has been carried out in several languages; most of them are annotated on top of Penn Treebank style phrase structure (Xue and Palmer, 2003; Palmer et al., 2008). However, a different grammatical analysis has been used for the Hindi PropBank annotation, dependency structure, which may be particularly suited for the analysis of flexible word order languages such as Hindi.

As a syntactic corpus, we use the Hindi Dependency Treebank (Bhatt et al., 2009). Using dependency structure has some advantages. First, semantic arguments[1] can be marked explicitly on the syntactic trees, so annotations of the predicate argument structure can be more consistent with the dependency structure. Second, the Hindi Dependency Treebank provides a rich set of dependency relations that capture the syntactic-semantic information. This facilitates mappings between syntactic dependents and semantic arguments. A successful mapping would reduce the annotation effort, improve the inter-annotator agreement, and guide a full fledged semantic role labeling task.

In this paper, we briefly describe our annotation work on the Hindi PropBank, and suggest mappings between syntactic and semantic arguments based on linguistic intuitions. We also present a probabilistic rule-based system that uses three types of rules to arrive at mappings between syntactic and semantic arguments. Our experiments show some promising results; these mappings illustrate how well those two frameworks are correlated, and can also be used to speed up the PropBank annotation.

2 Description of the Hindi PropBank

2.1 Background

The Hindi PropBank is part of a multi-dimensional and multi-layered resource creation effort for the Hindi-Urdu language (Bhatt et al., 2009). This multi-layered corpus includes both dependency annotation as well as lexical semantic information in the form of PropBank. The corpus also produces phrase structure representations in addition to de-

[1] The term 'semantic argument' is used to indicate all numbered arguments as well as modifiers in PropBank.

Proceedings of the Fifth Law Workshop (LAW V), pages 21–29,
Portland, Oregon, 23-24 June 2011. ©2011 Association for Computational Linguistics

pendency structure. The Hindi Dependency Treebank has created an annotation scheme for Hindi by adapting labels from Panini's Sanskrit grammar (also known as CPG: Computational Paninian Grammar; see Begum et al. (2008)). Previous work has demonstrated that the English PropBank tagset is quite similar to English dependency trees annotated with the Paninian labels (Vaidya et al., 2009). PropBank has also been mapped to other dependency schemes such as Functional Generative Description (Cinkova, 2006).

2.2 Hindi Dependency Treebank

The Hindi Dependency Treebank (HDT) includes morphological, part-of-speech and chunking information as well as dependency relations. These are represented in the Shakti Standard Format (SSF; see Bharati et al. (2007)). The dependency labels depict relations between chunks, which are "minimal phrases consisting of correlated, inseparable entities" (Bharati et al., 2006), so they are not necessarily individual words. The annotation of chunks also assumes that intra-chunk dependencies can be extracted automatically (Husain et al., 2010).

The dependency tagset consists of about 43 labels, which can be grouped into three categories: dependency relation labels, modifier labels, and labels for non-dependencies (Bharati et al., 2009). PropBank is mainly concerned with those labels depicting dependencies in the domain of locality of verb predicates. The dependency relation labels are based on the notion of 'karaka', defined as "the role played by a participant in an action". The karaka labels, `k1-5`, are centered around the verb's meaning. There are other labels such as `rt` (purpose) or `k7t` (location) that are independent of the verb's meaning.

2.3 Annotating the Hindi PropBank

The Hindi PropBank (HPB) contains the labeling of semantic roles, which are defined on a verb-by-verb basis. The description at the verb-specific level is fine-grained; e.g., 'hitter' and 'hittee'. These verb-specific roles are then grouped into broader categories using numbered arguments (`ARG#`). Each verb can also have modifiers not specific to the verb (`ARGM*`). The annotation process takes place in two stages: the creation of frameset files for individual verb types, and the annotation of predicate argument structures for each verb instance. As annotation tools, we use Cornerstone and Jubilee (Choi et al., 2010a; Choi et al., 2010b). The annotation is done on the HDT; following the dependency annotation, PropBank annotates each verb's syntactic dependents as their semantic arguments at the chunk level. Chunked trees are conveniently displayed for annotators in Jubilee. PropBank annotations generated in Jubilee can also be easily projected onto the SSF format of the original dependency trees.

The HPB currently consists of 24 labels including both numbered arguments and modifiers (Table 1). In certain respects, the HPB labels make some distinctions that are not made in some other language such as English. For instance, `ARG2` is subdivided into labels with function tags, in order to avoid `ARG2` from being semantically overloaded (Yi, 2007). `ARGC` and `ARGA` mark the arguments of morphological causatives in Hindi, which is different from the `ARG0` notion of 'causer'. We also introduce two labels to represent the complex predicate constructions: `ARGM-VLV` and `ARGM-PRX`.

Label	Description		
ARG0	agent, causer, experiencer		
ARG1	patient, theme, undergoer		
ARG2	beneficiary		
ARG3	instrument		
ARG2-ATR	attribute	ARG2-GOL	goal
ARG2-LOC	location	ARG2-SOU	source
ARGC	causer		
ARGA	secondary causer		
ARGM-VLV	verb-verb construction		
ARGM-PRX	noun-verb construction[2]		
ARGM-ADV	adverb	ARGM-CAU	cause
ARGM-DIR	direction	ARGM-DIS	discourse
ARGM-EXT	extent	ARGM-LOC	location
ARGM-MNR	manner	ARGM-MNS	means
ARGM-MOD	modal	ARGM-NEG	negation
ARGM-PRP	purpose	ARGM-TMP	temporal

Table 1: Hindi PropBank labels.

2.4 Empty arguments in the Hindi PropBank

The HDT and HPB layers have different ways of handling empty categories (Bhatia et al., 2010). HPB inserts empty arguments such as `PRO` (empty subject of a non-finite clause), `RELPRO` (empty relative pronoun), `pro` (pro-drop argument), and `gap-pro` (gapped argument). HPB annotates syntactic relations between its semantic roles, notably co-indexation of the empty argument `PRO` as well as `gap-pro`. The example in Figure 1 shows that *Mohan* and `PRO` are co-indexed; thus, *Mohan* becomes `ARG0` of *read* via the empty argument `PRO`. There is no dependency link between `PRO` and *read* because `PRO` is inserted only in the PropBank layer.

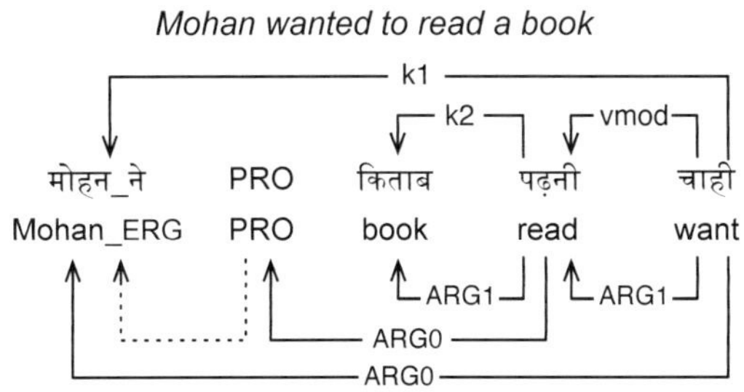

Figure 1: Empty argument example. The upper and lower edges indicate HDT and HPB labels, respectively.

3 Comparisons between syntactic and semantic arguments

In this section, we describe the mappings between HDT and HPB labels based on our linguistic intuitions. We show that there are several broad similarities between two tagsets. These mappings form the basis for our linguistically motivated rules in Section 4.2.3. In section 5.5, we analyze whether the intuitions discussed in this section are borne out by the results of our probabilistic rule-based system.

3.1 Numbered arguments

The numbered arguments correspond to `ARG0-3`, including function tags associated with `ARG2`. In PropBank, `ARG0` and `ARG1` are conceived as framework-independent labels, closely associated with Dowty's Proto-roles (Palmer et al., 2010). For instance, `ARG0` corresponds to the agent, causer, or experiencer, whether it is realized as the subject of an active construction or as the object of an adjunct (by phrase) of the corresponding passive. In this respect, `ARG0` and `ARG1` are very similar to `k1` and `k2` in HDT, which are annotated based on their semantic roles, not their grammatical relation. On the other hand, HDT treats the following sentences similarly, whereas PropBank does not:

- The boy *broke* the window.
- The window *broke*.

The boy and *the window* are both considered `k1` for HDT, whereas PropBank labels *the boy* as `ARG0` and *The window* as `ARG1`. *The window* is not considered a primary causer as the verb is unaccusative for Propbank. For HDT, the notion of unaccusativity is not taken into consideration. This is an important distinction that needs to be considered while carrying out the mapping. `k1` is thus ambiguous between `ARG0` and `ARG1`. Also, HDT makes a distinction between Experiencer subjects of certain verbs, labeling them as `k4a`. As PropBank does not make such a distinction, `k4a` maps to `ARG0`. The Experiencer subject information is included in the corresponding frameset files of the verbs. The mappings to `ARG0` and `ARG1` would be accurate only if they make use of specific verb information. The mappings for other numbered arguments as well as `ARGC` and `ARGA` are given in Table 2.

HDT label	HPB label
`k1` (karta); `k4a` (experiencer)	`Arg0`
`k2` (karma)	`Arg1`
`k4` (beneficiary)	`Arg2`
`k1s` (attribute)	`Arg2-ATR`
`k5` (source)	`Arg2-SOU`
`k2p` (goal)	`Arg2-GOL`
`k3` (instrument)	`Arg3`
`mk1` (causer)	`ArgC`
`pk1` (secondary causer)	`ArgA`

Table 2: Mappings to the HPB numbered arguments.

Note that in HDT annotation practice, `k3` and `k5` tend to be interpreted in a broad fashion such that they map not only to `ARG3` and `ARG2-SOU`, but also to `ARGM-MNS` and `ARGM-LOC` (Vaidya and Husain, 2011). Hence, a one-to-one mapping for these labels is not possible. Furthermore, the occurrence of morphological causatives (`ARGC` and `ARGA`) is fairly low so that we may not be able to test the accuracy of these mappings with the current data.

3.2 Modifiers

The modifiers in PropBank are quite similar in their definitions to certain HDT labels. We expect a fairly high mapping accuracy, especially as these are not verb-specific. Table 3 shows mappings between

HDT labels and HPB modifiers. A problematic mapping could be ARGM-MNR, which is quite coarse-grained in PropBank, applying not only to adverbs of manner, but also to infinitival adjunct clauses.

HDT label	HPB label
sent-adv (epistemic adv)	ArgM-ADV
rh (cause/reason)	ArgM-CAU
rd (direction)	ArgM-DIR
rad (discourse)	ArgM-DIS
k7p (location)	ArgM-LOC
adv (manner adv)	ArgM-MNR
rt (purpose)	ArgM-PRP
k7t (time)	ArgM-TMP

Table 3: Mappings to the HPB modifiers.

3.3 Simple and complex predicates

HPB distinguishes annotations between simple and complex predicates. Simple predicates consist of only a single verb whereas complex predicates consist of a light verb and a pre-verbal element. The complex predicates are identified with a special label ARGM-PRX (ARGument-PRedicating eXpresstion), which is being used for all light verb annotations in PropBank (Hwang et al., 2010). Figure 2 shows an example of the predicating noun *mention* annotated as ARGM-PRX, used with *come*. The predicating noun also has its own argument, *matter of*, indicated with the HDT label r6-k1. The HDT has two labels, r6-k1 and r6-k2, for the arguments of the predicating noun. Hence, the argument span for complex predicates includes not only direct dependents of the verb but also dependents of the noun.

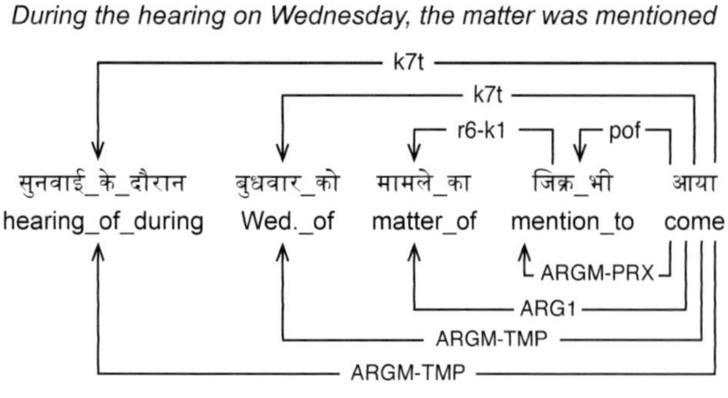

Figure 2: Complex predicate example.

The ARGM-PRX label usually overlaps with the HDT label pof, indicating a 'part of units' as pre-verbal elements in complex predicates. However, in certain cases, HPB has its own analysis for noun-verb complex predicates. Hence, not all the nominals labeled pof are labeled as ARGM-PRX. In the example in Figure 3, the noun chunk *important progress* is not considered to be an ARGM-PRX by HPB (in this example, we have *pragati hona*; (lit) progess be; to progress). The nominal for PropBank is in fact ARG1 of the verb *be*, rather than a composite on the verb. Additional evidence for this is that neither the nominal nor the light verb seem to project arguments of their own.

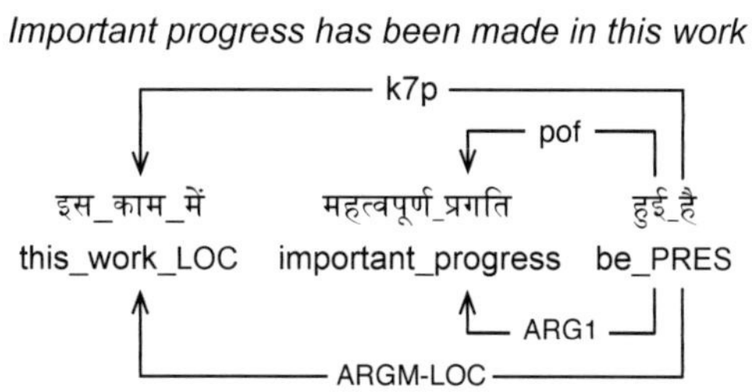

Figure 3: HDT vs. HPB on complex predicates.

4 Automatic mapping of HDT to HPB

Mapping between syntactic and semantic structures has been attempted in other languages. The Penn English and Chinese Treebanks consist of several semantic roles (e.g., locative, temporal) annotated on top of Penn Treebank style phrase structure (Marcus et al., 1994; Xue and Palmer, 2009). The Chinese PropBank specifies mappings between syntactic and semantic arguments in frameset files (e.g., SBJ → ARG0) that can be used for automatic mapping (Xue and Palmer, 2003). However, these Chinese mappings are limited to certain types of syntactic arguments (mostly subjects and objects). Moreover, semantic annotations on the Treebanks are done independently from PropBank annotations, which causes disagreement between the two structures.

Dependency structure transparently encodes relations between predicates and their arguments, which facilitates mappings between syntactic and semantic arguments. Hajičová and Kučerová (2002) tried to project PropBank semantic roles onto the Prague Dependency Treebank, and showed that the projection is not trivial. The same may be true to our case; however, our goal is not to achieve complete mappings between syntactic and semantic arguments, but to find a useful set of mappings that can speed up our annotation. These mappings will be applied to our future data as a pre-annotation stage, so that annotators do not need to annotate arguments that have already been automatically labeled by our system. Thus, it is important to find mappings with high precision and reasonably good recall.

In this section, we present a probabilistic rule-based system that identifies and classifies semantic arguments in the HPB using syntactic dependents in the HDT. This is still preliminary work; our system is expected to improve as we annotate more data and do more error analysis.

4.1 Argument identification

Identifying semantic arguments of each verb predicate is relatively easy given the dependency Treebank. For each verb predicate, we consider all syntactic dependents of the predicate as its semantic arguments (Figure 4). For complex predicates, we consider the syntactic dependents of both the verb and the predicating noun (cf. Section 3.3).

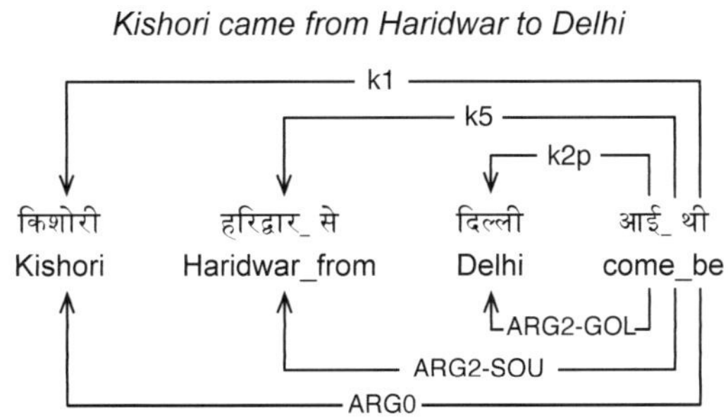

Figure 4: Simple predicate example.

With our heuristics, we get a precision of 99.11%, a recall of 95.50%, and an F1-score of 97.27% for argument identification. Such a high precision is expected as the annotation guidelines for HDT and HPB generally follow the same principles of identifying syntactic and semantic arguments of a verb. About 4.5% of semantic arguments are not identified by our method. Table 4 shows distributions of the most frequent non-identified arguments.

Label	Dist.	Label	Dist.	Label	Dist.
ARG0	3.21	ARG1	0.90	ARG2*	0.09

Table 4: Distributions of non-identified arguments caused by PropBank empty categories (in %).

Most of the non-identified argument are antecedents of PropBank empty arguments. As shown in Figure 1, the PropBank empty argument has no dependency link to the verb predicate. Identifying such arguments requires a task of empty category resolution, which will be explored as future work. Furthermore, we do not try to identify PropBank empty arguments for now, which will also be explored later.

4.2 Argument classification

Given the identified semantic arguments, we classify their semantic roles. Argument classification is done by using three types of rules. Deterministic rules are heuristics that are straightforward given dependency structure. Empirically-derived rules are generated by measuring statistics of dependency features in association with semantic roles. Finally, linguistically-motivated rules are derived from our linguistic intuitions. Each type of rule has its own strength; how to combine them is the art we need to explore.

4.2.1 Deterministic rule

Only one deterministic rule is used in our system. When an identified argument has a `pof` dependency relation with its predicate, we classify the argument as ARGM-PRX. This emphasizes the advantage of using our dependency structure: classifying ARGM-PRX cannot be done automatically in most other languages where there is no information provided for light verb constructions. This deterministic rule is applied before any other type of rule. Therefore, we do not generate further rules to classify the ARGM-PRX label.

4.2.2 Empirically-derived rules

Three kinds of features are used for the generation of empirically-derived rules: predicate ID, predicate's voice type, and argument's dependency label. The predicate ID is either the lemma or the roleset ID of the predicate. Predicate lemmas are already provided in HDT. When we use predicate lemmas, we assume no manual annotation of PropBank. Thus, rules generated from predicate lemmas can be applied to any future data without modification. When we use roleset ID's, we assume that sense annotations are already done. PropBank includes annotations of coarse verb senses, called roleset ID's, that differentiate each verb predicate with different senses (Palmer et al., 2005). A verb predicate can form several argument structures with respect to different senses. Using roleset ID's, we generate more fine-grained rules that are specific to those senses.

The predicate's voice type is either 'active' or 'passive', also provided in HDT. There are not many instances of passive construction in our current data, which makes it difficult to generate rules general enough for future data. However, even with the lack of training instances, we find some advantage of using the voice feature in our experiments. Finally, the argument's dependency label is the dependency label of an identified argument with respect to its predicate. This feature is straightforward for the case of simple predicates. For complex predicates, we use the dependency labels of arguments with respect to their syntactic heads, which can be pre-verbal elements. Note that rules generated with complex predicates contain slightly different features for predicate lemmas as well; instead of using predicate lemmas, we use joined tags of the predicate lemmas and the lemmas of pre-verbal elements.

ID	V	Drel	PBrel	#
come	a	`k1`	`ARG0`	1
come	a	`k5`	`ARG2-SOU`	1
come	a	`k2p`	`ARG2-GOL`	1
come_mention	a	`k7t`	`ARGM-TMP`	2
come_mention	a	`r6-k1`	`ARG1`	1

Table 5: Rules generated by the examples in Figures 4 and 2. The ID, V, and Drel columns show predicate ID, predicate's voice type, and argument's dependency label. The PBrel column shows the PropBank label of each argument. The # column shows the total count of each feature tuple being associated with the PropBank label. 'a' stands for active voice.

Table 5 shows a set of rules generated by the examples in Figures 4 (*come*) and 2 (*come_mention*). No rule is generated for `ARGM-PRX` because the label is already covered by our deterministic rule (Section 4.2.1). When roleset ID's are used in place of the predicate ID, *come* and *come_mention* are replaced with `A.03` and `A.01`, respectively. These rules can be formulated as a function $rule$ such that:

$$rule(id, v, drel) = \arg\max_i P(pbrel_i)$$

where $P(pbrel_i)$ is a probability of the predicted PropBank label $pbrel_i$, given a tuple of features $(id, v, drel)$. The probability is measured by estimating a maximum likelihood of each PropBank label being associated with the feature tuple. For example, a feature tuple (*come*, active, `k1`) can be associated with two PropBank labels, `ARG0` and `ARG1`, with counts of 8 and 2, respectively. In this case, the maximum likelihoods of `ARG0` and `ARG1` being associated with the feature tuple is 0.8 and 0.2; thus $rule$(*come*, active, `k1`) = `ARG0`.

Since we do not want to apply rules with low confidence, we set a threshold to $P(pbrel)$, so predictions with low probabilities can be filtered out. Finding the right threshold is a task of handling the precision/recall trade-off. For our experiments, we ran 10-fold cross-validation to find the best threshold.

4.2.3 Linguistically-motivated rules

Linguistically-motivated rules are applied to arguments that the deterministic rule and empirically-derived rules cannot classify. These rules capture general correlations between syntactic and semantic arguments for each predicate, so they are not as fine-grained as empirically-derived rules, but can be helpful for predicates not seen in the training data. The rules are manually generated by our annotators and specified in frameset files. Table 6 shows linguistically-motivated rules for the predicate 'A (*come*)', specified in the frameset file, 'A-v.xml'.[3]

Roleset	Usage	Rule
`A.01`	to come	`k1` → `ARG1` `k2p` → `ARG2-GOL`

`A.03`	to arrive	`k1` → `ARG1`
		`k2p` → `ARG2-GOL`
		`k5` → `ARG2-SOU`

`A.02`	light verb	No rule provided

Table 6: Rules for the predicate 'A (*come*)'.

The predicate 'A' has three verb senses and each sense specifies a different set of rules. For instance, the first rule of `A.01` maps a syntactic dependent with the dependency label `k1` to a semantic argument with the semantic label `ARG1`. Note that frameset files include rules only for numbered arguments. Most of these rules should already be included in the empirically-derived rules as we gain

[3]See Choi et al. (2010a) for details about frameset files.

more training data; however, for an early stage of annotation, these rules provide useful information.

5 Experiments

5.1 Corpus

All our experiments use a subset of the Hindi Dependency Treebank, distributed by the ICON'10 contest (Husain et al., 2010). Our corpus contains about 32,300 word tokens and 2,005 verb predicates, in which 546 of them are complex predicates. Each verb predicate is annotated with a verse sense specified in its corresponding frameset file. There are 160 frameset files created for the verb predicates. The number may seem small compared to the number of verb predicates. This is because we do not create separate frameset files for light verb constructions, which comprise about 27% of the predicate instances (see the example in Table 6).

All verb predicates are annotated with argument structures using PropBank labels. A total of 5,375 arguments are annotated. Since there is a relatively small set of data, we do not make a separate set for evaluations. Instead, we run 10-fold cross-validation to evaluate our rule-based system.

5.2 Evaluation of deterministic rule

First, we evaluate how well our deterministic rule classifies the `ARGM-PRX` label. Using the deterministic rule, we get a 94.46% precision and a 100% recall on `ARGM-PRX`. The 100% recall is expected; the precision implies that about 5.5% of the time, light verb annotations in the HPB do not agree with the complex predicate annotations (`pof` relation) in the HDT (cf. Section 3.3). More analysis needs to be done to improve the precision of this rule.

5.3 Evaluation of empirically-derived rules

Next, we evaluate our empirically-derived rules with respect to the different thresholds set for $P(pbrel_i)$. In general, the higher the threshold is, the higher and lower the precision and recall become, respectively. Figure 5 shows comparisons between precision and recall with respect to different thresholds. Notice that a threshold of 1.0, meaning that using only rules with 100% confidence, does not give the highest precision. This is because the model with this high of a threshold overfits to the training data. Rules that work well in the training data do not necessarily work as well on the test data.

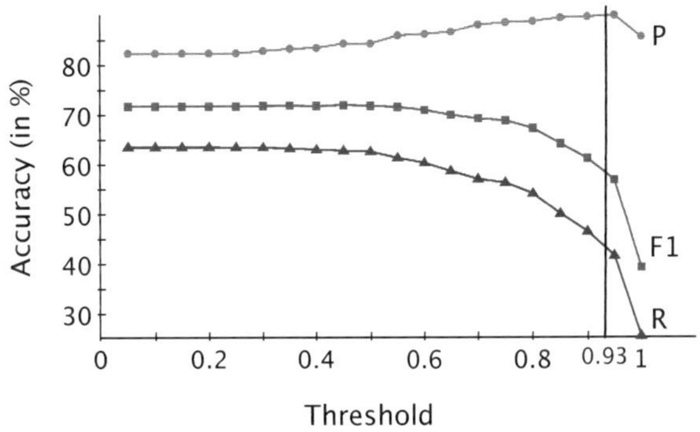

Figure 5: Accuracies achieved by the empirically derived rules using (lemma, voice, label) features. P, R, and F1 stand for precisions, recalls, and F1-scores, respectively.

We need to find a threshold that gives a high precision (so annotators do not get confused by the automatic output) while maintaining a good recall (so annotations can go faster). With a threshold of 0.93 using features (lemma, voice, dependency label), we get a precision of 90.37%, a recall of 44.52%, and an F1-score of 59.65%. Table 7 shows accuracies for all PropBank labels achieved by a threshold of 0.92 using roleset ID's instead of predicate's lemmas. Although the overall precision stays about the same, we get a noticeable improvement in the overall recall using roleset ID's. Note that some labels are missing in Table 7. This is because either they do not occur in our current data (`ARGC` and `ARGA`) or we have not started annotating them properly yet (`ARGM-MOD` and `ARGM-NEG`).

5.4 Evaluation of linguistically-motivated rules

Finally, we evaluate the impact of the linguistically-motivated rules. Table 8 shows accuracies achieved by the linguistically motivated rules applied after the empirically derived rules. As expected, the linguistically motivated rules improve the recall of `ARGN` significantly, but bring a slight decrease in the precision. This shows that our linguistic intuitions are generally on the right track. We may combine some of the empirically derived rules with linguistically motivated rules together in the frameset files so annotators can take advantage of both kinds of rules in the future.

	Dist.	P	R	F1
ALL	100.00	90.59	47.92	62.69
ARG0	17.50	95.83	67.27	79.05
ARG1	27.28	94.47	61.62	74.59
ARG2	3.42	81.48	37.93	51.76
ARG2-ATR	2.54	94.55	40.31	56.52
ARG2-GOL	1.61	64.29	21.95	32.73
ARG2-LOC	0.87	90.91	22.73	36.36
ARG2-SOU	0.83	78.26	42.86	55.38
ARG3	0.08	0.00	0.00	0.00
ARGM-ADV	3.50	31.82	3.93	7.00
ARGM-CAU	1.44	50.00	5.48	9.88
ARGM-DIR	0.43	100.00	18.18	30.77
ARGM-DIS	1.63	26.67	4.82	8.16
ARGM-EXT	1.42	0.00	0.00	0.00
ARGM-LOC	10.77	83.80	27.42	41.32
ARGM-MNR	6.00	57.14	9.18	15.82
ARGM-MNS	0.79	77.78	17.50	28.57
ARGM-PRP	2.15	65.52	17.43	27.54
ARGM-PRX	10.75	94.46	100.00	97.15
ARGM-TMP	7.01	74.63	14.04	23.64

Table 7: Labeling accuracies achieved by the empirically derived rules using (roleset ID, voice, label) features and a threshold of 0.92. The accuracy for ARGM-PRX is achieved by the deterministic rule. The Dist. column shows a distribution of each label.

	Dist.	P	R	F1
ALL	100.00	89.80	55.28	68.44
ARGN	54.12	91.87	72.36	80.96
ARGM	45.88	85.31	35.14	49.77
ARGN w/o LM		93.63	58.76	72.21

Table 8: Labeling accuracies achieved by the linguistically motivated rules. The ARGN and ARGM rows show statistics of all numbered arguments and modifiers combined, respectively. The 'ARGN w/o LM' row shows accuracies of ARGN achieved only by the empirically derived rules.

5.5 Error anlaysis

The precision and recall results for ARG0 and ARG1, are better than expected, despite the complexity of the mapping (Section 3.1). This is because they occur most often in the corpus, so enough rules can be extracted. The other numbered arguments are closely related to particular types of verbs (e.g., motion verbs for ARG2-GOL | SOU). Our linguistically motivated rules are more effective for these types of HPB labels. We would expect the modifiers to be mapped independently of the verb, but our experiments show that the presence of the verb lemma feature enhances the performance of modifiers. Although section 3.2 expects one-to-one mappings for modifiers, it is not the case in practice.

We observe that the interpretation of labels in annotation practice is important. For example, our system performs poorly for ARGM-ADV because the label is used for various sentential modifiers and can be mapped to as many as four HDT labels. On the other hand, HPB makes some fine-grained distinctions. For instance, means and causes are distinguished using ARGM-CAU and ARGM-MNS labels, a distinction that HDT does not make. In the example in Figure 6, we find that *aptitude_with* is assigned to ARGM-MNS, but gets the cause label rh in HDT.

Rajyapal can call upon any party with his aptitude

राज्यपाल अपने विवेक_से किसी_भी पार्टी_को बुला_सकता_है
Rajyapal his aptitude_with any_EMPH party_DAT call_can_be

Figure 6: Means vs. cause example.

6 Conclusion and future work

We provide an analysis of the Hindi PropBank annotated on the Hindi Dependency Treebank. There is an interesting correlation between dependency and predicate argument structures. By analyzing the similarities between the two structures, we find rules that can be used for automatic mapping of syntactic and semantic arguments, and achieve over 90% confidence for almost half of the data. These rules will be applied to our future data, which will make the annotation faster and possibly more accurate.

We plan to use different sets of rules generated by different thresholds to see which rule set leads to the most effective annotation. We also plan to develop a statistical semantic role labeling system in Hindi, once we have enough training data. In addition, we will explore the possibility of using existing lexical resource such as WordNet (Narayan et al., 2002) to improve our system.

Acknowledgements

This work is supported by NSF grants CNS- 0751089, CNS-0751171, CNS-0751202, and CNS-0751213. Any opinions, findings, and conclusions or recommendations expressed in this material are those of the authors and do not necessarily reflect the views of the National Science Foundation.

References

Rafiya Begum, Samar Husain, Arun Dhwaj, Dipti Misra Sharma, Lakshmi Bai, and Rajeev Sangal. 2008. Dependency annotation scheme for indian languages. In *In Proceedings of the 3rd International Joint Conference on Natural Language Processing*, IJCNLP'08.

Akshar Bharati, Dipti Misra Sharma, Lakshmi Bai, and Rajeev Sangal. 2006. AnnCorra: Guidelines for POS and Chunk Annotation for Indian Languages. Technical report, IIIT Hyderabad.

Akshar Bharati, Rajeev Sangal, and Dipti Misra Sharma. 2007. Ssf: Shakti standard format guide. Technical report, IIIT Hyderabad.

Akshara Bharati, Dipti Misra Sharma, Samar Husain, Lakshmi Bai, Rafiya Begam, and Rajeev Sangal. 2009. Anncorra : Treebanks for indian languages, guidelines for annotating hindi treebank. Technical report, IIIT Hyderabad.

Archna Bhatia, Rajesh Bhatt, Bhuvana Narasimhan, Martha Palmer, Owen Rambow, Dipti Misra Sharma, Michael Tepper, Ashwini Vaidya, and Fei Xia. 2010. Empty categories in a hindi treebank. In *Proceedings of the 7th International Conference on Language Resources and Evaluation (LREC'10)*, pages 1863–1870.

Rajesh Bhatt, Bhuvana Narasimhan, Martha Palmer, Owen Rambow, Dipti Sharma, and Fei Xia. 2009. A Multi-Representational and Multi-Layered Treebank for Hindi/Urdu. In *In the Proceedings of the Third Linguistic Annotation Workshop held in conjunction with ACL-IJCNLP 2009*.

Jinho D. Choi, Claire Bonial, and Martha Palmer. 2010a. Propbank frameset annotation guidelines using a dedicated editor, cornerstone. In *Proceedings of the 7th International Conference on Language Resources and Evaluation*, LREC'10, pages 3650–3653.

Jinho D. Choi, Claire Bonial, and Martha Palmer. 2010b. Propbank instance annotation guidelines using a dedicated editor, jubilee. In *Proceedings of the 7th International Conference on Language Resources and Evaluation*, LREC'10, pages 1871–1875.

Silvie Cinkova. 2006. From PropBank to EngVALLEX: Adapting PropBank-Lexicon to the Valency Theory of Functional Generative Description. In *Proceedings of the fifth International conference on Language Resources and Evaluation (LREC 2006), Genova, Italy*.

Eva Hajičová and Ivona Kučerová. 2002. Argument/valency structure in propbank, lcs database and prague dependency treebank: A comparative pilot study. In *Proceedings of the 3rd International Conference on Language Resources and Evaluation*, LREC'02, pages 846–851.

Samar Husain, Prashanth Mannem, Bharat Ram Ambati, and Phani Gadde. 2010. The ICON-2010 tools contest on Indian language dependency parsing. In *Proceedings of ICON-2010 Tools Contest on Indian Language Dependency Parsing*, ICON'10, pages 1–8.

Jena D. Hwang, Archna Bhatia, Claire Bonial, Aous Mansouri, Ashwini Vaidya, Nianwen Xue, and Martha Palmer. 2010. PropBank Annotation of Multilingual Light Verb Constructions. In *Proceedings of the Linguistic Annotation Workshop at ACL 2010*.

Mitchell Marcus, Grace Kim, Mary Ann Marcinkiewicz, Robert Macintyre, Ann Bies, Mark Ferguson, Karen Katz, and Britta Schasberger. 1994. The penn treebank: Annotating predicate argument structure. In *ARPA Human Language Technology Workshop*, pages 114–119.

Dipak Narayan, Debasri Chakrabarti, Prabhakar Pande, and Pushpak Bhattacharyya. 2002. An experience in building the indo wordnet - a wordnet for hindi. In *Proceedings of the 1st International Conference on Global WordNet*.

Martha Palmer, Daniel Gildea, and Paul Kingsbury. 2005. The proposition bank: An annotated corpus of semantic roles. *Computational Linguistics*, 31(1):71–106.

Martha Palmer, Olga Babko-Malaya, Ann Bies, Mona Diab, Mohamed Maamouri, Aous Mansouri, and Wajdi Zaghouani. 2008. A pilot arabic propbank. In *Proceedings of the 6th International Language Resources and Evaluation*, LREC'08, pages 28–30.

Martha Palmer, Daniel Gildea, and Nianwen Xue. 2010. Semantic role labeling. In Graeme Hirst, editor, *Synthesis Lectures on Human Language Technologies*. Morgan and Claypool.

Ashwini Vaidya and Samar Husain. 2011. A classification of dependencies in the Hindi/Urdu Treebank. In *Presented at the Workshop on South Asian Syntax and Semantics, Amherst, MA*.

Ashwini Vaidya, Samar Husain, and Prashanth Mannem. 2009. A karaka based dependency scheme for English. In *Proceedings of the CICLing-2009, Mexico City, Mexico*.

Nianwen Xue and Martha Palmer. 2003. Annotating the propositions in the penn chinese treebank. In *Proceedings of the 2nd SIGHAN workshop on Chinese language processing*, SIGHAN'03, pages 47–54.

Nianwen Xue and Martha Palmer. 2009. Adding semantic roles to the chinese treebank. *Natural Language Engineering*, 15(1):143–172.

Szu-Ting Yi. 2007. *Automatic Semantic Role Labeling*. Ph.D. thesis, University of Pennsylvania.

How Good is the Crowd at "real" WSD?

Jisup Hong
International Computer Science Institute
Berkeley, CA
jhong@icsi.berkeley.edu

Collin F. Baker
International Computer Science Institute
Berkeley, CA
collinb@icsi.berkeley.edu

Abstract

There has been a great deal of excitement recently about using the "wisdom of the crowd" to collect data of all kinds, quickly and cheaply (Howe, 2008; von Ahn and Dabbish, 2008). Snow *et al.* (Snow et al., 2008) were the first to give a convincing demonstration that at least some kinds of linguistic data can be gathered from workers on the web more cheaply than and as accurately as from local experts, and there has been a steady stream of papers and workshops since then with similar results. e.g. (Callison-Burch and Dredze, 2010).

Many of the tasks which have been successfully crowdsourced involve judgments which are similar to those performed in everyday life, such as recognizing unclear writing (von Ahn et al., 2008), or, for those tasks that require considerable judgment, the responses are usually binary or from a small set of responses, such as sentiment analysis (Mellebeek et al., 2010) or ratings (Heilman and Smith, 2010). Since the FrameNet process is known to be relatively expensive, we were interested in whether the FrameNet process of fine word sense discrimination and marking of dependents with semantic roles could be performed more cheaply and equally accurately using Amazon's Mechanical Turk (AMT) or similar resources. We report on a partial success in this respect and how it was achieved.

1 Defining the task

The usual FrameNet process for annotating examples of a particular **lexical unit (LU)**, is to first extract examples of this sense from a corpus, based on collocational and syntactic patterns, storing them in subcorpora; this process is called **subcorporation**. Given an LU, vanguarders begin by composing rules consisting of syntactic patterns and instructions as to whether to include or exclude the sentences that match them. An automated system extracts sentences containing uses of the LU's lemma, applies POS tagging and chunk parsing, and then matches the sentences against the rules in their specified order to allow for cascading effects. Ultimately, the result is a set of subcorpora, each corresponding to a pattern, and containing sentences likely to exhibit a use of the LU. More recently, a system has been developed in collaboration with the Sketch Engine ((Kilgarriff et al., July 2004) `http://www.sketchengine.co.uk`) to accelerate this process by giving annotators a graphical interface in which precomputed collocational pattern matches can be more directly assigned to the various LUs corresponding to a given lemma. The actual annotation of the **frame elements (FEs)** is facilitated by having pre-selected sets of sentences which are at least likely to contain the right sense of the word, and which share a syntactic pattern. Therefore, we first focused on the frame discrimination task (which in other contexts would be called word sense discrimination), which we assumed to be simpler to collect data for than the FE annotation task, and which is a prerequisite for it.

We began by evaluating the resources that AMT provides for designing and implementing **Human Intelligence Tasks (HITs)**; we quickly determined that the UI provided by AMT would not suffice for the task we planned. Specifically, it lacks the ability to:

- randomize the selection options,

Proceedings of the Fifth Law Workshop (LAW V), pages 30–37,

- present questions from a set one at a time,
- randomize the order in which a set of questions are presented, or
- record response times for each question.

We therefore decided to design our HITs using Amazon's "External Question HIT Type", and to serve the HITs from our own web server. In this system, when workers view or execute a HIT, the content of the HIT window is supplied from our server, and responses are stored directly in a database running our own server, rather than Amazon's. Workers log in through AMT and are ultimately paid through AMT, but the content of the tasks can be completely controlled though our web server.

The Frame Discrimination Task can be set up in a number of ways, such as:

1. Present a single sentence with the lemma highlighted. Workers must select a frame (or "none of the above") from a multiple-choice list of frames we provide.
2. Present a list of sentences all containing uses of the same lemma. Workers must check off all the sentences that contain uses of a given frame.
3. Present a list of sentences all containing uses of the same lemma. Provide one example sentence from each frame and ask users to categorize the sentences.

In order to get started as quickly as possible and get a baseline result, we chose the first of the above methods, which is the most straightforward from a theoretical point of view. For example, the lemma might be *gain*.v, which has two LUs, one in the **Change_position_on_a_scale** frame, and another in the **Getting** frame. The HIT displays one sentence at a time, with the lemma highlighted; below the sentence, a multiple-choice selection is presented with the Frame names:

```
You will have to GAIN their support,
if change is to be brought about.

   Change_position_on_a_scale
   Getting
   None of the above
```

When users mouse-over the name of a frame, a pop-up displays an example sentence from that Frame (from a different LU in the same frame). Users can also click the name of the frame, which causes the browser to open another window with the frame definition. This process repeats for 12 sentences, at which point the HIT is over, and results are entered into our database.

Sources of material for testing

We had no shortage of sentences for the frame discrimination task; we started with some of the many unannotated sentences already in the FrameNet database. In the usual process of subcorporation, each of the subcorpora matches one specific pattern; the goal is to extract roughly 20 examples of each collocational/syntactic pattern, and to annotate one or two of each. The following are examples from among the patterns used for *rip*.v in the **Removing** frame:

```
NP T NP [PP f="from"]
NP T NP [w "out"]
```

The first pattern would match sentences like, "I ripped the top from my pack of cigarettes," and the second, "She ripped the telephone out of the wall."

We do not presume, however, that we will always be able to define patterns for all of the possible valences of a predicator, so we also include two "other" subcorpora. The first of these (named "other-matched") contains 50 sentences (provided there are enough instances in the corpus) which matched any one of the preceding patterns but were left over after 20 had been extracted for each pattern. The second ("other-unmatched") contains sentences in which the lemma occurs (with the right POS) which did **not** match any of the earlier patterns. Vanguarders carefully check these "other" subcorpora to see if the lemma is used in a syntactic valence which was not foreseen; if they find any such new valences, they are annotated. Typically, this means that there are roughly 100 extra unannotated sentences for each LU. For this experiment, we extracted 10 sentences from the "other-matched" subcorpus of each of the LUs for the lemma, meaning that they had already matched some pattern which was designed for one of those LUs. In addition to the unannotated sentences, we randomly selected three annotated sentences from each LU, two to use as included gold-standard items

Frame name	Example
Cause_to_fragment	The revolution has RIPPED thousands of Cuban families apart ...
Damaging	... Mo's dress is RIPPED by a drunken admirer.
Removing	Sinatra then reportedly RIPPED the phone out of the wall ...
Self_motion	A tornado RIPPED through Salt Lake City ...
Judgment_communication	(no annotated examples–related to *rip into*.v)
Position_on_a_scale	Eggs, shellfish and cheese are all HIGH in cholesterol ...
Dimension	An adult tiger stands at least 3 ft (90 cm) HIGH at the shoulder.
Intoxication	Exhausted but HIGH on adrenalin, he would roam about the house...
Measurable_attributes	Finally we came to a HIGH plastic wall.
Evidence	Our results SHOW that unmodified oligonucleotides can provide ...
Reasoning	He uses economics to SHOW how this is so.
Obviousness	... sighting black mountain tops SHOWING through the ice-cap.
Cotheme	When they were SHOWN to their table, ...
Finish_competition	(no annotated examples– *Fair Lady placed in the second race at Aqueduct.*)
Cause_to_perceive	A second inner pylon SHOWS Ptolemy XIII paying homage to Isis ...

Table 1: LUs (senses) for *rip*.v, *high*.a, and *show*.v

for checking accuracy, and one to use as the example in the preview of the HIT. These sentences were randomized and separated into batches of 12 for each HIT; all of which were inserted into a database on a local web server. A local CGI script (reached from AMT) calls the database for the examples in each HIT and stores the workers' responses in the same database.

We ran three trials under this setup, for the lemmas *rip*.v, *high*.a, and *show*.v. Based on the success of earlier studies, our concern initially was to make our tasks be sufficiently challenging so as to be useful for evaluating AMT. Thus, we chose lemmas with four to five senses rather than just two or three. In addition, for these three lemmas, each of the senses appears with sufficient frequency in the corpus so that all senses are realistically available for consideration.[1] The frames for each of these lemmas are shown in Table 1; some of these distinctions are fairly subtle; we will discuss some examples below.

To combine responses, we took the modal response as the result for each item; in cases of ties, we chose randomly, and split the response count where necessary. On this basis, for *rip*.v, the workers had an accuracy of 32.16 correct out of 48 items (67%), for *high*.a, they got 22 out of 49 correct (46%), and for *show*.v, 37 out of 60 items (62%), as shown in Table 2. If we consider that FrameNet has four senses (LUs) for *rip*.v and *high*.a and five for *show*.v, this might not sound too awful, but if we think of this as pre-processing, so that the resulting sentences can be annotated in the correct frame, it leaves a lot to be desired. If we raise the agreement criteria, by filtering out items on which the margin between the modal response and the next highest is 35% or greater (i.e. those with high agreement among workers), we can get higher accuracy (shown in the right two columns of Table 2), at the expense of failing to classify $3/4$ of the items, hardly a solution to the problem.

Trials with CrowdFlower

We decided to try our task on CrowdFlower (`http://crowdflower.com`, formerly Dolores Labs), a company that provides tools and custom solutions to make crowdsourcing tasks easier to create and manage, including techniques to assure a certain level of quality in the results. While working with CrowdFlower, our tasks were running on AMT, although CrowdFlower also provides other labor pools, such as Samasource (`http://www.samasource.org`), depending on the nature of the task. We tried running the task for *rip*.v on Crowdflower's system, using the same HIT design as before, (recreated using

[1]An exception is the *show*.v in the **Finish_competition** frame, which we excluded for this reason, as in *Mucho Macho Man showed in the 2011 Kentucky Derby.*

Lemma	No. senses	No. Items	Accuracy	Filtered Items	Accuracy.
rip.v	4	48	67%	10	90%
high.a	4	48	46%	12	58%
show.v	5	60	62%	11	64%

Table 2: Results from Trial 1: *Rip*.v, *high*.a and *show*.v

their self-serve UI design tools), but with different sentences. Once again, we selected 12 sentences for each of the 4 LUs, for a total of 48 sentences. We wanted to collect 10 judgments per sentence, for a total of 480 judgments. Of the 12 sentences in each HIT, 2 were already annotated and used as a gold standard.

However, after starting this job, we found that the CrowdFlower system automatically halted the jobs after a few hours due to poor average performance on the gold standard items. After having the job halted repeatedly, we were finally able to force it to finish by suspending use of the gold standard to judge accuracy. In other words, the system was telling us that the task was too hard for the workers.

Revised CrowdFlower Trials

After our difficulties with the first trial on CrowdFlower's system, we visited their offices for an on-site consultation. We learned more about how CrowdFlower's system works, and received suggestions on how to improve performance:

- Run a larger set of data; they recommended at least 200 sentences for a job.
- Embed 20% gold standard items so that there is at least one per page of questions, since, without gold standard items, workers will answer randomly, or always choose the first option.
- Get rid of the frame names and use something easier to understand.
- Provide more detailed instructions that include examples.

Based on this consultation, we made the following changes in our HITs: (1) Replaced frame names with hand-crafted synonyms, (2) Renamed the task and rewrote all instructions to avoid jargon, (3) Removed links and roll-overs giving examples or referring people to external documentation, and (4) Extracted 60 sentences per LU, of which 10 are gold standard.

Although we planned to do this for *rip*.v, *high*.a, and *show*.v, we found that it was too difficult to come up with synonyms for *high*.a, so we ran trials only for *rip*.v and *show*.v. For *rip*.v, with four senses, we collected 10 judgments each on 240 sentences, for a total of 2400 judgments. For *show*.v, with five senses, we collected 10 judgments each on 300 sentences, for a total of 3000 judgments. In the final trials, the weighted majority response provided by CrowdFlower was found to be correct 75% for rip.v and 80% for show.v. This was encouraging, but we were concerned with the limitations of this method: (1) The calculation used to select the "weighted majority response" is proprietary to CrowdFlower, so that we could not know the details or change it, and (2) the final trials required handcrafted definitions, synonyms, and very clear definitions for each LU, which is at best time-consuming, and sometimes impossible (as is likely case for *high*.a), meaning the method will not scale well. As researchers, the first limitation is especially problematic as it is necessary to know exactly what methods we are using in our research and be able to share them openly. For these reasons, we decided to go back to building our own interfaces on AMT, and to look for approaches that would be more automatic.

Return to AMT

We redesigned the HIT around a pile-sorting model; instead of seeing one sentence and choosing between frames (whether by name or by synonym), workers are shown model sentences for each LU (i.e. in each frame), and then asked to categorize a list of sentences that are displayed all at once. Consequently, the worker generates a set of piles each corresponding to a frame/LU. The advantages of this approach are as follows:

- Workers can more easily exploit paradigmatic

contrasts across sentences to decide which category to put them in.

- Workers can recategorize sentences after initially putting them into a pile.
- Workers have example sentences using the LUs in question, which constitutes more information than the frame name (assuming that they were not going to the FrameNet website to peruse annotation).
- HITs can be generated automatically, without us having to manually create synonyms for each LU, which turned out to be quite difficult.

This approach, however, does have some disadvantages:

- We need to pre-annotate at least 1 sentence per LU in order to have example sentences.
- Having lots of sentences presented at once clutters up the screen and requires scrolling.
- The HIT interface is much more complex and potentially more fragile.

Because of the complexity of the new interface and the increased screen space required for each additional sense, we decided to begin trials on the lemma *justify*.v which (we believe) has just two senses, but still requires a fairly difficult distinction, between the **Deserving** frame, as in *The evolutionary analogy is close enough to JUSTIFY borrowing the term, ...* and the *Justifying* frame, as in *This final section allows Mr Hicks to JUSTIFY the implementation of abc as....* These two sentences were were annotated in the FrameNet data, and were randomly selected to serve as the models for the workers, illustrating the danger of choosing randomly in such cases!

For all HITs, the sentences were randomized in order, as well as the order of the example sentences. Example sentences retained the same colors, i.e. the frame/color correspondence was kept constant, so as not to confuse workers working on multiple HITs. Sentences were horizontally aligned so that the highlighted target word was centered and vertically aligned across the sentences. Each sentence had a drop-down box to its right where workers could select a category to place it in. Each sense category was represented by a model sentence with the frame name as a label for the category. We collected 10 judgments each on 132 sentences, with workers being asked to categorize 18 sentences in each HIT. In the first trial, accuracy was 55%. In trial 2, the model sentences were modified to also show frame element annotation, in the hope that the fact that the **Justifying** uses have an Agent as the subject, while the **Deserving** uses have a State of affairs as the subject would be clearer. An image of the HIT interface, with FE annotation displayed on the model sentences, is shown in Figure 1. Despite the added information, accuracy decreased to 45%.

Qualifying the prospects

In trial 3, we kept the HIT interface the same, including the model sentences, but added (1) a qualification test that was designed to evaluate the worker's ability in English, (2) required that the workers have registered a US address with Amazon and (3) required that workers have an overall HIT acceptance rate greater than 75%. Although over 100 workers took the qualification test, no workers accepted the HIT. In trial 4 we raised the rate of pay to $.25/HIT, but still got only 1 worker.

On the suspicion that our problem was partially caused by not having enough HITs to make it worth the workers' time to do them, in Trial 5 we posted the same HITs 3 times, amounting to 24 HITs, worth $6, from a worker's point of view; this raised the number of workers to 5 for all three HITs. Through the HITs completed by those workers, we collected 1 to 2 judgments on 107 of the 132 sentences posted, with 63% accuracy overall, and 86% accuracy on the gold sentences. Looking at their answers for each frame, workers correctly categorized 93% of cases of **Justifying** but only 52% of cases of **Deserving**.

In trial 6, we then customized the instructions (this time automatically, rather than manually) to refer to the lemma specifically rather than via a generic description like "the highlighted word." In addition, we removed the qualification test so as to make our HITs available to a much larger pool of workers, but kept the other two requirements. We ran HITs again with 18 sentences each, 2 of which were gold. We decided to try a different lemma with two sense distinctions, *top*.a, and to make it more worthwhile for workers to annotate our data by posting HITs simultaneously

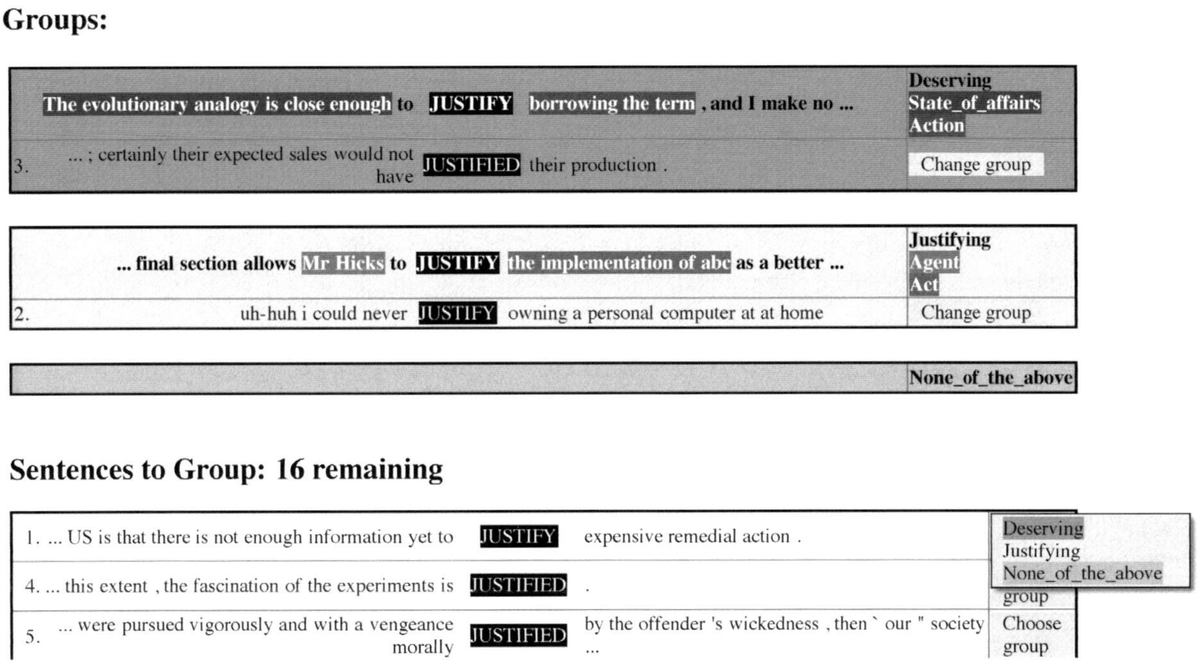

Figure 1: HIT Screen for *justify*.v (after two sentences have been categorized)

for *rip*.v and *high*.a. We posted 8 HITs for *top*.a, 16 HITs for *high*.a and 16 for *rip*.v, for a total of 40 HITs across all three lemmas, paying $.15/HIT and collecting 10 assignments/HIT.

These results were much more satisfactory, with accuracy as shown in Table 3. Filtering out items by raising the agreement criteria (as before) to 35% or greater between the modal response and the next highest, yielded even better accuracy, above 90% for all three lemmas, at the cost of failing to classify approximately 10% to 30% of the items.

In response to the relative success of this trial, we posted HITs for three additional lemmas: *thirst*.n, *range.n*, and *history.n*, with 3, 4, and 5 senses, respectively. We chose these lemmas to ascertain whether there would be an effect on performance from the number of senses. Thus all three lemmas were also of the name POS. For Trial 7, although we kept the same interface, we experimented with changing the pay, and offering bonuses in an effort to maintain good standing among AMT workers concerned with their HIT acceptance record. For previous HITs, workers had to correctly categorize both gold sentences in order to receive any payment. We changed this system so that the HIT is accepted if the worker categorizes 1 gold sentence correctly, and awards a bonus if they categorize both correctly. Our hope was that this change would enable us to experiment with posting difficult HITs without losing our credibility. The results from this trial, also presented in Table 3, show accuracy at 92%, 87%, and 73%, respectively for *thirst*.n, *range.n*, and *history.n*. These results seemed to suggest that increasing the number of senses to discriminate increases the difficulty of the HIT.

It will be recalled that on every item, the workers have a choice "none of the above". One of the difficulties is that this choice covers a variety of cases, including those where the word is the wrong part of speech (a fairly frequent occurrence, despite the high accuracy cited for POS tagging) and those where the needed sense has simply not been included in FrameNet. The latter was the case for the word *range*.n, which was run once with three senses and then again with five senses, after the LUs for *(firing, artillery) range* and the "stove" sense were added. With the two additional senses, the accuracy actually went up from 87% to 92%. Although it is possible that the improvement could be due to a training effect connected to an increase in the number of items, it suggests that having more sense distinctions does not necessarily increase difficulty of discrimination.

Lemma	No. senses	No. Items	Accuracy	Filtered Items	Accuracy
top.a	2	144	92%	134	96%
rip.v	4	288	85%	228	92%
high.a	4	288	80%	198	92%
thirst.n	2	144	92%	128	95%
range.n	3	216	87%	177	93%
history.n	4	288	73%	199	86%
range.n	5	360	92%	335	96%

Table 3: Results from recent trials, including accuracy after filtering on the basis of agreement

		Removing	Cause_to_fragment	Self_motion	Damaging	None_of_the_above
	N=	104	51	33	64	36
Removing	97	93	1	1	2	0
Cause_to_fragment	45	1	41	0	1	2
Self_motion	25	1	0	24	0	0
Damaging	84	8	9	7	58	2
None_of_the_above	37	1	0	1	3	32

Table 4: Confusion matrix for *rip*.v (rows=gold standard)

2 What we can learn from the Turkers' difficulties?

Consider the confusion matrix shown in Table 4; here each row represents the items grouped by the gold standard sense ("expected"); each column represents the items grouped by the most frequent worker judgment ("observed").

The accuracy on this HIT set was 85%, in accord with the much larger numbers along the diagonal, but the really interesting cases lie off the diagonal, where the plurality of the workers disagreed with the experts. In some cases, the workers are simply right, and the expert was wrong, as in *This new wave of anonymous buildings . . . has RIPPED the heart out of Hammersmith.*, which the gold standard has as Damaging, but where the workers voted 7 to 3 for Removing. In this case, the expert vanguarder appears to have classified the metaphorical use of *rip*.v using the target domain, rather than the source domain, as is the FrameNet policy on "productive" (rather than "lexicalized") metaphor (Ruppenhofer et al., 2006, Sec. 6.4)[2]. In practice, this classification would most likely have been corrected at the annotation phase, as the FEs are clearly those of the source domain, involving removing something (a Theme) out of something else (a Source). In other cases, such as *I ripped open the envelopes.*, the gold standard correctly has **Damaging**, while the workers have 4 **Removing**, 3 **Cause_to_fragment**, and 3 **Damaging**. There is a good possibility that the envelopes fragmented (although this is not implied, nor necessary to remove a letter from an envelope), and the purpose is likely to remove something from the envelopes, which might falsely suggest **Removing**.

[2]Available from the FrameNet website, `http://framenet.icsi.berkeley.edu`.

In other cases, the senses are so closely enmeshed, that is seems rather arbitrary to choose one: e.g. *I RIP up an old T-shirt of mine and offer it.* The shirt is certainly damaged and almost certainly fragmented as a result of the same action. *. . . the Oklahoma was RIPPED apart when seven torpedoes hit her.* strictly speaking, the ship is caused to fragment, but the military purpose is to damage her beyond repair, if possible. And there are fairly often examples where the sentence in isolation is ambiguous: *Rain RIPPED another piece of croissant*, *The sky RIPPED and hung in tatters , revealing plasterboard and lath behind.* Such cases are pushing us toward trying to incorporate blending of senses into our paradigm, along the lines of (Erk and McCarthy, 2009).

3 Conclusion

We have shown that it is possible to set up HITs on Amazon Mechanical Turk to discriminate the fairly fine sense distinctions used in FrameNet, if the right approach is taken, and that the results reach a level of accuracy that can be useful for further processing, as well as serving as a cross-check on the expert data and an invitation to re-think the task itself. Although the total amount of data collected may not be large by some standards, it has been sufficient to give a good sense of which techniques work for the type of WSD problems we are facing. We intend to continue investigating the general applicability of this system for frame disambiguation, including further analysis of our data to better understand the factors that make a disambiguation task more or less difficult for crowd workers. All the data collected in the course of this study, and the software used to collect and analyze it, will be made available on the FrameNet website.

Acknowledgments

This material is based upon work supported by the National Science Foundation under Grant No. 0947841 (CISE EAGER) "Crowdsourcing for NLP"; the Sketch Engine GUI was developed under NSF Grant IIS-00535297 "Rapid Development of a Frame-Semantic Lexicon".

References

Chris Callison-Burch and Mark Dredze, editors. 2010. *Proceedings of the NAACL HLT 2010 Workshop on Creating Speech and Language Data with Amazon's Mechanical Turk*, Los Angeles, June. Association for Computational Linguistics.

Katrin Erk and Diana McCarthy. 2009. Graded word sense assignment. In *Proceedings of the 2009 Conference on Empirical Methods in Natural Language Processing*, pages 440–449, Singapore, August. Association for Computational Linguistics.

Michael Heilman and Noah A. Smith. 2010. Rating computer-generated questions with Mechanical Turk. In *Proceedings of the NAACL HLT 2010 Workshop on Creating Speech and Language Data with Amazon's Mechanical Turk*, pages 35–40, Los Angeles, June. Association for Computational Linguistics.

Jeff Howe. 2008. *Crowdsourcing*. Crown Business, New York.

Adam Kilgarriff, Pavel Rychly, Pavel Smrz, and David Tugwell. July 2004. The Sketch Engine. In *Proceedings of EURALEX 2004*, Lorient, France.

Bart Mellebeek, Francesc Benavent, Jens Grivolla, Joan Codina, Marta R. Costa-Jussà, and Rafael Banchs. 2010. Opinion mining of spanish customer comments with non-expert annotations on mechanical turk. In *Proceedings of the NAACL HLT 2010 Workshop on Creating Speech and Language Data with Amazon's Mechanical Turk*, pages 114–121, Los Angeles, June. Association for Computational Linguistics.

Josef Ruppenhofer, Michael Ellsworth, Miriam R. L. Petruck, Christopher R. Johnson, and Jan Scheffczyk. 2006. *FrameNet II: Extended Theory and Practice*. International Computer Science Institute, Berkeley, California. Distributed with the FrameNet data.

Rion Snow, Brendan O'Connor, Daniel Jurafsky, and Andrew Ng. 2008. Cheap and fast — but is it good? Evaluating non-expert annotations for natural language tasks. In *Proceedings of the 2008 Conference on Empirical Methods in Natural Language Processing*, pages 254–263, Honolulu, Hawaii, October. Association for Computational Linguistics.

Luís von Ahn and Laura Dabbish. 2008. Designing games with a purpose. *Communications of the ACM*, 51:58–67., August.

Luís von Ahn, Benjamin Maurer, Colin McMillen, David Abraham, and Manuel Blum. 2008. reCAPTCHA: Human-based character recognition via web security measures. *Science*, 321(5895):1465–1468.

Consistency Maintenance in Prosodic Labeling for Reliable Prediction of Prosodic Breaks

Youngim Jung
Dept. Knowledge Resources at Korea Institute of Science and Technology Information/
245 Daehang-no Yuseong-gu,
305-806 Daejeon, Republic of Korea
acorn@kisti.re.kr

Hyuk-Chul Kwon
Dept. Computer Science and Engineering at
Pusan National University/
San 30, Jangjeon-dong, Geumjeon-gu
Busan, 609-735, Republic of Korea
hckwon@pusan.ac.kr

Abstract

For the implementation of the prosody prediction model, large scale annotated speech corpora have been widely applied. Reliability among transcribers, however, was too low for successful learning of an automatic prosodic prediction. This paper reveals our observations on performance deterioration of the learning model due to inconsistent tagging of prosodic breaks in the established corpora. Then, we suggest a method for consistent prosodic labeling among multiple transcribers. As a result, we obtain a corpus with consistent annotation of prosodic breaks. The estimated pairwise agreement of annotation of the main corpus is between 0.7477 and 0.7916, and the value of K is between 0.7057 and 0.7569. Considering the estimated K, annotation of the main corpus has reliable consistency among multiple transcribers.

1 Introduction

The naturalness and comprehensibility of text-to-speech (TTS) synthesis systems are strongly affected by the accuracy of prosody prediction from text input. For the implementation of the prosody prediction model, large annotated speech corpora have been widely applied to both linguistic research and speech processing technologies as in (Syrdal and McGory, 2000). Since an increasing number of annotated speech corpora become available, a number of self-learning or probabilistic models for prosodic prediction have been suggested. To obtain reliable results from data-driven models, the corpus must be large scale, noise-free and annotated consistently. However, due to the limited range of tagged data with prosodic breaks that is used to learn or establish stochastic models at present, reliable results cannot be obtained. Thus, the reliability among transcribers was too low for successful learning of a prosodic model (Wightman and Ostendorf, 1994). In addition, the performance of ASR systems degrades significantly when training data are limited or noisy as in (Alwan, 2008).

In this study we propose a new methodology of training transcribers, annotating a corpus by multiple transcribers, and validating the reliability of intertranscriber agreement. This paper is organized as follows: we review related work on corpus annotation for speech and language processing tasks and method of measuring the reliability of consistency among multiple annotators in Section 2. Section 3 describes our observations on performance deterioration of the learning model due to inconsistent tagging of prosodic breaks in the established corpora. In Section 4, we suggest a procedure of constructing a medium-scale corpus, which are aimed at maintaining consistency in prosodic labeling among multiple annotators. Through a series of experiments during the training phase, the improvement of the agreement of multiple annotators is shown. The final experiment is performed in order to guarantee labeling agreement among five annotators. A brief summary and future work are presented in the final section.

2 Related Work

As linguistically-annotated corpora became critical resources, science of corpus annotation has been highlighted and evolved to reflect various interests in the field as shown in (Ide, 2007). In order to annotate linguistic information to large-scale corpora, two methods have been used; existing natural lan-

Proceedings of the Fifth Law Workshop (LAW V), pages 38–46,
Portland, Oregon, 23-24 June 2011.

guage processing (NLP) tools such as part-of-speech taggers, syntactic parsers, sentence boundary recognizers, named entity recognizers as have been used to generate annotations for ANC data (Ide and Suderman, 2006). Big advantages of using existing tools are that much cost and time can be saved and that the annotation result is consistent. In addition, it could obtain reliable accuracies and reduce the prohibitive cost of hand-validation by combining results of multiple NLP tools. However, tagging for all other linguistic phenomena is still mainly a manual effort as presented in (Eugenio, 2000). Thus, human annotators are required for tagging, correcting or validating the linguistic information although human annotators are very expensive and inconsistent in various aspects.

Linguists and language engineers have recognized the importance of the consistency of annotation among multiple annotators while they construct a large-scale corpus and have focused on how to measure the inter-annotator agreement. Their annotators had difficulties in discriminating one annotation category from others that are closely related to each other. Fellbaum et al. (1999) who performed a semantic annotation project which aimed at linking each content word in a text to a corresponding synset in WordNet found out that, with increasing polysemy, both inter-annotator and annotator-expert matches decreased significantly. As to measure the rate of agreement, Fellbaum et al. (1999) used a very simple measurement, the percentage of agreement in semantic annotation task. A greedy algorithm for increasing the inter-annotator agreement has been suggested by Ng et al. (1999). However, automatic correction of the manual tagging cannot reflect natural linguistic information tagged by human.

On the other hand, in prosodic annotation, the reliable measurement of intertranscriber agreement was studied by Beckman et al. (1994) initially, since the goal of the original ToBI system designers was to design a system with 'reliability (agreement between different transcribers must be at least 80%)', 'coverage', 'learnability', and 'capability'. The designers and developers of adaptations of ToBI for other languages and dialects such as G-ToBI, GlaToBI and K-ToBI have proved the usability of their labeling system rather than have suggested the method of maintaining the intertranscriber agreement based on the aforementioned criteria (Grice et al., 1996; Mayo et al., 1996; Jun et al., 2000).

3 Problem Description

3.1 Obtaining a Large Scale Speech Annotated Corpus

In order to design and implement a prediction model of prosodic break, annotated corpus should be prepared. Recorded speech files and text scripts of Korean Broadcasting Station (KBS) News 9 were collected and manual annotation was conducted by two linguistic specialists. Each hand-labeled half of the selected script for prosodic breaks was cross-checked with the other half. The resultant corpus had 47,368 *eo-jeol*[1]s. The size of this corpus, however, does not seem to be sufficient. An easy way to construct a larger-scale corpus is using existing corpora in the field. To build a large volume of learning and testing data, annotated speech data from Postech speech groups were obtained. The Postech data included 122,025 *eo-jeols* from Munhwa Broadcasting Corporation (MBC) news. Three types of break, viz., major breaks, minor breaks and no breaks, were annotated after each *eo-jeol* in KBS data (our initial data) and MBC data.

3.2 Performance Deterioration of Learning Models due to Inconsistent Annotation

KBS and MBC news data were selected, to examine the effect of prosodic breaks in corpora constructed by different groups on learning and testing. Only 46,526 *eo-jeols* were randomly sampled from the MBC News corpus, whereas the entire KBS News data was used for learning and testing, to avoid potential side effects from the differing data size.

	KBS	MBC (Postech data)
Training Data	38,243	37,258
Testing Data	9,103	9,268

Table 1 Size of Training and Test data

[1] An *eo-jeol* in Korean can be composed up of one morpheme or several concatenated morphemes of different linguistic features which are equivalent to a phrase in English. This spacing unit is referred as an '*eo-jeol*', 'word', or 'morpheme cluster' in Koeran linguistic literatures. We adopt '*eo-jeol*' in order to refer to 'an alphanumeric cluster of morphemes with a space on either side'.

C4.5 and CRFs were adapted in this experiment. The learning and testing was conducted in two phases. First, learning and testing of the prosodic break prediction models used a corpus constructed by a single group. Five-fold cross-validation was used for evaluating the models. Second, learning and evaluation of the models used a different corpus constructed by each group. The ratio of training to testing data (held-out data) was four to one. The results obtained from the first and second phases of learning and testing are presented in Table 2.

Algorithm	1st Phase Precision (Learning -Testing)		2nd Phase Precision (Learning -Testing)	
	KBS-KBS	MBC-MBC	KBS-MBC	MBC-KBS
C4.5	85.30%	62.53%	38.78%	44.96%
CRFs	84.65%	67.52%	37.96%	45.01%

Table 2 Experimental Results for Impact Analysis of Inconsistent Tagging

The prediction models performed well with C4.5 and CRFs learning algorithms when the model was trained and tested with KBS news data. However, its performance decreased drastically when the model was initially trained with KBS news data and subsequently tested with MBC news data. The performance of the learning model trained with MBC news data also deteriorated when tested with KBS data. These results suggest that serious performance deterioration is caused by data inconsistency rather than by the learning algorithm per se.

3.3 Analysis on Inconsistent Annotation

The deterioration of the performance presented in Section 3.2 is quite considerable, despite the fact that the same genre and level of prosodic break labeling system was selected. After analyzing the data, we identified three main reasons as follows.

(1) Perceptual Prominence of Prosodic Labeling Systems

Despite the fact that three types of prosodic break have been commonly used in the speech engineering field for a considerable time as shown in (Ostendorf and Veilleux, 1994), they have not been clearly defined or referenced in standard prosodic labeling conventions. In particular, the notion of the minor break is rather vague, whereas those of no break and major break are intuitively clear as in (Mayo et al., 1996).

In the MBC news data labeled by Postech, sentences that had all prosodic breaks tagged as no break were frequently found, even if two long clauses exist in a sentence. Most sentences had been annotated only with no break. The speaking rate of news announcers on air is relatively fast and no obvious audible break seems to exist in their speech. However, Kim (1991) showed that even well-trained news announcers rarely read a sentence without breaks. Therefore, minor breaks need to be recognized not only by the duration of the break, but also by the tonal changes or lengthening of the final syllable as shown in (Kim, 1991; Jun, 2006; Jung et al., 2008).

(2) Different Perceptibility of Prosodic Breaks among Transcribers

Grice et al. (1996), Mayo et al. (1996) and Jun et al. (2000) have focused on reliability-agreement between different transcribers as the main criterion of evaluation. This fact indicates that individual labeling of a single utterance can differ, because each transcriber's recognition of the prosodic labeling system varies. And, the perceptibility of each transcriber differs. A large-scale corpus is necessary for modeling a data-driven framework, and the greater the number of transcribers cooperating, the poorer the intertranscriber agreement becomes. However, maintaining the intertranscriber agreements is often neglected as empirical work when researchers build and analyze a speech annotated corpus for implementation of the prosody model.

(3) Syntactic or Semantic Ambiguities

A single sentence with syntactic ambiguities has several different interpretations. In spoken language, prosody prevents garden path sentences and enables resolution of syntactic ambiguity as shown in (Kjelgaard and Speer, 1999; Schafer, 1997).

Sentences such as the one in the following example (E1) can be grammatically constructed with multiple syntactic structures[2].

(E1) 고속버스가 중앙선을 침범해 마주오던 승용차를 들이받았습니다.

a. *Gosogbeoseuga // jung-angseon-eul # chimbeom-hae /// maju-odeon # seung-yongchaleul // deul-ibad-ass-seubnida*

'An express bus drove over the center line and

[2] In examples, letters in italics denote phonetic transliteration of Korean; hyphens in transliteration are used for segmentation of syllables.

rammed into an oncoming car.'

b. *Gosogbeoseuga /// jung-angseon-eul # chim-beomhae // maju-odeon # seung-yongchaleul /// deul-ibad-ass-seubnida*
'An express bus rammed into an oncoming car which drove over the center line.'
#: no break, //: minor break, ///: major break

The prosodic phrasing in both (a) or (b) can be correct, depending on the sentence's syntactic structure. The pattern in (E1) is quite frequent in Korean, particularly in situations where the topic is broad. This kind of syntactic ambiguity needs to be resolved by semantic or pragmatic information, since it cannot be resolved using syntactic information only.

As we previously mentioned, three main problems arise when annotated speech data are both constructed by multiple labelers in a research group and the data are collected from different groups. Considering the impact of the quality of annotated corpora on the data-driven models, the overall procedure of corpus construction including the data collection and preprocess, labeling system selection and intertranscriber agreement maintenance should be designed and then evaluated as shown in Section 4.

4 Corpus Building

4.1 Selection of Prosodic Labeling System

In this paper, we define seven types of prosodic break in combination with phrasal boundary tones since a prosodic break cannot be separated from a boundary tone. Our seven types are defined as follows:

(1) **Major break with falling tone**: For cases with a strong phrasal disjuncture and a strong subjective sense of pause. The positions of major breaks generally correspond to the boundaries of intonational phrases (marked '///L').
(2) **Major break with rising tone**: For cases with a strong phrasal disjuncture but a weak subjective sense of pause length (marked '///H').
(3) **Major break with middle tone**: In real data, major breaks with middle tone (or major breaks without tonal change) are observed as in (Lee, 2004), although they have no definition or explanation in K-ToBI. They have been observed in very fast speech such as headline news utterances (marked '///M').
(4) **Minor break with rising tone**: For cases with a minimal phrasal disjuncture and no strong subjective sense of pause. The positions of minor breaks correspond to the boundaries of accentual phrases with rising tone. When an utterance is so fast that a pause cannot be recognized clearly, minor breaks are realized by tonal changes or segment lengthening of the final syllable (marked '//H').
(5) **Minor break with middle tone**: For cases with prosodic words in compound words, such as compound nouns or compound verbs. Breaks between noun groups in a compound word or between verbs in a compound verb may be realized when the overall length of a compound word is long, whereas a break is absent in a short compound word (marked '//M').
(6) **Minor break with falling tone**: For cases with minimal phrasal disjuncture and no strong subjective sense of pause. The positions of minor breaks correspond to the boundaries of accentual phrases with falling tone.
(7) **No break**: For internal phrase word boundaries. There is no prosodic break between one-word modifiers and their one-word partners or between a word-level argument and its predicate, because the two words are syntactically and semantically combined (marked '#').

The seven types of prosodic break are mapped to K-ToBI break indices, enabling further reusability of the corpus labeled by the suggested break types.

K-ToBI		Suggested Prosodic Breaks
Break Index	0	No Break (#)
	1	Minor Break (//L)
	2	Minor Break (//H, //M)
	3	Major Break (///H, ///M, ///L)
Tone Index	Ha, H%	H
	La, L%	L
	L+	M

Table 3 Mapping between break indices of K-ToBI and the suggested prosodic breaks

Jun et al. (2000) showed that the tonal pattern agreement for each word was approximately 36%

for all labelers and this low level of agreement appears to be due to the nature of the tonal pattern. Although fourteen possible AP (Accent Phrase) tonal patterns exist, these variations are neither meaningful nor phonologically correct. We concluded that the final phrasal tones are sufficient for the recognition of prosodic boundaries.

4.2 Data Selection and Preprocessing

In this study, KBS news scripts (issued January, 2005 ~ June, 2006) were collected as a raw corpus from web. Although the speech rate of TV news speech is faster than that of general read speech, announcers are trained to speak Standard Korean Language and to generate standard pronunciations, tones and breaks. In addition, individual stylistic variation is restricted in the announcer's speech.

The text formats of news scripts extracted from the web are unified. Then, sentences or expressions in news scripts differing from those in real sentences in multimedia files are revised according to the real utterances of the announcer. The selection and revision of the sentences is performed according to the following criteria.

1) Headline news sentences uttered by one female announcer are collected.
2) Minimum of five *eo-jeol*s are included in one sentence.
3) Real speech of news script read by the announcer is considered as primary source of prosodic break tagging for transcribers.
4) Sentences in the news script are deleted unless they are read by the announcer in real speech files.
5) Between 1-3 *eo-jeol*s in news scripts differing from those in speech files are revised according to the real speech if there is no semantic change.
6) Sentences in the news script differing considerably from those in speech files are deleted.
7) Words or phrases in the news script differing from those in speech files due to spelling/grammar errors are not corrected manually. They are corrected automatically by the PNU grammar checker, which shows over 95% accuracy as in (Kwon et al., 2004).

4.3 Training Transcribers

The most reliable method of maintaining the consistency and accuracy of prosodic breaks by multiple transcribers is for each well-trained transcriber to annotate prosodic breaks in the entire corpus. Then the majority of the tagging results among multiple transcribers are selected as an answer for the target *eo-jeol*. However, this method where all transcribers annotate the same corpus in depth is too time consuming and costly. Due to time and cost constraints, most related studies use a simpler method. If the size of the corpus is small, then a professional linguist annotates the entire corpus as in (Maragoudakis et al., 2003). If the size of corpus is large, more than two transcribers divide the corpus by the number of transcribers and each transcriber annotates his/her own part as in (Wightman and Ostendorf, 1994; Viana et al., 2003). Unless the transcribers are trained and the reliability of the intertranscriber agreement is validated, consistency of annotation by multiple transcribers cannot be assured. Hence, a method for maintaining the reliability of the intertranscriber agreement of prosodic breaks is suggested in this paper.

The overall procedure of training the transcribers, annotating the main corpus with prosodic breaks and validating the reliability of tagging consistency among multiple transcribers is illustrated in Figure 1.

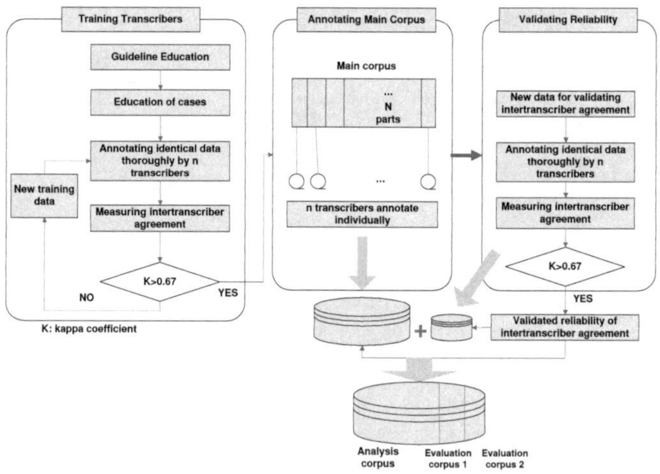

Figure 1 Overall Procedure of Corpus Building

Firstly, guidelines are provided for transcribers to familiarize themselves with the prosodic labeling system suggested in Section 4.1. Secondly, in order to improve the awareness of the length or strength of each prosodic break type in detail, transcribers repeatedly listen to speech files corresponding to several paragraphs in news scripts. In addition, WaveSurfer Version.1.8.5, which is an open source program for visualizing and manipulating speech, is utilized for transcribers to examine the pitch contour, waveform, and power plot of speech files.

In the training phase, five transcribers annotate the same data with prosodic breaks at the same time and then compare the results of their annotations, and discuss and repeatedly correct the various errors until reliable agreement among them is reached. The data used for this intertranscriber agreement training is given in Table 4.

	1st	2nd	3rd	4th
# *eo-jeols*	422	544	491	711
# sentences	35	49	42	32

Table 4 Data used in intertranscribers training

After mastering the guidelines and training with each data set, specific reasons for inconsistency among transcribers were analyzed and their solutions were educated as follows:

(1) Prosodic breaks were inserted due to announcers' emphasis on a certain *eo-jeol*, mistakes in reading the sentence or the habit of slowing down two or three *eo-jeol*s from the end of a sentence. Some transcribers recognized these as speakers' errors and corrected them in their annotations. On the other hand, others annotated prosodic breaks according to what they heard, regardless of errors. Due to these differing policies on annotation, the resultant annotation of prosodic breaks among transcribers is not consistent, as shown in example (E2).

(E2) 더욱 심각해지고 (///H, #)[3] 있습니다.
deo-ug simgaghaejigo iss-seubnida.
more serious become progress +EM[4]
"(sth) becomes more serious"

Inconsistency derived from these speakers' errors should be deleted.

(2) If the speech rate of the announcer is too fast for some transcribers to perceive audible breaks between two *eo-jeol*s, they omitted the minor break, whereas others put a minor break in the same place, as shown in (E3).

(E3) 그러나 (#, **//L**) 질병관리본부는
geuleona jilbyeonggwanlibonbu-neun
however Korea Center for Disease Control+TP and Prevention+TP
"However, the Korea Center for Disease Control and Prevention"

In this case, transcribers need to pay attention to whether the final tone of the target *eo-jeol* is rising or falling. In order to reduce inconsistency derived from missing breaks, transcribers repeatedly practice while listening to similar patterns.

(3) If only one annotator selects a different type of prosodic break than the others for the answer of the same place, he/she must change his approach in annotating prosodic breaks.

(4) Wightman and Ostendorf (1994) and Ross and Ostendorf (1996) have revealed that there is prosodic variability even for news speech data. The announcer showed variability in the location, strength or length, and tonal change in our news data as well. For example, the announcer occasionally put a minor break between two *eo-jeol*s consisting of a time expression, as shown in (E4).

(E4) a. 지난 //H 2002 년 오늘,
jinan //H 2002nyeon oneul,
past 2002year this day
"(on) this day 2002,"

b. 지난 # 2000 년 1 월
jinan # 2000nyeon 1wol
past 2000year January
"(in) January 2000,"

For a time expression including less than four *eo-jeol*s, no break should be marked in it.

Discussion and education such cases described above after annotating new training data sets repeats till the intertranscriber agreement is sufficiently high. The intertranscriber agreement in annotating seven-level prosodic breaks including tonal changes is shown in Table 5.

Agreement	**Cumulative rate (%)**

[3] The correct answer among different annotations is underlined.

[4] Notes on abbreviations of Korean grammatical morphemes are as follows: EM for ending markers, TP for topical postposition, LCM for locative case marker, OCM for objective case marker, PEC for pre-ending denoting continuous

	1st	2nd	3rd	4th
Five (all) agreed	43.84	50.55	55.80	57.67
At least four agreed	60.90	68.20	73.52	75.53
At least three agreed	81.75	87.50	90.84	91.70

Table 5 Intertranscriber agreement in training

The cumulative rate of agreement of more than half of the transcribers (n+1/2) is measured by approximate figures. Specifically, the rate of the intertranscriber agreement is calculated with the cumulative rate at which all five transcribers agreed, at least four of them agreed, and at least three of them agreed. The resultant agreement of the first experiment is quite low, though the first experiment was performed after the transcribers had familiarized themselves with the guidelines and studied many examples. The intertranscriber agreement in annotating data with seven-level prosodic breaks increases continuously with repeated training and experiments. This indicates that educating transcribers with guidelines and examples is not sufficient, and training of transcribers is required prior to annotation of the main corpus with specified tagging classes by multiple transcribers.

In order to review how accurately each individual transcriber annotates the corpus, the annotation accuracy of each individual transcriber is estimated. The prosodic break type for which at least three of them agreed is considered as the answer. The annotation result of each transcriber is compared to the answer, and then the accuracy is estimated by counting the number of annotations that match the answers. Table 6 shows the estimated annotation accuracy of five transcribers from the 1st to the 4th experiment.

Transcriber	Estimated accuracy (%)			
	1st	2nd	3rd	4th
A	94.51	84.00	86.32	91.56
B	78.03	85.26	89.24	93.25
C	78.03	93.05	94.39	94.02
D	88.44	90.32	90.36	90.64
E	82.37	83.79	84.08	89.11

Table 6 Estimated accuracy of each transcriber

Although there are individual variations, the estimated accuracy of the transcribers increases steadily.

After the four experiments, the cumulative rate of agreement of more than half of the transcribers reached 91.70% and the estimated accuracy of individual transcribers increased to 89.11~94.02%. Hence, an objective and reliable measurement for intertranscriber agreement is required in order to decide whether the training is sufficient.

The most commonly used methods to assess the level of agreement among transcribers are pairwise analysis and Kappa statistics. The reliability of intertranscriber agreement of the four experiments has been assessed with these two measurements and the result is given in Table 7.

Measurement	1st	2nd	3rd	4th
Pairwise analysis	0.6385	0.6969	0.7375	0.7477
Kappa statistics	0.5783	0.6464	0.6938	0.7057

Table 7 Reliability of intertranscriber agreement

Since the value of K is greater than 0.67 in the 3rd and 4th experiment, the intertranscriber agreement for annotating prosodic breaks is considered to have reached a reliable level as shown in (Carletta, 1996). Then annotation of the main corpus is performed.

The main corpus comprising 29,686 *eo-jeols* is divided into five parts. Each partition is assigned to the trained five transcribers and annotation is independently performed. WaveSurfer, which is used in the training phase, is also used in the annotation phase for the display and annotation of speech. Transcribers may openly discuss their annotations, even though they annotated different parts of the main corpus.

4.4 Validation of Reliability of Intertranscriber Agreement

Since each individual transcriber annotated a different part of the main corpus, the reliability of intertranscriber agreement cannot be measured directly. We assume that intranscriber agreement does not change dramatically before and after annotation of the main corpus.

Hence, another data set including 1,149 *eo-jeols* (46 sentences), with a size 1.5x larger than that of the data set used in the 4th experiment, is collected and used instead, in order to validate the reliability of agreement. Immediately after annotation of the main corpus, the final experiment is performed following the procedure performed in the training phase, except for the education steps. The five transcribers annotated the same data in depth, however, they worked independently. They were not allowed to discuss prosodic labeling. Pairwise analysis and Kappa statistics are used in measuring intertranscriber agreement on the validation data set. The pairwise agreement and K found in the validation experiment after annotation of the main corpus was 0.79 and 0.76, respectively.

Both agreement figures are greater than those found in the prior experiments, which were repeated four times in the training phase. Based on this result, annotation of the main corpus is also considered to be part of training of transcribers.

According to our assumption, the estimated intertranscriber agreement of annotation of the main corpus annotation is between the agreement of the prior and post experiments, as shown in Figure 2.

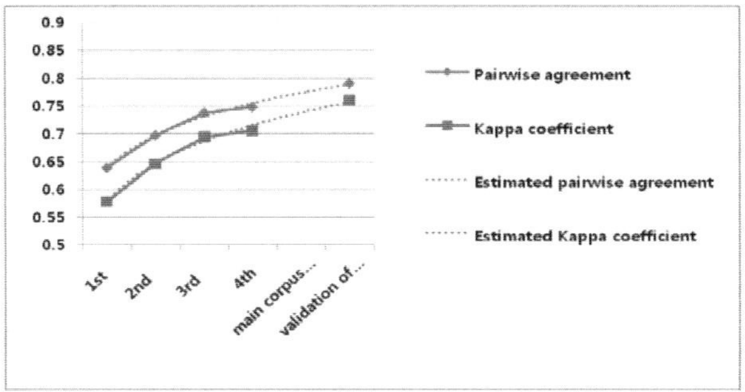

Figure 2 Estimated intertranscriber reliability in annotation of main corpus

The estimated pairwise agreement of annotation of the main corpus is between 0.7477 and 0.7916, and the value of K is between 0.7057 and 0.7569. Considering the estimated K, annotation of the main corpus has reliable consistency among multiple transcribers.

As a result, we obtained a corpus with consistent annotation of prosodic breaks. The data used in validation experiment is included as well. The statistics of the constructed corpus is shown in Table 8.

Data	# *eo-jeols*	# sentences
Data set from validation experiment	1,149	46
Main corpus	29,663	1,319
Total	30,812	1,365

Table 8 Size of resultant corpus

It took approximately three months for us to train transcribers, annotate main corpus and validate the reliability of intertranscriber agreement in the main corpus. Considering the size of the constructed corpus, three months might be regarded as a considerable amount of time for researchers who want to build a large-scale annotated corpus. However, most time was spent on analyzing the inconsistencies among transcribers in initial experiments during the training step. Hence, if transcribers are trained following the suggested method in this paper, the amount of time for transcribers to annotate the target corpus with reliable consistency will decrease dramatically compared with the time for all transcribers to annotate prosodic breaks in the entire corpus.

5 Conclusions

In this study, potential problems in the construction, collection and utilization of a speech annotation corpus have been identified, and a solution for each type of problem has been suggested. The overall procedure of training transcribers, tagging the main corpus and validating the reliability of intertranscriber agreement on the main corpus has also been specifically described. As a result, we obtained a corpus with consistent annotation of prosodic breaks. The estimated pairwise agreement of annotation of the main corpus is between 0.7477 and 0.7916 and K is between 0.7057 and 0.7569. The suggested method for constructing a consistently annotated corpus and validating the consistency of the resultant annotation must be applied prior to implementation of data-driven models for predicting prosodic breaks. As our future work, the resultant corpus will be used for building a robust prediction model of prosodic boundary.

In addition, the method can be utilized for semantic annotation tasks, discourse tagging and others, which have a similar problem due to the differing perceptions of transcribers in recognizing the closely related categories.

Acknowledgement

This work was supported by the National Research Foundation of Korea(NRF) grant funded by the Korea government(MEST) (2010-0028784).

References

Abeer Alwan. 2008. Dealing with Limited and Noisy Data in ASR: a Hybrid Knowledge-based and Statistical Approach, Proc. Interspeech 2008, Brisbane Australia, , pp. 11-15.

Amy J. Schafer. 1997. Prosodic Parsing: The Role of Prosody in Sentence Comprehension, University of Massachusetts.

Ann K. Syrdal and Julia McGory. 2000. Inter-transcriber Reliability of ToBI Prosodic Labeling, Proc.Interspeech 2000, pp. 235-238.

Barbara Di Eugenio. 2000. On the usage of Kappa to evaluate agreement on coding tasks, Proc. Second International Conference on Language Resources and Evaluation, pp.441-444.

Catherine Mayo, Matthew Aylett, D. Robert Ladd. 1996. Prosodic Transcription of Glasgow English: An Evaluation Study of GlaToBI, Proc. ESCA Workshop on Intonation: Theory, Models and Applications, Athens Greece, pp.231-234.

Christiane Fellbaum, Joachim Grabowski and Shari Landes. 1999. Performance and Confidence in a Semantic Annotation Task, WordNet: An Electronic Lexical Database etd. Fellbaum, MIT Press, London.

Colin W. Wightman and Mari Ostendorf. 1994. Automatic Labeling of Prosodic Patterns, IEEE Transactions on Speech and Audio Processing, 2(4):469-481.

Hee Tou Ng, Chung Yong Lim and Shou King Foo. 1999. A Case Study on Inter-Annotator Agreement for Word Sense Disambiguation, Proc. ACL SIGLEX Workshop on Standardizing Lexical Resources pp. 9-13.

Ho-Young Lee. 2004. H and L are Not Enough in Intonational Phonology, Korean Journal of Linguistics, 39:71-79.

Hyuk-Chul Kwon, Mi-young Kang and Sung-Ja Choi. 2004. Stochastic Korean Word Spacing with Smoothing Using Korean Spelling Checker, Computer Processing of Oriental Languages, 17:239-252.

Jean Carletta. 1996. Assessing Agreement on Classification Tasks: The Kappa Statistic, Computational Linguistics, 22(2):249-254.

K. Ross and M. Ostendorf. 1996. Prediction of abstract prosodic labels for speech synthesis, Computer Speech and Language, 10(3):155-185.

M. Céu Viana, Luís C. Oliveira and Ana I. Mata. 2003. Prosodic Phrasing: Machine and Human Evaluation, International Journal of Speech Technology, 6:83-94.

M. Maragoudakis, P. Zervas, N. Fakotakis and G. Kokkinakis. 2003. A Data-Driven Framework for Intonational Phrase Break Prediction, Lecture Notes in Computer Science, 2807: 189-197.

M. Ostendorf and N. Veilleux. 1994. A Hierarchical Stochastic Model for Automatic Prediction of Prosodic Boundary Location, Computational Linguistics, 20(1):27-54.

Margaret M. Kjelgaard and Shari R. Speer. 1999. Prosodic Facilitation and Interference in the Resolution of Temporary Syntactic Closure Ambiguity, Journal of Memory and Language, 40:153-194.

Martine Grice, Matthias Reyelt, Ralf Benzmuller, Jörg Mayer and Anton Batliner. 1996. Consistency in Transcription and Labelling of German Intonation with GToBI, Proc. Interspeech1996, pp. 1716-1719.

Mary E. Beckman, John F. Pitrelli and Julia Hirschberg. 1994. Evaluation of Prosodic Transcription Labeling Reliability in the ToBI Framework, Proc. Interspeech 1994, pp. 123-126.

Nancy Ide. 2007. Annotation Science From theory to Practice and Use: Data Structures for Linguistics Resources and Applications, Proc. Bienniel GLDV Conference, Tübingen, Germany.

Nancy Ide and Keith Suderman. 2006. Integrating Linguistic Resources: The American National Corpus Model, *Proceedings of the Fifth Language Resources and Evaluation Conference*, Genoa, Italy.

Sangjun Kim. 1991. Study on Broadcast Language, Hongwon, Seoul.

Sun-Ah Jun. 2006. Prosody in Sentence Processing: Korean vs. English, UCLA Working Papers in Phonetics, 104:26-45.

Sun-Ah Jun, Sook-Hyang Lee, Keeho Kim, Yong-Ju Lee. 2000. Labler agreement in Transcribing Korean Intonation with K-ToBI, Proc. Interspeech 2000, pp. 211-214.

Youngim Jung, Sunho Cho, Aesun Yoon and Hyuk-Chul Kwon. 2008. Prediction of Prosodic Break Using Syntactic Relations and Prosodic Features, Korean Journal of Cognitive Science, 19(1):89 -105.

WaveSurfer. WaveSurfer ver.1.8.5, http://crfpp.sourceforge.net/.

An Annotation Scheme for Automated Bias Detection in Wikipedia

Livnat Herzig, Alex Nunes and Batia Snir
Computer Science Department
Brandeis University
Waltham, MA, U.S.A.
lherzig, nunesa, bsnir @brandeis.edu

Abstract

BiasML is a novel annotation scheme with the purpose of identifying the presence as well as nuances of biased language within the subset of Wikipedia articles dedicated to service providers. Whereas Wikipedia currently uses only manual flagging to detect possible bias, our scheme provides a foundation for the automating of bias flagging by improving upon the methodology of annotation schemes in classic sentiment analysis. We also address challenges unique to the task of identifying biased writing within the specific context of Wikipedia's neutrality policy. We perform a detailed analysis of inter-annotator agreement, which shows that although the agreement scores for intra-sentential tags were relatively low, the agreement scores on the sentence and entry levels were encouraging (74.8% and 66.7%, respectively). Based on an analysis of our first implementation of our scheme, we suggest possible improvements to our guidelines, in hope that further rounds of annotation after incorporating them could provide appropriate data for use within a machine learning framework for automated detection of bias within Wikipedia.

1 Introduction

BiasML is an annotation scheme directed at detecting bias in the Wikipedia pages of service providers. Articles are judged as biased or non-biased at the sentential and document levels, and annotated on the intra-sentential level for a number of lexical and structural features.

2 Motivation and Background

2.1 Motivation

Neutral Point of View (NPOV) is one of three core tenets of Wikipedia's content policy. Wikipedia describes NPOV as "representing fairly, proportionately, and as far as possible without bias, all significant views that have been published by reliable sources" (Wikipedia, 2011a).

The collaborative design of Wikipedia is such that anyone can submit content, and so the detection and flagging of bias within articles is an essential and ongoing task in maintaining the quality and utility of Wikipedia. Currently, NPOV is enforced manually via the same open process that creates content on the site. Users can flag pages with suspect content as containing a "NPOV dispute". This is problematic: definitions of bias vary from editor to editor, and accusations of bias can themselves come from a biased perspective. Additionally, this practice is weighted towards the attention of Wikipedia users, such that the scrutiny an article receives is proportional to its broader popularity. For example, though the pages for Land of Israel and restaurant franchise Fresh to Order have both been flagged for NPOV disputes, they have been edited 1,480 and 46 times by 536 and 22 users, respectively (Wikipedia, 2011b; Wikipedia, 2011c). The average Wikipedia page receives just under 20 edits (Wikipedia, 2011d).

In light of this, an automated pass at bias detection is highly desirable. Instead of wholesale reliance on human editors, a system based on our annotation scheme could serve as an initial

Proceedings of the Fifth Law Workshop (LAW V), pages 47–55,
Portland, Oregon, 23-24 June 2011. ©2011 Association for Computational Linguistics

filter in monitoring user contributions. If integrated into the Wikipedia framework, this system could aid in the regulation of NPOV policy violations, e.g. tracking repeat offenders. With this goal in mind we have designed BiasML to flag NPOV issues in a specific subset of Wikipedia articles. We have constrained our task to the pages of service providers such as small businesses, schools, and hospitals. As a genre, the pages of service providers are especially worthy of scrutiny because they are both less likely to be closely vetted, and more likely to be edited by someone with a commercial interest in the reputation of the organization.

In addition, service provider pages are particularly appropriate for automatic POV-flagging because the bias complaints leveled against them tend to be much more systematic and objective compared with those of an especially controversial or divisive topic.

2.2 Background

Sentiment analysis efforts usually rely on the prior polarity of words (their polarity out of context). For example, Turney (2002) proposes a method to classify reviews as "recommended"/"not recommended", based on the average semantic orientation of the review. Semantic orientation is the mutual information measure of selected phrases with the word *excellent* minus their mutual information with the word *poor*. However, as Wilson et al. (2005) point out, even using a lexicon of positive/negative words marked for their prior polarity is merely a starting point, since a word's polarity in context might differ from its prior polarity.

The distinction between prior and contextual polarity is crucial for detecting bias, since words with a prior positive/negative polarity may or may not convey bias, depending on their context. Notably, the inverse is also true - generally neutral words can be used to create a favorable tone towards a sentence's topic, thereby expressing bias. An example of the latter case are the words *own* and *even* in the sentence *The hospital has its own pharmacy, maternity ward, and even a morgue*. Though generally neutral, their usage here contributes to the sentence's overall non-neutrality. In order to deal with contextual polarity, Wilson et al. propose a two-stage process that first uses clues marked with contextual polarity to determine whether the phrases containing these clues are polar or neutral. The second stage then determines the actual polarity of the phrases deemed non-neutral.

However, Wilson et al.'s approach would not suit our task of bias detection in Wikipedia, as the abovementioned example, taken from a Wikipedia entry, shows. Blatant expression of opinions or emotions is rare in the Wikipedia entries of service providers. Words which explicitly convey that an opinion/emotion is being expressed are rarely used (e.g. *I think*). Rather, bias is introduced either in more subtle ways (e.g. using words that are usually neutral) or in ways that differ from the ones addressed by previous approaches. For example, bias is introduced by preceding positive information about the provided service by phrases such as *it is widely believed*. Clearly, this phrase does not have contextual polarity, but it does introduce bias.

Within the realm of Wikipedia, phrases that create an impression that something specific and meaningful has been said when only a vague or ambiguous claim has been communicated, such as *it is widely believed*, are referred to as *weasels* (Wikipedia, 2011e). The recent CoNLL-2010 shared task (Farkas et al., 2010), aimed at detecting uncertainty cues in texts, focused on these phrases in trying to determine whether sentences contain uncertain information. In the same vein, we include weasel words as part of our annotation scheme to detect bias.

Finally, as Blitzer et al. (2007) point out, although the typical word-level analysis captures the finer-grained aspects of sentiment language, it falls short in capturing broader structurally or contextually-based bias. Bias can also be introduced by repetitive usage of words that in typical usage do not have prior polarity, but when used in a repetitive manner, create a favorable depiction of a sentence's topic. This cannot be captured by approaches such as those of Wilson et al. or Turney.

To tackle cases like those described above, our annotation scheme extends beyond lexical tags, and includes tags that capture dependencies between a word and its context, as well as tags that are aimed at capturing subtle expressions of bias.

3 Method

3.1 Corpus Selection and Preparation

The POV Wikipedia entries were selected from Wikipedia's list of entries that are classified as "NPOV dispute". Roughly 6,000 of the more than 3 million existing Wikipedia entries have been flagged this way (Wikipedia, 2011f). We went over these entries using a "get random article" feature, choosing ones that met our service provider criterion, i.e., they were either about a specific product or a service provider. The neutral entries were selected via a search through pages of products/service providers on Wikipedia that were evaluated by us as neutral. Our corpus ultimately consisted of 22 POV entries and 11 NPOV ones.

3.2 Annotation Scheme

Annotation Procedure and Tags: The annotation was performed using the MAE annotation tool (Stubbs, 2011), which is compliant with LAF guidelines (Ide and Romary, 2006). The annotation scheme uses standoff annotation and includes tagging on multiple levels - tagging biased words and linguistic structures; tagging the neutrality of each sentence; tagging the overall neutrality of the entry. The annotator is instructed to read through each sentence, and decide if it is written in a neutral point of view or not. At this point in the annotation process, a sentence is considered non-neutral if it is written in a non-neutral tone, or if it favors/disfavors its topic (regardless of whether the sentence is sourced). If a sentence is deemed neutral, it is tagged with a sentential level tag SENTENCE_POV, with the attribute NPOV, and no further tagging of it is required.

In the alternate case that a sentence is judged to contain non-neutral language, the annotator is asked to look for words/phrases that should be tagged with the word/phrase level tags (elaborated below) only within the scope of the current sentence. After tagging the word/phrase level tags, the sentence should be evaluated for its neutrality, and tagged SENTENCE_POV with one of two possible attributes (POV or NPOV), depending on the word/phrase level tags it has. After all the sentences are tagged with the SENTENCE_POV tag, the entire entry is tagged with the ENTRY_POV tag, whose attribute values are numeric, ranging between 1 and 4, where 1 is completely neutral and 4 is clearly non-neutral (i.e., written as an advertisement).

The annotation scheme is comprised of 4 word/phrase level extent tags that aim to capture biased language - POLAR_PHRASE, WEASEL, REPETITION, and PERSONAL_TONE. The POLAR_PHRASE tag is used to mark words/phrases that are used to express favor or disfavor within the sentential context, and contribute to the non-neutrality of the sentence. The annotator is advised to examine whether replacing the suspected word(s) results in a more neutral version of the sentence, without losing any of the sentence's content. If so, the word(s) should be tagged as POLAR_PHRASE (with a positive or negative attribute). For example, in the sentence *The new hospital <u>even</u> has a morgue*, *even* is tagged with the POLAR_PHRASE tag (the attribute value is positive), and the entire sentence's SENTENCE_POV tag receives the attribute POV.

The PERSONAL_TONE tag is used to tag words/phrases that convey a personal tone, which is commonly used in advertisements but is inappropriate in encyclopedic entries. The possible attribute values are first person (e.g. *we, our*), second person (e.g. *you, your*) and other (e.g. *here*). The REPETITION tag is used for two possible cases - when similar words are unnecessarily used to describe the same thing, all words except the first one should be considered a repetition; when there is unnecessary repetition that does not add new information (i.e., it is not elaboration, but mere repetition) about the service the service provider offers, or praise of the service provider, the repeated elements

Cedar Memorial is a cemetery located in Cedar Rapids, Iowa. In addition to the cemetery, a flower shop, funeral home, crematorium, family center, and a library containing materials on bereavement and genealogy are also on the grounds. This **unique** memorial park located on 1st Avenue between Cedar Rapids and Marion includes a wooded cemetery with many artistic features, a natural limestone funeral home, a modern cremation center, a family center and library, a full-service flower shop, and a chapel and mausoleum patterned after old world churches of England. The cemetery *is widely recognized* as **one of the finest** park cemeteries **in the country**. The park is 72 acres (290,000 m^2) in size, and offers traditional burial, lawn crypts, and mausoleum entombment. There are also several columbariums in the cemetery with niches for burial of cremated remains.

Figure 1: An annotated Wikipedia entry - POLAR_PHRASEs are underlined in bold, all of the positive type; WEASEL is italicized, and is of the pro type; REPETITION is underlined, receiving the attribute value 3. SENTENCE_POV for sentences no. 1, 2, 5 & 6 is NPOV, while it is POV for sentences no. 3 & 4. The ENTRY_POV is 3, which corresponds to POV.

should be considered repetition. For both cases, the attribute value will be the numeric value representing the number of repeated elements. To illustrate the former type of REPETITION and the PERSONAL_TONE tag, consider the sentence *The councils work to enhance and improve the quality of your local health service. Improve* is a case of REPETITION, since there is no need for both *enhance* and *improve* (the attribute value is 1). In addition, *your* is tagged with the PERSONAL_TONE tag (second person), and the sentence's SENTENCE_POV tag receives the attribute POV. The other type of REPETITION applies to cases where a sentence such as *The funeral home also offers a flower shop, crematorium, family center and library,* is subsequently followed by a sentence such as *This unique funeral home is built of natural limestone, and has a modern cremation center, a family center and library, a flower shop and a chapel.* While *unique* is tagged as a POLAR_PHRASE, the other underlined elements are all REPETITION, with the attribute value set to 3, since 3 elements are repeated unnecessarily, without adding new information. Note that although *crematorium* and *cremation center* refer to the same entity, it is not treated as a repetition, because the second mention adds that it is a modern crematorium. The second sentence's neutrality is therefore POV, while the first one's is NPOV.

As elaborated in the background section, weasel words also introduce bias, by presenting the appearance of support for statements while denying the reader the possibility to assess the viewpoint's source. These are usually general claims about what people think or feel, or what has been shown. These words/phrases are captured by the WEASEL tag. This tag has two possible attributes, pro, which captures "classic" WEASELs such as *is often credited*, and con, which would capture negative portrayal, as in *is never believed*. In contrast to the previously described word/phrase level tags, we also included a fifth tag, FACTIVE_PHRASE, which is inherently different. It is used to mark phrases that give objectivity to what is otherwise a biased description, usually a source. These phrases de-bias polar phrases and weasels.

The relation between a FACTIVE_PHRASE and the POLAR_PHRASE or WEASEL that it de-biases is captured by the LEGITIMIZE link tag. A sentence that was initially judged as non-neutral can eventually be tagged as NPOV, if each instance of its biased language is backed up by sources. Otherwise, it should be tagged as POV. For example, in the sentence *It is widely believed that John Smith started the tradition of pro-bono work.[1]*, the phrase *is widely believed* is tagged WEASEL, whereas *[1]* is tagged FACTIVE_PHRASE. In addition, a LEGITIMIZE tag will link these two elements, resulting in an overall neutral sentence, since its biased language is backed up by a source. The SENTENCE_POV tag will therefore have the attribute value NPOV (whereas it would be POV if there were no FACTIVE_PHRASE). To further illustrate this point, consider the sentence *Jones and Sons ranked number one in The American Lawyer's Annual Survey*. *Number one* is tagged as a POLAR_PHRASE (positive), *The American Lawyer's Annual Survey* is a FACTIVE_PHRASE, and there is a LEGITIMIZE link between them. The entire SENTENCE_POV tag's neutrality is therefore NPOV. This is in contrast to the sentence *Jones and Sons are the number one law firm* in Boston., which would have the attribute value POV, because its polar phrases have no factive phrase to back them up. Our framework also enables tagging a sentence as POV even if none of the possible tags apply to them. See Figure 1 for an example of an annotated entry.

BiasML Innovations: The annotation scheme elaborated above is an innovative yet practical answer to the theoretical linguistic considerations of sentiment analysis within the genre of Wikipedia. As previously mentioned, our scheme improves upon approaches that rely upon prior polarity (e.g. Turney, 2002) by identifying cases of biased language that stem from intra-sentential and cross-sentential dependencies, rather than isolated words. Our POLAR_PHRASE tag resembles phrases with non-neutral contextual polarity that Wilson et al.'s (2005) approach introduces, but it captures cases that their approach does not - namely, generally neutral words that nevertheless make a sentence biased.

Another innovation of our framework is enabling the legitimization of weasel words. Whereas the CoNLL-2010 shared task (Farkas et al., 2010) annotated all occurrences of weasels as uncertainty markers, we acknowledge the possibility of sources (e.g. citations) that actually nullify the weasel.

The multiple-level discourse association of our tag scheme also allows observation of shifts in polarity within the larger discourse of the article. The sentence-level POV tag allows the annotator to identify the overall neutrality of each sentence, thus producing a landscape of how biased language is distributed across the article. This landscape not only provides an indicator of where to look for contextual clues and dependencies among more local tags, but it is particularly relevant to Wikipedia's wiki platform, where it is likely that different authors contributed to different portions of the article, making it more prone to variance in biased tone.

While developing this scheme, we wanted to make sure it tapped into the capacity of the annotator to identify both subjective language use and objective linguistic phenomena. While tags like PERSONAL_TONE and WEASEL require the annotator to mark precise occurrences of language, the sentence and document-level POV tags allow the annotator to identify point of view without having to explicitly point to a specific linguistic structure. To preserve the value of the human annotator's subjective judgments, our scheme permitted the co-occurrence of a sentence or document POV tag with the absence of any local lexical tags. This allowed our scheme to recognize the difficult cases in sentiment analysis where one intuitively senses opinionated language, but is unable to formally define what makes it so.

Another aim of our work was to develop a scheme that captured the way information is portrayed in Wikipedia, while avoiding judgment on what information is actually communicated. A significant source of dispute within Wikipedia is disagreement as to the veracity of an article's content; however, identification of this is truly a different task then the one we have defined here. In order to tease apart these distinct types of evaluation, annotators were instructed to identify citations that legitimize statements that are potentially POV, but not to consider the truthfulness of the statement or validity of the source when tagging.

4 Results

Our corpus of 33 articles of varying degrees of neutrality was distributed among three annotators, each annotator receiving 2/3 of the entire corpus. The articles were presented as plain text in the annotation environment, and were stripped of images, titles, section headings, or other information extraneous to the main body of the text (inline references, however, were preserved). The annotators were graduate linguistics students. Their training consisted of a brief information session on the motivation of our work, a set of annotation guidelines, and optional question and answer sessions. Adjudication of the annotation was performed with the MAI adjudication tool (Stubbs, 2011).

4.1 Tag Analysis

For each tag, an average percent agreement score was calculated (for extents and attributes) per document, then averaged to get the agreement over all documents in the corpus. Note that extent agreement was defined as strictly as possible, requiring an exact character index match, meaning cases of overlap would not be considered agreement (e.g. *best* and *the best* would not be a match, even if they referred to the same instance of *best*). The percent agreement scores are displayed in Table 1. Note that calculations were not performed for the LEGITMIZE link tag, because it relies on the extent of other tags.

Tag	% Extent Agreement	% Attribute Agreement
POLAR_PHRASE	6.5	60
FACTIVE_PHRASE	9.3	NA
WEASEL	4.9	13.6
REPETITION	0	0
PERSONAL_TONE	33	57.1
SENTENCE_POV	94.6	74.8
ENTRY_POV	97	66.7

Table 1: Tag Analysis of IAA: Mean % Agreement

Agreement is notably stronger among the higher level tags, ENTRY_POV and SENTENCE_POV. For the ENTRY_POV neutrality attribute, we had decided to measure overall Entry_POV neutrality along a 4-point scale, after noticing our own hesitation to assign the same tag to both slightly preferential and flagrantly biased entries. However, this more nuanced system was at odds with our original objective of creating an annotation scheme for use in a binary classification of bias. Though it might manifest to different degrees, bias either is or is not present within an entry. Our intention in collapsing the scale after the fact was to recover a more organic division in Entry_POV judgments. With the built-in 4-way division, inter-annotator agreement on Entry_POV attributes stood at 42.42%. This number rose considerably when the scale was reduced to a 2-way division. To reflect the notion that any bias is unacceptable, we chose to divide ENTRY_POV into two groups: not-at-all-biased (ENTRY_POV=1) and containing bias (ENTRY_POV>1). This division yielded an inter-annotator agreement of 66.7%. In the case of the SENTENCE_POV attribute, which is binary, agreement on neutrality is even higher at 74.8%.

The strength of scores for attributes at the sentence and document levels suggest that annotators had similar perceptions of what kinds of discourse entailed a bias not fit for an encyclopedic entry. This in turn suggests that there is conceptual validity in our task on a higher level, as well as validity in how that concept was defined and conveyed to annotators.

Interestingly, agreement numbers decline for the intra-sentential tags. Both POLAR_PHRASE and PERSONAL_TONE have attribute agreement scores at or near 60%, but PERSONAL_TONE has an extent agreement of 33%, while POLAR_PHRASE has only 6.5% for extent. WEASEL and REPETITION have low scores for both extent and attribute, with REPETITION being 0% for both (note that extent agreement is a prerequisite for attribute agreement). FACTIVE_PHRASE also has low extent agreement, making extent agreement generally low across the board for intra-sentential tags.

Attribute agreement is expected to be high for the intra-sentential tags, given that attributes are almost always positive (pro/positive) within the service provider genre. Based on the adjudication process, we suspect that the main contributor to instances of attribute disagreement for these tags was simply a failure on the annotators' part to specify the attribute at all, perhaps because they encountered mainly positive/pro instances of POLAR_PHRASEs/WEASELs, thereby forgetting that an attribute is relevant. The annotators also reported confusion about cases where a generally negative word/phrase is used to support or promote the article's topic (in these cases, the attribute should be positive).

For POLAR_PHRASE, the lack of extent agreement is not entirely unexpected, as this tag was difficult to define. As previously discussed, we chose not to use a lexicon of positive/negative words with their prior polarity, because a word's polarity in these documents was highly contingent upon its context and particular usage. During adjudication, it was observed that one of the annotators consistently marked any term that was generally positive as a POLAR_PHRASE. For example, the word *modern* was chosen when used to describe *architecture*. Although this word has some sort of positive connotation, it does not meet the substitution criteria outlined for POLAR_PHRASE in the guidelines (for a word to qualify as a POLAR_PHRASE, there should be a comparable substitution possible that would reduce the non-neutrality of the sentence without losing any of its content). This annotator had set his/her acceptability threshold for this tag too low, which resulted in over-selection. This could hopefully be avoided in future annotation efforts by more exposure to correct and incorrect examples of polar phrases.

Low extent agreement for the WEASEL and REPETITION tags appears to be a result of a poor understanding of what the tags are meant to capture. In the case of the WEASEL tag, annotators tended to mark anything that had an obscured source, such as, *being overlooked for the position* and *a number of executives.* Although the passive voice in the first example and the vague specification in the second one do obscure a source, they do not present support for the topic at hand, which is part of the WEASEL definition. To aid future annotation, it appears that further emphasis is needed to convey the fact that a WEASEL consists of a targeted word/phrase (and not just a lack of citation) that is used to conceal the source of a favorable or unfavorable statement. A lexicon would be useful in this case, as most weasels are covered by just a handful of common phrases or constructions. For example, *the famous* _ is a common WEASEL that was missed by all annotators throughout the corpus.

The poor performance for the REPETITION tag is probably a result of it not being just literal echo, but rather a recurrence of information used for promotional purposes. Like POLAR_PHRASE, this makes its definition rather subjective, and thus prone to different interpretations. Throughout the corpus, all annotators tended to miss the REPETITION we had identified in the gold standard, and there were also cases of annotators marking literal repetitions that did not match the guidelines' criteria. Although the linguistic phenomenon that the REPETITION tag was intended to capture is indeed indicative of bias (especially for service provider articles), it is relatively rare. Its rarity and elusiveness, combined with the fact that agreement was 0%, would motivate us to exclude this as a tag in future versions of the annotation scheme.

4.2 Annotator Analysis

Table 2 reports how each annotator compares to the gold standard (which was determined by the authors). Overall, annotator B clearly outperformed the other two, with both strong precision and recall scores. For all the intra-sentential tags with the exception of WEASEL, there seems to be a consistent trend where annotator B has the highest scores, a second annotator has somewhat lower scores (either A or C), and the third one has very low scores. This trend suggests that for each of these tags, a single annotator tended to pull down its agreement scores, though not consistently the same annotator. For example, annotator C performed relatively poorly on FACTIVE_PHRASE and PERSONAL_TONE, while the same was true for annotator A on the POLAR_PHRASE and REPETITION tags. For the higher level tags (SENTENCE_POV and ENTRY_POV), performance was excellent for all annotators, which is consistent with the percent agreement scores from Table 1.

Tag	annotator_a	annotator_b	annotator_c
	pre., rec.	pre., rec.	pre., rec.
POLAR_PHRASE	0.2, 0.28	0.63, 0.89	0.55, 0.17
FACTIVE_PHRASE	0.29, 0.5	0.55, 0.86	0, 0
WEASEL	0.33, 0.28	0.85, 0.92	0.33, 0.6
REPETITION	0.06, 0.08	0.62, 1	0.44, 0.36
PERSONAL_TONE	0.64, 0.39	1, 1	0, 0
SENTENCE_POV	1, 0.97	1, 1	0.98, 0.97
ENTRY_POV	1, 1	1, 1	1, 1

Table 2: Per-Annotator Analysis: Precision and Recall

While the low individual scores on intra-sentential tags is disconcerting, the overall higher scores for annotator B are a positive indication that a decent understanding and execution of the scheme and guidelines are possible, and agreement could potentially improve greatly with better training for adherence to the guidelines in the case of the other two annotators.

4.3 Proposed Annotation Changes

Post-annotation analyses have provided a basis for changes to our annotation scheme, guidelines, and implementation process for the future. In addition to the changes to the guidelines we have suggested in the previous section, we believe that the greatest amount of improvement for our tag agreement could be achieved by conducting a training session for annotators, in which they study and then practice with positive and negative examples of the different tags. This would hopefully solidify understanding of the tagging scheme, since it became apparent during comparison with the gold standard that certain annotators had trouble with specific tags. Furthermore, it would be worth experimenting with less rigorous forms of extent matching, and perhaps allowing extents with a certain degree of overlap to qualify as agreement.

5 Conclusions and Future Work

The work presented here offers a new annotation scheme for the automatic detection of bias in the unique genre of Wikipedia entries. In addition to a tagset designed to identify linguistic characteristics associated with bias within an encyclopedic corpus, our scheme works beyond typical sentiment analysis approaches to capture cross-sentential linguistic phenomena that lead to encyclopedia bias. Strong agreement results for sentence and document levels bias tags (74.8% and 66.7%, respectively) indicate that there is conceptual validity in our task on a higher level, as well as validity in how that concept was defined and conveyed to annotators. While agreement for intra-sentential tags was lower, the fact that one annotator consistently scored high on agreement with the gold standard suggests that improved annotator training, and specification of unforeseen cases in the guidelines would provide more reliable annotator performance for these tags. It is our hope that upon implementing the suggested improvements outlined in this work, further rounds of annotation could provide appropriate data for use within a machine learning framework for automated detection of various sorts of bias within Wikipedia.

Acknowledgments

We would like to thank James Pustejovsky, Lotus Goldberg and Amber Stubbs for feedback on earlier versions of this paper and helpful advice along the execution of this project. We would also like to thank three anonymous reviewers for their comments.

References

John Blitzer, Mark Drezde , and Fernando Pereira. 2007. Biographies, Bollywood, Boom-boxes and Blenders: Domain Adaptation for Sentiment Classification. *Proceedings of the 45th Annual Meeting of the Association for Computational Linguistics*, 187–205. Prague, Czech Republic.

Richard Farkas, Veronika Vincze, Gyorgy Mora, Janos Csirik and Gyorgy Szarvas. 2010. The CoNLL-2010 Shared Task: Learning to Detect Hedges and their Scope in Natural Language Text.

Proceedings of the Fourteenth Conference on Computational Natural Language Learning: Shared Task, 1–12. Uppsala, Sweden.

Nancy Ide and Laurent Romary. 2006. Representing Linguistic Corpora and Their Annotations. *Proceedings of the Fifth Language Resources and Evaluation Conference*, Genoa, Italy.

Amber Stubbs. 2011. MAE and MAI: Lightweight Annotation and Adjudication Tools. *Proceedings of the Fifth Linguistic Annotation Workshop. LAW V*. Portland, Oregon.

Peter D. Turney. 2002. Thumbs Up or Thumbs Down? Semantic Orientation Applied to Unsupervised Classification fo Reviews. *Proceedings of the 40th Annual Meeting of the Association for Computational Linguistics*, 417–424. Philadelphia, Pennsylvania.

Wikipedia. 2011a. http://en.wikipedia.org/wiki/Wikipedia:Neutral_point_of_view. Accessed May 5, 2011.

Wikipedia. 2011b. http://toolserver.org/~soxred93/articleinfo/index.php?%20article=Land_of_Israel&lang=en&wiki=wikipedia. Accessed May 5, 2011.

Wikipedia. 2011c. http://toolserver.org/~soxred93/articleinfo/index.php?%20article=Fresh_to_Order&lang=en&wiki=wikipedia. Accessed May 5, 2011.

Wikipedia. 2011d. http://en.wikipedia.org/wiki/Special:Statistics. Accessed May 5, 2011.

Wikipedia. 2011e. http://en.wikipedia.org/wiki/Weasel_word. Accessed May 5, 2011.

Wikipedia. 2011f. http://en.wikipedia.org/wiki/Category:NPOV_disputes. Accessed May 5, 2011.

Theresa Wilson, Janyce Wiebe, and Paul Hoffman. 2005. Recognizing Contextual Polarity in Phrase-Level Sentiment Analysis. *Joint Human Language Technology Conference and the Conference on Empirical Methods in Natural Language Processing*, 347–354. Vancouver, Canada.

A Collaborative Annotation between Human Annotators and a Statistical Parser

Shun'ya Iwasawa **Hiroki Hanaoka** **Takuya Matsuzaki**
University of Tokyo
Tokyo, Japan
{iwasawa,hkhana,matuzaki}@is.s.u-tokyo.ac.jp

Yusuke Miyao
National Institute of Informatics
Tokyo, Japan
yusuke@nii.ac.jp

Jun'ichi Tsujii
Microsoft Research Asia
Beijing, P.R.China
jtsujii@microsoft.com

Abstract

We describe a new interactive annotation scheme between a human annotator who carries out simplified annotations on CFG trees, and a statistical parser that converts the human annotations automatically into a richly annotated HPSG treebank. In order to check the proposed scheme's effectiveness, we performed automatic pseudo-annotations that emulate the system's idealized behavior and measured the performance of the parser trained on those annotations. In addition, we implemented a prototype system and conducted manual annotation experiments on a small test set.

1 Introduction

On the basis of the success of the research on the corpus-based development in NLP, the demand for a variety of corpora has increased, for use as both a training resource and an evaluation data-set. However, the development of a richly annotated corpus such as an HPSG treebank is not an easy task, since the traditional two-step annotation, in which a parser first generates the candidates and then an annotator checks each candidate, needs intensive efforts even for well-trained annotators (Marcus et al., 1994; Kurohashi and Nagao, 1998). Among many NLP problems, adapting a parser for out-domain texts, which is usually referred to as domain adaptation problem, is one of the most remarkable problems. The main cause of this problem is the lack of corpora in that domain. Because it is difficult to prepare a sufficient corpus for each domain without reducing the annotation cost, research on annotation methodologies has been intensively studied.

There has been a number of research projects to efficiently develop richly annotated corpora with the help of parsers, one of which is called a discriminant-based treebanking (Carter, 1997). In discriminant-based treebanking, the annotation process consists of two steps: a parser first generates the parse trees, which are annotation candidates, and then a human annotator selects the most plausible one. One of the most important characteristics of this methodology is to use easily-understandable questions called discriminants for picking up the final annotation results. Human annotators can perform annotations simply by answering those questions without closely examining the whole tree. Although this approach has been successful in breaking down the difficult annotations into a set of easy questions, specific knowledge about the grammar, especially in the case of a deep grammar, is still required for an annotator. This would be the bottleneck to reduce the cost of annotator training and can restrict the size of annotations.

Interactive predictive parsing (Sánchez-Sáez et al., 2009; Sánchez-Sáez et al., 2010) is another approach of annotations, which focuses on CFG trees. In this system, an annotator revises the currently proposed CFG tree until he or she gets the correct tree by using a simple graphical user interface. Although our target product is a more richly annotated treebanks, the interface of CFG can be useful to develop deep annotations such as HPSG features by cooperating with a statistical deep parser. Since CFG is easier to understand than HPSG, it can re-

Proceedings of the Fifth Law Workshop (LAW V), pages 56–64,
Portland, Oregon, 23-24 June 2011.

duce the cost of annotator training; non-experts can perform annotations without decent training. As a result, crowd-sourcing or similar approach can be adopted and the annotation process would be accelerated.

Before conducting manual annotation, we simulated the annotation procedure for validating our system. In order to check whether the CFG-based annotations can lead to sufficiently accurate HPSG annotations, several HPSG treebanks were created with various qualities of CFG and evaluated by their HPSG qualities.

We further conducted manual annotation experiments by two human annotators to evaluate the efficiency of the annotation system and the accuracy of the resulting annotations. The causes of annotation errors were analyzed and future direction of the further development is discussed.

2 Statistical Deep Parser

2.1 HPSG

Head-Driven Phrase Structure Grammar (HPSG) is one of the lexicalized grammatical formalisms, which consists of lexical entries and a collection of schemata. The lexical entries represent the syntactic and semantic characteristics of words, and the schemata are the rules that construct larger phrases from smaller phrases. Figure 1 shows the mechanism of the bottom-up HPSG parsing for the sentence "Dogs run." First, a lexical entry is assigned to each word, and then, the lexical signs for "Dogs" and "run" are combined by Subject-Head schema. In this way, lexical signs and phrasal signs are combined until the whole sentence becomes one sign. Compared to Context Free Grammar (CFG), since each sign of HPSG has rich information about the phrase, such as subcategorization frame or predicate-argument structure, a corpus annotated in an HPSG manner is more difficult to build than CFG corpus. In our system, we aim at building HPSG treebanks with low-cost in which even non-experts can perform annotations.

2.2 HPSG Deep Parser

The Enju parser (Ninomiya et al., 2007) is a statistical deep parser based on the HPSG formalism. It produces an analysis of a sentence that includes the syntactic structure (i.e., parse tree) and the semantic structure represented as a set of predicate-argument dependencies. The grammar design is based on the standard HPSG analysis of English (Pollard and Sag, 1994). The parser finds a best parse tree scored by a maxent disambiguation model using a CKY-style algorithm and beam search. We used a toolkit distributed with the Enju parser for extracting a HPSG lexicon from a PTB-style treebank. The toolkit initially converts the PTB-style treebank into an HPSG treebank and then extracts the lexicon from it. The HPSG treebank converted from the test section is also used as the gold standard in the evaluation.

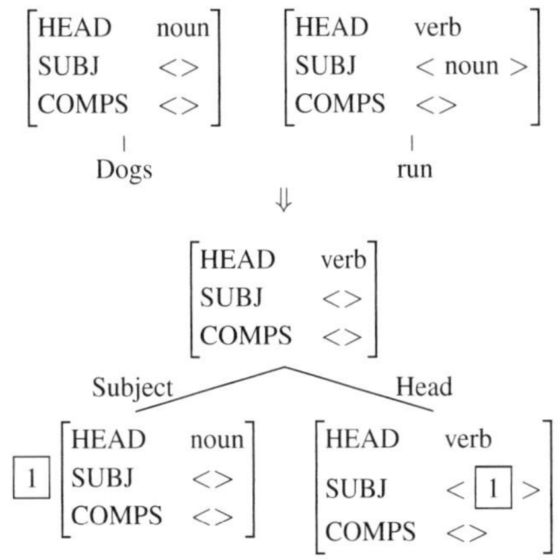

Figure 1: Example of HPSG parsing for "Dogs run."

2.3 Evaluation Metrics

In the experiments shown below, we evaluate the accuracy of an annotation result (i.e., an HPSG derivation on a sentence) by evaluating the accuracy of the semantic description produced by the derivation, as well as a more traditional metrics such as labeled bracketing accuracy of the tree structure. Specifically, we used labeled and unlabeled precision/recall/F-score of the predicate-argument dependencies and the labeled brackets compared against a gold-standard annotation obtained by using the Enju's treebank conversion tool. A predicate-argument dependency is represented as a tuple of $\langle w_p, w_a, r \rangle$, where w_p is the predicate word, w_a is the argument word, and r is the label of the predicate-argument relation, such as `verb-ARG1` (semantic subject of a verb) and `prep-MOD` (modifiee of a prepositional phrase). As for the bracketing accuracies, the label of a bracket is obtained by projecting the sign corresponding to the phrase into a simple phrasal labels such as S, NP, and VP.

3 Proposed Annotation System

In our system, a human annotator and a statistical deep parser cooperate to build a treebank. Our system uses CFG as user interface and bridges a gap between CFG and HPSG with a statistical CKY parser. Following the idea of the discriminant-based treebanking model, the parser first generates candidate trees and then an annotator selects the correct tree in the form of a packed forest. For selecting the correct tree, the annotator only edits a CFG tree projected from an HPSG tree through pre-defined set of operations, to eventually give the constraints onto HPSG trees. This is why annotators can annotate HPSG trees without HPSG knowledge. The current system is implemented based on the following client-server model.

3.1 Client: Annotator Interface

The client-side is an annotator's interface implemented with Ajax technique, on which annotator's revision is carried out through Web-Browser. When the client-side receives the data of the current best tree from the server-side, it shows an annotator the CFG representation of the tree. Then, an annotator adds revisions to the CFG tree using the same GUI, until the current best tree has the CFG structure that exactly matches the annotators' interpretation of the sentence. Finally, the client-side sends the annotator's revision as a CGI query to the server. Based on interactive predicative parsing system, two kinds of operations are implemented in our system: "span modification" and "label substitution", here abbreviated as "S" and "L" operations:

"S" operation $\mathit{modify\_span}(left, right)$
: An annotator can specify that a constituent in the tree after user's revision must match a specified span, by sequentially clicking the leaf nodes at the left and right boundaries.

"L" operation $\mathit{modify\_label}(pos, label)$
: An annotator can specify that a constituent in the tree after user's revision must match a specified label, by inputting a label and clicking the node position.

In addition to "S" and "L" operations, one more operation, "tree fixation", abbreviated "F", is implemented for making annotation more efficient. Our system computes the best tree under the current constraints, which are specified by the "S" and "L" operations that the annotator has given so far. It means other parts of the tree that are not constrained may change after a new operation by the annotator. This change may lead to a structure that the annotator does not want. To avoid such unexpected changes, an annotator can specify a subtree which he or she does not want to change by "tree fixation" operation:

"F" operation $\mathit{fix\_tree}(pos = i)$
: An annotator can specify a subtree as correct and not to be changed. The specified subtree does not change and always appears in the best tree.

3.2 Server: Parsing Constraints

In our annotation system, the server-side carries out the conversion of annotator's constraints into HPSG grammatical constraints on CKY chart and the recomputation of the current best tree under the constraints added so far. The server-side works in the following two steps. The first step is the conversion of the annotator's revision into a collection of dead edges or dead cells; a dead edge means the edge must not be a part of the correct tree, and a dead cell means all edges in the cell are dead. As mentioned in the background section, Enju creates a CKY chart during the parsing where all the terminal and nonterminal nodes are stored with the information of its sign and links to daughter edges. In our annotation system, to change the best tree according to the annotator's revision, we determine whether each edge in the chart is either alive or dead. The server-side re-constructs the best tree under the constraints that all the edges used in the tree are alive. The second step is the computation of the best tree by reconstructing the tree from the chart, under the constraint that the best tree contains only the alive edges as its subconstituents. Re-construction includes the following recursive process:

1. Start from the root edge.

2. Choose the link which has the highest probability among the links and whose daughter edges are all alive.
3. If there is such a link, recursively carry out the process for the daughter edge.
4. If all the links from the edge are dead, go back to the previous edge.

Note that our system parses a sentence only once, the first time, instead of re-parsing the sentence after each revision. Now, we are going to list the revision operations again and explain how the operations are interpreted as the constraints in the CKY chart. In the description below, `label`(x) means the CFG-symbol that corresponds to edge x. Note that there is in principle an infinite variety of possible HPSG signs. The label function maps this multitude of signs onto a small set of simple CFG nonterminal symbols.

"S" operation $span(left = i, right = j)$
When the revision type is "S" and the left and right boundary of the specified span is i and j in the CGI query, we add the cells which satisfy the following formula to the list of dead edges. Suppose the sentence length is L, then the set of new dead cells is defined as:

$$\{\texttt{cell}(a,b) \mid \begin{array}{l} 0 \le a < i, \\ i \le b < j \end{array}\} \bigcup \{\texttt{cell}(c,d) \mid \begin{array}{l} i+1 \le c \le j, \\ j+1 \le d \le n \end{array}\},$$

where the first set means the inhibition of the edges that span across the left boundary of the specified span. The second set means a similar conditions for the right span.

"L" operation *fix_label*$(position = i, label = l)$
When the revision type is "L", the node position is i and the label is l in the CGI query, we determine the set of new dead edges and dead cells as follows:

1. let `cell`(a,b) = the cell including i
2. mark those cells that are generated by `span`(a,b) as defined above to be dead, and
3. for each edge e' in `cell`(a,b), mark e' to be dead if `label`$(e') \neq l$

"F" operation *fix_tree*$(position = i)$
When the revision type is "F" and the target node position is i in the CGI query, we carry out the following process to determine the new dead edges and cells:

1. for each edge e in the subtree rooted at node i,
2. let `cell`(a,b) = the cell including e
3. mark those cells that are generated by `span`(a,b) as defined above to be dead
4. for each edge e' in `cell`(a,b), mark e' to be dead if `label`$(e') \neq$ `label`(e)

The above procedure adds the constraints so that the correct tree includes a subtree that has the same CFG-tree representation as the subtree rooted at i in the current tree.

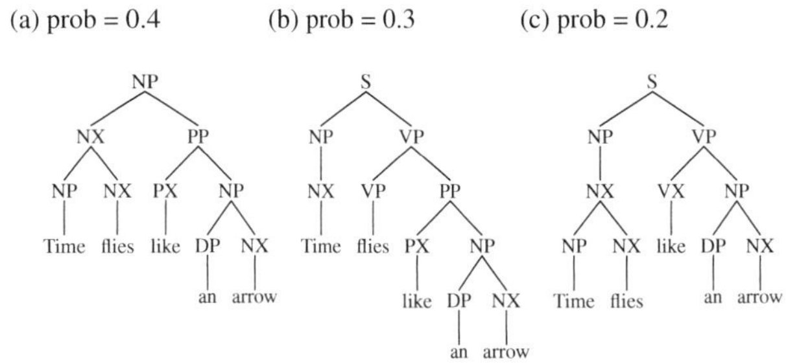

Figure 2: Three parse tree candidates of "Time flies like an arrow."

Finally we show how the best tree for the sentence "Time flies like an arrow." changes with the annotator's operations. Let us assume that the chart includes the three trees shown (in the CFG representation) in (Figure 2), and that there are no dead edges. Let us further assume that the probability of each tree is as shown in the figure and hence the current best tree is (a). If the annotator wants to select (b) as the best tree, s/he can apply "L" operation on the root node. The operation makes some of the edges dead, which include the root edge of tree (a) (see Figure 3). Accordingly, the best tree is now selected from (b), (c), etc., and tree (b) will be selected as the next best tree.

4 Validation of CFG-based Annotation

Because our system does not present HPSG annotations to the annotators, there is a risk that HPSG annotations are wrong even when their projections to CFG trees are completely correct. Our expecta-

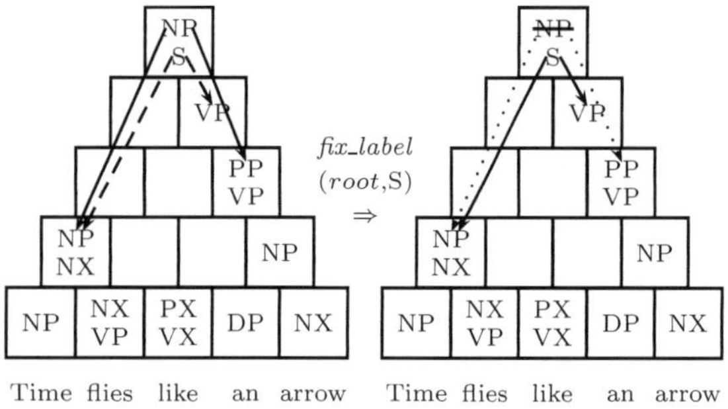

Figure 3: Chart constraints by "L" operation. Solid lines represent the link of the current best tree and dashed lines represent the second best one. Dotted lines stand for an unavailable link due to the death of the source edge.

tion is that the stochastic model of the HPSG parser properly resolves the remaining ambiguities in the HPSG annotation within the constraints given by a part of the CFG trees. In order to check the validity of this expectation and to measure to what extent the CFG-based annotations can achieve correct HPSG annotations, we performed a pseudo-annotation experiment.

In this experiment, we used bracketed sentences in the Brown Corpus (Kučera and Francis, 1967), and a court transcript portion of the Manually Annotated Sub-Corpus (MASC) (Ide et al., 2010). We automatically created HPSG annotations that mimic the annotation results by an ideal annotator in the following four steps. First, HPSG treebanks for these sentences are created by the treebank conversion program distributed with the Enju parser. This program converts a syntactic tree annotated by Penn Treebank style into an HPSG tree. Since this program cannot convert the sentences that are not covered by the basic design of the grammar, we used only those that are successfully converted by the program throughout the experiments and considered this converted treebank as the gold-standard treebank for evaluation. Second, the same sentences are parsed by the Enju parser and the results are compared with the gold-standard treebank. Then, CFG-level differences between the Enju parser's outputs and the gold-standard trees are translated into operation sequences of the annotation system. For example, "L" operation of NX $\rightarrow$ VP at the root node is obtained in the case of Figure 4. Finally, those operation sequences are executed on the annotation system and HPSG annotations are produced.

	total size	ave. s. l.	convertible
Brown	24,243	18.94	22,214
MASC	1,656	14.81	1,353

Table 1: Corpus and experimental data information (s. l. means "sentence length.")

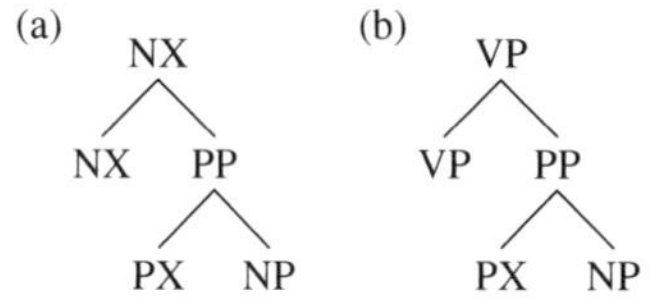

Figure 4: CFG representation of parser output (a) and gold-standard tree (b)

4.1 Relationship between CFG and HPSG Correctness

We evaluated the automatically produced annotations in terms of three measures: the labeled bracketing accuracies of their projections to CFG trees, the accuracy of the HPSG lexical entry assignments to the words, and the accuracy of the semantic dependencies extracted from the annotations. The CFG-labeled bracketing accuracies are defined in the same way as the traditional PARSEVAL measures. The HPSG lexical assignment accuracy is the ratio of words to which the correct HPSG lexical entry is assigned, and the semantic dependency accuracy is defined as explained in Section 2.3. In this experiment, we cut off sentences longer than 40 words for time reasons. We split the Brown Corpus into three parts: training, development test and evaluation, and evaluated the automatic annotation results only for the training portion.

We created three sets of automatic annotations as follows:

Baseline No operation; default parsing results are considered as the annotation results.

S-full Only "S" operations are used; the tree structures of the resulting annotations should thus be identical to the gold-standard annotations.

SL-full "S" and "L" operations are used; the labeled tree structures of the resulting annotations should thus be identical to the gold-standard annotations.

Before showing the evaluation results, splitting of the data should be described here. Our system assumes that the correct tree is included in the parser's

CKY chart; however, because of the beam-search limitation and the incomplete grammar coverage, it does not always hold true. In this paper, such situations are called "out-chart". Conversely, the situations in which the parser does include the correct tree in the CKY chart are "in-chart". The results of "in-chart" are here considered to be the results in the ideal situation of the perfect parser. In our experimental setting, the training portion of the Brown Corpus has 10,576 "in-chart" and 7,208 "out-chart" sentences, while the MASC portion has 864 "in-chart" and 489 "out-chart" sentences (Table 2). Under "out-chart" situations, we applied the operations greedily for calculating S-full and SL-full; that is, all operations are sequentially applied and an operation is skipped when there are no HPSG trees in the CKY chart after applying that operation.

Table 3 shows the results of our three measures: the CFG tree bracketing accuracy, the accuracy of HPSG lexical entry assignment and that of the semantic dependency. In both of S-full and SL-full, the improvement from the baseline is significant. Especially, SL-full for "in-chart" data has almost complete agreement with the gold-standard HPSG annotations. The detailed figures are shown in Table 4. Therefore, we can therefore conclude that high quality CFG annotations lead to high quality HPSG annotations when the are combined with a good statistical HPSG parser.

4.2 Domain Adaptation

We evaluated the parser accuracy adapted with the automatically created treebank on the Brown Corpus. In this experiment, we used the adaptation algorithm by (Hara et al., 2007), with the same hyper-parameters used there. Table 5 shows the result of the adapted parser. Each line of this table stands for the parser adapted with different data. "Gold" is the result adapted on the gold-standard annotations, and "Gold (only covered)" is that adapted on the gold data which is covered by the original Enju HPSG grammar that was extracted from the WSJ portion of the Penn Treebank. "SL-full" is the result adapted on our automatically created data. "Baseline" is the result by the original Enju parser, which is trained only on the WSJ-PTB and whose grammar was extracted from the WSJ-PTB. The table shows SL-full slightly improves the baseline results, which indicates our annotation system can be useful for domain adaptation. Because we used mixed data of "in-chart" and "out-chart" in this experiment, there still is much room for improvement by increasing the ratio of the "in-chart" sentences using a larger beam-width.

		#operations				
		S	L	F	Avg.	Time
Brown	A. 1	122	1	0	1.19	43.32
	A. 2	91	4	1	0.94	41.77
MASC	A. 1	275	2	5	2.76	33.33
	A. 2	52	2	0	0.51	35.13

Table 6: The number of operations and annotation time by human annotators. "Annotator" is abbreviated as A. Avg. is the average number of operations per sentence and Time is annotation time per sentence [sec.].

5 Interactive Annotation on a Prototype-system

We developed an initial version of the annotation system described in Section 3, and annotated 200 sentences in total on the system. Half of the sentences were taken from the Brown corpus and the other half were taken from a court-debate section of the MASC corpus. All of the sentences were annotated twice by two annotators. Both of the annotators has background in computer science and linguistics.

Table 6 shows the statistics of the annotation procedures. This table indicates that human annotators strongly prefer "S" operation to others, and that the manual annotation on the prototype system is at least comparable to the recent discriminant-based annotation system by (Zhang and Kordoni, 2010), although the comparison is not strict because of the difference of the text.

Table 7 shows the automatic evaluation results. We can see that the interactive annotation gave slight improvements in all accuracy metrics. The improvements were however not as much as we desired.

By classifying the remaining errors in the annotation results, we identified several classes of major errors:

1. Truly ambiguous structures, which require the context or world-knowledge to correctly resolve them.

	in	out	in+out
Brown (train.)	10,576 / 10,394	7,190 / 6,464	17,766 / 16,858
MASC	864 / 857	489 / 449	1,353 / 1,306

Table 2: The number of "in-chart" and "out-chart" sentences (total / 1-40 length)

		in	out	in+out
Brown	SL-full	100.00 / 99.31 / 99.60	88.67 / 83.95 / 82.00	94.91 / 92.21 / 92.24
	S-full	98.46 / 96.64 / 96.83	89.60 / 82.02 / 81.20	94.48 / 89.88 / 90.29
	Baseline	92.39 / 92.69 / 90.54	82.10 / 78.38 / 73.80	87.78 / 86.07 / 83.54
MASC	SL-full	100.00 / 99.13 / 99.30	85.91 / 80.75 / 78.80	93.38 / 90.55 / 91.02
	S-full	98.71 / 96.88 / 96.73	86.95 / 79.14 / 77.43	93.18 / 88.60 / 88.93
	Baseline	93.98 / 93.51 / 91.56	80.00 / 75.89 / 72.22	87.43 / 85.30 / 83.75

Table 3: Evaluation of the automatic annotation sets. Each cell has the score of CFG F1 / Lex. Acc. / Dep. F1.

	CFG tree accuracy	
	Brown	MASC
A. 1	90.55 / 90.83 / 90.69	90.62 / 90.80 / 90.71
A. 2	91.01 / 91.09 / 91.05	91.01 / 91.09 / 91.05
Enju	89.70 / 89.74 / 89.72	90.02 / 90.20 / 90.11
	PAS dependency accuracy	
	Brown	MASC
A. 1	87.48 / 87.55 / 87.52	86.02 / 86.02 / 86.02
A. 2	88.42 / 88.27 / 88.34	85.28 / 91.01 / 85.32
Enju	87.12 / 86.91 / 87.01	84.81 / 84.26 / 84.53

Table 7: Automatic evaluation of the annotation results (LP / LR / F1)

	CFG tree accuracy	
	in-chart	out-chart
A. 1	94.52 / 94.65 / 94.58	83.95 / 84.44 / 84.19
A. 2	95.07 / 95.14 / 95.10	84.22 / 84.32 / 84.27
Enju	94.44 / 94.37 / 94.40	81.81 / 82.00 / 81.90
	PAS dependency accuracy	
	in-chart	out-chart
A. 1	92.85 / 92.85 / 92.85	77.47 / 77.65 / 77.56
A. 2	93.34 / 93.34 / 93.34	79.17 / 78.80 / 78.98
Enju	92.73 / 92.73 / 92.73	76.57 / 76.04 / 76.30

Table 8: Automatic evaluation of the annotation results (LP/LR/F1); in-chart sentences (left-column) and out-chart sentences (right column) both from Brown

2. Purely grammar-dependent analyses, which require in-depth knowledge of the specific HPSG grammar behind the simplified CFG-tree representation given to the annotators.
3. Discrepancy between human intuition and the convention in the HPSG grammar introduced by the automatic conversion.
4. Apparently wrong analysis left untouched due to the limitation of the annotation system.

We suspect some of the errors of type 1 have been caused by the experimental setting of the annotation; we gave the test sentences randomly drawn from the corpus in a randomized order. This would have made it difficult for the annotators to interpret the sentences correctly. We thus expect this kind of errors would be reduced by doing the annotation on a larger chunk of text.

The second type of the errors are due to the fact that the annotators are not familiar with the details of the Enju English HPSG grammar. For example, one of the annotators systematically chose a structure like (NP (NP a cat) (PP on the mat)). This structure is however always analysed as (NP a (NP' cat (PP on the mat))) by the Enju grammar. The style of the analysis implemented in the grammar thus sometimes conflicts with the annotators' intuition and it introduces errors in the annotation results.

Our intention behind the design of the annotation system was to make the annotation system more accessible to non-experts and reduce the cost of the annotation. To reduce the type 2 errors, rather than the training of the annotators for a specific grammar, we plan to introduce another representation system in which the grammar-specific conventions become invisible to the annotators. For example, the above-shown difference in the bracketing structures of a determiner-noun-PP sequence can be hidden by showing the noun phrase as a ternary branch on the three children: (NP a cat (PP on the mat)).

The third type of the errors are mainly due to the rather arbitrary choice of the HPSG analysis introduced through the semi-automatic treebank conversion used to extract the HPSG grammar. For instance, the Penn Treebank annotates a structure including an adverb that intervenes an auxiliary verb

	Lex-Acc	Dep-LP	Dep-LR	Dep-UP	Dep-UR	Dep-F1	Dep-EM
Brown	99.26	99.61	99.59	99.69	99.67	99.60	95.80
MASC	99.13	99.26	99.33	99.42	99.49	99.30	95.68

Table 4: HPSG agreement of SL-full for "in-chart" data (EM means "Exact Match.")

	LP	LR	UP	UR	F1	EM
Gold	85.62	85.41	89.70	69.47	85.51	45.07
Gold (only covered)	84.32	84.01	88.72	88.40	84.17	42.52
SL-full	83.27	82.88	87.93	87.52	83.08	40.19
Baseline	82.64	82.20	87.50	87.03	82.42	37.63

Table 5: Domain Adaptation Results

and a following verb as in (VP is (ADVP already) installed). The attachment direction of the adverb is thus left unspecified. Such structures are however indistinguishably transformed to a binary structure like (VP (VP' is already) installed) in the course of the conversion to HPSG analysis since there is no way to choose the proper direction only with the information given in the source corpus. This design could be considered as a best-effort, systematic choice under the insufficient information, but it conflicts with the annotators' intuition in some cases.

We found in the annotation results that the annotators have left apparently wrong analyses on some sentences, either those remaining from the initial output proposed by the parser or a wrong structure appeared after some operations by the annotators (error type 4). Such errors are mainly due to the fact that for some sentences a correct analysis cannot be found in the parser's CKY chart. This can happen either when the correct analysis is not covered by the HPSG grammar, or the correct analysis has been pruned by the beam-search mechanism in the parser. To correct a wrong analysis from the insufficient grammar coverage, an expansion of the grammar is necessary, either in the form of the expansion of the lexicon, or an introduction of a new lexical type. For the other errors from the beam-search limitation, there is a chance to get a correct analysis from the parser by enlarging the beam size as necessary. The introduction of a new lexical type definitely requires a deep knowledge on the grammar and thus out of the scope of our annotation framework. The other cases can in principle be handled in the current framework, e.g., by a dynamic expansion of the lexicon (i.e., an introduction of a new association between a word and known lexical type), and by a dynamic tuning of the beam size.

To see the significance of the last type of the error, we re-evaluated the annotation results on the Brown sentences after classifying them into: (1) those for which the correct analyses were included in the parser's chart (in-chart, 65 sentences) and (2) those for which the correct analyses were not in the chart (out-chart, 35 sentences), either because of the pruning effect or the insufficient grammar coverage. The results shown in Table 8 clearly show that there is a large difference in the accuracy of the annotation results between these two cases. Actually, on the in-chart sentences, the parser has returned the correct analysis as the initial solution for over 50% of the sentences, and the annotators saved it without any operations. Thus, we believe it is quite effective to add the above-mentioned functionalities to reduce this type of errors.

6 Conclusion and Future Work

We proposed a new annotation framework for deep grammars by using statistical parsers. From the theoretical point of view, we can achieve significantly high quality HPSG annotations only by CFG annotations, and the products can be useful for the domain adaptation task. On the other hand, preliminary experiments of a manual annotation show some difficulties about CFG annotations for non-experts, especially grammar-specific ones. We hence need to develop some bridging functions reducing such difficulties. One possible strategy is to introduce another representation such as flat CFG than binary CFG. While we adopted CFG interface in our first prototype system, our scheme can be applied to another interface such as dependency as long as there exist some relatedness over syntax or semantics.

References

David Carter. 1997. The treebanker: a tool for supervised training of parsed corpora. In *Workshop On Computational Environments For Grammar Development And Linguistic Engineering*, pages 9–15.

Tadayoshi Hara, Yusuke Miyao, and Jun'ichi Tsujii. 2007. Evaluating impact of re-training a lexical disambiguation model on domain adaptation of an hpsg parser. In *Proceedings of the 10th International Conference on Parsing Technologies*, pages 11–22, Prague, Czech Republic.

Nancy Ide, Collin Baker, Christiane Fellbaum, and Rebecca Passonneau. 2010. The manually annotated sub-corpus: A community resource for and by the people. In *Proceedings of the ACL 2010 Conference Short Papers*, pages 68–73, Uppsala, Sweden, July.

Sadao Kurohashi and Makoto Nagao. 1998. Building a japanese parsed corpus while improving the parsing system. In *Proceedings of the NLPRS*, pages 719–724.

Henry Kučera and W. Nelson Francis. 1967. *Computational Analysis of Present Day American English*. Brown University Press, June.

Mitchell Marcus, Grace Kim, Mary Ann Marcinkiewicz, Robert MacIntyre, Ann Bies, Mark Ferguson, Karen Katz, and Britta Schasberger. 1994. The Penn treebank: Annotating predicate argument structure. In *Proceedings of the Workshop on Human Language Technology*, pages 114–119.

Takashi Ninomiya, Takuya Matsuzaki, Yusuke Miyao, and Jun'ichi Tsujii. 2007. A log-linear model with an n-gram reference distribution for accurate hpsg parsing. In *Proceedings of the 10th International Conference on Parsing Technologies*, pages 60–68.

Carl Pollard and Ivan A. Sag. 1994. *Head-Driven Phrase Structure Grammar*. University of Chicago Press.

Ricardo Sánchez-Sáez, Joan-Andreu Sánchez, and José-Miguel Benedí. 2009. Interactive predictive parsing. In *Proceedings of the 11th International Conference on Parsing Technologies*, pages 222–225.

Ricardo Sánchez-Sáez, Luis A. Leiva, Joan-Andreu Sánchez, and José-Miguel Benedí. 2010. Interactive predictive parsing using a web-based architecture. In *Proceedings of the NAACL HLT 2010 Demonstration Session*, pages 37–40.

Yi Zhang and Valia Kordoni. 2010. Discriminant ranking for efficient treebanking. In *Coling 2010: Posters*, pages 1453–1461, Beijing, China, August. Coling 2010 Organizing Committee.

Reducing the Need for Double Annotation

Dmitriy Dligach
Department of Computer Science
University of Colorado at Boulder
Dmitriy.Dligach@colorado.edu

Martha Palmer
Department of Linguistics
University of Colorado at Boulder
Martha.Palmer@colorado.edu

Abstract

The quality of annotated data is crucial for supervised learning. To eliminate errors in single annotated data, a second round of annotation is often used. However, is it absolutely necessary to double annotate every example? We show that it is possible to reduce the amount of the second round of annotation by more than half without sacrificing the performance.

1 Introduction

Supervised learning has become the dominant paradigm in NLP in recent years thus making the creation of high-quality annotated corpora a top priority in the field. A corpus where each instance is annotated by a single annotator unavoidably contains errors. To improve the quality of the data, one may choose to annotate each instance twice and adjudicate the disagreements thus producing the gold standard. For example, the OntoNotes (Hovy et al., 2006) project opted for this approach.

However, is it absolutely necessary to double annotate every example? In this paper, we demonstrate that it is possible to double annotate only a subset of the single annotated data and still achieve the same level of performance as with full double annotation. We accomplish this task by using the single annotated data to guide the selection of the instances to be double annotated.

We propose several algorithms that accept single annotated data as input. The algorithms select a subset of this data that they recommend for another round of annotation and adjudication. The single annotated data our algorithms work with can potentially come from any source. For example, it can be the single annotated output of active learning or the data that had been randomly sampled from some corpus and single annotated. Our approach is applicable whenever a second round of annotation is being considered to improve the quality of the data.

Our approach is similar in spirit to active learning but more practical in a double annotation multi-tagger environment. We evaluate this approach on OntoNotes word sense data. Our best algorithm detects 75% of the errors, while the random sampling baseline only detects less than a half of that amount. We also show that this algorithm can lead to a 54% reduction in the amount of annotation needed for the second round of annotation.

The rest of this paper is structured as follows: we discuss the relevant work in section 2, we explain our approach in section 3, we evaluate our approach in section 4, we discuss the results and draw a conclusion in section 5, and finally, we talk about our plans for future work in section 6.

2 Related Work

Active Learning (Settles, 2009; Olsson, 2009) has been the traditional avenue for reducing the amount of annotation. However, in practice, serial active learning is difficult in a multi-tagger environment (Settles, 2009) when many annotators are working in parallel (e.g. OntoNotes employs tens of taggers). At the same time, several papers recently appeared that used OntoNotes data for active learning experiments (Chen et al., 2006; Zhu, 2007; Zhong et al., 2008). These works all utilized OntoNotes gold standard labels, which were obtained via double annotation and adjudication. The implicit assumption, therefore, was that the same process of double anno-

Proceedings of the Fifth Law Workshop (LAW V), pages 65–73,
Portland, Oregon, 23-24 June 2011. ©2011 Association for Computational Linguistics

tation and adjudication could be reproduced in the process of active learning. However, this assumption is not very realistic and in practice, these approaches may not bring about the kind of annotation cost reduction that they report. For example, an instance would have to be annotated by two taggers (and each disagreement adjudicated) on each iteration before the system can be retrained and the next instance selected. Active learning tends to select ambiguous examples (especially at early stages), which are likely to cause an unusually high number of disagreements between taggers. The necessity of frequent manual adjudication would slow down the overall process. Thus, if the scenarios of (Chen et al., 2006; Zhu, 2007; Zhong et al., 2008) were used in practice, the taggers would have to wait on each other, on the adjudicator, and on the retraining, before the system can select the next example. The cost of annotator waiting time may undermine the savings in annotation cost.

The rationale for our work arises from these difficulties: because active learning is not practical in a double annotation scenario, the data is *single* annotated first (with the instances selected via active learning, random sampling or some other technique). After that, our algorithms can be applied to select a subset of the single annotated data for the second round of annotation and adjudication. Our algorithms select the data for repeated labeling in a single batch, which means the selection can be done off-line. This should greatly simplify the application of our approach in a real life annotation project.

Our work also borrows from the error detection literature. Researchers have explored error detection for manually tagged corpora in the context of pos-tagging (Eskin, 2000; Květoň and Oliva, 2002; Novák and Razímová, 2009), dependency parsing (Dickinson, 2009), and text-classification (Fukumoto and Suzuki, 2004). The approaches to error detection include anomaly detection (Eskin, 2000), finding inconsistent annotations (van Halteren, 2000; Květoň and Oliva, 2002; Novák and Razímová, 2009), and using the weights assigned by learning algorithms such as boosting (Abney et al., 1999; Luo et al., 2005) and SVM (Nakagawa and Matsumoto, 2002; Fukumoto and Suzuki, 2004) by exploiting the fact that errors tend to concentrate among the examples with large weights. Some of these works eliminate the errors (Luo et al., 2005). Others correct them automatically (Eskin, 2000; Květoň and Oliva, 2002; Fukumoto and Suzuki, 2004; Dickinson, 2009) or manually (Květoň and Oliva, 2002). Several authors also demonstrate ensuing performance improvements (Fukumoto and Suzuki, 2004; Luo et al., 2005; Dickinson, 2009). All of these researchers experimented with single annotated data such as Penn Treebank (Marcus et al., 1993) and they were often unable to hand-examine all the data their algorithms marked as errors because of the large size of their data sets. Instead, to demonstrate the effectiveness of their approaches, they examined a selected subset of the detected examples (e.g. (Abney et al., 1999; Eskin, 2000; Nakagawa and Matsumoto, 2002; Novák and Razímová, 2009)). In this paper, we experiment with fully double annotated and adjudicated data, which allows us to evaluate the effectiveness of our approach more precisely. A sizable body of work exists on using noisy labeling obtained from low-cost annotation services such as Amazon's Mechanical Turk (Snow et al., 2008; Sheng et al., 2008; Hsueh et al., 2009). Hsueh et al. (2009) identify several criteria for selecting high-quality annotations such as noise level, sentiment ambiguity, and lexical uncertainty. (Sheng et al., 2008) address the relationships between various repeated labeling strategies and the quality of the resulting models. They also propose a set of techniques for selective repeated labeling which are based on the principles of active learning and an estimate of uncertainty derived from each example's label multiset. These authors focus on the scenario where multiple (greater than two) labels can be obtained cheaply. This is not the case with the data we experiment with: OntoNotes data is double annotated by expensive human experts. Also, unfortunately, Sheng et al. simulate multiple labeling (the noise is introduced randomly). However, human annotators may have a non-random annotation bias resulting from misreading or misinterpreting the directions, or from genuine ambiguities. The data we use in our experiments is annotated by humans.

3 Algorithms

In the approach to double annotation we are proposing, the reduction in annotation effort is achieved by double annotating only the examples selected by our algorithms instead of double annotating the entire data set. If we can find most or all the errors made during the first round of labeling and show that double annotating only these instances does not sacrifice performance, we will consider the outcome of this study positive. We propose three algorithms for selecting a subset of the single annotated data for the second round of annotation.

Our **machine tagger** algorithm draws on error detection research. Single annotated data unavoidably contains errors. The main assumption this algorithm makes is that a machine learning classifier can form a theory about how the data should be labeled from a portion of the single annotated data. The classifier can be subsequently applied to the rest of the data to find the examples that contradict this theory. In other words, the algorithm is geared toward detecting inconsistent labeling within the single annotated data. The machine tagger algorithm can also be viewed as using a machine learning classifier to simulate the second human annotator. The machine tagger algorithm accepts single annotated data as input and returns the instances that it believes are labeled inconsistently.

Our **ambiguity detector** algorithm is inspired by uncertainty sampling (Lewis and Gale, 1994), a kind of active learning in which the model selects the instances for which its prediction is least certain. Some instances in the data are intrinsically ambiguous. The main assumption the ambiguity detector algorithm makes is that a machine learning classifier trained using a portion of the single annotated data can be used to detect ambiguous examples in the rest of the single annotated data. The algorithm is geared toward finding hard-to-classify instances that are likely to cause problems for the human annotator. The ambiguity detector algorithm accepts single annotated data as input and returns the instances that are potentially ambiguous and thus are likely to be controversial among different annotators.

It is important to notice that the machine tagger and ambiguity detector algorithms target two different types of errors in the data: the former detects inconsistent labeling that may be due to inconsistent views among taggers (in a case when the single annotated data is labeled by more than one person) or the same tagger tagging inconsistently. The latter finds the examples that are likely to result in disagreements when labeled multiple times due to their intrinsic ambiguity. Therefore, our goal is not to compare the performance of the machine tagger and ambiguity detector algorithms, but rather to provide a viable solution for reducing the amount of annotation on the second round by detecting as much noise in the data as possible. Toward that goal we also consider a **hybrid** approach, which is a combination of the first two.

Still, we expect some amount of overlap in the examples detected by the two approaches. For example, the ambiguous instances selected by the second algorithm may also turn out to be the ones that the first one will identify because they are harder to classify (both by human annotators and machine learning classifiers). The three algorithms we experiment with are therefore (1) the machine tagger, (2) the ambiguity detector, and (3) the hybrid of the two. We will now provide more details about how each of them is implemented.

3.1 General Framework

All three algorithms accept single annotated data as input. They output a subset of this data that they recommend for repeated labeling. All algorithms begin by splitting the single annotated data into N sets of equal size. They proceed by training a classifier on $N-1$ sets and applying it to the remaining set, which we will call the *pool*[1]. The cycle repeats N times in the style of N-fold cross-validation. Upon completion, each single annotated instance has been examined by the algorithm. A subset of the single annotated data is selected for the second round of annotation based on various criteria. These criteria are what sets the algorithms apart. Because of the time constraints, for the experiments we describe in this paper, we set N to 10. A larger value will increase the running time but may also result in an improved performance.

[1]Notice that the term *pool* in active learning research typically refers to the collection of *unlabeled* data from which the examples to be labeled are selected. In our case, this term applies to the data that is *already labeled* and the goal is to select data for *repeated* labeling.

3.2 Machine Tagger Algorithm

The main goal of the machine tagger algorithm is finding inconsistent labeling in the data. This algorithm operates by training a discriminative classifier and making a prediction for each instance in the *pool*. Whenever this prediction disagrees with the human-assigned label, the instance is selected for repeated labeling.

For classification we choose a support vector machine (SVM) classifier because we need a high-accuracy classifier. The state-of-the art system we use for our experiments is SVM-based (Dligach and Palmer, 2008). The specific classification software we utilize is LibSVM (Chang and Lin, 2001). We accept the default settings ($C = 1$ and linear kernel).

3.3 Ambiguity Detector Algorithm

The ambiguity detector algorithm trains a probabilistic classifier and makes a prediction for each instance in the *pool*. However, unlike the previous algorithm, the objective in this case is to find the instances that are potentially hard to annotate due to their ambiguity. The instances that lie close to the decision boundary are intrinsically ambiguous and therefore harder to annotate. We hypothesize that a human tagger is more likely to make a mistake when annotating these instances.

We can estimate the proximity to the class boundary using a classifier confidence metric such as the prediction margin, which is a simple metric often used in active learning (e.g. (Chen et al., 2006)). For an instance x, we compute the prediction margin as follows:

$$Margin(x) = |P(c_1|x) - P(c_2|x)| \quad (1)$$

Where c_1 and c_2 are the two most probable classes of x according to the model. We rank the single annotated instances by their prediction margin and select *selectsize* instances with the smallest margin. The *selectsize* setting can be manipulated to increase the recall. We experiment with the settings of *selectsize* of 20% and larger.

While SVM classifiers can be adapted to produce a calibrated posterior probability (Platt and Platt, 1999), for simplicity, we use a maximum entropy classifier, which is an intrinsically probabilistic classifier and thus has the advantage of being able to output the probability distribution over the class labels right off-the-shelf. The specific classification software we utilize is the python maximum entropy modeling toolkit (Le, 2004) with the default options.

3.4 Hybrid Algorithm

We hypothesize that both the machine tagger and ambiguity detector algorithms we just described select the instances that are appropriate for the second round of human annotation. The hybrid algorithm simply unions the instances selected by these two algorithms. As a result, the amount of data selected by this algorithm is expected to be larger than the amount selected by each individual algorithm.

4 Evaluation

For evaluation we use the word sense data annotated by the OntoNotes project. The OntoNotes data was chosen because it is fully double-blind annotated by human annotators and the disagreements are adjudicated by a third (more experienced) annotator. This type of data allows us to: (1) Simulate single annotation by using the labels assigned by the first annotator, (2) Simulate the second round of annotation for selected examples by using the labels assigned by the second annotator, (3) Evaluate how well our algorithms capture the errors made by the first annotator, and (4) Measure the performance of the corrected data against the performance of the double annotated and adjudicated gold standard.

We randomly split the gold standard data into ten parts of equal size. Nine parts are used as a *pool* of data from which a subset is selected for repeated labeling. The rest is used as a test set. Before passing the *pool* to the algorithm, we "single annotate" it (i.e. relabel with the labels assigned by the first annotator). The test set always stays double annotated and adjudicated to make sure the performance is evaluated against the gold standard labels. The cycle is repeated ten times and the results are averaged.

Since our goal is finding errors in single annotated data, a brief explanation of what we count as an error is appropriate. In this evaluation, the errors are the disagreements between the first annotator and the gold standard. The fact that our data

Sense Definition	Sample Context
Accept as true without verification	I *assume* his train was late
Take on a feature, position, responsibility, right	When will the new President *assume* office?
Take someone's soul into heaven	This is the day when Mary was *assumed* into heaven

Table 1: Senses of *to assume*

is double annotated allows us to be reasonably sure that most of the errors made by the first annotator were caught (as disagreements with the second annotator) and resolved. Even though other errors may still exist in the data (e.g. when the two annotators made the same mistake), we assume that there are very few of them and we ignore them for the purpose of this study.

4.1 Task

The task we are using for evaluating our approach is word sense disambiguation (WSD). Resolution of lexical ambiguities has for a long time been viewed as an important problem in natural language processing that tests our ability to capture and represent semantic knowledge and and learn from linguistic data. More specifically, we experiment with verbs. There are fewer verbs in English than nouns but the verbs are more polysemous, which makes the task of disambiguating verbs harder. As an example, we list the senses of one of the participating verbs, *to assume*, in Table 1.

The goal of WSD is predicting the sense of an ambiguous word given its context. For example, given a sentence *When will the new President assume office?*, the task consists of determining that the verb *assume* in this sentence is used in the *Take on a feature, position, responsibility, right, etc.* sense.

4.2 Data

We selected the 215 most frequent verbs in the OntoNotes data and discarded the 15 most frequent ones to make the size of the dataset more manageable (the 15 most frequent verbs have roughly as many examples as the next 200 frequent verbs). We ended up with a dataset containing 58,728 instances of 200 frequent verbs. Table 2 shows various important characteristics of this dataset averaged across the 200 verbs.

Inter-annotator agreement	86%
Annotator1-gold standard agreement	93%
Share of the most frequent sense	71%
Number of classes (senses) per verb	4.44

Table 2: Evaluation data at a glance

Observe that even though the annotator1-gold standard agreement is high, it is not perfect: about 7% of the instances are the errors the first annotator made. These are the instances we are targeting. OntoNotes double annotated *all* the instances to eliminate the errors. Our goal is finding them automatically.

4.3 System

Our word sense disambiguation system (Dligach and Palmer, 2008) includes three groups of features. Lexical features include open class words from the target sentence and the two surrounding sentences; two words on both sides of the target verb and their POS tags. Syntactic features are based on constituency parses of the target sentence and include the information about whether the target verb has a subject/object, what their head words and POS tags are, whether the target verb has a subordinate clause, and whether the target verb has a PP adjunct. The semantic features include the information about the semantic class of the subject and the object of the target verb. The system uses Libsvm (Chang and Lin, 2001) software for classification. We train a single model per verb and average the results across all 200 verbs.

4.4 Performance Metrics

Our objective is finding errors in single annotated data. One way to quantify the success of error detection is by means of precision and recall. We compute **precision** as the ratio of the number of errors in the data that the algorithm selected and the total number of instances the algorithm selected. We compute **recall** as the ratio of the number of errors in the data that the algorithm selected to the total number of errors in the data. To compute baseline precision and recall for an algorithm, we count how many instances it selected and randomly draw the same number of instances from the single annotated data. We then compute precision and recall for the randomly selected data.

We also evaluate each algorithm in terms of classification accuracy. For each algorithm, we measure the accuracy on the test set when the model is trained on: (1) Single annotated data only, (2) Single annotated data with a random subset of it double annotated[2] (of the same size as the data selected by the algorithm), (3) Single annotated data with the instances selected by the algorithm double annotated, and (4) Single annotated data with all instances double annotated.

4.5 Error Detection Performance

In this experiment we evaluate how well the three algorithms detect the errors. We split the data for each word into 90% and 10% parts as described at the beginning of section 4. We relabel the 90% part with the labels assigned by the first tagger and use it as a pool in which we detect the errors. We pass the pool to each algorithm and compute the precision and recall of errors in the data the algorithm returns. We also measure the random baseline performance by drawing the same number of examples randomly and computing the precision and recall. The results are in the top portion of Table 3.

Consider the second column, which shows the performance of the machine tagger algorithm. The algorithm identified as errors 16.93% of the total number of examples that we passed to it. These selected examples contained 60.32% of the total number of errors found in the data. Of the selected examples, 23.81% were in fact errors. By drawing the same number of examples (16.93%) randomly we recall only 16.79% of the single annotation errors. The share of errors in the randomly drawn examples is 6.82%. Thus, the machine tagger outperforms the random baseline both with respect to precision and recall.

The ambiguity detector algorithm selected 20% of the examples with the highest value of the prediction margin and beat the random baseline both with respect to precision and recall. The hybrid algorithm also beat the random baselines. It recalled 75% of errors but at the expense of selecting a larger set of examples, 30.48%. This is the case because it selects both the data selected by the machine tagger and the ambiguity detector. The size selected, 30.48%, is smaller than the sum, 16.93% + 20.01%, because there is some overlap between the instances selected by the first two algorithms.

4.6 Model Performance

In this experiment we investigate whether double annotating and adjudicating selected instances improves the accuracy of the models. We use the same pool/test split (90%-10%) as was used in the previous experiment. The results are in the bottom portion of Table 3.

Let us first validate empirically an assumption this paper makes: we have been assuming that full double annotation is justified because it helps to correct the errors the first annotator made, which in turn leads to a better performance. If this assumption does not hold, our task is pointless. In general repeated labeling does not always lead to better performance (Sheng et al., 2008), but it does in our case. We train a model using only the single annotated data and test it. We then train a model using the double annotated and adjudicated version of the same data and evaluate its performance.

As expected, the models trained on fully double annotated data perform better. The performance of the fully double annotated data, 84.15%, is the ceiling performance we can expect to obtain if we detect all the errors made by the first annotator. The performance of the single annotated data, 82.84%, is the hard baseline. Thus, double annotating is beneficial, especially if one can avoid double annotating everything by identifying the single annotated instances where an error is suspected.

All three algorithms beat both the hard and the random baselines. For example, by double annotating the examples the hybrid algorithm selected we achieve an accuracy of 83.82%, which is close to the full double annotation accuracy, 84.15%. By double annotating the same number of randomly selected instances, we reach a lower accuracy, 83.36%. The differences are statistically significant for all three

[2]Random sampling is often used as a baseline in the active learning literature (Settles, 2009; Olsson, 2009).

Metric	Machine Tagger, %	Ambiguity Detector, %	Hybrid, %
Actual size selected	16.93	20.01	30.48
Error detection precision	23.81	10.61	14.70
Error detection recall	60.32	37.94	**75.14**
Baseline error detection precision	6.82	6.63	6.86
Baseline error detection recall	16.79	19.61	29.06
Single annotation only accuracy	82.84	82.84	82.84
Single + random double accuracy	83.23	83.09	83.36
Single + selected double accuracy	83.58	83.42	**83.82**
Full double annotation accuracy	84.15	84.15	84.15

Table 3: Results of performance evaluation. Error detection performance is shown at the top part of the table. Model performance is shown at the bottom.

algorithms ($p < 0.05$).

Even though the accuracy gains over the random baseline are modest in absolute terms, the reader should keep in mind that the maximum possible accuracy gain is 84.15% - 82.84% = 1.31% (when all the data is double annotated). The hybrid algorithm came closer to the target accuracy than the other two algorithms because of a higher recall of errors, 75.14%, but at the expense of selecting almost twice as much data as, for example, the machine tagger algorithm.

4.7 Reaching Double Annotation Accuracy

The hybrid algorithm performed better than the baselines but it still fell short of reaching the accuracy our system achieves when trained on fully double annotated data. However, we have a simple way of increasing the recall of error detection. One way to do it is by increasing the number of instances with the smallest prediction margin the ambiguity detector algorithm selects, which in turn will increase the recall of the hybrid algorithm. In this series of experiments we measure the performance of the hybrid algorithm at various settings of the selection size. The goal is to keep increasing the recall of errors until the performance is close to the double annotation accuracy.

Again, we split the data for each word into 90% and 10% parts. We relabel the 90% part with the labels assigned by the first tagger and pass it to the hybrid algorithm. We vary the selection size setting between 20% and 50%. At each setting, we compute the precision and recall of errors in the data the algorithm returns as well as in the random baseline. We also measure the performance of the models trained on on the single annotated data with its randomly and algorithm-selected subsets double annotated. The results are in Table 4.

As we see at the top portion of the Table 4, as we select more and more examples with a small prediction margin, the recall of errors grows. For example, at the 30% setting, the hybrid algorithm selects 37.91% of the total number of single annotated examples, which contain 80.42% of all errors in the single annotated data (more than twice as much as the random baseline).

As can be seen at the bottom portion of the Table 4, with increased recall of errors, the accuracy on the test set also grows and nears the double annotation accuracy. At the 40% setting, the algorithm selects 45.80% of the single annotated instances and the accuracy with these instances double annotated reaches 84.06% which is not statistically different ($p < 0.05$) from the double annotation accuracy.

5 Discussion and Conclusion

We proposed several simple algorithms for reducing the amount of the second round of annotation. The algorithms operate by detecting annotation errors along with hard-to-annotate and potentially error-prone instances in single annotated data. We evaluate the algorithms using OntoNotes word sense data. Because OntoNotes data is double annotated and adjudicated we were able to evaluate the error detection performance of the algorithms as well as their accuracy on the gold standard test set. All three al-

Metric	Selection Size			
	20%	30%	40%	50%
Actual size selected	30.46	37.91	45.80	54.12
Error detection precision	14.63	12.81	11.40	10.28
Error detection recall	75.65	80.42	83.95	87.37
Baseline error detection precision	6.80	6.71	6.78	6.77
Baseline error detection recall	29.86	36.23	45.63	53.30
Single annotation only accuracy	83.04	83.04	83.04	83.04
Single + random double accuracy	83.47	83.49	83.63	83.81
Single + selected double accuracy	83.95	83.99	84.06	84.10
Full double annotation accuracy	84.18	84.18	84.18	84.18

Table 4: Performance at various sizes of selected data.

gorithms outperformed the random sampling baseline both with respect to error recall and model performance.

By progressively increasing the recall of errors, we showed that the hybrid algorithm can be used to replace *full* double annotation. The hybrid algorithm reached accuracy that is not statistically different from the full double annotation accuracy with approximately 46% of data double annotated. Thus, it can potentially save 54% of the second pass of annotation effort without sacrificing performance.

While we evaluated the proposed algorithms only on word sense data, the evaluation was performed using 200 distinct word type datasets. These words each have contextual features that are essentially unique to that word type and consequently, 200 distinct classifiers, one per word type, are trained. Hence, these could loosely be considered 200 distinct annotation and classification tasks. Thus, it is likely that the proposed algorithms will be widely applicable whenever a second round of annotation is being contemplated to improve the quality of the data.

6 Future Work

Toward the same goal of reducing the cost of the second round of double annotation, we will explore several research directions. We will investigate the utility of more complex error detection algorithms such as the ones described in (Eskin, 2000) and (Nakagawa and Matsumoto, 2002). Currently our algorithms select the instances to be double annotated in one batch. However it is possible to frame the selection more like batch active learning, where the next batch is selected only after the previous one is annotated, which may result in further reductions in annotation costs.

Acknowledgements

We gratefully acknowledge the support of the National Science Foundation Grant NSF-0715078, Consistent Criteria for Word Sense Disambiguation, and the GALE program of the Defense Advanced Research Projects Agency, Contract No. HR0011-06-C-0022, a subcontract from the BBN-AGILE Team. Any opinions, findings, and conclusions or recommendations expressed in this material are those of the authors and do not necessarily reflect the views of the National Science Foundation.

References

Steven Abney, Robert E. Schapire, and Yoram Singer. 1999. Boosting applied to tagging and pp attachment. In *Proceedings of the Joint SIGDAT Conference on Empirical Methods in Natural Language Processing and Very Large Corpora*, pages 38–45.

Chih-Chung Chang and Chih-Jen Lin, 2001. *LIBSVM: a library for support vector machines.*

Jinying Chen, Andrew Schein, Lyle Ungar, and Martha Palmer. 2006. An empirical study of the behavior of active learning for word sense disambiguation. In *Proceedings of the main conference on Human Language Technology Conference of the North American Chapter of the Association of Computational Linguistics*, pages 120–127, Morristown, NJ, USA. Association for Computational Linguistics.

Markus Dickinson. 2009. Correcting dependency annotation errors. In *EACL '09: Proceedings of the 12th Conference of the European Chapter of the Association for Computational Linguistics*, pages 193–201, Morristown, NJ, USA. Association for Computational Linguistics.

Dmitriy Dligach and Martha Palmer. 2008. Novel semantic features for verb sense disambiguation. In *HLT '08: Proceedings of the 46th Annual Meeting of the Association for Computational Linguistics on Human Language Technologies*, pages 29–32, Morristown, NJ, USA. Association for Computational Linguistics.

Eleazar Eskin. 2000. Detecting errors within a corpus using anomaly detection. In *Proceedings of the 1st North American chapter of the Association for Computational Linguistics conference*, pages 148–153, San Francisco, CA, USA. Morgan Kaufmann Publishers Inc.

Fumiyo Fukumoto and Yoshimi Suzuki. 2004. Correcting category errors in text classification. In *COLING '04: Proceedings of the 20th international conference on Computational Linguistics*, page 868, Morristown, NJ, USA. Association for Computational Linguistics.

Eduard Hovy, Mitchell Marcus, Martha Palmer, Lance Ramshaw, and Ralph Weischedel. 2006. Ontonotes: the 90% solution. In *NAACL '06: Proceedings of the Human Language Technology Conference of the NAACL, Companion Volume: Short Papers on XX*, pages 57–60, Morristown, NJ, USA. Association for Computational Linguistics.

Pei-Yun Hsueh, Prem Melville, and Vikas Sindhwani. 2009. Data quality from crowdsourcing: a study of annotation selection criteria. In *HLT '09: Proceedings of the NAACL HLT 2009 Workshop on Active Learning for Natural Language Processing*, pages 27–35, Morristown, NJ, USA. Association for Computational Linguistics.

Pavel Květoň and Karel Oliva. 2002. (semi-)automatic detection of errors in pos-tagged corpora. In *Proceedings of the 19th international conference on Computational linguistics*, pages 1–7, Morristown, NJ, USA. Association for Computational Linguistics.

Zhang Le, 2004. *Maximum Entropy Modeling Toolkit for Python and C++.*

David D. Lewis and William A. Gale. 1994. A sequential algorithm for training text classifiers. In *SIGIR '94: Proceedings of the 17th annual international ACM SIGIR conference on Research and development in information retrieval*, pages 3–12, New York, NY, USA. Springer-Verlag New York, Inc.

Dingsheng Luo, Xinhao Wang, Xihong Wu, and Huisheng Chi. 2005. Learning outliers to refine a corpus for chinese webpage categorization. In *ICNC (1)*, pages 167–178.

Mitchell P. Marcus, Mary Ann Marcinkiewicz, and Beatrice Santorini. 1993. Building a large annotated corpus of english: the penn treebank. *Comput. Linguist.*, 19(2):313–330.

Tetsuji Nakagawa and Yuji Matsumoto. 2002. Detecting errors in corpora using support vector machines. In *Proceedings of the 19th international conference on Computational linguistics*, pages 1–7, Morristown, NJ, USA. Association for Computational Linguistics.

Václav Novák and Magda Razímová. 2009. Unsupervised detection of annotation inconsistencies using apriori algorithm. In *ACL-IJCNLP '09: Proceedings of the Third Linguistic Annotation Workshop*, pages 138–141, Morristown, NJ, USA. Association for Computational Linguistics.

Fredrik Olsson. 2009. A literature survey of active machine learning in the context of natural language processing. In *Technical Report, Swedish Institute of Computer Science.*

John C. Platt and John C. Platt. 1999. Probabilistic outputs for support vector machines and comparisons to regularized likelihood methods. In *Advances in Large Margin Classifiers*, pages 61–74. MIT Press.

Burr Settles. 2009. Active learning literature survey. In *Computer Sciences Technical Report 1648 University of Wisconsin-Madison.*

Victor S. Sheng, Foster Provost, and Panagiotis G. Ipeirotis. 2008. Get another label? improving data quality and data mining using multiple, noisy labelers. In *KDD '08: Proceeding of the 14th ACM SIGKDD international conference on Knowledge discovery and data mining*, pages 614–622, New York, NY, USA. ACM.

Rion Snow, Brendan O'Connor, Daniel Jurafsky, and Andrew Y. Ng. 2008. Cheap and fast—but is it good?: evaluating non-expert annotations for natural language tasks. In *EMNLP '08: Proceedings of the Conference on Empirical Methods in Natural Language Processing*, pages 254–263, Morristown, NJ, USA. Association for Computational Linguistics.

Hans van Halteren. 2000. The detection of inconsistency in manually tagged text. In *Proceedings of LINC-00, Luxembourg.*

Z. Zhong, H.T. Ng, and Y.S. Chan. 2008. Word sense disambiguation using OntoNotes: An empirical study. In *Proceedings of the Conference on Empirical Methods in Natural Language Processing*, pages 1002–1010. Association for Computational Linguistics.

Jingbo Zhu. 2007. Active learning for word sense disambiguation with methods for addressing the class imbalance problem. In *In Proceedings of ACL*, pages 783–790.

Crowdsourcing Word Sense Definition

Anna Rumshisky[†*]
[†] Computer Science and Artificial Intelligence Laboratory
Massachusetts Institute of Technology
Cambridge, MA
arum@csail.mit.edu
[*]Department of Computer Science
Brandeis University
Waltham, MA

Abstract

In this paper, we propose a crowdsourcing methodology for a single-step construction of both an empirically-derived sense inventory and the corresponding sense-annotated corpus. The methodology taps the intuitions of non-expert native speakers to create an expert-quality resource, and natively lends itself to supplementing such a resource with additional information about the structure and reliability of the produced sense inventories. The resulting resource will provide several ways to empirically measure distances between related word senses, and will explicitly address the question of fuzzy boundaries between them.

1 Introduction

A number of recent initiatives has focused on creating sense-annotated gold standards for word sense disambiguation and induction algorithms. However, such work has frequently come under criticism over the lack of a satisfactory set of standards for creating consistent, task-independent sense inventories. More systematic efforts to replace ad hoc lexicographic procedures for sense inventory construction have often focused on working with existing sense inventories, attempting to resolve the specific associated problems (e.g. sense granularity, overlapping senses, etc.) Methodologically, defining a robust procedure for sense definition has remained an elusive task.

In this paper, we propose a method for creating a sense inventory from scratch for any polysemous word, simultaneously with the corresponding sense-annotated lexical sample. The methodology we propose explicitly addresses the question of related word senses and fuzzy boundaries between them, without trying to establish hard divisions where empirically there are none.

The proposed method uses Amazon's Mechanical Turk for sense annotation. Over the last several of years, Mechanical Turk, introduced by Amazon as "artificial artificial intelligence", has been used successfully for a number of NLP tasks, including robust evaluation of machine translation systems by reading comprehension (Callison-Burch, 2009), and other tasks explored in the recent NAACL workshop (Callison-Burch and Dredze, 2010b). Mechanical Turk has also been used to create labeled data sets for word sense disambiguation (Snow et al., 2008) and even to modify sense inventories. But the original sense inventory construction has always been left to the experts. In contrast, in the annotation method we describe, the expert is eliminated from the annotation process. As has been the case with using Mechanical Turk for other NLP tasks, the proposed annotation is quite inexpensive and can be done very quickly, while maintaining expert-level annotation quality.

The resulting resource will produce several ways to empirically measure distances between senses, and should help to address some open research questions regarding word sense perceptions by native speakers. We describe a set of pilot annotation studies needed to ensure reliability of this methodology and test the proposed quality control mechanisms.

The outcome will be a lexicon where sense inventories are represented as clusters of instances, and an explicit quantitative representation of sense con-

Proceedings of the Fifth Law Workshop (LAW V), pages 74–81,
Portland, Oregon, 23-24 June 2011.

sistency, distance between senses, and sense overlap is associated with the senses for each word. The goal is to provide a more accurate representation the way speakers of a language conceptualize senses, which can be used for training and testing of the automated WSD systems, as well as to automatically induce semantic and syntactic context patterns that represent usage norms and permit native speakers to perform sense disambiguation.

2 The Problem of Sense Definition

The quality of the annotated corpora depends directly on the selected sense inventory, so, for example, SemCor (Landes et al., 1998), which used WordNet synsets, inherited all the associated problems, including using senses that are too fine-grained and in many cases poorly distinguished. At the Senseval competitions (Mihalcea et al., 2004; Snyder and Palmer, 2004; Preiss and Yarowsky, 2001), the choice of a sense inventory also frequently presented problems, spurring the efforts to create coarser-grained sense inventories (Navigli, 2006; Hovy et al., 2006; Palmer et al., 2007). Inventories derived from WordNet by using small-scale corpus analysis and by automatic mapping to top entries in Oxford Dictionary of English were used in the recent workshops on semantic evaluation, including Semeval-2007 and Semeval-2010 (Agirre et al., 2007; Erk and Strapparava, 2010).

Several current resource-oriented projects attempt to formalize the procedure of creating a sense inventory. FrameNet (Ruppenhofer et al., 2006) attempts to organize lexical information in terms of script-like semantic frames, with semantic and syntactic combinatorial possibilities specified for each frame-evoking lexical unit (word/sense pairing). Corpus Pattern Analysis (CPA) (Hanks and Pustejovsky, 2005) attempts to catalog norms of usage for individual words, specifying them in terms of context patterns. Other large-scale resource-building projects also use corpus analysis techniques. In PropBank (Palmer et al., 2005), verb senses were defined based on their use in Wall Street Journal corpus and specified in terms of framesets which consist of a set of semantic roles for the arguments of a particular sense. In the OntoNotes project (Hovy et al., 2006), annotators use small-scale corpus analysis to create sense inventories derived by grouping together WordNet senses, with the procedure restricted to maintain 90% inter-annotator agreement.

Importantly, most standard WSD resources contain no information about the clarity of distinctions between different senses in the sense inventory. For example, OntoNotes, which was used for evaluation in the word sense disambiguation and sense induction tasks in the latest SemEval competitions contains no information about sense hierarchy, related senses, or difficulty and consistency of a given set of senses.

3 Characteristics of the Proposed Lexical Resource

The lexical resource we propose to build is a sense-disambiguated lexicon which will consist of an empirically-derived sense inventory for each word in the language, and a sense-tagged corpus annotated with the derived inventories. The resource will be assembled from "the ground up" using the intuitions of non-expert native speakers about the similarity between different uses of the same word. Each sense will be represented as a cluster of instances grouped together in annotation. The following information will be associated with each sense cluster:

1. Consistency rating for each sense cluster, including several of the following measures:
    - *Annotator agreement*, using the inter-annotator agreement measures for the sense cluster (e.g. Fleiss' Kappa);
    - *Cluster tightness*, determined from the distributional contextual features associated with instance comprising the cluster;
2. Distances to other sense clusters derived for the same word, using several distance measures, including:
    - *Cluster overlap*, determined from the percentage of instances associated with both clusters;
    - *Translation similarity*, determined as the number existing different lexicalizations in an aligned multilingual parallel corpus, using a measurement methodology similar to Resnik and Yarowsky (1999).

The resource would also include a *Membership rating* for each instance within a given sense cluster, which would represent how typical this example is for the associated sense cluster. The instances whose membership in the cluster was established with minimal disagreement between the annotators, and which do not have multiple sense cluster membership will be designated as the core of the sense cluster. The membership ratings would be based on (1) inter-annotator agreement for that instance (2) distance from the core elements of the cluster.

Presently, the evaluation of automated WSD and WSI systems does not take into account the relative difficulty of sense distinctions made within a given sense inventories. In the proposed resource, for every lexical item, annotator agreement values will be associated with each sense separately, as well as with the full sense inventory for that word, providing an innate measure of disambiguation difficulty for every lexical item.

Given that the fluidity of senses is such a pervasive problem for lexical resources and that it creates severe problems for the usability of the systems trained using these resources, establishing the reliability and consistency of each sense cluster and the "prototypicality" of each example associated with that sense is crucial for any lexical resource. Similarly crucial is the information about the overlap between senses in a sense inventory as well as the similarity between senses. And yet, none of the existing resources contain this information.[1] As a result, the systems trained on sense-tagged corpora using the existing sense inventories attempt to make sense distinctions where empirically no hard division between senses exist. And since the information about consistency and instance typicality is not available, the standard evaluation paradigm currently used in the field for the automated WSD/WSI systems does not take it into account. In contrast, the methodology we propose here lends itself naturally to quantitative analysis needed to explicitly address the question of related word senses and fuzzy boundaries between them.

[1]One notable exception is the sense-based inter-annotator agreement available in OntoNotes.

4 Annotation Methodology

In traditional annotation settings, the quality of annotation directly depends on how well the annotation task is defined. The effects of felicitous or poor task design are greatly amplified when one is targeting untrained non-expert annotators.

Typically for the tasks performed using Mechanical Turk, complex annotation is split into simpler steps. Each step is farmed out to the non-expert annotators employed via Mechanical Turk (henceforth, MTurkers) in a form of a HIT (Human Intelligence Task), a term used to refer to the tasks that are hard to perform automatically, yet very easy to do for humans.

4.1 Prototype-Based Clustering

We propose a simple HIT design intended to imitate the work done by a lexicographer in corpus-based dictionary construction, of the kind used in Corpus Pattern Analysis (CPA, 2009). The task is designed as a sequence of annotation rounds, with each round creating a cluster corresponding to one sense. MTurkers are first given a set of sentences containing the target word, and one sentence that is randomly selected from this set as a target sentence. They are then asked to identify, for each sentence, whether the target word is used in the same way as in the target sentence. If the sense is unclear or it is impossible to tell, they are instructed to pick the "unclear" option. After the first round of annotation is completed, the sentences that are judged as similar to the target sentence by the majority vote are set apart into a separate cluster corresponding to one sense, and excluded from the set used in further rounds. The procedure is repeated with the remaining set, i.e. a new target sentence is selected, and the remaining examples are presented to the annotators. This cycle is repeated until all the remaining examples are classified as "unclear" by the majority vote, or no examples remain.

4.2 Proof-of-Concept Study

A preliminary proof-of-concept study for this task design has been reported on previously (Rumshisky et al., 2009). In that study, the proposed task design was tested on a chosen polysemous verb of medium difficulty. The results were then evaluated against the groupings created by a professional lexicographer, giving the set-matching F-score of 93.0 and the entropy of the two clustering solutions of 0.3. The example sentences were taken from the CPA verb lexicon for *crush*. Figure 1 shows the first screen displayed to MTurkers for the HIT, with ten examples presented on each screen. Each example was annotated by 5 MTurkers.

The prototype sentences associated with each cluster obtained for the verb *crush* are shown below:

C1 By appointing Majid as Interior Minister, President Saddam placed him in charge of **crushing** the southern rebellion.

C2 The lighter woods such as balsa can be **crushed** with the finger.

C3 This time the defeat of his hopes didn't **crush** him for more than a few days.

Each round took approximately 30 minutes to an hour to complete, depending on the number of sentences in that round. Each set of 10 sentences took on the average 1 minute, and the annotator received $0.03 USD as compensation. The experiment was conducted using 5-way annotation, and the total sum spent was less than $10 USD. It should be noted that in a large-scale annotation effort, the cost of the annotation for a single word will certainly vary depending on the number of senses it has. However, time is less of an issue, since the annotators can work in parallel on many words at the same time.

4.3 Removing Prototype Impact

Prototype-based clustering produces hard clusters, without explicit information about the origin of boundary cases or the potentially overlapping senses. One of the possible alternatives to having instances judged against a single prototype, with multiple iterations, is to have pairs of concordance lines evaluated against each other. This is in effect more realistic, since (1) each sentence is effectively a prototype, and (2) there is no limitation on the types of similarity judgments allowed; "cross-cluster" connections can be retained.

Whether obtained in a prototype-based setup, or in pairs, the obtained data lends itself well to a graph representation. The pairwise judgments induce an undirected graph, in which judgments can be thought of as edges connecting the instance nodes, and interconnected clusters of nodes correspond to the derived sense inventory (cf. Figure 2).

In the pairwise setup, results do not depend on the selection of a prototype sentence, so it provides a natural protection against a single unclear sentence having undue impact on cluster results, and does so without having to introduce an additional step into the annotation process. It also protects against directional similarity evaluation bias. However, one of the disadvantages is the number of judgments required to collect. The prototype-based clustering of N instances requires between $N(N-1)/2$ and $N-1$ judgments (depending on the way instances split between senses), which gives $O(N^2)$ for 1 cluster 1 instance case vs. $O(N)$ for 1 cluster 1 word case. A typical sense inventory has < 10 senses, so that gives us an estimate of about $10N$ judgments to cluster N concordance lines, to be multiplied by the number of annotators for each pair. In order to bypass prototyping, we must allow same/different judgments for every pair of examples. For N examples, this gives $O(N^2)$ judgments, which makes collecting all pair judgments, from multiple annotators, too expensive.

One of the alternatives for reducing the number of judgments is to use a partial graph approximation. The idea behind it is that rather than collecting repeat judgments (multiple annotations) of the same instance, one would collect a random subset of edges from the full graph, and then perform clustering on the obtained sparse graph. Full pairwise annotation will need to be performed on a small cross-section of English vocabulary in order to get an idea of how sparse the judgment graph can be to obtain results comparable to those we obtained with prototype-based clustering using good prototypes.

Some preliminary experiments using Markov Clustering (MCL) on a sparse judgment graph suggest that the number of judgments collected in the proof-of-concept experiment above by Rumshisky et al. (2009) in order to cluster 350 concordance lines would only be sufficient to reliably cluster about 140 concordance lines.

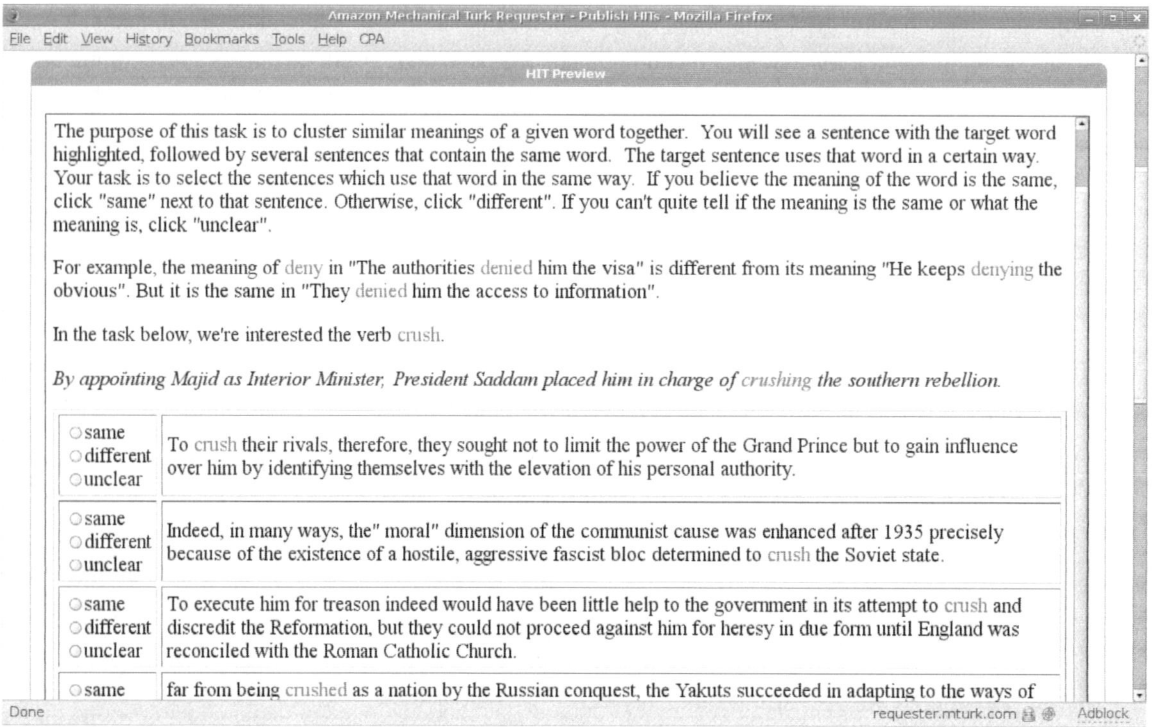

Figure 1: Task interface and instructions for the HIT presented to the non-expert annotators in proof-of-concept experiment.

5 Pilot Annotations

In this section, we outline the pilot studies that need to be conducted prior to applying the described methodology in a large-scale annotation effort. The goal of the pilot studies we propose is to establish the best MTurk annotation practice that would ensure the reliability of obtained results while minimizing the required time and cost of the annotation. The anticipated outcome of these studies is a robust methodology which can be applied to unseen data during the construction of the proposed lexical resource.

5.1 Testing the validity of obtained results

The goal of the first set of studies is to establish the validity of sense groupings obtained using non-expert annotators. We propose to use the procedure outlined in Sec 4 on the data from existing sense-tagged corpora, in particular, OntoNotes, PropBank, NomBank, and CPA.

This group of pilot studies would involve performing prototype-based annotation for a selected set of words representing a cross-section of English vocabulary. A concordance for each selected word will be extracted from the gold standard provided by an expert-tagged sense-annotated corpus. The initial set of selected content words would be evenly split between verbs and nouns. Each group will consist of a set of words with different degrees of polysemy. The lexical items would need to be prioritized according to corpus frequencies, with more frequent words from each group being given preference.

For example, for verbs, a preliminary study done within the framework of the CPA project suggested that out of roughly 6,000 verbs in a language, 30% have one sense, with the rest evenly split between verbs having 2-3 senses and verbs having more than 4 senses. About 20 light verbs have roughly 100 senses each. The chosen lexical sample will therefore need to include low-polysemy verbs, mid-range verbs with 3-10 senses, lighter verbs with 10-20 senses, and several light verbs. Degree of polysemy would need to be obtained from the existing lexical resource used as a gold standard. The annotation procedure could also be tested additionally on a small number of adjectives and adverbs.

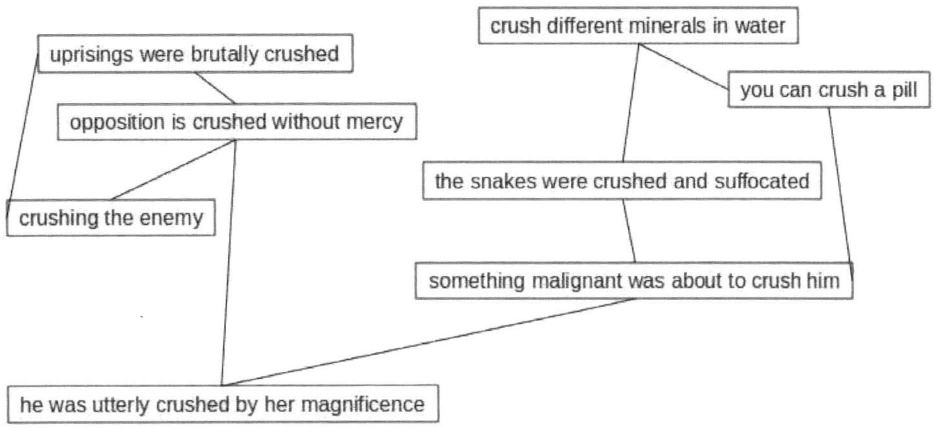

Figure 2: Similarity judgment graph

A smaller subset of the re-annotated data would then need to be annotated using full pairwise annotation. The results of this annotation would need to be used to investigate the quality of the clusters obtained using a partial judgment graph, induced by a subset of collected judgments. The results of both types of annotation could then be used to evaluate different measures of sense consistency and as well as for evaluation of distance between different senses of a lexical item.

5.2 Testing quality control mechanisms

The goal of this set of studies is to establish reliable quality control mechanisms for the annotation. A number of mechanisms for quality control have been proposed for use with Mechanical Turk annotation (Callison-Burch and Dredze, 2010a). We propose to investigate the following mechanisms:

- Multiple annotation. A subset of the data from existing resources would need to be annotated by a larger number of annotators, (e.g. 10 MTurkers. The obtained clustering results would need to be compared to the gold standard data from the existing resource, while varying the number of annotators producing the clustering through majority voting. Results from different subsets of annotators for each subset size would need to be aggregated to evaluate the consistency of annotation for each value. For example, for 3-way annotation, the clusterings obtained from by the majority vote within all possible triads of annotators would be evaluated and the results averaged.

- Checking annotator work against gold standard. Using the same annotated data set, we could investigate the effects of eliminating the annotators performing poorly on the judgments of similarity for the first 50 examples from the gold standard. The judgments of the remaining annotators would need to be aggregated to produce results through a majority vote.

- Checking annotator work against the majority vote. Using a similar approach, we can investigate the effects of eliminating the annotators performing poorly against the majority vote. The data set obtained above would allow us to experiment with different thresholds for eliminating annotators, in each case evaluating the resulting improvement in cluster quality.

- Using prototype-quality control step. We would need to re-annotate a subset of words using an additional step, during which poor quality prototype sentences will be eliminated. This step would be integrated with the main annotation as follows. For each candidate prototype sentence, we would collect the first few similarity judgments from the selected number of annotators. If a certain percentage of judgments are logged as unclear, the sentence is eliminated from the set, and another prototype sentence is selected. We would evaluate the results of this modification, using different thresholds for the number of judgments collected and the percentage of "unclear" ratings.

5.3 Using translation equivalents to compute distances between senses

The goal of this set of studies is to investigate the viability of computing distances between the sense clusters obtained for a given word by using its translation equivalents in other languages. If this methodology proves viable, then the proposed lexical resource can be designed to include some data from multilingual parallel corpora. This would provide both a methodology for measuring relatedness of derived senses and a ready set of translation equivalents for every sense.

Resnik and Yarowsky (1999) used human annotators to produce cross-lingual data in order to measure distances between different senses in a monolingual sense inventory and derive a hierarchy of senses, at different levels of sense granularity. Two methods were tested, where the first one involved asking human translators for the "best" translation for a given polysemous word in a monolingual sense-annotated lexical sample data set. The second method involved asking the human translators, for each pair of examples in the lexical sample, to provide different lexicalizations for the target word, if they existed in their language. The distances between different senses were then determined from the number of languages in which different lexicalizations were preferred (or existed) for different senses of the target word.

In the present project, we propose to obtain similar information by using the English part of a word-aligned multilingual parallel corpus for sense annotation. The degree of cross-lingual lexicalization of the target word in instances associated with different sense classes could then be used to evaluate the distance between these senses. We propose the following to be done as a part of this pilot study. For a selected sample of polysemous words:

- Extract several hundred instances for each word from the English part of a multilingual corpus, such as the Europarl (Koehn, 2005); [2]
- Use the best MTurk annotation procedure as established in Sec 5.2 to cluster the extracted instances;
- Obtain translation equivalents for each instance of the target word using word-alignment produced with Giza++ (Och and Ney, 2000);
- Compute the distances between the obtained clusters by estimating the probability of different lexicalization of the two senses from the word-aligned parallel corpus.

The distances would then be computed using a multilingual cost function similar to the one used by Resnik and Yarowsky (1999), shown in Figure 5.3.

The Europarl corpus contains Indo-European languages (except for Finnish), predominantly of the Romanic and Germanic family. These languages often have parallel sense distinctions. If that proves to be the case, a small additional parallel corpus with the data from other non-European languages would need to be used to supplement the data from Europarl.

6 Conclusion

In this paper, we have presented a proposal for a new annotation strategy for obtaining sense-annotated data WSD/WSI applications, together with the corresponding sense inventories, using non-expert annotators. We have described a set of pilot studies that would need to be conducted prior to applying this strategy in a large-scale annotation effort. We outlined the provisional design of the lexical resource that can be constructed using this strategy, including the native measures for sense consistency and difficulty, distance between related senses, sense overlap, and other parameters necessary for the hierarchical organization of sense inventories.

Acknowledgments

I would like to thank James Pustejovsky and David Tresner-Kirsch for their contributions to this project.

[2] If necessary, the instance set for selected words may be supplemented with the data from other corpora, such as the JRC-Acquis corpus (Steinberger et al., 2006).

$$\text{Cost}(sense_i, sense_j) = \frac{1}{|Languages|} \sum_{L \in Languages} P_L(\text{diff-lexicalization}|sense_i, sense_j)$$

Figure 3: Multilingual cost function for distances between senses.

References

E. Agirre, L. Màrquez, and R. Wicentowski, editors. 2007. *Proceedings of the Fourth International Workshop on Semantic Evaluations (SemEval-2007)*. ACL, Prague, Czech Republic, June.

Chris Callison-Burch and Mark Dredze. 2010a. Creating speech and language data with amazon's mechanical turk. In *Proceedings of the NAACL HLT 2010 Workshop on Creating Speech and Language Data with Amazon's Mechanical Turk*, pages 1–12, Los Angeles, June. ACL.

Chris Callison-Burch and Mark Dredze, editors. 2010b. *Proceedings of the NAACL HLT 2010 Workshop on Creating Speech and Language Data with Amazon's Mechanical Turk*. ACL, Los Angeles, June.

Chris Callison-Burch. 2009. Fast, cheap, and creative: Evaluating translation quality using amazon's mechanical turk. In *Proceedings of the Conference on Empirical Methods in Natural Language Processing (EMNLP 2009)*.

CPA. 2009. Corpus Pattern Analysis.

Katrin Erk and Carlo Strapparava, editors. 2010. *Proceedings of the 5th International Workshop on Semantic Evaluation*. ACL, Uppsala, Sweden, July.

P. Hanks and J. Pustejovsky. 2005. A pattern dictionary for natural language processing. *Revue Française de Linguistique Appliquée*.

E. Hovy, M. Marcus, M. Palmer, L. Ramshaw, and R. Weischedel. 2006. OntoNotes: The 90% solution. In *Proceedings of the Human Language Technology Conference of the NAACL, Companion Volume: Short Papers*, pages 57–60, New York City, USA, June. ACL.

P. Koehn. 2005. Europarl: A parallel corpus for statistical machine translation. In *MT summit*, volume 5. Citeseer.

S. Landes, C. Leacock, and R.I. Tengi. 1998. Building semantic concordances. In C. Fellbaum, editor, *Wordnet: an electronic lexical database*. MIT Press, Cambridge (Mass.).

R. Mihalcea, T. Chklovski, and A. Kilgarriff. 2004. The Senseval-3 English lexical sample task. In Rada Mihalcea and Phil Edmonds, editors, *Senseval-3: Third International Workshop on the Evaluation of Systems for the Semantic Analysis of Text*, pages 25–28, Barcelona, Spain, July. ACL.

R. Navigli. 2006. Meaningful clustering of senses helps boost word sense disambiguation performance. In *Proceedings of the 21st International Conference on Computational Linguistics and 44th Annual Meeting of the Association for Computational Linguistics*, pages 105–112, Sydney, Australia, July. ACL.

F. J. Och and H. Ney. 2000. Improved statistical alignment models. pages 440–447, Hongkong, China, October.

M. Palmer, D. Gildea, and P. Kingsbury. 2005. The Proposition Bank: An annotated corpus of semantic roles. *Computational Linguistics*, 31(1):71–106.

M. Palmer, H. Dang, and C. Fellbaum. 2007. Making fine-grained and coarse-grained sense distinctions, both manually and automatically. *Journal of Natural Language Engineering*.

J Preiss and D. Yarowsky, editors. 2001. *Proceedings of the Second Int. Workshop on Evaluating WSD Systems (Senseval 2)*. ACL2002/EACL2001.

P. Resnik and D. Yarowsky. 1999. Distinguishing systems and distinguishing senses: new evaluation methods for word sense disambiguation. *Natural Language Engineering*, 5(2):113–134.

A. Rumshisky, J. Moszkowicz, and M. Verhagen. 2009. The holy grail of sense definition: Creating a sense-disambiguated corpus from scratch. In *Proceedings of 5th International Conference on Generative Approaches to the Lexicon (GL2009)*, Pisa, Italy.

J. Ruppenhofer, M. Ellsworth, M. Petruck, C. Johnson, and J. Scheffczyk. 2006. *FrameNet II: Extended Theory and Practice*.

R. Snow, B. OConnor, D. Jurafsky, and A.Y. Ng. 2008. Cheap and fastbut is it good? evaluating non-expert annotations for natural language tasks. In *Proceedings of the Conference on Empirical Methods in Natural Language Processing (EMNLP 2008)*.

B. Snyder and M. Palmer. 2004. The english all-words task. In Rada Mihalcea and Phil Edmonds, editors, *Senseval-3: Third International Workshop on the Evaluation of Systems for the Semantic Analysis of Text*, pages 41–43, Barcelona, Spain, July. ACL.

R. Steinberger, B. Pouliquen, A. Widiger, C. Ignat, T. Erjavec, D. Tufis, and D. Varga. 2006. The JRC-Acquis: A multilingual aligned parallel corpus with 20+ languages. *Arxiv preprint cs/0609058*.

A scaleable automated quality assurance technique for semantic representations and proposition banks

K. Bretonnel Cohen
Computational Bioscience Program
U. of Colorado School of Medicine
Department of Linguistics
University of Colorado at Boulder
kevin.cohen@gmail.com

Lawrence E. Hunter
Computational Bioscience Program
U. of Colorado School of Medicine
larry.hunter@ucdenver.edu

Martha Palmer
Department of Linguistics
University of Colorado at Boulder
martha.palmer@colorado.edu

Abstract

This paper presents an evaluation of an automated quality assurance technique for a type of semantic representation known as a predicate argument structure. These representations are crucial to the development of an important class of corpus known as a proposition bank. Previous work (Cohen and Hunter, 2006) proposed and tested an analytical technique based on a simple discovery procedure inspired by classic structural linguistic methodology. Cohen and Hunter applied the technique manually to a small set of representations. Here we test the feasibility of automating the technique, as well as the ability of the technique to scale to a set of semantic representations and to a corpus many times larger than that used by Cohen and Hunter. We conclude that the technique is completely automatable, uncovers missing sense distinctions and other bad semantic representations, and does scale well, performing at an accuracy of 69% for identifying bad representations. We also report on the implications of our findings for the correctness of the semantic representations in PropBank.

1 Introduction

It has recently been suggested that in addition to more, bigger, and better resources, we need a science of creating them (Palmer et al., Download date December 17 2010).

The corpus linguistics community has arguably been developing at least a nascent science of annotation for years, represented by publications such as (Leech, 1993; Ide and Brew, 2000; Wynne, 2005; Cohen et al., 2005a; Cohen et al., 2005b) that address architectural, sampling, and procedural issues, as well as publications such as (Hripcsak and Rothschild, 2005; Artstein and Poesio, 2008) that address issues in inter-annotator agreement. However, there is not yet a significant body of work on the subject of quality assurance for corpora, or for that matter, for many other types of linguistic resources. (Meyers et al., 2004) describe three error-checking measures used in the construction of NomBank, and the use of inter-annotator agreement as a quality control measure for corpus construction is discussed at some length in (Marcus et al., 1993; Palmer et al., 2005). However, discussion of quality control for corpora is otherwise limited or nonexistent.

With the exception of the inter-annotator-agreement-oriented work mentioned above, none of this work is quantitative. This is a problem if our goal is the development of a true science of annotation.

Work on quality assurance for computational lexical resources other than ontologies is especially lacking. However, the body of work on quality assurance for ontologies (Kohler et al., 2006; Ceusters et al., 2004; Cimino et al., 2003; Cimino, 1998; Cimino, 2001; Ogren et al., 2004) is worth considering in the context of this paper. One common theme in that work is that even manually curated lexical resources contain some percentage of errors.

The small size of the numbers of errors uncovered in some of these studies should not be taken as a significance-reducing factor for the development of quality assurance measures for lexical resources—

Proceedings of the Fifth Law Workshop (LAW V), pages 82–91,
Portland, Oregon, 23-24 June 2011. ©2011 Association for Computational Linguistics

rather, the opposite: as lexical resources become larger, it becomes correspondingly more difficult to locate errors in them. Finding problems in a very errorful resource is easy; finding them in a mostly correct resource is an entirely different challenge.

We present here an evaluation of a methodology for quality assurance for a particular type of lexical resource: the class of semantic representation known as a predicate argument structure (PAS). Predicate argument structures are important in the context of resource development in part because they are the fundamental annotation target of the class of corpus known as a proposition bank. Much of the significance claim for this work comes from the significance of proposition banks themselves in recent research on natural language processing and computational lexical semantics. The impact of proposition banks on work in these fields is suggested by the large number of citations of just the three publications (Kingsbury and Palmer, 2002; Kingsbury et al., 2002; Palmer et al., 2005)—at the time of writing, 290, 220, and 567, respectively. Additional indications of the impact of PropBank on the field of natural language processing include its use as the data source for two shared tasks ((Carreras and Màrquez, 2005)).

The methodology consists of looking for arguments that never coöccur with each other. In structural linguistics, this property of non-coöccurrence is known as *complementary distribution*. Complementary distribution occurs when two linguistic elements never occur in the same environment. In this case, the environment is defined as any sentence containing a given predicate. Earlier work showed a proof-of-concept application to a small set of rolesets (defined below) representing the potential PAS of 34 biomedical predicates (Cohen and Hunter 2006). The only inputs to the method are a set of rolesets and a corpus annotated with respect to those rolesets. Here, we evaluate the ability of the technique to scale to a set of semantic representations 137 times larger (4,654 in PropBank versus 34 in Cohen and Hunter's pilot project) and to a corpus about 1500 times larger (1M words in PropBank versus about 680 in Cohen and Hunter's pilot project) than that considered in previous work. We also use a set of independent judges to assess the technique, where in the earlier work, the results were only assessed by one of the authors.

Novel aspects of the current study include:

- Investigating the feasibility of automating the previously manual process
- Scaling up the size of the set of semantic representations evaluated
- Scaling up the size of the corpus against which the representations are evaluated
- Using independent judges to assess the predictions of the method

1.1 Definitions

For clarity, we define the terms *roleset, frame file,* and *predicate* here. A *roleset* is a 2-tuple of a sense for a predicate, identified by a combination of a lemma and a number—e.g., *love.01*—and a set of individual thematic roles for that predicate—e.g., *Arg0 lover* and *Arg1 loved.* A *frame file* is the set of all rolesets for a single lemma—e.g., for *love,* the rolesets are *love.01* (the sense whose antonym is *hate*) and *love.02*, the "semi-modal" sense in *whether it be melancholy or gay, I love to recall it* (Austen, 1811). Finally, we refer to sense-labelled predicates (e.g. *love.01*) as *predicates* in the remainder of the paper.

PropBank rolesets contain two sorts of thematic roles: (core) arguments and (non-core) adjuncts. Arguments are considered central to the semantics of the predicate, e.g. the Arg0 *lover* of *love.01*. Adjuncts are not central to the semantics and can occur with many predicates; examples of adjuncts include negation, temporal expressions, and locations.

In this paper, the *arity* of a roleset is determined by its count of arguments, disregarding adjuncts.

1.2 The relationship between observed argument distributions and various characteristics of the corpus

This work is predicated on the hypothesis that argument distributions are affected by goodness of the fit between the argument set and the actual semantics of the predicate. However, the argument distributions that are observed in a specific data set can be affected by other factors, as well. These include at least:

- Inflectional and derivational forms attested in the corpus

- Sublanguage characteristics
- Incidence of the predicate in the corpus

A likely cause of derivational effects on observed distributions is nominalization processes. Nominalization is well known for being associated with the omission of agentive arguments (Koptjevskaja-Tamm, 1993). A genre in which nominalization is frequent might therefore show fewer coöccurrences of Arg0s with other arguments. Since PropBank does not include annotations of nominalizations, this phenomenon had no effect on this particular study.

Sublanguage characteristics might also affect observed distributions. The sublanguage of recipes has been noted to exhibit rampant deletions of definite object noun phrases both in French and in English, as has the sublanguage of technical manuals in English. (Neither of these sublanguages have been noted to occur in the PropBank corpus. The sublanguage of stock reports, however, presumably does occur in the corpus; this sublanguage *has* been noted to exhibit distributional subtleties of predicates and their arguments that might be relevant to the accuracy of the semantic representations in PropBank, but the distributional facts do not seem to include variability in argument coöccurrence so much as patterns of argument/predicate coöccurrence (Kittredge, 1982).)

Finally, incidence of the predicate in the corpus could affect the observed distribution, and in particular, the range of argument coöccurrences that are attested: the lower the number of observations of a predicate, the lower the chance of observing any two arguments together, and as the number of arguments in a roleset increases, the higher the chance of failing to see any pair together. That is, for a roleset with an arity of three and an incidence of n occurrences in a corpus, the likelihood of never seeing any two of the three arguments together is much lower than for a roleset with an arity of six and an incidence of n occurrences in the corpus. The number of observations required in order to be able to draw conclusions about the observed argument distributions with some degree of confidence is an empirical question; prior work (Cohen and Hunter 2006) suggests that as few as ten tokens can be sufficient to uncover erroneous representations for rolesets with an arity of four or less, although that number of observations of one roleset with an arity of four showed multiple non-coöccurring arguments that were not obviously indicative of problems with the representation (i.e., a false positive finding).

Besides the effects of these aspects of the corpus contents on the observed distributions, there are also a number of theoretical and practical issues in the design and construction of the corpus (as distinct from the rolesets, or the distributional characteristics of the contents) which have nontrivial implications for the methodology being evaluated here. In particular, the implications of the argument/adjunct distinction, of the choice of syntactic representation, and of annotation errors are all discussed in Section 4. Note that we are aware that corpus-based studies generally yield new lexical items and usages any time a new corpus is introduced, so we do not make the naive assumption that PropBank will give complete coverage of all coöccurring arguments, and in fact our evaluation procedure took this into account explicitly, as described in Section 2.3.

2 Materials and Methods

2.1 Materials

We used Rev. 1.0 of the PropBank I corpus, and the associated framesets in the `frames` directory.

2.2 Methods

2.2.1 Determining the distribution of arguments for a roleset

In determining the possible coöccurring argument pairs for a roleset, we considered only arguments, not adjuncts. As we discuss in Section 4.1, this is a non-trivial decision with potential implications for the ability of the algorithm to detect problematic representations in general, and with implications for PropBank in particular. The rationale behind the choice to consider only arguments is that our goal is to evaluate the representation of the semantics of the predicates, and that by definition, the PropBank arguments are essential to defining that semantics, while by definition, the adjuncts are not.

In the first processing step, for each roleset, we used the corresponding framefile as input and generated a look-up table of the possible argument pairs for that predicate. For example, the predicate *post.01* has the three arguments *Arg0, Arg1,* and

Arg2; we generated the set {<Arg0, Arg1>, <Arg0, Arg2>, <Arg1, Arg2>} for it.

In the second processing step, we iterated over all annotations in the PropBank corpus, and for each token of each predicate, we extracted the complete set of arguments that occurred in association with that token. We then constructed the set of coöccurring arguments for that annotation, and used it to increment the counts of each potential argument pair for the predicate in question. For example, the PropBank annotation for *Oils and fats also did well, posting a 5.3% sales increase* (`wsj/06/wsj_0663.mrg`) contains an Arg0 and an Arg1, so we incremented the count for that argument pair by 1; it contains no other argument pairs, so we did not increment the counts for <Arg0, Arg2> or <Arg1, Arg2>.

The output of this step was a table with the count of occurrence of every potential pair of arguments for every roleset; members of pairs whose count was zero were then output as arguments in complementary distribution. For example, for *post.01*, the pairs <Arg0, Arg2> and <Arg1, Arg2> never occurred, even as traces, so the arguments Arg0 and Arg2 are in complementary distribution for this predicate, as are the arguments Arg1 and Arg2.

To manipulate the data, we used Scott Cotton's Java API, with some extensions, which we documented in the API's Javadoc.

2.3 Determining the goodness of rolesets exhibiting complementary distribution

In (Cohen and Hunter, 2006), determinations of the goodness of rolesets were made by pointing out the distributional data to the corpus creators, showing them the corresponding data, and reaching consensus with them about the appropriate fixes to the representations. For this larger-scale project, one of the goals was to obtain goodness judgements from completely independent third parties.

Towards that end, two judges with experience in working with PropBank were assigned to judge the predictions of the algorithm. Judge 1 had two years of experience, and Judge 2 had four years of experience. The judges were then given a typology of classification to assign to the predicates: good, bad, and conditionally bad. The definitions of these categories, with the topology of the typology, were:

- **Good:** This label is assigned to predicates that the algorithm predicted to have bad representations, but that are actually good. They are false positives for the method.
- **Not good:** (This label was not actually assigned, but rather was used to group the following two categories.)
  - **Bad:** This label is assigned to predicates that the algorithm predicted to have bad representations and that the judges agreed were bad. They are true positives for the method.
  - **Conditionally bad:** This label is assigned to predicates that the algorithm predicted to have bad representations and that the judges agreed were bad based on the evidence available in PropBank, but that the judges thought might be good based on native speaker intiution or other evidence. In all of these cases, the judges did suggest changes to the representations, and they were counted as not good, per the typology, and are also true positives.

Judges were also asked to indicate whether bad representations should be fixed by splitting predicates into more word senses, or by eliminating or merging one or more arguments.

We then took the lists of all predicted bad predicates that appeared at least 50, 100, or 200 times in the PropBank corpus. These were combined into a single list of 107 predicates and randomized. The judges then split the list into halves, and each judge examined half of the list. Additionally, 31 predicates, or 29% of the data set, were randomly selected for double annotation by both judges to assess interjudge agreement. Judges were shown both the predicates themselves and the sets of non-coöccurring arguments for each predicate.

3 Results

3.1 Accuracy

The overall results were that out of 107 predicates, 33 were judged GOOD, i.e. were false positives. 44 were judged BAD and 30 were judged CONDITIONAL, i.e. were true positives. This yields a ratio of 2.24 of true positives to false positives: the pro-

Table 1: Ratios of BAD plus CONDITIONAL to GOOD for the pooled judgements as broken down by arity

Arity	Ratio
3	1.29
4	1.47
5	4.0
6	8.0
7	None found

cedure returns about two true positives for every one false positive. Expressed in terms of accuracy, this corresponds to 69% for correctly labelling true positives.

We broke down the data by (1) arity of the roleset, and (2) minimum number of observations of a role set. This allowed us to test whether predictive power decreased as arity increased, and to test the dependency of the algorithm on the minimum number of observations; we suspected that it might be less accurate the fewer the number of observations.

Table 1 shows the ratios of true positives to false positives, broken down by arity. The data confirms that the algorithm is effective at finding bad representations, with the number of true positives outnumbering the number of false positives at every arity. This data is also important because it allows us to test a hypothesis: is it the case that predictive power becomes worse as arity increases? As the table shows, the ratio of true positives to false positives actually increases as the arity of the predicate increases. Therefore, the data is consistent with the hypothesis that not only does the predictive power of the algorithm not lessen as arity increases, but rather it actually becomes greater.

Table 2 shows the ratios of true positives to false positives again, this time broken down by minimum number of occurrences of the predicates. Again, the data confirms that the algorithm is effective at finding bad representations—it returns more bad representations than good representations at every level of minimum number of observations. This data is also important because it allows us to test the hypothesis of whether or not predictive power of the algorithm decreases with the minimum number of observations. As we hypothesized, it does show that the predictive power decreases as the minimum number

Table 2: Ratios of BAD plus CONDITIONAL to GOOD for the pooled judgements as broken down by minimum number of observations

	ratio
Minimum 50	1.88
Minimum 100	2.63
Minimum 200	2.63

of observations decreases, with the ratio of true positives to false positives dropping from 2.63 with a minimum of 200 or 100 observations to 1.88 with a minimum of 50 observations. However, the ratio of true positives to false positives remains close to 2:1 at every level.

3.2 Suggested fixes to the representations

Of the 74 true positives, the judges felt that 17 of the bad representations should be fixed by splitting the predicate into multiple senses. For the 57 remaining true positives, the judges felt that an argument should be removed from the representation or converted to an adjunct. This demonstrates that the method is applicable both to the problem of revealing missing sense distinctions and to the problem of identifying bad arguments.

3.3 Scalability

The running time was less than one and a half minutes for all 4,654 rolesets on the 1-million-word corpus.

3.4 Inter-judge agreement

A subset of 31 predicates was double-annotated by the two judges to examine inter-judge agreement. The judges then examined the cases on which they initially disagreed, and came to a consensus where possible. Initially, the judges agreed in 63.3% of the cases, which is above chance but not the 80% agreement that we would like to see. The judges then went through a reconciliation process. They were able to come to a consensus in all cases.

3.5 Putting the results in context

To help put these results in context, we give here the distribution of arities in the PropBank rolesets and the minimum number of observations of each in the PropBank corpus.

Table 3: Distribution of arities by percentage and by count in the 4,654 PropBank rolesets.

Arity	percentage (count)
0	0.28% (13)
1 (Arg0)	155
1 (Arg1)	146
1 (all)	6.5% (301)
2	45.14% (2,101)
3	37.02% (1,723)
4	7.05% (328)
5	3.5% (163)
6	0.5% (24)
7	0.0002% (1)
Total	100% (4,654)

Table 3 shows the distribution of arities in the PropBank rolesets. It distinguishes between non-ergatives and ergatives (although for the purpose of calculating percentages, they are combined into one single-arity group). The mode is an arity of 2: 45.14% of all rolesets (2,101/4,654) have an arity of 2. 3 is a close second, with 37.02% (1,723/4,654). (The single roleset with an arity of seven is *notch.02*, with a gloss of "move incrementally.")

Table 4 gives summary statistics for the occurrence of complementary distribution, showing the distribution of rolesets in which there were at least one argument pair in complementary distribution and of the total number of argument pairs in complementary distribution. Since (as noted in Section 1.2) the incidence of a predicate has a potential effect on the incidence of argument pairs in apparent complementary distribution, we display the counts separately for four cut-offs for the minimum number of observations of the predicate: 200, 100, 50, and 10.

To further explicate the operation of the discovery procedure, we give here some examples of rolesets that were found to have arguments in complementary distribution.

3.5.1 *accept.01*

Accept.01 is the only roleset for the lemma *accept*. Its sense is *take willingly*. It has four arguments:

- Arg0 acceptor
- Arg1 thing accepted
- Arg2 accepted-from
- Arg3 attribute

Table 4: Summary statistics: counts of predicates with at least one argument pair in complementary distribution and of total argument pairs in complementary distribution for four different minimum numbers of observations of the predicates.

Minimum observations	Predicates	Argument pairs
200	29	69
100	58	125
50	107	268
10	328	882

The predicate occurs 149 times in the corpus. The algorithm found Arg2 and Arg3 to be in complementary distribution.

Manual investigation showed the following distributional characteristics for the predicate and its arguments:

- (Arg0 or Arg1) and Arg2: 5 tokens
- (Arg0 or Arg1) and Arg3: 8 tokens
- Arg2 with neither Arg0 nor Arg1: 0 tokens
- Arg3 with neither Arg0 nor Arg1: 0 tokens
- Arg0 or Arg1 with neither Arg2 nor Arg 3: 136 tokens

Examination of the 5 tokens in which Arg2 coöccurred with Arg0 or Arg1 and the 8 tokens in which Arg3 coöccurred with Arg0 or Arg1 suggested an explanation for the complementary distribution of arguments Arg2 and Arg3. When Arg2 appeared, the sense of the verb seemed to be one of physical transfer: Arg2 coöccurred with Arg1s like *substantial gifts* (`wsj_0051.mrg`) and *a $3 million payment* (`wsj_2071.mrg`). In contrast, when Arg3 appeared, the sense was not one of physical transfer, but of some more metaphorical sense—Arg3 coöccurred with Arg1s like *the war* (`wsj_0946.mrg`) and *Friday's dizzying 190-point plunge* (`wsj_2276.mrg`). There is no *accept.02*; creating one with a 3-argument roleset including the current Arg3 seems warranted. Keeping the Arg3 for *accept.01* might be warranted, as well, but probably as an adjunct (to account for usages like *John accepted it as a gift*.)

3.5.2 *affect.01*

Affect.01 is one of two senses for the lemma *affect.* Its sense is *have an effect on.* It has three arguments:

- Arg0 thing affecting
- Arg1 thing affected
- Arg2 instrument

The predicate occurs 149 times in the corpus. The algorithm found Arg0 and Arg2, as well as Arg1 and Arg2, to be in complementary distribution.

Manual investigation revealed that in fact, Arg2 never appears in the corpus at all. Presumably, either Arg0 and Arg2 should be merged, or—more likely—Arg2 should not be an argument, but rather an adjunct.

3.6 Incidental findings

3.6.1 Mistakes uncovered in frame files

In the process of calculating the set of possible argument pairs for each predicate in the PropBank frame files, we found a roleset that erroneously had two Arg1s. The predicate in question was *proscribe.01*. The roles in the frame file were:

- Arg0 causer
- Arg1 thing proscribed
- Arg1 proscribed from

It was clear from the annotations in the example sentence that the "second" Arg1 was intended to be an Arg2: *[The First Amendment$_{Arg0}$] proscribes [the government$_{Arg1}$] from [passing laws abridging the right to free speech$_{\mathbf{Arg2}}$].*

3.6.2 Unlicensed arguments used in the corpus

We found eighteen tokens in the corpus that were annotated with argument structures that were not licensed by the roleset for the corresponding predicate. For example, the predicate *zip.01* has only a single argument in its semantic representation—Arg0, described as *entity in motion.* However, the corpus contains a token of *zip.01* that is annotated with an Arg0 and an Arg1.

4 Discussion/Conclusions

4.1 The effect of the argument/adjunct distinction

The validity and usefulness of the distinction between arguments and adjuncts is an ongoing controversy in biomedical computational lexical semantics. The BioProp project (Chou et al., 2006; Tsai et al., 2006) makes considerable use of adjuncts, essentially identically to PropBank; however, most biomedical PAS-oriented projects have relatively larger numbers of arguments and lesser use of adjuncts (Wattarujeekrit et al., 2004; Kogan et al., 2005; Shah et al., 2005) than PropBank. Overall, one would predict fewer non-coöccurring arguments with a set of representations that made a stronger distinction between arguments and adjuncts; overall arity of rolesets would be smaller (see above for the effect of arity on the number of observations required for a predicate), and the arguments for such a representation might be more "core" to the semantics of the predicate, and might therefore be less likely to not occur overall, and therefore less likely to not coöccur.

4.2 The effect of syntactic representation on observed argument distributions

The original work by Cohen and Hunter assumed a very simple, and very surface, syntactic representation. In particular, there was no representation of traces. In contrast, PropBank is built on Treebank II, which does include representation of traces, and arguments can, in fact, be filled by traces. This could be expected to reduce the number of tokens of apparently absent arguments, and thereby the number of non-coöoccurring arguments. This doesn't seem to have had a strong enough effect to interfere with the ability of the method to uncover errors.

4.3 The effect of arity

The mode for distribution of arities in the PropBank framefiles was 2 (see Table 3). In contrast, the modes for distribution of rolesets with at least one argument pair in complementary distribution across arities and for distribution of argument pairs in complementary distribution across arities was 4 or 5 for the full range of minimum observations of the predicates from 200 to 10 (data omitted for space).

This supports the initial assumption that higher-arity predicates are more likely to have argument pairs in complementary distribution—see Section 1.2 above.

One aspect of a granular analysis of the data is worth pointing out with respect to the effects of arity: as a validation check, note that for all arities, the number of predicates and the number of argument pairs rises as the minimum required number of tokens of the predicate in the corpus goes down.

4.4 Conclusions

The goals of this study were to investigate the automatability and scalability of a technique for PAS quality assurance that had previously only been shown to work for a small lexical resource and a small corpus, and to use it to characterize the quality of the shallow semantic representations in the PropBank framefiles. The evaluation procedure was found to be automatable: the process of finding argument pairs in complementary distribution is achievable by running a single Java application. In addition, the use of a common representation for argument sets in a framefile and argument sets in a PropBank annotation enabled the fortuitous discovery of a number of problems in the framefiles and in the corpus (see Section 3.6) as a side-effect of application of the technique.

The process was also found to scale well, with a running time of less than one and a half minutes for a set of 4,654 rolesets and a 1-million-word corpus on a moderately priced laptop; additionally, the resource maintainer's efforts can easily be focussed towards the most likely and the most prevalent error sources by adjusting the minimum number of observations required before reporting a case of complementary distribution. The process was also found to be able to identify missing sense distinctions and to identify bad arguments.

In addition to our findings regarding the quality assurance technique, a granular breakdown of the errors found by the algorithm by arity and minimum number of observations (data not shown due to space) allows us to estimate the number of errors in the PropBank framefiles. A reasonable upper-bound estimate for the number of errorful rolesets is the number of predicates that were observed at least 10 times and were found to have at least one pair of arguments in complementary distribution (the bottom row of Table 4), adjusted by the accuracy of the technique that we reported in Section 3.1, i.e. 0.69. This yields a worst-case scenario of (0.69*328)/4,654 rolesets, or 4.9% of the rolesets in PropBank, being in need of revision. The best-case scenario would assume that we can only draw conclusions about the predicates with high numbers of observations and high arity, again adjusted downward for the accuracy of the technique; taking 5 or more arguments as high arity, this yields a best-case scenario of (0.69*17)/4,654 rolesets, or 0.3% of the rolesets in PropBank, being in need of revision. A different sort of worst-case scenario assumes that the major problem in maintaining a proposition bank is not fixing inadequate representations, but *finding* them. On this assumption, the problematic representations are the ones with small numbers of tokens and low arity. Taking 3 or fewer arguments as low arity yields a worst-case scenario of 99/4,654 rolesets (no adjustment for accuracy required), or 2.13% of the rolesets in PropBank, being essentially uncharacterizable as to the goodness of their semantic representation[1].

Besides its obvious role in quality assurance for proposition banks, there may be other uses for this technique, as well. The output of the technique may also be useful in sense grouping and splitting and in detecting metaphorical uses of verbs (e.g. the *accept* example). As the PropBank model is extended to an increasingly large set of languages (currently Arabic, Basque, Catalan, Chinese, Hindi, Korean, and Russian), the need for a quality assurance mechanism for proposition banks—both to ensure the quality of their contents, and to assure funding agencies that they are evaluatable—will only grow larger.

References

Ron Artstein and Massimo Poesio. 2008. Inter-coder agreement for computational linguistics. *Computational Linguistics*, 34(4):555–596.

Jane Austen. 1811. *Sense and Sensibility*.

Xavier Carreras and Lluís Màrquez. 2005. Introduction to the CoNLL-2005 shared task: semantic role label-

[1]The situation is arguably actually somewhat worse than this, since it does not take into account predicates which occur fewer than ten times in the corpus; however, there is a reasonable counter-argument that those predicates are too rare for any individual roleset to have a large impact on the overall goodness of the resource.

ing. In *Proceedings of the 9th conference on computational natural language learning*, pages 152–164.

Werner Ceusters, Barry Smith, Anand Kumar, and Christoffel Dhaen. 2004. Mistakes in medical ontologies: where do they come from and how can they be detected? In D.M. Pisanelli, editor, *Ontologies in medicine: proceedings of the workshop on medical ontologies*, pages 145–163. IOS Press.

Wen-Chi Chou, Richard Tzong-Han Tsai, Ying-Shan Su, Wei Ku, Ting-Yi Sung, and Wen-Lian Hsu. 2006. A semi-automatic method for annotating a biomedical proposition bank. In *Proceedings of the workshop on frontiers in linguistically annotated corpora 2006*, pages 5–12. Association for Computational Linguistics.

J.J. Cimino, H. Min, and Y. Perl. 2003. Consistency across the hierarchies of the UMLS Semantic Network and Metathesaurus. *Journal of Biomedical Informatics*, 36:450–461.

James J. Cimino. 1998. Auditing the Unified Medical Language System with semantic methods. *Journal of the American Medical Informatics Association*, 5:41–51.

James J. Cimino. 2001. Battling Scylla and Charybdis: the search for redundancy and ambiguity in the 2001 UMLS Metathesaurus. In *Proc. AMIA annual symposium*, pages 120–124.

K. Bretonnel Cohen and Lawrence Hunter. 2006. A critical revew of PASBio's argument structures for biomedical verbs. *BMC Bioinformatics*, 7(Suppl. 3).

K. B. Cohen, Lynne Fox, Philip V. Ogren, and Lawrence Hunter. 2005a. Corpus design for biomedical natural language processing. In *Proceedings of the ACL-ISMB workshop on linking biological literature, ontologies and databases*, pages 38–45. Association for Computational Linguistics.

K. Bretonnel Cohen, Lynne Fox, Philip V. Ogren, and Lawrence Hunter. 2005b. Empirical data on corpus design and usage in biomedical natural language processing. In *AMIA 2005 symposium proceedings*, pages 156–160.

George Hripcsak and Adam S. Rothschild. 2005. Agreement, the F-measure, and reliability in information retrieval. *Journal of the American Medical Informatics Association*, 12(3):296–298.

Nancy Ide and Chris Brew. 2000. Requirements, tools, and architectures for annotated corpora. In *Proc. data architectures and software support for large corpora*, pages 1–5.

Paul Kingsbury and Martha Palmer. 2002. From TreeBank to PropBank. In *Proceedings of the LREC*.

Paul Kingsbury, Martha Palmer, and Mitch Marcus. 2002. Adding semantic annotation to the Penn TreeBank. In *Proceedings of the Human Language Technology Conference*.

Richard Kittredge. 1982. Variation and homogeneity of sublanguages. In Richard Kittredge and John Lehrberger, editors, *Sublanguage: studies of language in restricted semantic domains*, pages 107–137.

Yacov Kogan, Nigel Collier, Serguei Pakhomov, and Michael Krauthammer. 2005. Towards semantic role labeling & IE in the medical literature. In *AMIA 2005 Symposium Proceedings*, pages 410–414.

Jacob Kohler, Katherine Munn, Alexander Ruegg, Andre Skusa, and Barry Smith. 2006. Quality control for terms and definitions in ontologies and taxonomies. *BMC Bioinformatics*, 7(1).

Maria Koptjevskaja-Tamm. 1993. *Nominalizations*. Routledge.

Geoffrey Leech. 1993. Corpus annotation schemes. *Literary and linguistic computing*, pages 275–281.

Mitchell P. Marcus, Mary A. Marcinkiewicz, and Beatrice Santorini. 1993. Building a large annotated corpus of English: the Penn Treebank. *Computational Linguistics*, 19(2):313–330.

Adam Meyers, Ruth Reeves, Catherine Macleod, Rachel Szekely, Veronika Zielinska, Brian Young, and Ralph Grishman. 2004. Annotating noun argument structure for NomBank. In *Proceedings of Language Resources and Evaluation, LREC*.

Philip V. Ogren, K. Bretonnel Cohen, George K. Acquaah-Mensah, Jens Eberlein, and Lawrence Hunter. 2004. The compositional structure of Gene Ontology terms. *Pacific Symposium on Biocomputing*, pages 214–225.

Martha Palmer, Paul Kingsbury, and Daniel Gildea. 2005. The Proposition Bank: an annotated corpus of semantic roles. *Computational Linguistics*, 31(1):71–106.

Martha Palmer, Stephanie Strassel, and Randee Tangi. Download date December 17, 2010. Historical development and future directions in data resource development. In *MINDS 2006–2007*.

Parantu K. Shah, Lars J. Jensen, Stéphanie Boué, and Peer Bork. 2005. Extraction of transcript diversity from scientific literature. *PLoS Computational Biology*, 1(1):67–73.

Richard Tzong-Han Tsai, Wen-Chi Chou, Yu-Chun Lin, Cheng-Lung Sung, Wei Ku, Ying-Shan Su, Ting-Yi Sung, and Wen-Lian Hsu. 2006. BIOSMILE: adapting semantic role labeling for biomedical verbs: an exponential model coupled with automatically generated template features. In *Proceedings of the BioNLP Workshop on Linking Natural Language Processing and Biology*, pages 57–64. Association for Computational Linguistics.

Tuangthong Wattarujeekrit, Parantu K. Shah, and Nigel Collier. 2004. PASBio: predicate-argument structures for event extraction in molecular biology. *BMC Bioinformatics*, 5(155).

Martin Wynne, editor. 2005. *Developing linguistic corpora: a guide to good practice*. David Brown Book Company.

Proposal for an Extension of Traditional Named Entities: From Guidelines to Evaluation, an Overview

Cyril Grouin[α], Sophie Rosset[α], Pierre Zweigenbaum[α]
Karën Fort[β,γ], Olivier Galibert[δ], Ludovic Quintard[δ]
[α]LIMSI–CNRS, France [β]INIST–CNRS, France [γ]LIPN, France [δ]LNE, France
{cyril.grouin,sophie.rosset,pierre.zweigenbaum}@limsi.fr
karen.fort@inist.fr, {olivier.galibert,ludovic.quintard}@lne.fr

Abstract

Within the framework of the construction of a fact database, we defined guidelines to extract named entities, using a taxonomy based on an extension of the usual named entities definition. We thus defined new types of entities with broader coverage including substantive-based expressions. These extended named entities are hierarchical (with types and components) and compositional (with recursive type inclusion and metonymy annotation). Human annotators used these guidelines to annotate a 1.3M word broadcast news corpus in French. This article presents the definition and novelty of extended named entity annotation guidelines, the human annotation of a global corpus and of a mini reference corpus, and the evaluation of annotations through the computation of inter-annotator agreements. Finally, we discuss our approach and the computed results, and outline further work.

1 Introduction

Within the framework of the Quaero project—a multimedia indexing project—we organized an evaluation campaign on named entity extraction aiming at building a fact database in the news domain, the first step being to define what kind of entities are needed. This campaign focused on broadcast news corpora in French. While traditional named entities include three major classes (persons, locations and organizations), we decided to extend the coverage of our campaign to new types of entities and to broaden their main parts-of-speech from proper names to substantives, this extension being necessary for ever-increasing knowledge extraction from documents. We thus produced guidelines to specify the way corpora had to be annotated, and launched the annotation process.

In this paper, after covering related work (Section 2), we describe the taxonomy we created (Section 3) and the annotation process and results (Section 4), including the corpora we gathered and the tools we developed to facilitate annotation. We then present inter-annotator agreement measures (Section 5), outline limitations (Section 6) and conclude on perspectives for further work (Section 7).

2 Related work

2.1 Named entity definitions

Named Entity recognition was first defined as recognizing proper names (Coates-Stephens, 1992). Since MUC-6 (Grishman and Sundheim, 1996; SAIC, 1998), named entities have been proper names falling into three major classes: persons, locations and organizations.

Proposals were made to sub-divide these entities into finer-grained classes. The "politicians" subclass was proposed for the "person" class by (Fleischman and Hovy, 2002) while the "cities" subclass was added to the "location" class by (Fleischman, 2001; Lee and Lee, 2005).

The CONLL conference added a miscellaneous type that includes proper names falling outside the previous classes. Some classes have thus sometimes been added, e.g. the "product" class by (Bick, 2004; Galliano et al., 2009).

Proceedings of the Fifth Law Workshop (LAW V), pages 92–100,
Portland, Oregon, 23-24 June 2011. ©2011 Association for Computational Linguistics

Specific entities are proposed and handled in some tasks: "language" or "shape" for question-answering systems in specific domains (Rosset et al., 2007), "email address" or "phone number" to process electronic messages (Maynard et al., 2001). Numeric types are also often described and used. They include "date", "time", and "amount" types ("amount" generally covers money and percentage). In specific domains, entities such as gene, protein, are also handled (Ohta, 2002), and campaigns are organized for gene detection (Yeh et al., 2005). At the same time, extensions of named entities have been proposed: (Sekine, 2004) defined a complete hierarchy of named entities containing about 200 types.

2.2 Named Entities and Annotation

As for any other kind of annotation, some aspects are known to lead to difficulties in obtaining coherence in the manual annotation process (Ehrmann, 2008; Fort et al., 2009). Three different classes of problems are distinguished: (1) selecting the correct category in cases of ambiguity, where one entity can fall into several classes, depending on the context ("*Paris*" can be a town or a person name); (2) detecting the boundaries (in a person designation, is only the proper name to be annotated or the trigger "*Mr*" too?) and (3) annotating metonymies ("*France*" can be a sports team, a country, etc.).

In the ACE Named Entity task (Doddington et al., 2004), a complex task, the obtained inter-annotator agreement was 0.86 in 2002 and 0.88 in 2003. Some tasks obtain better agreement. Desmet and Hoste (2010) described the Named Entity annotation realized within the Sonar project, where Named Entity are clearly simpler. They follow the MUC Named Entity definition with the subtypes as proposed by ACE. The agreement computed over the Sonar Dutch corpus ranges from 0.91 to 0.97 (kappa values) depending of the emphasized elements (span, main type, subtype, etc.).

3 Taxonomy

3.1 Guidelines production

Having in mind the objective of building a fact database through the extraction of named entities from texts, we defined a richer taxonomy than those used in other information extraction works.

Following (Bonneau-Maynard et al., 2005; Alex et al., 2010), the annotation guidelines were first written from December 2009 to May 2010 by three researchers managing the manual annotation campaign. During guidelines production, we evaluated the feasibility of this specific annotation task and the usefulness of the guidelines by annotating a small part of the target corpus. Then, these guidelines were delivered to the annotators. They consist of a description of the objects to annotate, general annotation rules and principles, and more than 250 prototypical and real examples extracted from the corpus (Rosset et al., 2010). Rules are important to set the general way annotations must be produced. Additionally, examples are essential for human annotators to grasp the annotation rationale more easily.

Indeed, while producing the guidelines, we knew that the given examples would never cover all possible cases because of the specificity of language and of the ambiguity of formulations and situations described in corpora, as shown in (Fort et al., 2009). Nevertheless, guidelines examples must be considered as a way to understand the final objective of the annotation work. Thanks to numerous meetings from May to November 2010, we gathered feedback from the annotators (four annotators plus one annotation manager). This feedback allowed us to clarify and extend the guidelines in several directions. The guidelines are 72 pages long and consist of 3 major parts: general description of the task and the principles (25% of the overall document), presentation of each type of named entity (57%), and a simpler "cheat sheet" (18%).

3.2 Definition

We decided to use the three general types of named entities: *name* (person, location, organization) as described in (Grishman and Sundheim, 1996; SAIC, 1998), *time* (date and duration), and *quantity* (amount). We then included named entities extensions proposed by (Sekine, 2004; Galliano et al., 2009) (respectively products and functions) and we extended the definition of named entities to expressions which are not composed of proper names (e.g., phrases built around substantives). The extended named entities we defined are both hierarchical and compositional. For example, type *pers* (person) is split into two subtypes, *pers.ind* (indi-

<table>
<tr><th colspan="6">Person</th><th colspan="6">Function</th></tr>
<tr><td colspan="3">pers.ind (individual person)</td><td colspan="3">pers.coll (group of persons)</td><td colspan="3">func.ind (individual function)</td><td colspan="3">func.coll (collectivity of functions)</td></tr>
<tr><th colspan="6">Location</th><th colspan="6">Product</th></tr>
<tr><td colspan="2" rowspan="3">administrative (loc.adm.town, loc.adm.reg, loc.adm.nat, loc.adm.sup)</td><td colspan="2" rowspan="3">physical (loc.phys.geo, loc.phys.hydro, loc.phys.astro)</td><td colspan="2" rowspan="3">facilities (loc.fac), oronyms (loc.oro), address (loc.add.phys, loc.add.elec)</td><td colspan="2">prod.object (manufactured object)</td><td colspan="2">prod.serv (transportation route)</td><td colspan="2">prod.fin (financial products)</td></tr>
<tr><td colspan="2">prod.doctr (doctrine)</td><td colspan="2">prod.rule (law)</td><td colspan="2">prod.soft (software)</td></tr>
<tr><td colspan="2">prod.art</td><td colspan="2">prod.media</td><td colspan="2">prod.award</td></tr>
<tr><th colspan="6">Organization</th><th colspan="6">Time</th></tr>
<tr><td colspan="3">org.adm (administration)</td><td colspan="3">org.ent (services)</td><td colspan="3" rowspan="3">time.date.abs (absolute date), time.date.rel (relative date)</td><td colspan="3" rowspan="3">time.hour.abs (absolute hour), time.hour.rel (relative hour)</td></tr>
<tr><th colspan="6">Amount</th></tr>
<tr><td colspan="6">amount (with unit or general object), including duration</td></tr>
</table>

Table 1: Types (in bold) and subtypes (in italic)

vidual person) and *pers.coll* (collective person), and *pers* entities are composed of several components, among which are *name.first* and *name.last*.

3.3 Hierarchy

We used two kinds of elements: types and components. The types with their subtypes categorize a named entity. While types and subtypes were used before (ACE, 2000; Sekine, 2004; ACE, 2005; Galliano et al., 2009), we consider that structuring the contents of an entity (its components) is important too. Components categorize the elements inside a named entity.

Our taxonomy is composed of 7 main types (*person, function, location, product, organization, amount* and *time*) and 32 subtypes (Table 1). Types and subtypes refer to the general category of a named entity. They give general information about the annotated expression. Almost each type is then specified using subtypes that either mark an opposition between two major subtypes (individual person vs. collective person), or add precisions (for example for locations: administrative location, physical location, etc.).

This two-level representation of named entities, with types and components, constitutes a novel approach.

Types and subtypes To deal with the intrinsic ambiguity of named entities, we defined two specific transverse subtypes: 1. *other* for entities with a different subtype than those proposed in the taxonomy (for example, *prod.other* for games), and 2. *unknown* when the annotator does not know which subtype to use.

Types and subtypes constitute the first level of annotation. They refer to a general segmentation of the world into major categories. Within these categories, we defined a second level of annotation we call *components*.

Components Components can be considered as clues that help the annotator to produce an annotation: either to determine the named entity type (e.g. a first name is a clue for the *pers.ind* named entity subtype), or to set the named entity boundaries (e.g. a given token is a clue for the named entity, and is within its scope, while the next token is not a clue and is outside its scope). Components are second-level elements, and can never be used outside the scope of a type or subtype element. An entity is thus composed of components that are of two kinds: transverse components and specific components (Table 2). Transverse components can be used in several types of entities, whereas specific components can only be used in one type of entity.

Transverse components			
name (name of the entity), *kind* (hyperonym of the entity), *qualifier* (qualifying adjective), *demonym* (inhabitant or ethnic group name), *demonym.nickname* (inhabitant or ethnic group nickname), *val* (a number), *unit* (a unit), *extractor* (an element in a series), *range-mark* (range between two values), *time-modifier* (a time modifier).			
pers.ind	**loc.add.phys**	**time.date.abs/rel**	**amount**
name.last, name.first, name.middle, pseudonym, name.nickname, title	*address-number, po-box, zip-code, other-address-component*	*week, day, month, year, century, millennium, reference-era*	*object*
			prod.award
			award-cat

Table 2: Transverse and specific components

3.4 Composition

Another original point in this work is the compositional nature of the annotations. Entities can be compositional for three reasons: (i) a type contains a component; (ii) a type includes another type, used as a component; and (iii) in cases of metonymy. During the Ester II evaluation campaign, there was an attempt to use compositionality in named entities for two categories: persons and functions, where a person entity could contain a function entity.

<pers.hum> <func.pol> *président* </func.pol> <pers.hum> *Chirac* </pers.hum> </pers.hum>

Nevertheless, the Ester II evaluation did not take this inclusion into account and only focused on the encompassing annotation (<pers.hum> *président Chirac* </pers.hum>). We drew our inspiration from this experience, and allowed the annotators and the systems to use compositionality in the annotations.

Cases of inclusion can be found in the *function* type (Figure 1), where type *func.ind*, which spans the whole expression, includes type *org.adm*, which spans the single word "*budget*". In this case, we consider that the designation of this function ("*ministre du budget*") includes both the kind ("*ministre*") and the name ("*budget*") of the ministry, which itself is typed as is relevant (*org.adm*). Recursive cases of embedding can be found when a subtype includes another named entity annotated with the same subtype (*org.ent* in Figure 2).

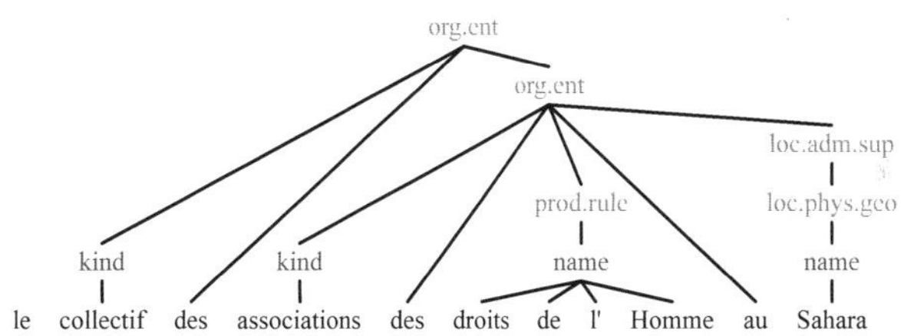

Figure 2: Recursive embedding of the same subtype: *Collective of the Human Rights Organizations in Sahara.*

Cases of metonymy include strict metonymy (a term is substituted with another one in a relation of contiguity) and antonomasia (a proper name is used as a substantive or vice versa). In such cases, the entity must be annotated with both types, first (inside) with the intrinsic type of the entity, then (outside) with the type that corresponds to the result of the metonymy. Basically, country names correspond to "national administrative" locations (*loc.adm.nat*) but they can also designate the administration (*org.adm*) of the country (Figure 3).

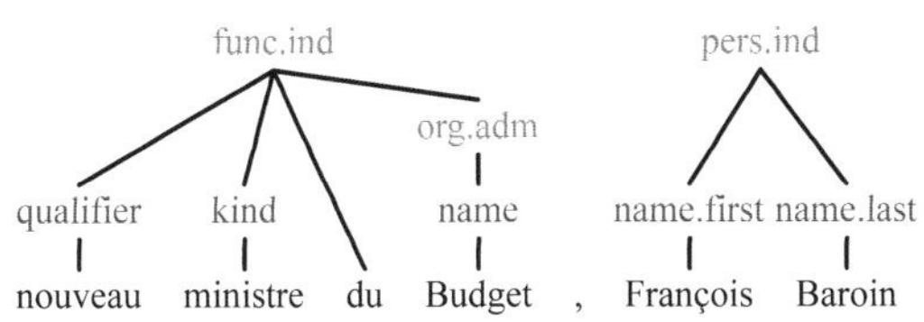

Figure 1: Multi-level annotation of entity types (red tags) and components (blue tags): *new minister of budget , François Baroin.*

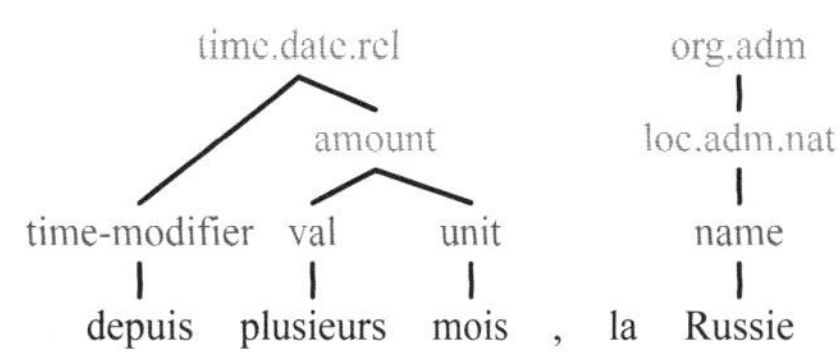

Figure 3: Annotation with a metonymic use of country "Russia" as its government: *for several months , Russia...*

3.5 Boundaries

Our definition of the scope of entities excludes relative clauses, subordinate clauses, and interpolated clauses: the annotation of an entity must end before these clauses. If an interpolated clause occurs inside an entity, its annotation must be split. Moreover, two distinct persons sharing the same last name must be annotated as two separate entities (Figure 4); we intend to use relations between entities to gather these segments in the next step of the project.

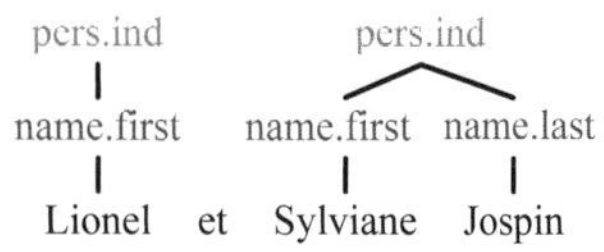

Figure 4: Separate (coordinated) named entities.

4 Annotation process

4.1 Corpus

We managed the annotation of a corpus of about one hundred hours of transcribed speech from several French-speaking radio stations in France and Morocco. Both news and entertainment shows were transcribed, including dialogs, with speaker turns.[1]

Once annotated, the corpus was split into a development corpus: one file from a French radio station;[2] a training corpus: 188 files from five French stations[3] and one Moroccan station;[4] and a test corpus: 18 files from two French stations already studied in the training corpus[5] and from unseen sources, both radio[6] and television,[7] in order to evaluate the robustness of systems. These data have been used in the 2011 Quaero named entity evaluation campaign.

This corpus allows us to perform different evaluations, depending of the knowledge the systems have of the source (source seen in the training corpus vs. unseen source), the kind of show (news vs. entertainment), the language style (popular vs. refined), and the type of media (radio vs. television).

4.2 Tools for annotators

To perform our test annotations (see Section 2.2), we developed a very simple annotation tool as an interface based on XEmacs. We provided the human annotators with this tool and they decided to use it for the campaign, despite the fact that it is very simple and that we told them about other, more generic, annotation tools such as GATE[8] or Glozz.[9] This is probably due to the fact that apart from being very simple to install and use, it has interesting features.

The first feature is the insertion of annotations using combinations of keyboard shortcuts based on the initial of each type, subtype and component name. For example, combination F2 key + initial keys is used to annotate a subtype (*pers.ind*, etc.), F3 + keys for a transverse component (*name, kind*, etc.), F4 + keys for a specific component (*name.first*, etc.), and F5 to delete the annotation selected with the cursor (both opening and closing tags).

The second feature is boundary management: if the annotator puts the cursor over the token to annotate, the annotation tool will handle the boundaries of this token; opening and closing tags will be inserted around the token.

However, it presents some limitations: tags are inserted in the text (which makes visualization more complex, especially for long sentences or in cases of multiple annotations on the same entity), no personalization is offered (tags are of only one color), and there is no function to express annotator uncertainty (the user must choose among several possible tags the one that fits the best;[10] while producing the guidelines, we did not consider it could be of interest: as a consequence, no uncertainty management was implemented). Therefore, this tool allows users to insert tags rapidly into a text, but it offers no external resources, as real annotation tools (e.g. GATE) often do.

[1] Potential named entities may be split across several segments or turns.

[2] News from France Culture.

[3] News from France Culture (refined language), France Info (news with short news headlines), France Inter (generalist radio station), Radio Classique (classical music and economic news), RFI (international radio broadcast out of France).

[4] News from RTM (generalist French speaking radio).

[5] News from France Culture, news and entertainment from France Inter.

[6] A popular entertainment show from Europe 1.

[7] News from Arte (public channel with art and culture), France 2 (public generalist channel), and TF1 (private generalist popular channel).

[8] `http://gate.ac.uk/`

[9] `http://www.glozz.org/`

[10] Uncertainty can be found in cases of lack of context.

These simplistic characteristics combined with a fast learning curve allow the annotators to rapidly annotate the corpora. Annotators were allowed not to annotate the transverse component *name* (only if it was the only component in the annotated phrase, e.g. "Russia" in Figure 3, blue tag) and to annotate events, even though we do not focus on this type of entity as of yet. We therefore also provided a normalization tool which adds the transverse component *name* in these instances, and which removes event annotations.

4.3 Corpus annotation

Global annotation It took four human annotators two months and a half to annotate the entire corpus (10 man-month). These annotators were hired graduate students (MS in linguistics). The overall corpus was annotated in duplicate. Regular comparisons of annotations were performed and allowed the annotators to develop a methodology, which was subsequently used to annotate the remaining documents.

Mini reference corpus To evaluate the global annotation, we built a mini reference corpus by randomly selecting 400 sentences from the training corpus and distributing them into four files. These files were annotated by four graduate human annotators from two research institutes (Figure 5) with two humans per institute, in about 10 hours per annotator.

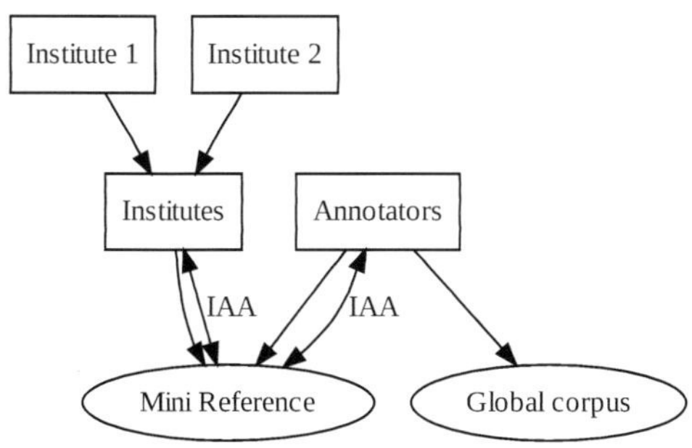

Figure 5: Creation of mini reference corpus and computation of inter-annotator agreement. Institute 1 = LIMSI–CNRS, Institute 2 = INIST–CNRS

First, we merged the annotations of each file within a given institute (1.5h per pair of annotators), then merged the results across the two institutes (2h). Finally, we merged the results with the annotations of the hired annotators (8h). We thus spent about 90 hours to annotate and merge annotations in this mini reference corpus (0.75 man-month).

4.4 Annotation results

Our broadcast news corpus includes 1,291,225 tokens, among which there are 954,049 non-punctuation tokens. Its annotation contains 113,885 named entities and 146,405 components (Table 3), i.e. one entity per 8.4 non-punctuation tokens, and one component per 6.5 non-punctuation tokens. There is an average of 6 annotations per line.

Inf. \ Data	Training	Test
# shows	188	18
# lines	43,289	5,637
# words	1,291,225	108,010
# entity types	113,885	5,523
# distinct types	41	32
# components	146,405	8,902
# distinct comp.	29	22

Table 3: Statistics on annotated corpora.

5 Inter-Annotator Agreement

5.1 Procedure

During the annotation campaign, we measured several criteria on a regular basis: inter-annotator agreement and disagreement. We used them to correct erroneous annotations, and mapped these corrections to the original annotations. We also used these measures to give the annotators feedback on the encountered problems, discrepancies, and residual errors. Whereas we performed these measurements all along the annotation campaign, this paper focuses on the final evaluation on the mini reference corpus.

5.2 Metrics

Because human annotation is an interpretation process (Leech, 1997), there is no "truth" to rely on. It is therefore impossible to really evaluate the validity of an annotation. All we can and should do is to evaluate its reliability, i.e. the consistency of the annotation across annotators, which is achieved through computation of the inter-annotator agreement (IAA).

The best way to compute it is to use one of the Kappa family coefficients, namely Cohen's Kappa (Cohen, 1960) or Scott's Pi (Scott, 1955), also known as Carletta's Kappa (Carletta, 1996),[11] as they take chance into account (Artstein and Poesio, 2008). However, these coefficients imply a comparison with a "random baseline" to establish whether the correlation between annotations is statistically significant. This baseline depends on the number of "markables", i.e. all the units that *could* be annotated.

In the case of named entities, as in many others, this "random baseline" is known to be difficult—if not impossible—to identify (Alex et al., 2010). We wish to analyze this in more detail, to see how we could actually compute these coefficients and what information it would give us about the annotation.

Markables	Annotators	Both institutes
	F = 0.84522	F = 0.91123
U1: n-grams	$\kappa = 0.84522$ $\pi = 0.81687$	$\kappa = 0.91123$ $\pi = 0.90258$
U2: n-grams ≤ 6	$\kappa = 0.84519$ $\pi = 0.81685$	$\kappa = 0.91121$ $\pi = 0.90257$
U3: NPs	$\kappa = 0.84458$ $\pi = 0.81628$	$\kappa = 0.91084$ $\pi = 0.90219$
U4: Ester entities	$\kappa = 0.71300$ $\pi = 0.71210$	$\kappa = 0.82607$ $\pi = 0.82598$
U5: Pooling	$\kappa = 0.71300$ $\pi = 0.71210$	$\kappa = 0.82607$ $\pi = 0.82598$

Table 4: Inter-Annotator Agreements (κ stands for Cohen's Kappa, π for Scott's Pi, and F for F-measure). IAA values were computed by taking as the reference the hired annotators' annotation or that obtained by merging from both institutes (see Figure 5).

In the present case, we could consider that, potentially, all the noun phrases can be annotated (row U3 in Table 4, based on the PASSAGE campaign (Vilnat et al., 2010)). Of course, this is a wrong approximation as named entities are not necessarily noun phrases (e.g., "à partir de l'automne prochain", *from next autumn*).

We could also consider all n-grams of tokens in the corpus (row U1). However, it would be more relevant to limit their size. For a maximum size of six, we get the results shown in row U2. All this, of course, is artificial, as the named entity annotation process is not random.

To obtain results that are closer to reality, we could use numbers of named entities from previous named entity annotation campaigns (row U4 based on the Ester II campaign (Galliano et al., 2009)), but as we consider here a largely extended version of those, the results would again be far from reality.

Another solution is to consider as "markables" all the units annotated by at least one of the annotators (row U5). In this particular case, units not annotated by any of the annotators (i.e. silence) are overlooked.

The lowest IAA will be the one computed with this last solution, while the highest IAA will be equal to the F-measure (i.e. the measure computed with all the markables as shown in row U1 in Table 4). We notice that the first two solutions (U1 and U2 with n-grams) are not acceptable because they are far from reality; even extended named entities are sparse annotations, and just considering all tokens as 'markables' is not suitable. The last three ones seem to be more relevant because they are based on an observed segmentation on similar data. Still, the U3 solution (NPs) overrates the number of markables because not all noun phrases are extended named entities. Although the U4 solution (Ester entities) is based on the same corpus used for a related task, it underrates the number of markables because that task produced 16.3 times less annotations. Finally the U5 solution (pooling) gives the lower bound for the κ estimation which is an interesting information but may easily undervalue the quality of the annotation.

As (Hripcsak and Rothschild, 2005) showed, in our case κ tends towards the F-measure when the number of negative cases tends towards infinity. Our results show that it is hard to build a justifiable hypothesis on the number of markables which is larger than the number of actually annotated entities while keeping κ significantly under the F-measure. But building no hypothesis leads to underestimating the κ value.

This reinforces the idea of using the F-measure as the main inter-annotator agreement measure for named entity annotation tasks.

[11]For more details on terminology issues, we refer to the introduction of (Artstein and Poesio, 2008).

6 Limitations

We used syntax to define some components (e.g. a *qualifier* is an adjective) and to set the scope of entities (e.g. stop at relative clauses). Nevertheless, this syntactic definition cannot fit all named entities, which are mainly defined according to semantics: the phrase "*dans les mois qui viennent*" ("*in the coming months*") expresses an entity of type *time.date.rel* where the relative clause "*qui viennent*" is part of the entity and contributes the *time-modifier* component.

The distinction between some types of entities may be fuzzy, especially for the organizations (is the Social Security an administrative organization or a company?) and for context-dependent annotations (is *lemonde.fr* a URL, a media, or a company?). As a consequence, some entity types might be converted into specific components in a future revision, e.g. the *func* type could become a component of the *pers* type, where it would become a description of the function itself instead of the person who performs this function (Figure 6).

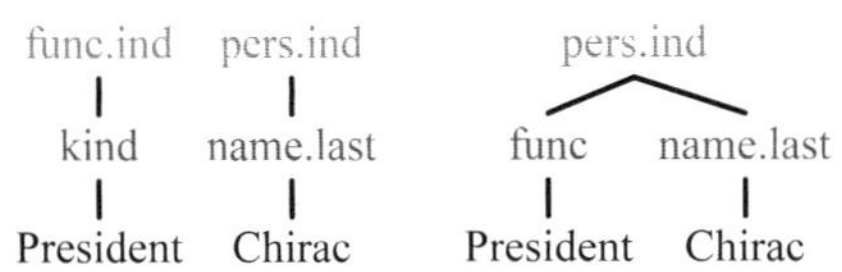

Figure 6: Possible revision: current annotation (left), transformation of *func* from entity to component (right).

7 Conclusion and perspectives

In this paper, we presented an extension of the traditional named entity categories to new types (functions, civilizations) and new coverage (expressions built over a substantive). We created guidelines that were used by graduate annotators to annotate a broadcast news corpus.

The organizers also annotated a small part of the corpus to build a mini reference corpus. We evaluated the human annotations with our mini-reference corpus: the actual computed κ is between 0.71 et 0.85 which, given the complexity of the task, seems to indicate a good annotation quality. Our results are consistent with other studies (Dandapat et al., 2009) in demonstrating that human annotators' training is a key asset to produce quality annotations.

We also saw that guidelines are never fixed, but evolve all along the annotation process due to feedback between annotators and organizers; the relationship between guidelines producers and human annotators evolved from "parent" to "peer" (Akrich and Boullier, 1991). This evolution was observed during the annotation development, beyond our expectations. These data have been used for the 2011 Quaero Named Entity evaluation campaign.

Extensions and revisions are planned. Our first goal is to add a new type of named entity for all kinds of events; guidelines are being written and human annotation tests are ongoing. We noticed that some subtypes are more difficult to disambiguate than others, especially *org.adm* and *org.ent* (definition and examples in the guidelines are not clear enough). We shall make decisions about this kind of ambiguity, either by merging these subtypes or by reorganizing the distinctions within the *organization* type. We also plan to link the annotated entities using relations; further work is needed to define more precisely the way we will perform these annotations. Moreover, the taxonomy we defined was applied to a broadcast news corpus, but we intend to use it in other corpora. The annotation of an old press corpus was performed according to the same process. Its evaluation will start in the coming months.

Acknowledgments

We thank all the annotators who did such a great work on this project, as well as Sabine Barreaux (INIST–CNRS) for her work on the reference corpus.

This work was partly realized as part of the Quaero Programme, funded by Oseo, French State agency for innovation and by the French ANR Etape project.

References

ACE. 2000. Entity detection and tracking, phase 1, ACE pilot study. Task definition. http://www.nist.gov/speech/tests/ace/phase1/doc/summary-v01.htm.

ACE. 2005. ACE (Automatic Content Extraction) English annotation guidelines for entities version 5.6.1 2005.05.23. http://www.ldc.upenn.edu/Projects/ACE/docs/English-Entities-Guidelines_v5.6.1.pdf.

Madeleine Akrich and Dominique Boullier. 1991. Le mode d'emploi, genèse, forme et usage. In Denis Chevallier, editor, *Savoir faire et pouvoir transmettre*, pages 113–131. éd. de la MSH (collection Ethnologie de la France, Cahier 6).

Beatrice Alex, Claire Grover, Rongzhou Shen, and Mijail Kabadjov. 2010. Agile Corpus Annotation in Practice: An Overview of Manual and Automatic Annotation of CVs. In *Proc. of the Fourth Linguistic Annotation Workshop*, pages 29–37, Uppsala, Sweden. ACL.

Ron Artstein and Massimo Poesio. 2008. Inter-Coder Agreement for Computational Linguistics. *Computational Linguistics*, 34(4):555–596.

Eckhard Bick. 2004. A named entity recognizer for danish. In *LREC'04*.

Hélène Bonneau-Maynard, Sophie Rosset, Christelle Ayache, Anne Kuhn, and Djamel Mostefa. 2005. Semantic Annotation of the French Media Dialog Corpus. In *InterSpeech*, Lisbon.

Jean Carletta. 1996. Assessing Agreement on Classification Tasks: the Kappa Statistic. *Computational Linguistics*, 22:249–254.

Sam Coates-Stephens. 1992. The analysis and acquisition of proper names for the understanding of free text. *Computers and the Humanities*, 26:441–456.

Jacob Cohen. 1960. A Coefficient of Agreement for Nominal Scales. *Educational and Psychological Measurement*, 20(1):37–46.

Sandipan Dandapat, Priyanka Biswas, Monojit Choudhury, and Kalika Bali. 2009. Complex Linguistic Annotation - No Easy Way Out! A Case from Bangla and Hindi POS Labeling Tasks. In *Proc. of the Third Linguistic Annotation Workshop*, Singapour. ACL.

Bart Desmet and Véronique Hoste. 2010. Towards a balanced named entity corpus for dutch. In *LREC*.

George Doddington, Alexis Mitchell, Mark Przybocki, Lance Ramshaw, Stephanie Strassel, and Ralph Weischedel. 2004. The automatic content extraction (ACE) program tasks, data, and evaluation. In *Proc. of LREC*.

Maud Ehrmann. 2008. *Les entités nommées, de la linguistique au TAL : statut théorique et méthodes de désambiguïsation*. Ph.D. thesis, Univ. Paris 7 Diderot.

Michael Fleischman and Eduard Hovy. 2002. Fine grained classification of named entities. In *Proc. of COLING*, volume 1, pages 1–7. ACL.

Michael Fleischman. 2001. Automated subcategorization of named entities. In *Proc. of the ACL 2001 Student Research Workshop*, pages 25–30.

Karën Fort, Maud Ehrmann, and Adeline Nazarenko. 2009. Towards a Methodology for Named Entities Annotation. In *Proceeding of the 3rd ACL Linguistic Annotation Workshop (LAW III)*, Singapore.

Sylvain Galliano, Guillaume Gravier, and Laura Chaubard. 2009. The ESTER 2 evaluation campaign for the rich transcription of French radio broadcasts. In *Proc of Interspeech 2009*.

Ralph Grishman and Beth Sundheim. 1996. Message Understanding Conference - 6: A brief history. In *Proc. of COLING*, pages 466–471.

George Hripcsak and Adam S. Rothschild. 2005. Technical brief: Agreement, the f-measure, and reliability in information retrieval. *JAMIA*, 12(3):296–298.

Seungwoo Lee and Gary Geunbae Lee. 2005. Heuristic methods for reducing errors of geographic named entities learned by bootstrapping. In *IJCNLP*, pages 658–669.

Geoffrey Leech. 1997. Introducing corpus annotation. In Geoffrey Leech Roger Garside and Tony McEnery, editors, *Corpus annotation: Linguistic information from computer text corpora*, pages 1–18. Longman, London.

Diana Maynard, Valentin Tablan, Cristian Ursu, Hamish Cunningham, and Yorick Wilks. 2001. Named entity recognition from diverse text types. In *Recent Advances in NLP 2001 Conference, Tzigov Chark*.

Tomoko Ohta. 2002. The genia corpus: An annotated research abstract corpus in molecular biology domain. In *Proc. of HLTC*, pages 73–77.

Sophie Rosset, Olivier Galibert, Gilles Adda, and Eric Bilinski. 2007. The LIMSI participation to the QAst track. In *Working Notes for the CLEF 2007 Workshop*, Budapest, Hungary.

Sophie Rosset, Cyril Grouin, and Pierre Zweigenbaum. 2010. Entités nommées : guide d'annotation Quaero, November. T3.2, presse écrite et orale.

SAIC. 1998. Proceedings of the seventh message understanding conference (MUC-7).

William A Scott. 1955. Reliability of Content Analysis: The Case of Nominal Scale Coding. *Public Opinion Quaterly*, 19(3):321–325.

Satoshi Sekine. 2004. Definition, dictionaries and tagger of extended named entity hierarchy. In *Proc. of LREC*.

Anne Vilnat, Patrick Paroubek, Eric Villemonte de la Clergerie, Gil Francopoulo, and Marie-Laure Guénot. 2010. Passage syntactic representation: a minimal common ground for evaluation. In *Proc. of LREC*.

Alex Yeh, Alex Morgan, Marc Colosimo, and Lynette Hirschman. 2005. BioCreAtIvE task 1A: gene mention finding evaluation. *BMC Bioinformatics*, 6(1).

Assessing the Practical Usability of an Automatically Annotated Corpus

Md. Faisal Mahbub Chowdhury † ‡ **and Alberto Lavelli** ‡
‡ Human Language Technology Research Unit, Fondazione Bruno Kessler, Trento, Italy
† Department of Information Engineering and Computer Science, University of Trento, Italy
{chowdhury, lavelli}@fbk.eu

Abstract

The creation of a gold standard corpus (GSC) is a very laborious and costly process. Silver standard corpus (SSC) annotation is a very recent direction of corpus development which relies on multiple systems instead of human annotators. In this paper, we investigate the practical usability of an SSC when a machine learning system is trained on it and tested on an unseen benchmark GSC. The main focus of this paper is how an SSC can be maximally exploited. In this process, we inspect several hypotheses which might have influenced the idea of SSC creation. Empirical results suggest that some of the hypotheses (e.g. a positive impact of a large SSC despite of having wrong and missing annotations) are not fully correct. We show that it is possible to automatically improve the quality and the quantity of the SSC annotations. We also observe that considering only those sentences of SSC which contain annotations rather than the full SSC results in a performance boost.

1 Introduction

The creation of a **gold standard corpus (GSC)** is not only a very laborious task due to the manual effort involved but also a costly and time consuming process. However, the importance of the GSC to effectively train machine learning (ML) systems cannot be underestimated. Researchers have been trying for years to find alternatives or at least some compromise. As a result, self-training, co-training and unsupervised approaches targeted for specific tasks (such as word sense disambiguation, syntactic parsing, etc) have emerged. In the process of these researches, it became clear that the size of the (manually annotated) training corpus has an impact on the final outcome.

Recently an initiative is ongoing in the context of the European project CALBC[1] which aims to create a large, so called **silver standard corpus (SSC)** using harmonized annotations automatically produced by multiple systems (Rebholz-Schuhmann et al., 2010; Rebholz-Schuhmann et al., 2010a; Rebholz-Schuhmann et al., 2010b). The basic idea is that independent biomedical named entity recognition (BNER) systems annotate a large corpus of biomedical articles without any restriction on the methodology or external resources to be exploited. The different annotations are automatically harmonized using some criteria (e.g. minimum number of systems to agree on a certain annotation) to yield a consensus based corpus. This consensus based corpus is called silver standard corpus because, differently from a GSC, it is not created exclusively by human annotators. Several factors can influence the quantity and quality of the annotations during SSC development. These include varying performance, methodology, annotation guidelines and resources of the SSC annotation systems (henceforth **annotation systems**).

The annotation of SSC in the framework of the CALBC project is focused on (bio) entity mentions (a specific application of the named entity recognition (NER)[2] task). However, the idea of SSC creation might also be applied to other types of annotations, e.g. annotation of relations among entities, annotation of treebanks and so on. Hence, if it can be

[1] http://www.ebi.ac.uk/Rebholz-srv/CALBC/project.html

[2] Named entity recognition is the task of locating boundaries of the entity mentions in a text and tagging them with their corresponding semantic types (e.g. person, location, disease and so on).

Proceedings of the Fifth Law Workshop (LAW V), pages 101–109, shown that an SSC is a useful resource for the NER task, similar resources can be developed for annotation of information other than entities and utilized for the relevant natural language processing (NLP) tasks.

The primary objective of SSC annotation is to compensate the cost, time and manual effort required for a GSC. The procedure of SSC development is inexpensive, fast and yet capable of yielding huge amount of annotated data. These advantages trigger several hypotheses. For example:

- The size of annotated training corpus always plays a crucial role in the performance of ML systems. If the annotation systems have very high precision and somewhat moderate recall, they would be also able to annotate automatically a huge SSC which would have a good quality of annotations. So, one might assume that, even if such an SSC may contain wrong and missing annotations, a relatively 15 or 20 times bigger SSC than a smaller GSC should allow an ML based system to ameliorate the adverse effects of the erroneous annotations.

- Rebholz-Schuhmann et al. (2010) hypothesized that an SSC might serve as an approximation of a GSC.

- In the absence of a GSC, it is expected that ML systems would be able to exploit the harmonised annotations of an SSC to annotate unseen text with reasonable accuracy.

- An SSC could be used to semi-automate the annotations of a GSC. However, in that case, it is expected that the annotation systems would have very high recall. One can assume that converting an SSC into a GSC would be less time consuming and less costly than developing a GSC from scratch.

All these hypotheses are yet to be verified. Nevertheless, once we have an SSC annotated with certain type of information, the main question would be *how this corpus can be maximally exploited* given the fact that it might be created by annotation systems that used different resources and possibly not the same annotation guidelines. This question is directly related to the practical usability of an SSC, which is the focus of this paper.

Taking the aforementioned hypotheses into account, our goal is to investigate the following research questions which are fundamental to the maximum exploitation of an SSC:

1. How can the annotation quality of an SSC be improved automatically?

2. How would a system trained on an SSC perform if tested on an unseen benchmark GSC?

3. Can an SSC combined with a GSC produce a better trained system?

4. What would be the impact on system performance if *unannotated sentences*[3] are removed from an SSC?

5. What would be the effects of the variation in the size of an SSC on precision and recall?

Our goal is not to judge the procedure of SSC creation, rather our objective is to examine how an SSC can be exploited *automatically* and *maximally* for a specific task. Perhaps this would provide useful insights to re-evaluate the approach of SSC creation.

For our experiments, we use a benchmark GSC called the BioCreAtIvE II GM corpus (Smith et al., 2008) and the CALBC SSC-I corpus (Rebholz-Schuhmann et al., 2010a). Both of these corpora are annotated with genes. Our motivation behind the choice of a gene annotated GSC for the SSC evaluation is that ML based BNER for genes has already achieved a sufficient level of maturity. This is not the case for other important bio-entity types, primarily due to the absence of training GSC of adequate size. In fact, for many bio-entity types there exist no GSC. If we can achieve a reasonably good baseline for gene mention identification by maximizing the exploitation of SSC, we might be able to apply almost similar strategies to exploit SSC for other bio-entity types, too.

The remaining of this paper is organised as follows. Section 2 includes brief discussion of the related work. Apart from mentioning the related literature, this section also underlines the difference of

[3]For the specific SSC that we use in this work, *unannotated sentences* correspond to those sentences that contain no gene annotation.

SSC development with respect to approaches such as self-training and co-training. Then in Section 3, we describe the data used in our experiments and the experimental settings. Following that, in Section 4, empirical results are presented and discussed. Finally, we conclude with a description of what we learned from this work in Section 5.

2 Related Work

As mentioned, the concept of SSC has been initiated by the CALBC project (Rebholz-Schuhmann et al., 2010a; Rebholz-Schuhmann et al., 2010). So far, two versions of SSC have been released as part of the project. The CALBC SSC-I has been harmonised from the annotations of the systems provided by the four project partners. Three of them are dictionary based systems while the other is an ML based system. The systems utilized different types of resources such as GENIA corpus (Kim et al., 2003), Entrez Genes[4], Uniprot[5], etc. The CALBC SSC-II corpus has been harmonised from the annotations done by the 11 participants of the first CALBC challenge and the project partners.[6] Some of the participants have used the CALBC SSC-I versions for training while others used various gene databases or benchmark GSCs such as the BioCreAtIvE II GM corpus.

One of the key questions regarding an SSC would be how close its annotation quality is to a corresponding GSC. On the one hand, every GSC contains its special view of the correct annotation of a given corpus. On the other hand, an SSC is created by systems that might be trained with resources having different annotation standards. So, it is possible that the annotations of an SSC significantly differ with respect to a manually annotated (i.e., gold standard) version of the same corpus. This is because human experts are asked to follow specific annotation guidelines.

Rebholz-Schuhmann and Hahn (2010c) did an intrinsic evaluation of the SSC where they created an SSC and a GSC on a dataset of 3,236 Medline[7] abstracts. They were not able to make any specific conclusion whether the SSC is approaching to the GSC. They were of the opinion that SSC annotations are more similar to terminological resources.

Hahn et al. (2010) proposed a policy where silver standards can be dynamically optimized and customized on demand (given a specific goal function) using a gold standard as an oracle. The gold standard is used for optimization only, not for training for the purpose of SSC annotation. They argued that the nature of diverging tasks to be solved, the levels of specificity to be reached, the sort of guidelines being preferred, etc should allow prospective users of an SSC to customize one on their own and not stick to something that is already prefabricated without concrete application in mind.

Self-training and co-training are two of the existing approaches that have been used for compensating the lack of a training GSC with adequate size in several different tasks such as word sense disambiguation, semantic role labelling, parsing, etc (Ng and Cardie, 2003; Pierce and Cardie, 2004; McClosky et al., 2006; He and Gildea, 2006). According to Ng and Cardie (2003), self-training is the procedure where a committee of classifiers are trained on the (gold) annotated examples to tag unannotated examples independently. Only those new annotations to which all the classifiers agree are added to the training set and classifiers are retrained. This procedure repeats until a stop condition is met. According to Clark et al. (2003), self-training is a procedure in which "a tagger is retrained on its own labeled cache at each round". In other words, a single classifier is trained on the initially (gold) annotated data and then applied on a set of unannotated data. Those examples meeting a selection criterion are added to the annotated dataset and the classifier is retrained on this new data set. This procedure can continue for several rounds as required.

Co-training is another weakly supervised approach (Blum and Mitchell, 1998). It applies for those tasks where each of the two (or more) sets of features from the initially (gold) annotated training data is sufficient to classify/annotate the unannotated data (Pierce and Cardie, 2001; Pierce and Cardie,

[4]http://jura.wi.mit.edu/entrez_gene/

[5]http://www.uniprot.org/

[6]See proceedings of the 1st CALBC Workshop, 2010, Editors: Dietrich Rebholz-Schuhmann and Udo Hahn (http://www.ebi.ac.uk/Rebholz-srv/CALBC/docs/FirstProceedings.pdf) for details.

[7]http://www.nlm.nih.gov/databases/databases_medline.html

2004; He and Gildea, 2006). As with SSC annotation and self-training, it also attempts to increase the amount of annotated data by making use of unannotated data. The main idea of co-training is to represent the initially annotated data using two (or more) separate feature sets, each called a "view". Then, two (or more) classifiers are trained on those views of the data which are then used to tag new unannotated data. From this newly annotated data, the most confident predictions are added to the previously annotated data. This whole process may continue for several iterations. It should be noted that, by limiting the number of views to one, co-training becomes self-training.

Like the SSC, the multiple classifier approach of self-training and co-training, as described above, adopts the same vision of utilizing automatic systems for producing the annotation. Apart from that, SSC annotation is completely different from both self-training and co-training. For example, classifiers in self-training and co-training utilizes the same (manually annotated) resource for their initial training. But SSC annotation systems do not necessarily use the same resource. Both self-training and co-training are weakly supervised approaches where the classifiers are based on supervised ML techniques. In the case of SSC annotation, the annotation systems can be dictionary based or rule based. This attractive flexibility allows SSC annotation to be a completely unsupervised approach since the annotation systems do not necessarily need to be trained.

3 Experimental settings

We use the BioCreAtIvE II GM corpus (henceforth, only the GSC) for evaluation of an SSC. The training corpus in the GSC has in total 18,265 gene annotations in 15,000 sentences. The GSC test data has 6,331 annotations in 5,000 sentences.

Some of the CALBC challenge participants have used the BioCreAtIvE II GM corpus for training to annotate gene/protein in the CALBC SSC-II corpus. We wanted our benchmark corpus and benchmark corpus annotation to be totally unseen by the systems that annotated the SSC to be used in our experiments so that there is no bias in our empirical results. SSC-I satisfies this criteria. So, we use the SSC-I (henceforth, we would refer the CALBC SSC-I as simply the SSC) in our experiments despite the fact that it is almost 3 times smaller than the SSC-II. The SSC has in total 137,610 gene annotations in 316,869 sentences of 50,000 abstracts.

Generally, using a customized dictionary of entity names along with annotated corpus boosts NER performance. However, since our objective is to observe to what extent a ML system can learn from SSC, we avoid the use of any dictionary. We use an open source ML based BNER system named BioEnEx[8] (Chowdhury and Lavelli, 2010). The system uses conditional random fields (CRFs), and achieves comparable results (F_1 score of 86.22% on the BioCreAtIvE II GM test corpus) to that of the other state-of-the-art systems without using any dictionary or lexicon.

One of the complex issues in NER is to come to an agreement regarding the boundaries of entity mentions. Different annotation guidelines have different preferences. There may be tasks where a longer entity mention such as "human IL-7 protein" may be appropriate, while for another task a short one such as "IL-7" is adequate (Hahn et al., 2010).

However, usually evaluation on BNER corpora (e.g., the BioCreAtIvE II GM corpus) is performed adopting exact boundary match. Given that we have used the official evaluation script of the BioCreAtIvE II GM corpus, we have been forced to adopt exact boundary match. Considering a relaxed boundary matching (i.e. the annotations might differ in uninformative terms such as *the*, *a*, *acute*, etc.) rather than exact boundary matching might provide a slightly different picture of the effectiveness of the SSC usage.

4 Results and analyses

4.1 Automatically improving SSC quality

The CALBC SSC-I corpus has a negligible number of overlapping gene annotations (in fact, only 6). For those overlapping annotations, we kept only the longest ones. Our hypothesis is that a certain token in the same context can refer to (or be part of) only one concept name (i.e. annotation) of a certain semantic group (i.e. entity type). After removing these few overlaps, the SSC has 137,604 annotations. We

[8]Freely available at http://hlt.fbk.eu/en/people/chowdhury/research

will refer to this version of the SSC as the **initial SSC (ISSC)**.

We construct a list[9] using the lemmatized form of 132 frequently used words that appear in gene names. These words cannot constitute a gene name themselves. If (the lemmatized form of) all the words in a gene name belong to this list then that gene annotation should be discarded. We use this list to remove erroneous annotations in the ISSC. After this purification step, the total number of annotations is reduced to 133,707. We would refer to this version as the **filtered SSC (FSSC)**.

Then, we use the post-processing module of BioEnEx, first to further filter out possible wrong gene annotations in the FSSC and then to automatically include potential gene mentions which are not annotated. It has been observed that some of the annotated mentions in the SSC-I span only part of the corresponding token[10]. For example, in the token "IL-2R", only "IL-" is annotated. We extend the post-processing module of BioEnEx to automatically identify all such types of annotations and expand their boundaries when their neighbouring characters are alphanumeric.

Following that, the extended post-processing module of BioEnEx is used to check in every sentence whether there exist any potential unannotated mentions[11] which differ from any of the annotated mentions (in the same sentence) by a single character (e.g. "IL-2L" and "IL-2R"), number (e.g. "IL-2R" and "IL-345R") or Greek letter (e.g. "IFN-alpha" and "IFN-beta"). After this step, the total number of gene annotations is 144,375. This means that *we were able to remove/correct some specific types of errors and then further expand the total number of annotations (by including entities not annotated in the original SSC) up to **4.92%** with respect to the ISSC*. We will refer to this expanded version of the SSC as the **processed SSC (PSSC)**.

When BioEnEx is trained on the above versions

[9]The words are collected from http://pir.georgetown.edu/pirwww/iprolink/general_name and the annotation guideline of GENETAG (Tanabe et al., 2005).

[10]By *token* we mean a sequence of consecutive non-whitespace characters.

[11]Any token or sequence of tokens is considered to verify whether it should be annotated or not, if its length is more than 2 characters excluding digits and Greek letters.

	TP	FP	FN	P	R	F_1
ISSC	2,396	594	3,935	80.13	37.85	51.41
FSSC	2,518	557	3,813	81.89	39.77	53.54
PSSC	2,606	631	3,725	80.51	41.16	54.47

Table 1: The results of experiments when trained with different versions of the SSC and tested on the GSC test data.

of the SSC and tested on the GSC test data, we observed an increase of more than 3% of F_1 score because of the filtering and expansion (see Table 1). One noticeable characteristic in the results is that the number of annotations obtained (i.e. TP+FP[12]) by training on any of the versions of the SSC is almost half of the actual number annotations of the GSC test data. This has resulted in a low recall. There could be mainly two reasons behind this outcome:

- First of all, it might be the case that a considerable number of gene names are not annotated inside the SSC versions. As a result, the features shared by the annotated gene names (i.e. TP) and unnannotated gene names (i.e. FN) might not have enough influence.

- There might be a considerable number of wrong annotations which are actually not genes (i.e. FP). Consequently, a number of bad features might be collected from those wrong annotations which are misleading the training process.

To verify the above conditions, it would be required to annotate the huge CALBC SSC manually. This would be not feasible because of the cost of human labour and time. Nevertheless, we can try to measure the state of the above conditions roughly by using only *annotated sentences* (i.e. sentences containing at least one annotation) and varying the size of the corpus, which are the subjects of our next experiments.

[12]TP (true positive) = corresponding annotation done by the system is correct, FP (false positive) = corresponding annotation done by the system is incorrect, FN (false negative) = corresponding annotation is correct but it is not annotated by the system.

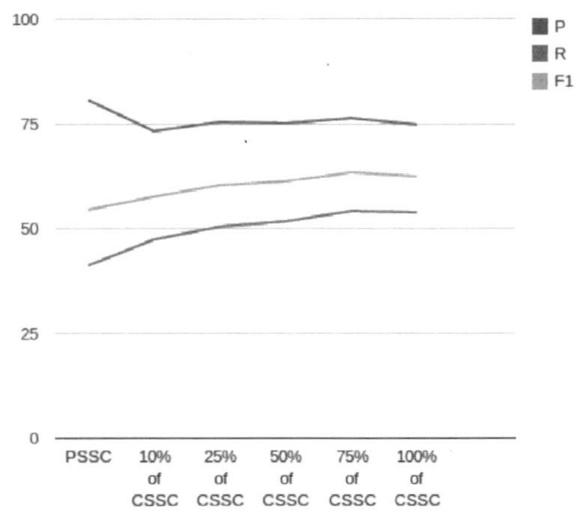

Figure 1: Graphical representation of the experimental results with varying size of the CSSC.

4.2 Impact of annotated sentences and different sizes of the SSC

We observe that only 77,117 out of the 316,869 sentences in the PSSC contain gene annotations. We will refer to the sentences having at least one gene annotation collectively as the **condensed SSC (CSSC)**. Table 2 and Figure 1 show the results when we used different portions of the CSSC for training.

There are four immediate observations on the above results:

- Using the full PSSC, we obtain total (i.e. TP+FP) 3,237 annotations on the GSC test data. But when we use only annotated sentences of the PSSC (i.e. the CSSC), the total number of annotations is 4,562, i.e. there is an increment of 40.93%.
- Although we have a boost in F_1 score due to the increase in recall using the CSSC in place of the PSSC, there is a considerable drop in precision.
- The number of FP is almost the same for the usage of 10-75% of the CSSC.
- The number of FN kept decreasing (and TP kept increasing) for 10-75% of the CSSC.

These observations can be interpreted as follows:

- Unannotated sentences inside the SSC in reality contain many gene annotations; so the inclusion of such sentences misleads the training process of the ML system.
- Some of the unannotated sentences actually do not contain any gene names, while others would contain such names but the automatic annotations missed them. As a consequence, the former sentences contain true negative examples which could provide useful features that can be exploited during training so that less FPs are produced (with a precision drop using the CSSC). So, instead of simply discarding all the unannotated sentences, we could adopt a filtering strategy that tries to distinguish between the two classes of sentences above.
- The experimental results with the increasing size of the CSSC show a decrease in both precision (74.55 vs 76.17) and recall (53.72 vs 54.04). We plan to run again these experiments with different randomized splits to better assess the performance.
- Even using only 10% of the whole CSSC does not produce a drastic difference with the results when the full CSSC is used. This indicates that perhaps the more CSSC data is fed, the more the system tends to overfit.
- It is evident that the more the size of the CSSC increases, the lower the improvement of F_1 score, if the total number of annotations in the newly added sentences and the accuracy of the annotations are not considerably higher. It might be not surprising if, after the addition of more sentences in the CSSC, the F_1 score drops further rather than increasing. The assumption that having a huge SSC would be beneficiary might not be completely correct. There might be some optimal limit of the SSC (depending on the task) that can provide maximum benefits.

4.3 Training with the GSC and the SSC together

Our final experiments were focused on whether it is possible to improve performance by simply merging the GSC training data with the PSSC and the CSSC. The PSSC has almost 24 times the number of sentences and almost 8 times the number of gene annotations than the GSC. There is a possibility that, when we do a simple merge, the weight of the

	Total tokens in the corpus	No of annotated genes	TP	FP	FN	P	R	F_1
PSSC	6,955,662	144,375	2,606	631	3,725	80.51	41.16	54.47
100% of CSSC	1,983,113	144,375	3,401	1,161	2,930	74.55	53.72	62.44
75% of CSSC	1,487,823	108,213	3,421	1,070	2,910	76.17	54.04	63.22
50% of CSSC	992,392	72,316	3,265	1,095	3,066	74.89	51.57	61.08
25% of CSSC	494,249	35,984	3,179	1,048	3,152	75.21	50.21	60.22
10% of CSSC	196,522	14,189	2,988	1,097	3,343	73.15	47.20	57.37

Table 2: The results of SSC experiments with varying size of the CSSC = condensed SSC (i.e. sentences containing at least one annotation). SSC size = 316,869 sentences. CSSC size = 77,117.

	TP	FP	FN	P	R	F_1
GSC	5,373	759	958	87.62	84.87	86.22
PSSC + GSC	3,745	634	2,586	85.52	59.15	69.93
PSSC + GSC * 8	4,163	606	2,168	87.29	65.76	75.01
CSSC + GSC * 8	4,507	814	1,824	84.70	71.19	77.36

Table 3: The results of experiments by training on the GSC training data merged with the PSSC and the CSSC.

gold annotations would be underestimated. So, apart from doing a simple merge, we also try to balance the annotations of the two corpora. There are two options to do this – (i) by duplicating the GSC training corpus 8 times to make its total number of annotations equal to that of the PSSC, or (ii) by choosing randomly a portion of the PSSC that would have almost similar amount of annotations as that of the GSC. We choose the 1st option.

Unfortunately, when an SSC (i.e. the PSSC or the CSSC) is combined with the GSC, the result is far below than that of using the GSC only (see Table 3). Again, low recall is the main issue partly due to the lower number of annotations (i.e. TP+FP) done by the system trained on an SSC and the GSC instead of the GSC only. As we know, a GSC is manually annotated following precise guidelines, while an SSC is annotated with automatic systems that do not necessarily follow the same guidelines as a GSC. So, it would not have been surprising if the number of annotations were high (since we have much bigger training corpus due to SSC) but precision were low. But in practice, precision obtained by combining an SSC and the GSC is almost as high as the precision achieved using the GSC.

One reason for the lower number of annotations might be the errors that have been propagated inside the SSC. Some of the systems that have been used for the annotation of the SSC might have low recall. As a result, during harmonization of their annotations several valid gene mentions might not have been included[13].

One other possible reason could be the difference in the entity name boundaries in the GSC and an SSC. We have checked some of the SSC annotations randomly. It appears that in those annotated entity names some relevant (neighbouring) words (in the corresponding sentences) are not included. It is most likely that the SSC annotation systems had disagreements on those words.

When the annotations of the GSC were given higher preference (by duplicating), there is a substantial improvement in the F_1 score, although still lower than the result with the GSC only.

5 Conclusions

The idea of SSC development is simple and yet attractive. Obtaining better results on a test dataset by combining output of multiple (accurate and diverse[14]) systems is not new (Torii et al., 2009; Smith et al., 2008). But adopting this strategy for cor-

[13]There can be two reasons for this – (i) when a certain valid gene name is not annotated by any of the annotation systems, and (ii) when only a few of those systems have annotated the valid name but the total number of such systems is below than the minimum required number of agreements, and hence the gene name is not considered as an SSC annotation.

[14]A system is said to be accurate if its classification performance is better than a random classification. Two systems are considered diverse if they do not make the same classification mistakes. (Torii et al., 2009)

pus development is a novel and unconventional approach. Some natural language processing tasks (especially the new ones) lack adequate GSCs to be used for the training of ML based systems. For such tasks, domain experts can provide patterns or rules to build systems that can be used to annotate an initial version of SSC. Such systems might lack high recall but are expected to have high precision. Already available task specific lexicons or dictionaries can also be utilized for SSC annotation. Such an initial version of SSC can be later enriched using automatic process which would utilize existing annotations in the SSC.

With this vision in mind, we pose ourselves several questions (see Section 1) regarding the practical usability and exploitation of an SSC. Our experiments are conducted on a publicly available biomedical SSC developed for the training of biomedical NER systems. For the evaluation of a state-of-the-art ML system trained on such an SSC, we use a widely used benchmark biomedical GSC.

In the search of answers for our questions, we accumulate several important empirical observations. We have been able to automatically reduce the number of erroneous annotations from the SSC and include unannotated potential entity mentions simply using the annotations that the SSC already provides. Our techniques have been effective for improving the annotation quality as there is a considerable increment of F_1 score (almost 11% higher when we use CSSC instead of using ISSC; see Table 1 and 2).

We also observe that it is possible to obtain more than 80% of precision using the SSC. But recall remains quite low, partly due to the low number of annotations provided by the system trained with the SSC. Perhaps, the entity names in the SSC that are missed by the annotation systems is one of the reasons for that.

Perhaps, the most interesting outcome of this study is that, if only annotated sentences (which we call *condensed* corpus) are considered, then the number of annotations as well as the performance increases significantly. This indicates that many unannotated sentences contain annotations missed by the automatic annotation systems. However, it appears that correctly unannotated sentences influence the achievement of high precision. Maybe a more sophisticated approach should be adopted instead of completely discarding the unannotated sentences, e.g. devising a filter able to distinguish between relevant unannotated sentences (i.e., those that should contain annotations) from non-relevant ones (i.e., those that correctly do not contain any annotation). Measuring lexical similarity between annotated and unannotated sentences might help in this case.

We notice the size of an SSC affects performance, but increasing it above a certain limit does not always guarantee an improvement of performance (see Figure 1). This rejects the hypothesis that having a much larger SSC should allow an ML based system to ameliorate the effect of having erroneous annotations inside the SSC.

Our empirical results show that combining GSC and SSC do not improve results for the particular task of NER, even if GSC annotations are given higher weights (through duplication). We assume that this is partly due to the variations in the guidelines of entity name boundaries[15]. These impact the learning of the ML algorithm. For other NLP tasks where the possible outcome is boolean (e.g. relation extraction, i.e. whether a particular relation holds between two entities or not), we speculate the results of such combination might be better.

We use a CRF based ML system for our experiments. It would be interesting to see whether the observations are similar if a system with a different ML algorithm is used.

To conclude, this study suggests that an automatically pre-processed SSC might already contain annotations with reasonable quality and quantity, since using it we are able to reach more than 62% of F_1 score. This is encouraging since in the absence of a GSC, an ML system would be able to exploit an SSC to annotate unseen text with a moderate (if not high) accuracy. Hence, SSC development might be a good option to semi-automate the annotation of a GSC.

Acknowledgments

This work was carried out in the context of the project "eOnco - Pervasive knowledge and data management in cancer care". The authors would like to thank Pierre Zweigenbaum for useful discussion, and the anonymous reviewers for valuable feedback.

[15]For example, "human IL-7 protein" vs "IL-7".

References

Avrim Blum and Tom Mitchell. 1998. Combining labeled and unlabeled data with co-training. In *Proceedings of the 11th Annual Conference on Computational learning theory (COLT'98)*, pages 92–100.

Md. Faisal Mahbub Chowdhury and Alberto Lavelli. 2010. Disease mention recognition with specific features. In *Proceedings of the Workshop on Biomedical Natural Language Processing (BioNLP 2010), 48th Annual Meeting of the Association for Computational Linguistics*, pages 83–90, Uppsala, Sweden, July.

Stephen Clark, James R. Curran, and Miles Osborne. 2003. Bootstrapping POS taggers using unlabelled data. In *Proceedings of the 7th Conference on Natural Language Learning (CoNLL-2003)*, pages 49–55.

Udo Hahn, Katrin Tomanek, Elena Beisswanger, and Erik Faessler. 2010. A proposal for a configurable silver standard. In *Proceedings of the 4th Linguistic Annotation Workshop, 48th Annual Meeting of the Association for Computational Linguistics*, pages 235–242, Uppsala, Sweden, July.

Shan He and Daniel Gildea. 2006. Self-training and co-training for semantic role labeling: Primary report. Technical report, University of Rochester.

Jin-Dong Kim, Tomoko Ohta, Yuka Tateisi, and Jun'ichi Tsujii. 2003. Genia corpus - semantically annotated corpus for bio-textmining. *Bioinformatics*, 19(Suppl 1):i180–182.

David McClosky, Eugene Charniak, and Mark Johnson. 2006. Reranking and self-training for parser adaptation. In *Proceedings of the 21st International Conference on Computational Linguistics*, pages 337–344, Sydney, Australia.

Vincent Ng and Claire Cardie. 2003. Weakly supervised natural language learning without redundant views. In *Proceedings of the 2003 Human Language Technology Conference of the North American Chapter of the Association for Computational Linguistics (HLT-NAACL-2003)*, pages 173–180.

David Pierce and Claire Cardie. 2001. Limitations of co-training for natural language learning from large datasets. In *Proceedings of the 2001 Conference on Empirical Methods in Natural Language Processing (EMNLP-2001)*, pages 1–9.

David Pierce and Claire Cardie. 2004. Co-training and self-training for word sense disambiguation. In *Proceedings of the 8th Conference on Computational Natural Language Learning (CoNLL-2004)*, pages 33–40.

Dietrich Rebholz-Schuhmann and Udo Hahn. 2010c. Silver standard corpus vs. gold standard corpus. In *Proceedings of the 1st CALBC Workshop*, Cambridge, U.K., June.

Dietrich Rebholz-Schuhmann, Antonio Jimeno, Chen Li, Senay Kafkas, Ian Lewin, Ning Kang, Peter Corbett, David Milward, Ekaterina Buyko, Elena Beisswanger, Kerstin Hornbostel, Alexandre Kouznetsov, Rene Witte, Jonas B Laurila, Christopher JO Baker, Chen-Ju Kuo, Simon Clematide, Fabio Rinaldi, Richrd Farkas, Gyrgy Mra, Kazuo Hara, Laura Furlong, Michael Rautschka, Mariana Lara Neves, Alberto Pascual-Montano, Qi Wei, Nigel Collier, Md. Faisal Mahbub Chowdhury, Alberto Lavelli, Rafael Berlanga, Roser Morante, Vincent Van Asch, Walter Daelemans, José Luís Marina, Erik van Mulligen, Jan Kors, and Udo Hahn. 2010. Assessment of NER solutions against the first and second CALBC silver standard corpus. In *Proceedings of the fourth International Symposium on Semantic Mining in Biomedicine (SMBM'2010)*, October.

Dietrich Rebholz-Schuhmann, Antonio José Jimeno-Yepes, Erik van Mulligen, Ning Kang, Jan Kors, David Milward, Peter Corbett, Ekaterina Buyko, Elena Beisswanger, and Udo Hahn. 2010a. CALBC silver standard corpus. *Journal of Bioinformatics and Computational Biology*, 8:163–179.

Dietrich Rebholz-Schuhmann, Antonio José Jimeno-Yepes, Erik van Mulligen, Ning Kang, Jan Kors, David Milward, Peter Corbett, Ekaterina Buyko, Katrin Tomanek, Elena Beisswanger, and Udo Hahn. 2010b. The CALBC silver standard corpus for biomedical named entities – a study in harmonizing the contributions from four independent named entity taggers. In *Proceedings of the 7th International conference on Language Resources and Evaluation (LREC'10)*, Valletta, Malta, May.

Larry Smith, Lorraine Tanabe, Rie Ando, Cheng-Ju Kuo, I-Fang Chung, Chun-Nan Hsu, Yu-Shi Lin, Roman Klinger, Christoph Friedrich, Kuzman Ganchev, Manabu Torii, Hongfang Liu, Barry Haddow, Craig Struble, Richard Povinelli, Andreas Vlachos, William Baumgartner, Lawrence Hunter, Bob Carpenter, Richard Tsai, Hong-Jie Dai, Feng Liu, Yifei Chen, Chengjie Sun, Sophia Katrenko, Pieter Adriaans, Christian Blaschke, Rafael Torres, Mariana Neves, Preslav Nakov, Anna Divoli, Manuel Mana-Lopez, Jacinto Mata, and W John Wilbur. 2008. Overview of BioCreAtIvE II gene mention recognition. *Genome Biology*, 9(Suppl 2):S2.

Lorraine Tanabe, Natalie Xie, Lynne Thom, Wayne Matten, and W John Wilbur. 2005. GENETAG: a tagged corpus for gene/protein named entity recognition. *BMC Bioinformatics*, 6(Suppl 1):S3.

Manabu Torii, Zhangzhi Hu, Cathy H Wu, and Hongfang Liu. 2009. Biotagger-GM: a gene/protein name recognition system. *Journal of the American Medical Informatics Association : JAMIA*, 16:247–255.

Subjectivity and Sentiment Annotation of Modern Standard Arabic Newswire

Muhammad Abdul-Mageed
Department of Linguistics &
School of Library & Info. Science,
Indiana University,
Bloomington, USA
mabdulma@indiana.edu

Mona T. Diab
Center for Computational Learning Systems,
Columbia University,
NYC, USA
mdiab@ccls.columbia.edu

Abstract

Subjectivity and sentiment analysis (SSA) is an area that has been witnessing a flurry of novel research. However, only few attempts have been made to build SSA systems for *morphologically-rich languages (MRL)*. In the current study, we report efforts to partially bridge this gap. We present a newly labeled corpus of Modern Standard Arabic (MSA) from the news domain manually annotated for subjectivity and domain at the sentence level. We summarize our linguistically-motivated annotation guidelines and provide examples from our corpus exemplifying the different phenomena. Throughout the paper, we discuss expression of subjectivity in natural language, combining various previously scattered insights belonging to many branches of linguistics.

1 Introduction

As the volume of web data continues to phenomenally increase, researchers are becoming more interested in mining that data and making the information therein accessible to end-users in various innovative ways. As a result, searches and processing of data beyond the limiting level of surface words are becoming increasingly important (Diab et al., 2009). The sentiment expressed in Web data specifically continues to be of high interest and value to internet users, businesses, and governmental bodies. Thus, the area of *Subjectivity and sentiment analysis (SSA)* has been witnessing a flurry of novel research. *Subjectivity* in natural language refers to aspects of language used to express opinions, feelings, evaluations, and speculations (Banfield, 1982; Wiebe, 1994) and it, thus, incorporates *sentiment*. The process of *subjectivity classification* refers to the task of classifying texts into either *Objective* (e.g., *More than 1000 tourists have visited Tahrir Square, in downtown Cairo, last week.*) or *Subjective*. Subjective text is further classified with *sentiment* or *polarity*. For sentiment classification, the task refers to identifying whether a subjective text is *positive* (e.g., *The Egyptian revolution was really impressive!*), *negative* (e.g., *The bloodbaths that took place in Tripoli were horrifying!*), *neutral* (e.g., *The company may release the software next month.*), and, sometimes, *mixed* (e.g., *I really like this labtop, but it is prohibitively expensive.*). SSA sometimes incorporates identifying the *holder(s)*, *target(s)*, and *strength (e.g., low, medium, high)* of the expressed sentiment.

In spite of the great interest in SSA, only few studies have been conducted on *morphologically-rich languages (MRL)* (i.e., languages in which significant information concerning syntactic units and relations are expressed at the word-level (Tsarfaty et al., 2010)). Arabic, Hebrew, Turkish, Czech, and Basque are examples of MRLs. SSA work on MRLs has been hampered by lack of annotated data. In the current paper we report efforts to manually annotate a corpus of Modern Standard Arabic (MSA), a morphologically-rich variety of Arabic, e.g., (Diab et al., 2007; Habash et al., 2009). The corpus is a collection of documents from the newswire genre covering several domains such as politics and sports. We label the data at the sentence level. Our annotation guidelines explicitly incorporate linguistically-motivated information.

Proceedings of the Fifth Law Workshop (LAW V), pages 110–118,
Portland, Oregon, 23-24 June 2011. ©2011 Association for Computational Linguistics

The rest of the paper is organized as follows: In Section 2, we motivate work on the news genre. In Section 3, we summarize our linguistically-motivated annotation guidelines. In Section 4, we introduce the domain annotation task. In Section 5 we provide examples from our dataset. We present related work in Section 6. We conclude in Section 7.

2 Subjectivity and Sentiment in the News

Most work on SSA has been conducted on data belonging to highly subjective, user-generated genres such as blogs and product or movie reviews where authors express their opinions quite freely (Balahur and Steinberger, 2009). In spite of the important role news play in our lives (e.g., as an influencer of the social construction of reality (Fowler, 1991), (Chouliaraki and Fairclough, 1999), (Wodak and Meyer, 2009)), the news genre has received much less attention within the SSA community. This role of news and the connection between news-making and social contexts and practices motivates the task of building SSA system. In addition, the many novel ways online news-making is becoming an interactive process (Abdul-Mageed, 2008) further motivates investigating the newswire genre. News-makers reproduce some of the views of their readers (e.g., by quoting them) and they devote full stories about the interactions of web users on social media outlets[1]. Although subjectivity in news articles has traditionally tended to be implicit, the fact that news stories have their own biases (e.g., hiding agents behind negative or positive events via use of passive voice, variation in lexical choice) has been pointed out by e.g., (Van Dijk, 1988). The growing trend to foster interactivity and more heavily report communication of internet users within the body of news articles is likely to make expression of subjectivity in news articles more explicit.

3 Subjectivity and Sentiment Annotation (SSA)

Two graduate level educated native speakers of Arabic annotated 2855 sentences from Part 1 V 3.0 of the Penn Arabic TreeBank (PATB) (Maamouri et al., 2004). The sentences make up the first 400 documents of that part of PATB amounting to a total of 54.5% of the PATB Part 1 data set. The task was to annotate MSA news articles at the sentence level. Each article has been processed such that coders are provided sentences to label. We prepared annotation guidelines for this SSA task focusing specifically on the newswire genre. We summarize the guidelines next, illustrating related and relevant literature.

	OBJ	S-POS	S-NEG	S-NEUT	Total
OBJ	1192	21	57	11	1281
S-POS	47	439	2	3	491
S-NEG	69	0	614	6	689
S-NEUT	115	2	9	268	394
Total	1423	462	682	288	2855

Table 1: Agreement for SSA sentences

3.1 SSA Categories

For each sentence, each annotator assigned one of 4 possible labels: (1) Objective (OBJ), (2) Subjective-Positive (S-POS), (3) Subjective-Negative (S-NEG), and (4) Subjective-Neutral (S-NEUT). We followed (Wiebe et al., 1999) in operationalizing the subjective vs. the objective categories. In other words, if the primary goal of a sentence is perceived to be the objective reporting of information, it was labeled OBJ. Otherwise, a sentence would be a candidate for one of the three subjective classes.[2] Table 1 shows the contingency table for the two annotators judgments. Overall agreement is 88.06%, with a Kappa (k) value of 0.38.

To illustrate, a sentence such as "The Prime Minister announced that he will visit the city, saying that he will be glad to see the injured", has two authors (the story writer and the Prime Minister indirectly quoted). Accordingly to our guidelines, this sentence should be annotated S-POS tag since the part related to the person quoted (the Prime Minis-

[1]This trend has increased especially in Arab news organizations like Al-Jazeera and Al-Arabiya with the hightened attention to social media as a result of ongoing revolutions and protests in the Arab world

[2]It is worth noting that even though some SSA researchers include subjective mixed categories, we only saw such categories attested in less than $<$ 0.005% which is expected since our granularity level is the sentence. If we are to consider larger units of annotation, we believe mixed categories will become more frequent. Thus we decided to tag the very few subjective mixed sentences as S-NEUT.

ter) expresses a positive subjective sentiment, "glad" which is a *private state* (i.e., a state that is not subject to direct verification) (Quirk et al., 1974).

3.2 Good & Bad News

News can be good or bad. For example, whereas "Five persons were killed in a car accident" is bad news, "It is sunny and warm today in Chicago" is good news. Our coders were instructed not to consider *good* news *positive* nor bad news *negative* if they think the sentences expressing them are objectively reporting information. Thus, bad news and good news can be OBJ as is the case in both examples.

3.3 Perspective

Some sentences are written from a certain *perspective* (Lin et al., 2006) or point of view. Consider the two sentences (1) "Israeli soldiers, our heroes, are keen on protecting settlers" and (2) "Palestinian freedom fighters are willing to attack these Israeli targets". Sentence (1) is written from an Israeli perspective, while sentence (2) is written from a Palestinian perspective. The perspective from which a sentence is written interplays with how sentiment is assigned. Sentence (1) is considered positive from an Israeli perspective, yet the act of protecting settlers is considered negative from a Palestinian perspective. Similarly, attacking Israeli targets may be positive from a Palestinian vantage point, but will be negative from an Israeli perspective. Coders were instructed to assign a tag based on their understanding of the type of sentiment, if any, the author of a sentence is trying to communicate. Thus, we have tagged the sentences from the perspective of their authors. As it is easy for a human to identify the perspective of an author (Lin et al., 2006), this measure facilitated the annotation task. Thus, knowing that the sentence (1) is written from an Israeli perspective the annotator assigns it a S-POS tag.

3.4 Epistemic Modality

Epistemic modality serves to reveal how confident writers are about the truth of the ideational material they convey (Palmer, 1986). Epistemic modality is classified into *hedges* and *boosters*. *Hedges* are devices like *perhaps* and *I guess* that speakers employ to reduce the degree of liability or responsibility they might face in expressing the ideational material. *Boosters*[3] are elements like *definitely, I assure that*, and *of course* that writers or speakers use to emphasize what they really believe. Both hedges and boosters can (1) turn a given unit of analsysis from objective into subjective and (2) modify polarity (i.e., either strengthen or weaken it). Consider, for example, the sentences (1) "Gaddafi has murdered hundreds of people", (2) "Gaddafi may have murdered hundreds of people", and (3) "Unfortunately, Gaddafi has definitely murdered hundreds of people". While (1) is OBJ, since it lacks any subjectivity cues), (2) is S-NEUT because the proposition is not presented as a fact but rather is softened and hence offered as subject to counter-argument, (3) is a strong S-NEG (i.e., it is S-NEG as a result of the use of "unfortnately", and *strong* due to the use of the booster *definitely*). Our annotators were explicitly alerted to the ways epistemic modality markers interact with subjectivity.

3.5 Illocutionary Speech Acts

Occurrences of language expressing (e.g. *apologies, congratulations, praise*, etc. are referred to as *illocutionary speech acts* (ISA) (Searle, 1975). We believe that ISAs are relevant to the expression of sentiment in natural language. For example, the two categories *expressives* (e.g., congratulating, thanking, apologizing and *commisives* (e.g., promising) of (Searle, 1975)'s taxonomy of ISAs are specially relevant to SSA. In addition, (Bach and Harnish, 1979) define an ISA as a medium of communicating attitude and discuss ISAs like *banning, bidding, indicting, penalizing, assessing* and *convicting*. For example, the sentence "The army should never do that again" is a *banning* act and hence is S-NEG. Although our coders were not required to assign ISA tags to the sentences, we have brought the the concept of ISAs to their attention as we believe a good understanding of the concept facilitates annotating data for SSA.

3.6 Annotator's Background Knowledge

The type of sentiment expressed may vary based on the type of background knowledge of an annota-

[3] (Polanyi and Zaenen, 2006) call these *intensifiers*.

Domain	# of Cases
Politics	1186
Sports	530
Military & political violence	435
Disaster	228
Economy	208
Culture	78
Light news	72
Crime	62
This day in history	56
Total	**2855**

Table 2: Domains

tor/reader (Balahur and Steinberger, 2009). For example, the sentence "Secularists will be defeated", may be positive to a reader who opposes secularism. However, if the primary intention of the author is judged to be communicating negative sentiment, annotators are supposed to assign a S-NEG tag. In general, annotators have been advised to avoid interpreting the subjectivity of text based on their own economic, social, religious, cultural, etc. background knowledge.

4 Domain Annotation

The same two annotators also manually assigned each sentence a domain label. The domain labels are from the news genre and are adopted from (Abdul-Mageed, 2008). The set of domain labels is as follows: {*Light news, Military and political violence, Sport, Politics, Crime, Economy, Disaster, Arts and culture, This day in history*}. Table 2 illustrates the number of sentences deemed for each domain. Domain annotation is an easier task than subjectivity annotation. Inter-annotator agreement for domain label assignment is at 97%. The two coders discussed differences and a total agreement was eventually reached. Coders disagreed most on cases belonging to the *Military and political violence* and *Politics* domains. For example, the following is a case where the two raters disagreed (and which was eventutally assigned a *Military and political violence* domain):

طلب رئيس الوزراء السابق في جزر فيدجي ماهندرا شودري الذي أطيح به في ١٩ أيار مايو إثر حركة انقلابية، اليوم السبت باعادة حكومته إلى السلطة.

Transliteration: Tlb r}ys AlwzrA' AlsAbq fy jzr fydjy mAhndrA $wdry Al*y OTyH bh fy 19 OyAr mAyw Ivr Hrkp AnqlAbyp, Alywm Alsbt bIEAdp Hkwmth IlY AlslTp.

English: Former Prime Minister of Fiji Mahendra Chaudhry, who was ousted in May 19 after a revolutionary movement, asked on Saturday to return to office.

5 Examples of SSA categories from MSA news

We illustrate examples of each category in our annotation scheme. We also show and discuss examples for each category where the annotators differed in their annotations. Importantly, the two annotators discussed and adjudicated together the differences.

5.1 Objective Sentences

Sentences where no opinion, sentiment, speculation, etc. is expressed are tagged as OBJ. Typically such sentences relay factual information, potentially expressed by an official source, like examples 1-3 below:
(1)

(١) ويبلغ عدد المشردين في كنتية لوس انجلس نحو ٨٤ الف شخص.

Transliteration:[4] wyblg Edd Alm$rdyn fy kwntyp lws Onjlys nHw 84 Olf $xS.

English: The number of homeless in Los Angeles County is about 48 thousand.

(٢) طهران ٧-١٥ (أف ب) - وقع ١٦ انفجارا مساء اليوم السبت في وزارة الاستخبارات حيث استدعيت العديد من سيارات الاسعاف كما أكد شاهد عيان لوكالة فرانس برس.

Transliteration: ThrAn 15-7 (A f b) - wqE 16 AnfjArA msA' Alywm Alsbt fy wzArp AlAstxbArAt Hyv. AstdEyt AlEdyd mn syArAt AlIsEAf kmA Okd $Ahd EyAn lwkAlp frAns brs.

[4]We use here Buckwalter transliteration www.qamus.org.

English: Tehran 15-7 (AFP) - An eye witness affirmed to AFP that 16 explosions occurred late Saturday at the Ministry of Intelligence where many ambulances were summoned.

(٣) أعلن السائق الأيرلندي أيدي أيرفاين (جاغوار) انسحابه من سباق جائزة النمسا الكبرى.

Transliteration: AEln AlsA}q AlIyrlndy Iydy IyrfAyn (jAgwAr) {nsHAbh mn sbAq jA}zp AlnmsA AlkbrY.

English: The Irish driver Eddie Irvine (Jaguar) announced his withdrawal from the Austrian Grand Prix.

Examples 1-3 show that objective sentences can have some implicitly negative words/phrases like انسحاب "{nsHAb" ("withdrawl"). In addition, although these 3 examples convey *bad* news, they are annotated with an OBJ tag since the sentences are judged as facts, although one annotator did initially tag example 1 as S-NEG before it was resolved later. In a similar vein, the OBJ tag was also assigned to *good* news as in example 4 below:

(٤) وتوءكد أولغا صاحبة المجمع أن كل شيء ينتج محليا باستثناء الطحين والسكر والمشروبات التي يتم شراوءها من السوق.

Transliteration wtWkd AwlgA SAHbp AlmjmE An kl $y' yntj mHlyA b{stvnA' AlTHyn wAlskr wAlm$rwbAt Alty ytm $rAWhA mn Alswq.

English: Olga, the owner of the restaurant, asserts that everything is produced locally except flour, sugar and beverages, which are purchased from the market.

The OBJ tag was also assigned to sentences which are neither *good* nor *bad* news, as example 5 below:

(٥) وسبق لكامبوس الذي كان يشرف على الريان القطري في الموسم الماضي أن درب الشباب في مطلع التسعينيات.

Transliteration: wsbq lkAmbws Al*y kAn y$rf ElY AlryAn AlqTry fy Almwsm AlmADy On drb Al$bAb fy mTlE AltsEynyAt.

English: Previously, Campos, who acted as the coach of Al Rayyan in Qatar last season, coached Al Shabab in the early nineties.

5.2 Subjective Positive Sentences

Sentences that were assigned a S-POS tag included ones with positive *private states* (Quirk et al., 1974) (i.e., states that are not subject to verification). Examples 6 and 7 below are cases in point where the phrase انتعشت الآمال "AntE$t Al—mAl" ("hopes revived") and the word اطمئنان "TmnAn" ("relief") stand for unverifiable private states:

(٦) وانتعشت الآمال بالافراج عن الرهائن في الساعات الـ ٢٤ الأخيرة مع تدخل ليبيا.

Transliteration: wAntE$t Al—mAl bAlIfrAj En AlrhA}n fy AlsAEAt Al 24 AlAxyrp mE tdxl lybyA.

English: Hopes for the release of hostages revived in the last 24 hours with the intervention of Libya.

(٧) و أبدى صلات حسن اطمئنانه إلى عودة النظام والاستقرار إلى بلاده.

Transliteration: wAbdY SlAt Hsn TmnAnh IlY Ewdp AlnZAm wAlstqrAr IlY blAdh.

English: Silaat Hasan expressed relief for the return of order and stability to his country.

The subtle nature of subjectivity as expressed in the news genre is reflected in some of the positive examples, especially in directly or indirectly quoted content when quoted people express their emotion or support their cause (via e.g., using modifiers). For instance, the use of the phrases \" من أجل نهضة الصومال\" "mn Ajl nhDp Al-SwmAl" ("for the advancement of Somalia") and إلى الأبد "IlY AlAbd" ("for ever") in examples 8 and 9, respectively, below turn what would have otherwise been OBJ sentences into S-POS sentences. Again, one annotator initially tagged example 8 as OBJ).:

(٨) دعا الرئيس الصومالي مساء أمس السبت الدول المانحة وخصوصا أعضاء الجامعة العربية والاتحاد

الأوروبي إلى تقديم مساعدات إلى بلاده "\من أجل نهضة الصومال "\.

Transliteration: dEA Alr}ys AlSwmAly msA' Ams Alsbt Aldwl AlmAnHp wxSwSA AEDA' Al-jAmEp AlErbyp wAl{tHAd AlAwrwby IlY tqdym msAEdAt IlY blAdh "mn Ajl nhDp AlSwmAl".
English: The Somali President, on Saturday evening, called on the donor countries, especially members of the Arab League and the European Union, to provide assistance to his country "for the advancement of Somalia".

(٩) وأكد [الرئيس] أن صفحة الحرب الأهلية قد أنتهت إلى الأبد، ويعود ذلك بشكل أساسي إلى انتهاء التدخلات الخارجية.

Transliteration: wAkd [Alrys] An SfHp AlHrb AlAhlyp qd Antht IlY AlAbd, wyEwd *'lk b$kl AsAsy IlY AnthA' AltdxlAt AlxArjyp.
English: He [The president] affirmed that was over for ever mainly because of the end of foreign/external interference.

Quoted content sometimes was in the form of *speech acts* (Searle, 1975). For example, (10) is an *expressive speech act* where the quoted person is thanking another party:

(١٠) [وأضاف:] "\شكرا من أعماق قلبي لهذا الشرف الذي يمتد مدى الحياة. "\

Transliteration: [wADAf:] "$krA mn AEmAq qlby lh'*A Al$rf Al*y ymtd mdY AlHyAp".
English: [He added:] Thank you from all my heart for this life-long honor.

Positive content was also sometimes explicitly expressed in the text belonging to the story author, especially in stories belonging to the Sports domain as is shown in (11).

(١١) ويمكن اعتبار ماتشالا (٥٠ عاما) من أنجح المدربين في القارة الآسيوية وتحديدا في منطقة الخليج، ويكفي أنه قاد المنتخب الكويتي إلى أحراز لقب كأس الخليج مرتين متاليتين عام ٩٦ وعام ٩٨.

Transliteration: wymkn AEtbAr mAt$AlA (50 EAmA) mn AnjH Almdrbyn fy AlqArp AlAsywyp wtHdydA fy mnTqp Alxlyj, wykfy Anh qAd Almntxb Alkwyty IlY IHrAz lqb kAs Alxlyj mrtyn mttAlytyn EAmy 96 w 98
English: Máčala, 50 years old, is one of the most successful coaches in Asia, more specifically in the Gulf area, and it is enough that he lead the Kuwaiti team to winning the Gulf Cup twice in a row in 96 and 98.

5.3 Subjective Negative Sentences

Again, the more explicit negative content was found to be frequent in sentences with quoted content (as is illustrated in examples 12-14). (12) shows how the S-NEG S-POS sentiment can be very strong as is illustrated by the use of the noun phrase إصرار شيطاني "ISrAr $yTAny" ("diabolical insistence"):

(١٢) ورد أحد محامي أندريوتي جيواكينو على قرار النيابة في باليرمو واصفا إياه بأنه "\إصرار شيطاني "\ من قبل الاتهام.

Transliteration: wrd AHd mHAmy Andrywty jywAkynw sbAky ElY qrAr AlnyAbp fy bAlyrmw wASfA IyAh bAnh "ISrAr $yTAny" mn qbl AlAthAm.
English: One of lawyers of Andreotti Jjoaquino responded to the prosecutor's decision in Palermo, describing it as a "diabolical insistence" on the acusser's part.

(13) shows how political parties express their political stance toward events via use of private state expressions (e.g., بقلق كبير "bqlq kbyr" ["with great concern"]).

(١٣) وأوضح بيان لوزارة الخارجية التركية أن: "\تركيا تتابع بقلق كبير هجمات الارهابيين التي حدثت في الأيام الأخيرة في أوزبكستان وقرغيزستان "\.

Transliteration: wAwDH byAn l- wzArp AlxArjyp Altrkyp An "trkyA ttAbE bqlq kbyr hjmAt AlArhAbyyn Alty Hdvt fy AlAyAm AlAxyrp fy AwzbkstAn wqrgyzstAn".

English: A statement from the Turkish Foreign Ministry indicated that "Turkey follows with great concern the terrorist attacks that have occurred in recent days in Uzbekistan and Kyrgyzstan".

Speech acts have also been used to express negative sentiment. For example, (14) is a direct quotation where a political figure denounces the acts of hearers. The speech act is intensified through the use of the adverb حتى "HtY" ("even"):

(١٤) وقال شارون من منصة الكنيست متوجها إلى نواب حزب العمل: "\لقد تخليتم حتى عن القسم الأكبر من المدينة القديمة "\.

Buckwalter: wqAl $Arwn mn mnSp Alknyst mtwjhA AlY nwAb Hzb AlEml "lqd txlytm HtY En Alqsm AlAkbr mn Almdynp Alqdymp."

English: Sharon, addressing Labour MPs from the Knesset, said: "You have even abandoned the biggest part of the old city".

Majority of the sentences pertaining to the *military and political violence* domain were OBJ, however, some of the sentences belonging to this specific domain were annotated S-NEG. News reporting is supposed to be objective, story authors sometimes used very negative modifiers, sometimes metaphorically as is indicated in (15). Example 15, however, was labeled OBJ by one of the annotators, and later agrrement was reached that it is more of an S-NEG case.

(١٥) وكان شهر تموز (يوليو) دمويا بشكل خاص مع سقوط نحو ٣٠٠ قتيل.

Transliteration: wkAn $hr tmwz ywlyw dmwyA b$kl xAS mE sqwT nHw 300 qtyl.
English: The month of July was especially bloody, with the killing of 300 people.

Again, authors of articles sometimes evaluated the events they reported. Sentences 16 and 17 are examples:

(١٦) وبات موقف فريق الأهلي صعبا للغاية في البطولة الأفريقية التي يسعى للفوز بلقبها وتضع جماهيره أيديها على قلوبها خشية انهياره.

Transliteration: wbAt mwqf fryq AlAhly SEbA lAlgAyp fy AlbTwlp AlIfryqyp Alty ysEY lAlfwz blqbhA wtDE jmAhyrh AydyhA ElY qlwbhA x$yp nhyArh.
English: The position of Al-Ahly in the African Championship, which the team seeks to win, became extremely difficult; and the team's fans hold their breath in fear of its defeat.

(١٧) وجاء اعتداء هشام حنفي على زميله شادي محمد على مرأى ومسمع الجميع أثناء مباراة الأهلي والاسماعيلي في نصف نهائي الكأس الأسبوع الماضي ليوءكد تفكك الفريق.

Transliteration: wjA' AEtdA' h$Am Hnfy ElY zmylh $Ady mHmd ElY mrAY wmsmE AljmyE AvnA' mbArAp AlAhly wAlAsmAEyly fy nSf nhA}y AlkAs AlAsbwE AlmADy lyWkd tfkk Alfryq.
English: Hesham Hanafi's attack on his colleague Shadi Muhammad, in front of everyone during the game between Al-Ahli and Al-Ismaili in the semi-finals last week, confirms the disintegration of the team.

5.4 Subjective Neutral Sentences

Some of the S-NEUT cases were speculations about the future, as is illustrated by sentences 18 and 19:

(١٨) ويتوقع أن يعود إلى الولايات المتحدة في ٢٥ تموز (يوليو).

Transliteration: wytwqE An yEwd IlY AlwlAyAt AlmtHdp fy 25 tmwz (ywlyw).
English: And he is expected to return to the United States on July 25.

(١٩) وكل الموءشرات تفيد أن هذا الوضع لن يتغير بعد الانتخابات.

Transliteration: wkl AlmW$rAt tfyd In h'*A AlwDE ln ytgyr bEd AlAntxAbAt.
English: All indications are that this situation will not change after the elections.

Hedges were also used to show cautious commitment to propositions, and hence turn OBJ sentences to S-NEUT ones. Sentences (20) and (21) are examples, with the occurrence of the hedge trigger word يبدو "ybdw" ("it seems") in (20) and على الأرجح "ElY AlArjH" ("it is most likely") in (21):

(٢٠) و يبدو أن التكتم الذي أحاط بزيارة بيريز إلى أندونيسيا كان يهدف إلى تفادي إثارة ردود فعل معادية في البلاد.

Transliteration: w ybdw An Altktm Al*y AHAT bzyArp byryz AlY AndwnysyA kAn yhdf AlY tfAdy AvArp rdwd fEl mEAdyp fy AlblAd.
English: It seems that the secrecy surrounding Peres's visit to Indonesia was aimed at avoiding negative reactions in the country.

(٢١) وعلى الأرجح أن قبطان الغواصة أعطى الأمر بإطفاء كل الآلات على متنها.

Transliteration: wElY AlArjH An qbTAn AlgwASp AETY AlAmr bATfA' kl AlAlAt ElY mtnhA.
English: Most likely the submarine's captain ordered turning off all the machines on board.

Some S-NEUT cases are examples of *arguing* that something is true or should be done (Somasundaran et al., 2007). (22) is an illustrative example:

(٢٢) قلتها، وأكررها، فالمشكلة ليست في النفط الخام وإنما في المشتقات النفطية.

Transliteration: qlthA, wAkrrhA, fAlm$klp lyst fy AlnfT AlxAm wInmA fy Alm$tqAt AlnfTyp.
English: I said, and I repeat it, the problem is not in crude oil but rather in oil derivatives.

Example 22 was, however, initially tagged as OBJ. Later, the two annotators agreed to assign it an S-NEUT tag.

6 Related Work

There are a number of datasets annotated for SSA. Most relevant to us is work on the news genre. (Wiebe et al., 2005) describe a fine-grained news corpus manually labeled for SSA[5] at the word and phrase levels. Their annotation scheme involves identifying the *source* and *target* of sentiment as well as other related properties (e.g., the *intensity* of expressed sentiment). Our work is less fine grained on the one hand, but we label our data for domain as well as subjectivity.

(Balahur et al., 2009) report work on labeling quotations from the news involving one person mentioning another entity and maintain that quotations typically contain more sentiment expressions than other parts of news articles. Our work is different from that of (Balahur et al., 2009) in that we label all sentences regardless whether they include quotations or not. (Balahur et al., 2009) found that entities mentioned in quotations are not necessarily the target of the sentiment, and hence we believe that SSA systems built for news are better if they focus on all the sentences of articles rather than quotations alone (since the target of sentiment may be outside the scope of a quotation, but within that of the sentence to which a quotation belongs)..

The only work on Arabic SSA we are aware of is that of Abbasi et al. (2008) who briefly describe labeling a collection of documents from Arabic Web forums. (Abbasi et al., 2008)'s dataset, however, is not publicly available and detailed information as to how the data was annotated is lacking. Our work is different from (Abbasi et al., 2008)'s in that we label instances at the sentence level. We believe that documents contain mixtures of OBJ and SUBJ cases and hence sentence-level annotation is more fine-grained. In addition, (Abbasi et al., 2008) focus on a specific domain of 'dark Web forums'.

7 Conclusion

In this paper, we present a novel annotation layer of SSA to an already labeled MSA data set, the PATB Part 1 ver. 3.0. To the best of our knowledge, this layer of annotation is the first of its kind on MSA data of the newswire genre. We will make that collection available to the community at large. We motivate SSA for news and summarize our linguistics-motivated guidelines for data annotation and provide examples from our data set.

[5]They use the term *private states* (Quirk et al., 1974) to refer to expressions of subjectivity.

References

A. Abbasi, H. Chen, and A. Salem. 2008. Sentiment analysis in multiple languages: Feature selection for opinion classification in web forums. *ACM Trans. Inf. Syst.*, 26:1–34.

M. Abdul-Mageed. 2008. Online News Sites and Journalism 2.0: Reader Comments on Al Jazeera Arabic. *tripleC-Cognition, Communication, Co-operation*, 6(2):59.

K. Bach and R.M. Harnish. 1979. Linguistic communication and speech acts.

A. Balahur and R. Steinberger. 2009. Rethinking Sentiment Analysis in the News: from Theory to Practice and back. *Proceeding of WOMSA*.

A. Balahur, R. Steinberger, E. van der Goot, B. Pouliquen, and M. Kabadjov. 2009. Opinion mining on newspaper quotations. In *2009 IEEE/WIC/ACM International Conference on Web Intelligence and Intelligent Agent Technology*, pages 523–526. IEEE.

A. Banfield. 1982. *Unspeakable Sentences: Narration and Representation in the Language of Fiction*. Routledge Kegan Paul, Boston.

L. Chouliaraki and N. Fairclough. 1999. *Discourse in late modernity: Rethinking critical discourse analysis*. Edinburgh Univ Pr.

M. Diab, K. Hacioglu, and D. Jurafsky. 2007. Automatic processing of Modern Standard Arabic text. *Arabic Computational Morphology*, pages 159–179.

M.T. Diab, L. Levin, T. Mitamura, O. Rambow, V. Prabhakaran, and W. Guo. 2009. Committed belief annotation and tagging. In *Proceedings of the Third Linguistic Annotation Workshop*, pages 68–73. Association for Computational Linguistics.

R. Fowler. 1991. *Language in the News: Discourse and Ideology in the Press*. Routledge.

N. Habash, O. Rambow, and R. Roth. 2009. Mada+tokan: A toolkit for arabic tokenization, diacritization, morphological disambiguation, pos tagging, stemming and lemmatization. In *Proceedings of the 2nd International Conference on Arabic Language Resources and Tools (MEDAR)*, Cairo, Egypt.

S. Kim and E. Hovy. 2004. Determining the sentiment of opinions. In *Proceedings of the 20th International Conference on Computational Linguistics*, pages 1367–1373.

W.H. Lin, T. Wilson, J. Wiebe, and A. Hauptmann. 2006. Which side are you on?: identifying perspectives at the document and sentence levels. In *Proceedings of the Tenth Conference on Computational Natural Language Learning*, pages 109–116. Association for Computational Linguistics.

M. Maamouri, A. Bies, T. Buckwalter, and W. Mekki. 2004. The penn arabic treebank: Building a large-scale annotated arabic corpus. In *NEMLAR Conference on Arabic Language Resources and Tools*, pages 102–109.

F. Palmer. 1986. *Mood and Modality. 1986*. Cambridge: Cambridge University Press.

L. Polanyi and A. Zaenen. 2006. Contextual valence shifters. *Computing attitude and affect in text: Theory and applications*, pages 1–10.

R. Quirk, S. Greenbaum, R.A. Close, and R. Quirk. 1974. *A university grammar of English*, volume 1985. Longman.

J.R. Searle. 1975. A taxonomy of speech acts. In K. Gunderson, editor, *Language, mind, and knowledge*, pages 344–369. Minneapolis: University of Minnesota Press.

S. Somasundaran, J. Ruppenhofer, and J. Wiebe. 2007. Detecting arguing and sentiment in meetings. In *Proceedings of the SIGdial Workshop on Discourse and Dialogue*, volume 6. Citeseer.

H. Tanev. 2007. Unsupervised learning of social networks from a multiple-source news corpus. *MuLTI-SOuRcE, MuLTILINguAL INfORMATION ExTRAcTION ANd SuMMARIzATION*, page 33.

R. Tsarfaty, D. Seddah, Y. Goldberg, S. Kuebler, Y. Versley, M. Candito, J. Foster, I. Rehbein, and L. Tounsi. 2010. Statistical parsing of morphologically rich languages (spmrl) what, how and whither. In *Proceedings of the NAACL HLT 2010 First Workshop on Statistical Parsing of Morphologically-Rich Languages*, Los Angeles, CA.

T.A. Van Dijk. 1988. *News as discourse*. Lawrence Erlbaum Associates.

J. Wiebe, R. Bruce, and T. O'Hara. 1999. Development and use of a gold standard data set for subjectivity classifications. In *Proc. 37th Annual Meeting of the Assoc. for Computational Linguistics (ACL-99)*, pages 246–253, University of Maryland: ACL.

J. Wiebe, T. Wilson, and C. Cardie. 2005. Annotating expressions of opinions and emotions in language. *Language Resources and Evaluation*, 39(2):165–210.

J. Wiebe. 1994. Tracking point of view in narrative. *Computional Linguistics*, 20(2):233–287.

R. Wodak and M. Meyer. 2009. Critical discourse analysis: History, agenda, theory and methodology. *Methods of critical discourse analysis*, pages 1–33.

Creating an Annotated Tamil Corpus as a Discourse Resource

Ravi Teja Rachakonda
International Institute of
Information Technology
Hyderabad, India
raviteja.r@research.iiit.ac.in

Dipti Misra Sharma
International Institute of
Information Technology
Hyderabad, India
dipti@iiit.ac.in

Abstract

We describe our efforts to apply the Penn Discourse Treebank guidelines on a Tamil corpus to create an annotated corpus of discourse relations in Tamil. After conducting a preliminary exploratory study on Tamil discourse connectives, we show our observations and results of a pilot experiment that we conducted by annotating a small portion of our corpus. Our ultimate goal is to develop a Tamil Discourse Relation Bank that will be useful as a resource for further research in Tamil discourse. Furthermore, a study of the behavior of discourse connectives in Tamil will also help in furthering the cross-linguistic understanding of discourse connectives.

1 Introduction

The study of discourse structure in natural language processing has its applications in emerging fields such as coherence evaluation, question answering, natural language generation and textual summarization. Such a study is possible in a given human language only if there are sufficient discourse annotated resources available for that language. The Penn Discourse Treebank (PDTB) is a project whose goal is to annotate the discourse relations holding between events described in a text. The PDTB is a lexically grounded approach where discourse relations are anchored in lexical items wherever they are explicitly realized in the text (Miltsakaki et al. 2004, Prasad et al., 2008). To foster cross-linguistic studies in discourse relations, projects similar to the PDTB in discourse annotation were initiated in Czech (Mladová et al., 2008), Chinese (Xue, 2005), Turkish (Zeyrek and Webber, 2008) and Hindi (Prasad et al., 2008). We explore how the underlying framework and annotation guidelines apply to Tamil, a morphologically rich, agglutinative, free word order language.

In this paper, we present how a corpus of Tamil texts was created on which we performed our pilot experiment. Next, in Section 3 we cover the basics of the PDTB guidelines that we followed during our annotation process. In Section 4, we show various categories of Tamil discourse connectives that we identified after a preliminary study on discourse connectives in Tamil, illustrating each with examples. In Section 5, we discuss some interesting issues specific to Tamil that we encountered during discourse annotation and present the results of the pilot experiment that we performed on our source corpus. We conclude this paper in Section 6 by discussing about challenges that were unique to our work and our plans for the future.

2 Source Corpus

We collected Tamil encyclopedia articles from the June 2008 edition of the Wikipedia static HTML dumps[1]. Elements such as HTML metadata, navigational links, etc. were then removed until only the text of the articles remained. A corpus was then built by collecting the texts from all the articles in the dump. The corpus thus created consists of

[1] http://static.wikipedia.org/

Proceedings of the Fifth Law Workshop (LAW V), pages 119–123,
Portland, Oregon, 23-24 June 2011. ©2011 Association for Computational Linguistics

about 2.2 million words from approximately 200,000 sentences.

Since the texts used in building the corpus were all encyclopedia articles featured in the Tamil language version of Wikipedia, the corpus covers a wide variety of topics including arts, culture, biographies, geography, society, history, etc., written and edited by volunteers from around the world.

3 Penn Discourse Treebank Guidelines

The PDTB is a resource built on discourse structure in (Webber and Joshi, 1998) where discourse connectives are treated as discourse-level predicates that always take exactly two *abstract objects* such as events, states and propositions as their arguments. We now describe the types of connectives and their senses from the PDTB framework and provide examples from Tamil sentences.

3.1 Annotation Process

The process of discourse annotation involves identifying discourse connectives in raw text and then annotating their arguments and semantics. Discourse connectives are identified as being *explicit*, *implicit*, *AltLex*, *EntRel* or *NoRel* (Prasad et al. 2008). These classes are described in detail in Section 4. By convention, annotated *explicit* connectives are underlined and *implicit* connectives are shown by the marker, "(Implicit=)". As can be seen in example (1), one of the arguments is shown enclosed between { } and the other argument is shown in []. The *AltLex*, *EntRel* or *NoRel* relations are shown by underlining, i.e., as "(AltLex=)", "(EntRel)" and "(NoRel)", respectively.

(1) {eN kAl uDaindadaN}Al [eNNAl viLayADa muDiyAdu].
'{My leg broke}, hence [I cannot play].'

3.2 Sense Hierarchy

The semantics of discourse relations are termed as *senses* and are then classified hierarchically using four top-level *classes* 'Comparison', 'Contingency', 'Expansion' and 'Temporal'. Each class is refined by its component *types* and these, in turn, are further refined by the *subtype* level.

It is interesting to note that some connectives have multiple senses. In example (2) the affixed –*um* connective carries the sense of type *Expansion:Conjunction* 'also' whereas in example (3) the same affix carries the sense of the subtype *Contingency:Concession* 'however'.

(2) {idaN mUlam avar oru nAL pOttiyil oNbadAyiram OttangaLai kaDanda pattAvadu vIrar eNra perumaiyai pettrAr}. [inda OttangaLai kaDanda mudal teNNAppirikka vIrar eNra sAdaNaiyaiy]um [nigaztiNAr].
'{By this, he became the tenth player to cross nine thousand runs in one-day internationals}. [He] also [attained the record of becoming the first South African player to cross these many runs].'

(3) {seNra murai kirikket ulagakkOppaiyiN pOthu pangu pattriyadai vida iraNDu aNigaL immurai kUDudalAga pangu pattriya pOd}um, [motthap pOttigaL inda muraiyil kuraivANadAgum.]
'Though {two more teams participated when compared to last Cricket World Cup}, [the total matches played during this time were fewer].'

4 Discourse Connectives in Tamil

Tamil is an *agglutinative language* where morphemes are affixed to the roots of individual words, a trait that it shares with many other Dravidian languages and languages like Turkish, Estonian and Japanese. Here, each affix represents information such as *discourse connective, gender, number*, etc. We now describe how we try to capture various types of Tamil discourse connectives using a proposed scheme which is based on the existing PDTB guidelines proposed by (Prasad et al., 2007).

4.1 Explicit Discourse Connectives

Explicit discourse connectives are lexical items present in text that are used to anchor the discourse relations portrayed by them. In Tamil, they are found as affixes to the verb, as in example (4) where the affix *-Al* conveys the meaning 'so'. This is in a way similar to the *simplex subordinators* in Turkish, as described in (Zeyrek and Webber, 2008). However, like in English, explicit discourse connectives are also realized as unbound lexical items, as can be seen in example (5) where the word *eNavE* means 'hence'.

(4) {avaradu uDalnalam sariyillAmaiy}Al [nAngu mAdangaL avarAl viLayADa iyalavillai].
'{He was suffering from ill health} so [he could not play for four months].'

(5) {tirukkuraL aNaittu madattiNarum paDittu payaNaDaiyum vagaiyil ezudappattuLLadu}. eNavE [innUl palarAl pArAttappaDuginradu].
'{Thirukkural has been written in such a way that people from all religions can benefit from it}. Hence, [this book is praised by many].'

Syntactically, explicit connectives can be *coordinating conjunctions* e.g., *alladu* ('or'), *subordinating conjunctions* e.g., *-Al* ('so'), *sentential relatives* e.g., *-adaNAl* ('because of which'), *particles* e.g., *-um* ('also') or *adverbials* e.g., *-pOdu* ('just then').

Explicit connectives also occur as *conjoined connectives* where two or more instances of connectives share the same two arguments. Such connectives are annotated as distinct types and are annotated discontinuously, as seen in example (6) where the connectives *-um* and *-um* are paired together to share the same arguments.

(6) {mANavargaLukku sattuNavu aLikkav}um [avargaL sariyAga uDarpayirchi seiyyav]um arasup paLLigaL udava vENDum.
'Government schools should help in {providing nutritious food to the students} and [making sure they perform physical exercises].

4.2 Implicit Discourse Connectives

Implicit discourse connectives are inserted between adjacent sentence pairs that are not related explicitly by any of the syntactically defined set of explicit connectives. In such a case, we attempted to infer a discourse relation between the sentences and a connective expression that best conveys the inferred relation is inserted. In example (7), the implicit expression *uthAraNamAga* ('for example') has been inserted as an inferred discourse relation between the two sentences.

(7) {IyOrA iNa makkaLiN moziyil irundu iNru Angilattil vazangum sorkaL uLLaNa}. (Implicit=uthAraNamAga) [dingO, vUmErA, vAlabi pONra sorkaL IyOravilirindu tONriya sorkaL dAN].
'{There are words that are present in English that originated from the language of the Eora people}. (Implicit= For example) [Dingo, Woomera and Wallaby are words with their origins in Eora].'

4.3 AltLex, EntRel and NoRel

In cases where no implicit connective was appropriately found to be placed between adjacent sentence-pairs, we now look at three distinct classes. *AltLex* relations, as seen in example (8) are discourse relations where the insertion of an implicit connective leads to a redundancy in its expression as the relation is already alternatively lexicalized by some other expression that cannot be labeled as an explicit connective. Example (9) shows an *EntRel* relation where no discourse relation can be inferred and the second sentence provides further description of an entity realized in the first sentence. When neither a discourse relation nor entity-based coherence can be inferred between the two adjacent sentences, it is described as a *NoRel*, shown in example (10).

(8) {mudalAvadAga mAgim, jOgEshwari, pUrivilla rayil nilayangaLil guNDu vedittadu}. (AtlLex=idai toDarndu) [mErku rayilvEyiN aNaittu rayilgaLum niruttappaTTaNa].
'{Initially, bombs exploded in Mahim, Jogeshwari and Poorivilla}. (AltLex=following this) [all the trains from the western railway were halted].'

(9) {ivvANDu kirikket ulagakkOppai mErkindiyat tIvugaLil mArc padimUnril irundu Epral irubattu-ettu varai naDaipettradu}. (EntRel) [indap pOttiyil pangupattriya padiNAru nADugaLaic cArnda aNigaLum ovvoru kuzuvilum nANgu aNigaL vIdamAga nANgu kuzukkaLAga pirikkapattu pOttigaL iDampettraNa].
'{This year's Cricket World Cup was held in West Indies from the thirteenth of March to the twenty-eight of April}. (EntRel) [In this competition, the teams representing the sixteen nations were grouped into four groups with four teams in each group].'

(10) {caccin TeNdUlkar ulagiNilEyE migac ciranda mattai vIccALarAga karudappadugirAr}. (NoRel) [indiya pandu vIccALargaL sariyANa muraiyil payirci peruvadillai].
'{Sachin Tendulkar is considered the best batsman in the world}. (NoRel) [Indian bowlers are not being given proper coaching].'

5 Observations and Results

5.1 Combined connectives

There is a paired connective *-um ... -um (...)* that sometimes expresses an *Expansion:Conjunction* relation between the events where each *-um* is suffixed to the verb that describes each event (see example (6)). Also, there is a connective *-Al* which usually never occurs more than once and sometimes expresses a *Contingency:Cause* relation between two events.

It is interesting to see that in sentences like (11), the *-Al* combines with the *-um ... -um* to express something like a new type of relation. In the process, the *-um ... -um* causes the *-Al*, which is usually not doubled, to become doubled, thereby forming an *-Alum ... -Alum*. We call this special type of connectives as *combined connectives*, as shown in example (11).

(11) {kirikket viLayADiyad}Alum {uDarpayirci seidad}Alum [sOrvaDaindEN].
'Because {I played cricket} and because {I did exercise} [I am tired].'

5.2 Redundant connectives

The connective *-O ... -O (...)* that conveys a *dubitative* relation also combines with the *-Al* connective in a way similar to what was shown in Section 5.1 to form the combined connective *-AlO ... -AlO (...)*.

However, in example (12), *alladu*, an equivalent of the *-O ... -O* connective has also occurred in addition to the combined *-AlO ... -AlO* connective. This may be purely redundant, or could serve a purpose to emphasize the dubitative relation expressed by both *alladu* and *-O ... -O*.

(12) {pOtti samappatt}AlO alladu {muDivu perapaDAmal pON}AlO [piNvarum muraigaL mUlam aNigaL tarappaDuttapaDum].
'If {a game is tied} or if {there is no result}, [the qualified teams are chosen using the following rules].'

5.3 Results of Pilot Study

In this experiment, we looked at 511 sentences from the corpus mentioned in Section 2 and annotated a total of 323 connectives. Table 1 shows the distribution of the annotated connectives across the different types such as Explicit, Implicit, EntRel, AltLex and NoRel.

Connective Type	Count	Count (unique)	Count (%)	Senses
Explicit	269	96	83.3	18
Implicit	28	16	8.6	13
EntRel	16	-	5.0	-
AltLex	8	5	2.5	4
NoRel	2	-	0.6	-

Table 1: Results of Pilot Experiment

While a higher percentage of the connectives annotated are those of the Explicit type, it can also be seen that there is a higher proportion of unique connectives in the Implicit and AltLex types. Note that since EntRel and NoRel connectives are not associated with a sense relation or a lexical item, their counts are left blank.

6 Challenges and Future Work

The agglutinative nature of the Tamil language required a deeper analysis to look into suffixes that act as discourse connectives in addition to those that occur as unbounded lexical items. We also found certain interesting examples that were distinct from those observed during similar approaches in relatively less morphologically rich languages like English.

While this was a first attempt at creating a discourse annotated Tamil corpus, we are planning to conduct future work involving multiple annotators which would yield information on annotation metrics like inter-annotator agreement, for example. Our work and results would also be useful for similar approaches in other morphologically rich and related South Indian languages such as Malayalam, Kannada, Telugu, etc.

We will also work on a way in which the discourse annotations have been performed will help in augmenting the information provided during dependency annotations at the sentence-level.

Acknowledgments

We are grateful to Prof. Aravind Joshi and Prof. Rashmi Prasad of University of Pennsylvania and Prof. Bonnie Webber of University of Edinburgh for their valuable assistance and feedback.

We would like to thank Prof. Rajeev Sangal of IIIT Hyderabad for his timely guidance and useful inputs. We also acknowledge the role of Sudheer Kolachina in the discussions we had in the writing of this paper.

References

Eleni Miltsakaki, Rashmi Prasad, Aravind Joshi and Bonnie Webber. 2004. The Penn Discourse Treebank. Proceedings of LREC-2004.

Rashmi Prasad, Samar Husain, Dipti Mishra Sharma and Aravind Joshi. 2008. Towards an Annotated Corpus of Discourse Relations in Hindi. Proceedings of IJCNLP-2008.

Rashmi Prasad, Eleni Miltsakaki, Nikhil Dinesh, Alan Lee, Aravind Joshi, Livio Robaldo and Bonnie Webber. 2007. The Penn Discourse Tree Bank 2.0 Annotation Manual. December 17, 2007.

Bonnie Webber and Aravind Joshi. 1998. Anchoring a lexicalized tree-adjoining grammar for discourse. In Manfred Stede, Leo Wanner, and Eduard Hovy, editors, Discourse Relations and Discourse Markers: Proceedings of the Conference, pages 86-92. Association of Computational Linguistics.

Nianwen Xue. 2005. Annotating Discourse Connectives in the Chinese Treebank. Proceedings of the ACL Workshop on Frontiers in Corpus Annotation II: Pie in the Sky.

Deniz Zeyrek and Bonnie Webber. 2008. A Discourse Resource for Turkish: Annotating Discourse Connectives in the METU Corpus. Proceedings of IJCNLP-2008.

A Gold Standard Corpus of Early Modern German

Silke Scheible, Richard J. Whitt, Martin Durrell and **Paul Bennett**
School of Languages, Linguistics, and Cultures
University of Manchester
Silke.Scheible, Richard.Whitt@manchester.ac.uk
Martin.Durrell, Paul.Bennett@manchester.ac.uk

Abstract

This paper describes an annotated gold standard sample corpus of Early Modern German containing over 50,000 tokens of text manually annotated with POS tags, lemmas, and normalised spelling variants. The corpus is the first resource of its kind for this variant of German, and represents an ideal test bed for evaluating and adapting existing NLP tools on historical data. We describe the corpus format, annotation levels, and challenges, providing an example of the requirements and needs of smaller humanities-based corpus projects.

1 Introduction

This paper describes work which is part of a larger project whose goal is to develop a representative corpus of Early Modern German from 1650-1800. The GerManC corpus was born out of the need for a resource to facilitate comparative studies of the development and standardisation of English and German in the 17th and 18th centuries. One major goal is to annotate GerManC with linguistic information in terms of POS tags, lemmas, and normalised spelling variants. However, due to the lexical, morphological, syntactic, and graphemic peculiarities characteristic of Early Modern German, automatic annotation of the texts poses a major challenge. Most existing NLP tools are tuned to perform well on modern language data, but perform considerably worse on historical, non-standardised data (Rayson et al., 2007). This paper describes a gold standard subcorpus of GerManC which has been manually annotated by two human annotators for POS tags, lemmas, and normalised spelling variants. The corpus will be used to test and adapt modern NLP tools on historical data, and will be of interest to other current corpus-based projects in historical linguistics (Jurish, 2010; Fasshauer, 2011; Dipper, 2010).

2 Corpus design

2.1 GerManC

In order to enable corpus-linguistic investigations, the GerManC corpus aims to be representative on three different levels. First of all, the corpus includes a range of text types: four orally-oriented genres (dramas, newspapers, letters, and sermons), and four print-oriented ones (narrative prose, and humanities, scientific, and legal texts). Secondly, in order to enable historical developments to be traced, the period has been divided into three fifty year sections (1650-1700, 1700-1750, and 1750-1800). The combination of historical and text-type coverage should enable research on the evolution of style in different genres (cf. Biber and Finegan, 1989). Finally, the corpus also aims to be representative with respect to region, including five broad dialect areas: North German, West Central, East Central, West Upper (including Switzerland), and East Upper German (including Austria). Per genre, period, and region, three extracts of around 2000 words are selected, yielding a corpus size of nearly a million words. The structure of the GerManC corpus is summarised in Table 1.

2.2 GerManC-GS

In order to facilitate a thorough linguistic investigation of the data, the final version of the Ger-

Proceedings of the Fifth Law Workshop (LAW V), pages 124–128,
Portland, Oregon, 23-24 June 2011. ©2011 Association for Computational Linguistics

Periods	Regions	Genres
1650-1700	North	Drama
1700-1750	West Central	Newspaper
1750-1800	East Central	Letter
	West Upper	Sermon
	East Upper	Narrative
		Humanities
		Scientific
		Legal

Table 1: Structure of the GerManC corpus

ManC corpus aims to provide the following linguistic annotations: 1.) Normalised spelling variants; 2.) Lemmas; 3.) POS tags. However, due to the non-standard nature of written Early Modern German, and the additional variation introduced by the three variables of 'genre', 'region', and 'time', automatic annotation of the corpus poses a major challenge. In order to assess the suitability of existing NLP tools on historical data, and with a view to adapting them to improve their performance, a manually annotated gold standard subcorpus has been developed, which aims to be as representative of the main corpus as possible (GerManC-GS). To remain manageable in terms of annotation times and cost, the subcorpus considers only two of the three corpus variables, 'genre' and 'time', as they alone were found to display as much if not more variation than 'region'. GerManC-GS thus only includes texts from the North German dialect region, with one sample file per genre and time period. Table 2 provides an overview of GerManC-GS, showing publication year, file name, and number of tokens for each genre/period combination. It contains 57,845 tokens in total, which have been manually annotated as described in the following sections.

2.3 Corpus format

As transcription of historical texts needs to be very detailed with regard to document structure, glossing, damaged or illegible passages, foreign language material and special characters such as diacritics and ligatures, the raw input texts have been annotated according to the guidelines of the Text Encoding Initiative (TEI)[1] during manual transcription. The TEI have published a set of XML-based encoding conventions recommended for meta-textual markup to minimise inconsistencies across projects and to maximise mutual usability and data interchange.

The GerManC corpus has been marked up using the TEI P5 Lite tagset, which serves as standard for many humanities-based projects. Only the most relevant tags have been selected to keep the document structure as straightforward as possible. Figure 1 shows structural annotation of a drama excerpt, including headers, stage directions, speakers, as well as lines.

```
<div type="act" n="2"><head>Anderer Handlung.</head>
<div type="scene" n="1"><head>Erster Auftritt.</head>
 <head>Ein Ko&#868;niglicher Hof.</head>
 <stage>Telamides.</stage>
 <sp who="Telemides">
  <l>IHr Go&#868;tter ach mit was Vergnu&#868;gen/</l>
  <l>hab ich <hi rend="antiqua">Aspasien</hi>
   geho&#868;ret und gesehn?</l>
  <l>wiewol es nicht vor mich geschehn/</l>
  <l>was ich mit ihr geredt. Weil ich aus treuen Muth/</l>
  <l>allein des Freundes Liebes-Bluth</l>
  <l>ihr auf das beste vorgestellt/</l>
  <l>und meine selbst dabey verschwiegen</l>
  <l>vor ein verliebtes Hertze/ fa&#868;llt</l>
  <l>zwar die Berrichtung schwer.</l>
```

Figure 1: TEI annotation of raw corpus

3 Linguistic annotation

GerManC-GS has been annotated with linguistic information in terms of normalised word forms, lemmas, and POS tags. To reduce manual labour, a semi-automatic approach was chosen whose output was manually corrected by two trained annotators. The following paragraphs provide an overview of the annotation types and the main challenges encountered during annotation.

3.1 Tokenisation and sentence boundaries

As German orthography was not yet codified in the Early Modern period, word boundaries were difficult to determine at times. Clitics and multi-word tokens are particularly difficult issues: lack of standardisation means that clitics can occur in various different forms, some of which are difficult to tokenise (e.g. *wirstu* instead of *wirst du*). Multi-word tokens, on the other hand, represent a problem as the same expression may be sometimes treated as compound (e.g. *obgleich*), but written separately at other times (*ob gleich*). Our tokenisation scheme takes clitics into account, but does not yet deal with multiword tokens. This means that whitespace characters usually act as token boundaries.

[1] http://www.tei-c.org

Genre	P	Year	File name	Tokens	Genre	P	Year	File name	Tokens
	1	1673	Leonilda	2933		**1**	1659	Herkules	2345
DRAM	**2**	1749	AlteJungfer	2835	**NARR**	**2**	1706	SatyrischerRoman	2379
	3	1767	Minna	3037		**3**	1790	AntonReiser	2551
	1	1667	Ratseburg	2563		**1**	1666	Berlin1	1132
HUMA	**2**	1737	Königstein	2308	**NEWS**	**2**	1735	Berlin	2273
	3	1772	Ursprung	2760		**3**	1786	Wolfenbuettel1	1506
	1	1673	BergOrdnung	2534		**1**	1672	Prognosticis	2323
LEGA	**2**	1707	Reglement	2467	**SCIE**	**2**	1734	Barometer	2438
	3	1757	Rostock	2414		**3**	1775	Chemie	2303
	1	1672	Guericke	2473		**1**	1677	LeichSermon	2585
LETT	**2**	1748	Borchward	2557	**SERM**	**2**	1730	JubelFeste	2523
	3	1798	Arndt	2314		**3**	1770	Gottesdienst	2292
								Total number of tokens	**57,845**

Table 2: GerManC-GS design

Annotation of sentence boundaries is also affected by the non-standard nature of the data. Punctuation is not standardised in Early Modern German and varies considerably across the corpus. For example, the virgule symbol "/" was often used in place of both comma and full-stop, which proves problematic for sentence boundary detection.

3.2 Normalising spelling variants and lemmatisation

One of the key challenges in working with historical texts is the large amount of spelling variation they contain. As most existing NLP tools (such as POS-taggers or parsers) are tuned to perform well on modern language data, they are not usually able to account for variable spelling, resulting in lower overall performance (Rayson et al., 2007). Likewise, modern search engines do not take spelling variation into account and are thus often unable to retrieve all occurrences of a given historical search word. Both issues have been addressed in previous work through the task of spelling normalisation. Ernst-Gerlach and Fuhr (2006) and Pilz and Luther (2009) have created a tool that can generate variant spellings for historical German to retrieve relevant instances of a given modern lemma, while Baron and Rayson (2008) and Jurish (2010) have implemented tools which normalise spelling variants in order to achieve better performance of NLP tools such as POS taggers (by running the tools on the normalised input). Our annotation of spelling variants aims to compromise between these two approaches by allowing for historically accurate linguistic searches, while also aiming to maximise the performance of automatic annotation tools. We treat the task of normalising spelling variation as a type of pre-lemmatisation, where each word token occurring in a text is labelled with a normalised head variant. As linguistic search requires a historically accurate treatment of spelling variation, our scheme has a preference for treating two seemingly similar tokens as separate items on historical grounds (e.g. *etwan* vs. *etwa*). However, the scheme normalises variants to a modernised form even where the given lexical item has since died out (e.g. obsolete verbs ending in *-iren* are normalised to *-ieren*), in order to support automatic tools using morphological strategies such as suffix probabilities (Schmid, 1994).

Lemmatisation resolves the normalised variant to a base lexeme in modern form, using Duden[2] pre-reform spelling. With obsolete words, the leading form in Grimm's Deutsches Wörterbuch[3] is taken.

3.3 POS-Tagging

We introduce a modified version of the STTS tagset (Schiller et al., 1999), the STTS-EMG tagset, to account for important differences between modern and Early Modern German (EMG), and to facilitate more accurate searches. The tagset merges two categories, as the criteria for distinguishing them are not applicable in EMG (1.), and provides a number of additional ones to account for special EMG constructions (2. to 6.):

[2]http://www.duden.de/

[3]http://www.dwb.uni-trier.de/

1. **PIAT** (merged with **PIDAT**): Indefinite determiner (occurring on its own, or in conjunction with another determiner), as in '*viele solche* *Bemerkungen*'
2. **NA**: Adjectives used as nouns, as in '*der* ***Gesandte***'
3. **PAVREL**: Pronominal adverb used as relative, as in '*die Puppe,* ***damit*** *sie spielt*'
4. **PTKREL**: Indeclinable relative particle, as in '*die Fälle,* ***so*** *aus Schwachheit entstehen*'
5. **PWAVREL**: Interrogative adverb used as relative, as in '*der Zaun,* ***worüber*** *sie springt*'
6. **PWREL**: Interrogative pronoun used as relative, as in '*etwas,* ***was*** *er sieht*'

Around 2.0% (1132) of all tokens in the corpus have been tagged with one of the above POS categories, of which the merged PIAT class contains the majority (657 tokens). The remaining 475 cases occur as NA (291), or as one of the new relative markers PWAVREL (69), PWREL (57), PTKREL (38), and PAVREL (20).

4 Annotation procedure and agreement

In order to produce the gold standard annotations in GerManC-GS we used the GATE platform, which facilitates automatic as well as manual annotation (Cunningham et al, 2002). Initially, GATE's German Language plugin[4] was used to obtain word tokens and sentence boundaries. The output was manually inspected and corrected by one annotator, who manually added a layer of normalised spelling variants (NORM). This annotation layer was then used as input for the TreeTagger (Schmid, 1994), obtaining annotations in terms of lemmas (LEMMA) and POS tags (POS). All annotations (NORM, LEMMA, and POS) were subsequently corrected by two annotators, and all disagreements were reconciled to produce the gold standard. Table 3 shows the overall agreement for the three annotation types across GerManC-GS (measured in accuracy).

The agreement values demonstrate that normalised word forms and lemmas are relatively easy to determine for the annotators, with 96.9% and 95.5% agreement, respectively. POS tags, on the other, represent more of a challenge with only 91.6%

[4]http://gate.ac.uk/sale/tao/splitch15.html

	NORM	**LEMMA**	**POS**
Agreed tokens (out of 57,845)	56,052	55,217	52,959
Accuracy (%)	**96.9%**	**95.5%**	**91.6%**

Table 3: Inter-annotator agreement

agreement between two annotators, which is considerably lower than the agreement level reported for annotating a corpus of modern German using STTS, at 98.6% (Brants, 2000a). While a more detailed analysis of the results remains to be carried out, an initial study shows that POS agreement is lower in earlier texts (89.3% in Period P1) compared to later ones (93.1% in P3). It is likely that a substantial amount of disagreements in the earlier texts are due to the larger number of unfamiliar word forms and variants on the one hand, and foreign word tokens on the other. These represent a problem as from a modern view point it is not always easy to decide which words were 'foreign' to a language and which ones 'native'.

5 Future work

The gold standard corpus described in this paper will be used to test and adapt modern NLP tools on Early Modern German data. Initial experiments focus on utilising the layer of normalised spelling variants to improve tagger performance, and investigating to what extent normalisation can be reliably automated (Jurish, 2010). We further plan to retrain state-of-the-art POS taggers such as the TreeTagger and TnT Tagger (Brants, 2000b) on our data.

Finally, we plan to investigate how linguistic annotations can be automatically integrated in the TEI-annotated version of the corpus to produce TEI-conformant output. Currently, both structural and linguistic annotations are merged in GATE stand-off XML format, which, as a consequence, is no longer TEI-conformant. In the interest of interoperability and comparative studies between corpora we aim to contribute towards the development of clearer procedures whereby structural and linguistic annotations might be merged (Scheible et al., 2010).

References

Alistair Baron and Paul Rayson. 2008. VARD 2: A tool for dealing with spelling variation in historical corpora. *Proceedings of the Postgraduate Conference in Corpus Linguistics, Birmingham, UK.*

Douglas Biber and Edward Finegan. 1989. Drift and the evolution of English style: a history of three genres. *Language 65. 487-517.*

Torsten Brants. 2000a. Inter-annotator agreement for a German newspaper corpus. *Second International Conference on Language Resources and Evaluation (LREC 2000), Athens, Greece.*

Torsten Brants. 2000b. TnT – a statistical part-of-speech tagger. *Proceedings of the 6th Applied NLP Conference, ANLP-2000, Seattle, WA.*

Hamish Cunningham, Diana Maynard, Kalina Bontcheva, and Valentin Tablan. 2002. GATE: A framework and graphical development environment for robust NLP tools and applications. *Proceedings of the 40th Anniversary Meeting of the Association for Computational Linguistics.*

Stefanie Dipper. 2010. POS-Tagging of historical language data: First experiments in semantic approaches in Natural Language Processing. *Proceedings of the 10th Conference on Natural Language Processing (KONVENS-10). Saarbrücken, Germany. 117-121.*

Andrea Ernst-Gerlach and Norbert Fuhr. 2006. Generating search term variants for text collections with historic spellings. *Proceedings of the 28th European Conference on Information Retrieval Research (ECIR 2006), London, UK.*

Vera Fasshauer. 2011. http://www.indogermanistik.uni-jena.de/index.php?auswahl=184
Accessed 30/03/2011.

Bryan Jurish. 2010. Comparing canonicalizations of historical German text. *Proceedings of the 11th Meeting of the ACL Special Interest Group on Computational Morphology and Phonology (SIGMORPHON), Uppsala, Sweden. 72-77.*

Thomas Pilz and Wolfram Luther. 2009. Automated support for evidence retrieval in documents with nonstandard orthography. *The Fruits of Empirical Linguistics. Sam Featherston and Susanne Winkler (eds.). 211–228.*

Paul Rayson, Dawn Archer, Alistair Baron, Jonathan Culpeper, and Nicholas Smith. 2007. Tagging the Bard: Evaluating the accuracy of a modern POS tagger on Early Modern English corpora. *Proceedings of the Corpus Linguistics Conference (CL2007), University of Birmingham, UK.*

Silke Scheible, Richard J. Whitt, Martin Durrell, and Paul Bennett. 2010. Annotating a Historical Corpus of German: A Case Study. *Proceedings of the LREC 2010 Workshop on Language Resources and Language Technology Standards, Valletta, Malta.*

Anne Schiller, Simone Teufel, Christine Stöckert, and Christine Thielen. 1999. Guidelines für das Tagging deutscher Textcorpora mit STTS. *Technical Report. Institut für maschinelle Sprachverarbeitung, Stuttgart.*

Helmut Schmid. 1994. Probabilistic part-of-speech tagging using decision trees. *International Conference on New Methods in Language Processing, Manchester, UK. 44–49.*

MAE and MAI: Lightweight Annotation and Adjudication Tools

Amber Stubbs
Department of Computer Science
Brandeis University MS 018
Waltham, Massachusetts, 02454 USA
astubbs@cs.brandeis.edu

Abstract

MAE and MAI are lightweight annotation and adjudication tools for corpus creation. DTDs are used to define the annotation tags and attributes, including extent tags, link tags, and non-consuming tags. Both programs are written in Java and use a stand-alone SQLite database for storage and retrieval of annotation data. Output is in stand-off XML.

1 Introduction

The use of machine learning for natural language processing tasks has been steadily increasing over the years: text processing challenges such as those associated with the SemEval workshops (Erk and Strapparava, 2010) and the I2B2 medical informatics shared tasks (i2b2 team, 2011) are well known, and tools for training and testing algorithms on corpora, such as the Natural Language Tool Kit (Bird et al., 2009) and the WEKA tools (Hall et al., 2009) are widely used.

However, a key component for training a machine for a task is having sufficient data for the computer to learn from. In order to create these corpora, human researchers must define the tasks that they wish to accomplish and find ways to encode the necessary information, usually in some form of XML, then have relevant data annotated with XML tags.

The necessity of corpus annotation has led to a number of useful tools, as well as assessments for tool usability and standards for linguistic annotation. A recent survey (Dipper et al., 2004) examined what attributes an annotation tool should have for it to be most useful, and the Linguistic Annotation Framework (LAF) describes the desired properties of an annotation framework to ensure interoperability and utility (Ide and Romary, 2006).

The Multi-purpose Annotation Environment (MAE), and the Multi-document Adjudication Interface (MAI) were designed to be easy to begin using, but have enough flexibility to provide a starting point for most annotation tasks. Both programs are written in Java and use a stand-alone SQLite database[1] for storage and retrieval of annotation data, and output standoff XML that is compliant with the abstract LAF model. Both of these tools are available from http://pages.cs.brandeis.edu/~astubbs/

2 Related Work

As previously mentioned, there are already a number of annotation tools in use—Dipper et al. examined five different programs; additionally Knowtator (Ogren, 2006), GATE (Cunningham et al., 2010), Callisto (MITRE, 2002), and BAT (Verhagen, 2010) have been used for various annotation tasks; and the list goes on[2]. However, as Kaplan et al. noted in a paper about their own annotation software, SLAT 2.0 (2010), much annotation software is not generic, either because it was designed for a specific annotation task, or designed to be used in a particular way. BAT, for example, utilizes a layered annotation framework, which allows for adjudication at each step of the annotation process, but this makes

[1] http://www.zentus.com/sqlitejdbc/

[2] See http://annotation.exmaralda.org/index.php/Tools for a reasonably up-to-date list of annotation software

Proceedings of the Fifth Law Workshop (LAW V), pages 129–133,
Portland, Oregon, 23-24 June 2011.

tasks difficult to modify and is best suited for use when the schema is not likely to change. GATE was built primarily as a tool for automated annotation, and Callisto, while excellent for annotating contiguous portions of texts, cannot easily create links—it requires the user to create an entire task-specific plug-in. Knowtator provides links and extent tagging, but comes as a plug-in for Protégé[3], a level of overhead that users may find daunting. Similarly, the Apache UIMA system (Apache, 2006) is well developed and supported but presents a very steep learning curve for task creation.

As for adjudication, while some software has built-in judgment capabilities (GATE, BAT, Knowtator, and SLAT, for example), that functionality does not stand alone, but rather relies on the annotations being done in the same environment.

All of the tools mentioned are well-suited for their purposes, but it seems that there is room for an annotation tool that allows for reasonably complex annotation tasks without requiring a lot of time for setup.

3 Simple Task Creation

One of the defining factors that Dipper et al. (2004) identified in evaluating annotation tools is simplicity of use–how long does it take to start annotating? Upon examining various existing annotation tools, they found that there was often a trade-off between simplicity and data quality assurance: tools that have an open interface and loose restrictions for tag sets tended to have lower quality data output, while tools that require a specification could output better data, but took a little longer to get running.

MAE and MAI attempt to find a middle ground between the two extremes: they require task definitions in the form of slightly customized Document Type Definition (DTD) files, which are used to define the tags and their attributes but are not difficult to create or modify[4].

There are two types of tags that are primarily used in annotation: extent tags (sometimes called 'segments' (Noguchi et al., 2008)) which are used to mark a contiguous portion of text as having a specific characteristic, and link tags, which are used to create a relationship between two extent tags. MAE and MAI support both of these tag types, and additionally support non-consuming extent tags, which can be useful for having an annotator mark explicitly whether or not a particular phenomena appears in the document being annotated.

DTD creation is quite simple. If, for example, an annotator wanted to look at nouns and mark their types, they could define the following:

```
<!ELEMENT NOUN (#PCDATA)>
<!ATTLIST NOUN type
  (person|place|thing|other)>
```

The "#PCDATA" in the first line informs the software that NOUN is an extent tag, and the second line gives NOUN an attribute called "type", with the possible values defined in the list in parenthesis.

Creating a link is equally simple:

```
<!ELEMENT ACTION EMPTY >
<!ATTLIST ACTION relationship
   (performs|performed_by)>
```

The "EMPTY" marker indicates that the tag is a link, and the attributes and attribute values work the same way as for extent tags.

4 MAE

Once the DTD is created and files are preprocessed, the user loads the DTD and a file into MAE. The text to be annotated appears in the window, and a window at the bottom of the screen holds a table for each tag (see Figure 1). When a user selects an extent and creates a tag, some information about the tag is automatically added to the table: the start and end locations of the tag, and the text of the extent. Additionally, MAE will automatically generate a document-unique ID number for that tag so that it can easily be referenced in links.

The user can then add in any information about the attributes by filling in the table at the bottom of the screen. In the text window, the color of the extent that has been tagged is changed to the color associated with that tag. If there are multiple tags in a location, the text is underlined as well. Highlighting tagged text in the window will also highlight any table rows associated with that tag, including link tags. This makes it easy for the annotator to see what information has already been added about that text.

[3]http://protege.stanford.edu/

[4]In the future, a GUI will be added to MAE that will make the DTD creation process easier.

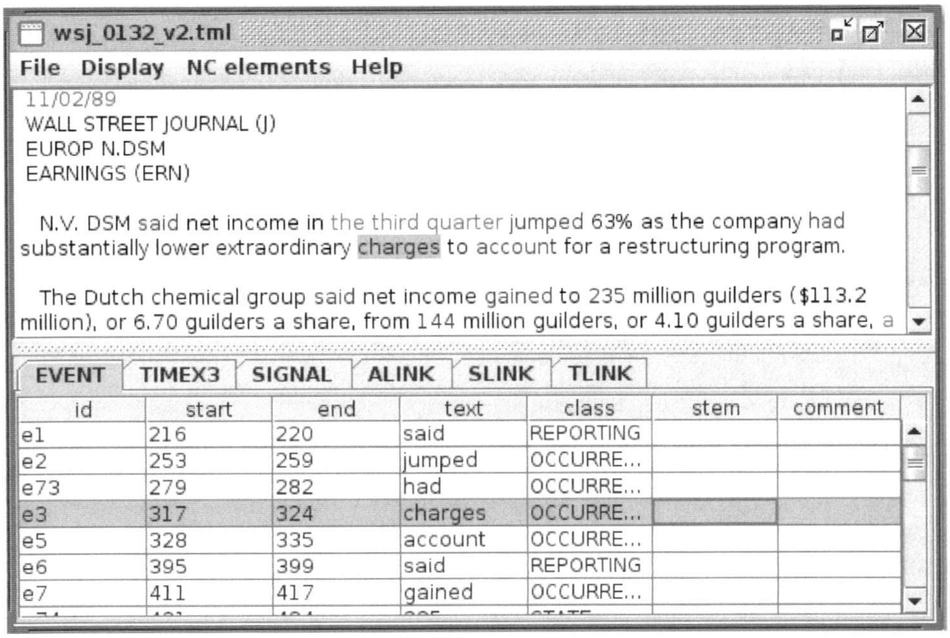

Figure 1: TimeML annotation in MAE.

Non-consuming tags are created from the menu at the top of the screen. Links are created by holding down the control key (or the command key on Macs) and clicking on the two tags that will be linked. A window pops up that allows the user to link either to the tags at the specified locations, or to any non-consuming tags that have been created in the document.

5 Output

Once the user is done annotating, they can save their work in an XML file. MAE outputs (and takes as input) UTF-8 encoded files, so it can be used to annotate any character set that is representable in UTF-8, including Chinese. The output is compliant with the LAF guidelines (Ide and Romary, 2006).

5.1 System testing

MAE is currently being used for a variety of annotation tasks: medical record annotation, eligibility criteria assessment, and for a university course on corpus creation. Annotation tasks in that course range from opinion annotation to tense and aspect in Chinese verbs. It is currently being used on Windows, Mac, and Linux.

6 MAI

MAI is built on the same back-end code as MAE, making them easily compatible. Like MAE, using MAI begins with loading a DTD. Then the adjudicator can load each annotation of a text that they would like to create a gold standard for. As each new document is added, MAI loads the tag information for each annotation into the database for quick reference.

Once all the files are loaded, the adjudicator selects the tag they want to review from the left part of the screen. The text is then color-coded to reflect the agreement of the annotators: blue if all the annotators agree that a tag of the selected type should be at a location, red if only a subset would place a tag there, and black for locations where no tag is present (see Figure 2).

When text is highlighted by the adjudicator, the information about each annotator's tag and attributes for that location is filled in on a table to the right of the screen. From there, the annotator can either fill in the values for the gold standard by hand, or copy the values from one annotator directly into the gold standard column and modifying them as needed. Once the adjudicator is satisfied with the gold standard they can add the annotation to the database by

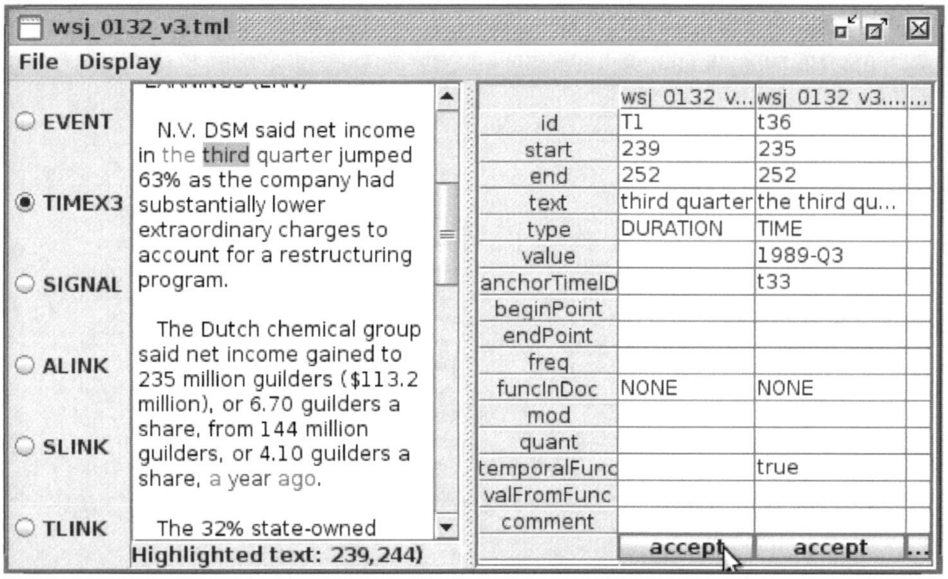

Figure 2: The extent adjudication table in MAI

clicking the "accept/modify" button at the bottom of the gold standard column. At this point, MAI will generate a new ID for that tag, and the color of the adjudicated font will become green.

At the time of this writing, the algorithms for link and non-consuming tag adjudication have not been fully worked out for use inside of MAI. However, once the extent tags have been adjudicated, the annotator can choose to export the non-consuming tags and link tags that involve "approved" extent tags into an XML file, along with the adjudicated extents. This partially-judged file can then be loaded into MAE, where it is easier to display and modify all the relevant information.

6.1 System testing

As with MAE, MAI has been used for the various annotation projects for a course on corpus creation, as well as a medical record annotation task. This program is still under development, but so far adjudications tasks with MAI have proved successful.

7 Conclusions and Future Work

While MAE and MAI do not represent a new frontier in annotation software, I believe that their ease of use, portability, and clean visualization will make them useful tools for annotation projects that do not want to invest in the time required to use other existing software, and for adjudicators that want an easy way to fix discrepancies between annotators. Admittedly, tasks involving heirarchical annotations would require one of the more sophisticated tools that are currently available, but there are still many tasks that do not require that level of complexity that MAE and MAI can be used for.

There is room for improvement in both of these programs: fully implementing link adjudication in MAI, allowing for more customization in the visualizations would make them more enjoyable to use, and expanding the functionality to make them more useful for more tasks (for example, allowing links with multiple anchors instead of just two). Both MAE and MAI are under development, and improvements to both will be made over the coming months.

Acknowledgments

Funding for this project development was provided by NIH grant NIHR21LM009633-02, PI: James Pustejovsky

Many thanks to the annotators who helped me identify bugs in the software, particularly Cornelia Parkes, Cheryl Keenan, BJ Harshfield, and all the students in the Brandeis University Spring 2011 Computer Science 216 class.

References

Apache. 2006. Unstructured information management architecture. http://uima.apache.org/.

Steven Bird, Ewan Klein, and Edward Loper. 2009. *Natural Language Processing with Python*. O'Reilly Media Inc, Sebastopol, CA, first edition edition.

Hamish Cunningham, Diana Maynard, Kalina Bontcheva, Valentin Tablan, Niraj Aswani, and Ian Roberts, 2010. *Developing Language Processing Components with GATE*, 5 edition, July.

Stefanie Dipper, Michael Götze, and Manfred Stede. 2004. Simple annotation tools for complex annotation tasks: an evaluation. In *Proceedings of the LREC Workshop on XML-based Richly Annotated Corpora*, pages 54–62, Lisbon, Portugal.

Katrin Erk and Carlo Strapparava. 2010. Semeval-2. http://semeval2.fbk.eu/semeval2.php.

Mark Hall, Eibe Frank, Geoffrey Holmes, Bernhard Pfahringer, Peter Reutemann, and Ian H. Witten. 2009. The weka data mining software: An update. *SIGKDD Explorations*, 11(1).

i2b2 team. 2011. i2b2 shared task. https://www.i2b2.org/NLP/Coreference/Main.php. accessed Feb. 2011.

Nancy Ide and Laurent Romary. 2006. Representing linguistic corpora and their annotations. In *Proceedings of the Fifth Language Resources and Evaluation Conference (LREC*.

Dain Kaplan, Ryu Iida, and Takenobu Tokunaga. 2010. Slat 2.0: Corpus construction and annotation process management. In *Proceedings of the 16th Annual Meeting of The Association for Natural Language Processing*, pages pp.510 – 513.

MITRE. 2002. Callisto website. http://callisto.mitre.org/index.html. accessed Dec. 17, 2010.

Masaki Noguchi, Kenta Miyoshi, Takenobu Tokunaga, Ryu Iida, Mamoru Komachi, and Kentaro Inui. 2008. Multiple purpose annotation using slat - segment and link-based annotation tool -. In *Proceedings of 2nd Linguistic Annotation Workshop*, pages pp.61 – 64.

Philip V. Ogren. 2006. Knowtator: a protégé plug-in for annotated corpus construction. In *Proceedings of the 2006 Conference of the North American Chapter of the Association for Computational Linguistics on Human Language Technology*, pages 273–275, Morristown, NJ, USA. Association for Computational Linguistics.

Marc Verhagen. 2010. The brandeis annotation tool. In Nicoletta Calzolari (Conference Chair), Khalid Choukri, Bente Maegaard, Joseph Mariani, Jan Odijk, Stelios Piperidis, Mike Rosner, and Daniel Tapias, editors, *Proceedings of the Seventh conference on International Language Resources and Evaluation (LREC'10)*, Valletta, Malta, may. European Language Resources Association (ELRA).

Empty Categories in Hindi Dependency Treebank: Analysis and Recovery

Chaitanya GSK
Intl Institute of Info. Technology
Hyderabad, India
chaitanya.gsk
@research.iiit.ac.in

Samar Husain
Intl Institute of Info. Technology
Hyderabad, India
samar
@research.iiit.ac.in

Prashanth Mannem
Intl Institute of Info. Technology
Hyderabad, India
prashanth
@research.iiit.ac.in

Abstract

In this paper, we first analyze and classify the empty categories in a Hindi dependency treebank and then identify various discovery procedures to automatically detect the existence of these categories in a sentence. For this we make use of lexical knowledge along with the parsed output from a constraint based parser. Through this work we show that it is possible to successfully discover certain types of empty categories while some other types are more difficult to identify. This work leads to the state-of-the-art system for automatic insertion of empty categories in the Hindi sentence.

1 Introduction

Empty categories play a crucial role in the annotation framework of the Hindi dependency treebank[1] (Begum et al., 2008; Bharati et al., 2009b). They are inserted in a sentence in case the dependency analysis does not lead to a fully connected tree. In the Hindi treebank, an empty category (denoted by a NULL node) always has at least one child. These elements have essentially the same properties (e.g. case-marking, agreement, etc.) as an overtly realized element and they provide valuable information (such as predicate-argument structure, etc.). A different kind of motivation for postulating empty categories comes from the demands of natural lan- guage processing, in particular parsing. There are several types of empty categories in the Hindi dependency treebank serving different purposes. The presence of these elements can be crucial for correct automatic parsing. Traditional parsing algorithms do not insert empty categories and require them to be part of the input. The performance of such parser will be severely affected if one removes these elements from the input data. Statistical parsers like MaltParser (Nivre, 2003), MSTParser (McDonald, 2005), as well as Constraint Based Hybrid Parser (CBHP) (Bharati et al., 2009a) produce incorrect parse trees once the empty categories are removed from the input data. Hence there is a need for automatic detection and insertion of empty categories in the Hindi data. Additionally, it is evident that successful detection of such nodes will help the annotation process as well.

There have been many approaches for the recovery of empty categories in the treebanks like Penn treebank, both ML based (Collins, 1997; Johnson, 2002; Dienes and Dubey, 2003a,b; Higgins, 2003) and rule based (R Campbell, 2004). Some approaches such as Yang and Xue (2010) follow a post processing step of recovering empty categories after parsing the text.

In this paper we make use of lexical knowledge along with the parsed output from a constraint based parser to successfully insert empty category in the input sentence, which may further be given for parsing or other applications. Throughout this paper, we use the term recovery (of empty categories) for the insertion of different types of empty categories into the input sentence.

The paper is arranged as follows, Section 2 discusses the empty nodes in the treebank and classifies

[1] The dependency treebank is part of a Multi Representational and Multi-Layered Treebank for Hindi/Urdu (Palmer et al., 2009).

Proceedings of the Fifth Law Workshop (LAW V), pages 134–142,
Portland, Oregon, 23-24 June 2011. ©2011 Association for Computational Linguistics

NULL_NP tokens	69
NULL_VG tokens	68
NULL_CCP tokens	32
Sentences with more than one empty category in them	159

Table 1: Empty categories in Hindi Tree bank

them based on their syntactic type. In section 3 we provide an algorithm to automatically recover these elements. Section 4 shows the performance of our system and discusses the results. We conclude the paper in section 5.

2 An overview of Empty Categories in Hindi dependency Treebank

Begum et al., (2008) proposed a dependency framework in which an empty node is introduced during the annotation process only if its presence is required to build the dependency tree for the sentence (Figures 1, 2, 3) [2]. Empty categories such as those discussed in Bhatia et al. (2010) which would be leaf nodes in the dependency tree are not part of the dependency structure and are added during Propbanking[3]. Consequently, the empty categories in Hindi treebank do not mark displacement as in Penn treebank (Marcus et al., 1993) rather, they represent undisplaced syntactic elements which happen to lack phonological realization. In the Hindi dependency treebank, an empty category is represented by a 'NULL' word. Sentences can have a missing VG or NP or CCP [4]. These are represented by 'NULL' token and are marked with the appropriate Part-of-speech tag along with marking the chunk tag such as NULL_NP, NULL_VGF, NULL_CCP, etc. in Table 2

[2]Due to space constraints, sentences in all the figures only show chunk heads. Please refer to examples 1 to 6 for entire sentences with glosses

[3]These empty categories are either required to correctly capture the argument structure during propbanking or are required to successfully convert the dependency structure to phrase structure (Xia et al., 2009)

[4]VG is Verb Group, NP is Noun Phrase and CCP is Conjunct Phrase.

Type of empty categories	**Instances**	**Chunk tag** (CPOS)
Empty subject	69	NULL_NP
Backward gapping	29	NULL_VG
Forward gapping	21	NULL_VG
Finite verb ellipses	18	NULL_VG
Conjunction ellipses (verbs)	20	NULL_CCP
Conjunction ellipses (nouns)	12	NULL_CCP
Total	169	

Table 2: Empty category types.

2.1 Empty category types

From the empty categories recovery point of view, we have divided the empty categories in the treebank into six types (Table 2).

The first type of empty category is *Empty Subject (Figure 1), example.1* where a clause *'rava ke kaaran hi manmohan singh rajaneeti me aaye'* is dependent on the missing subject of the verb *'hai'* (is).

(1) NULL gaurtalab hai ki raao
NULL 'noticeable' 'is' 'that' 'Rao'
ke kaaran hi manmohan sing
'because' 'only' 'Manmohan' 'singh'
raajaniiti me aaye
'politics' 'in' 'came.

'it is noticeable that because of Rao, Manmohan Singh came in politics'

The second type of empty category is due to *Backward Gapping (Figure 2), example.2* where the verb is absent in the clause that occurs before a co-ordinating conjunct.

(2) doosare nambara para misa roosa
'second' 'position' 'on' 'miss' 'Russia'
natasha NULL aur tiisare nambara
'Natasha' NULL 'and' 'third' 'position'
para misa lebanan sendra rahiim .
'on' 'miss' 'Lebanan' 'Sandra' were' .

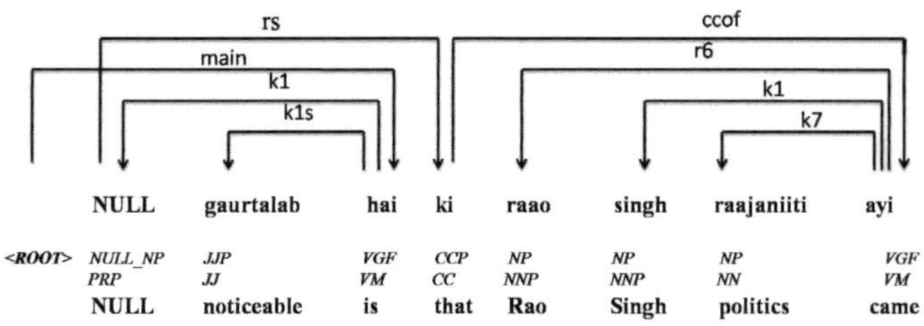

Figure 1: Empty Subject.

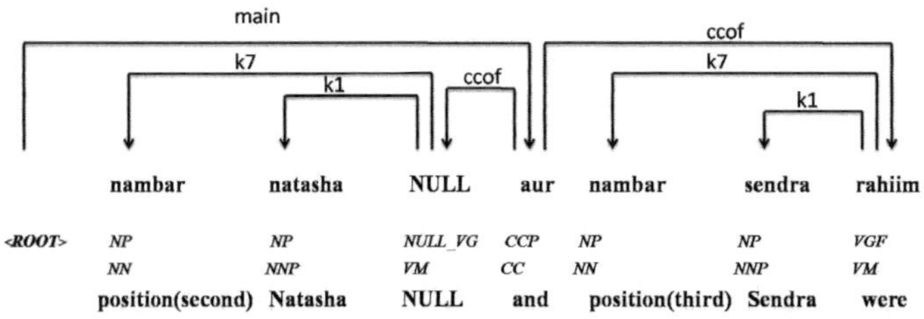

Figure 2: Backward Gapping.

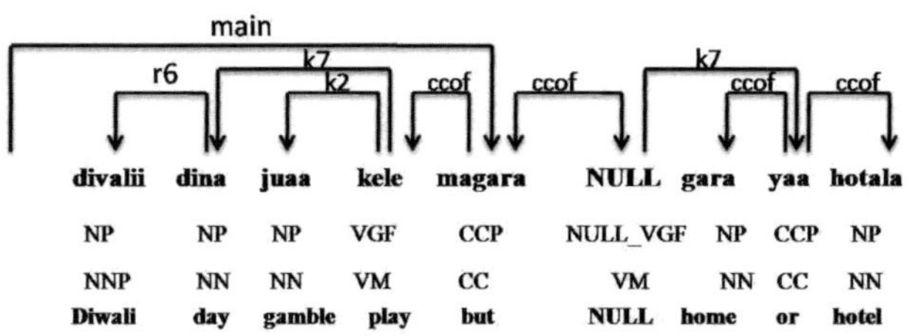

Figure 3: Forward Gapping.

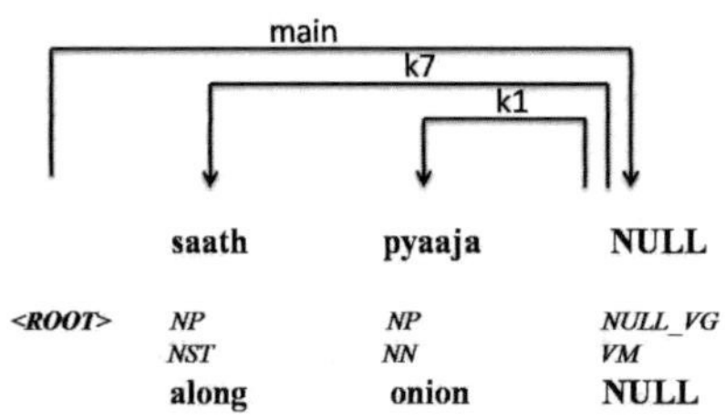

Figure 4: Finite verb ellipses.

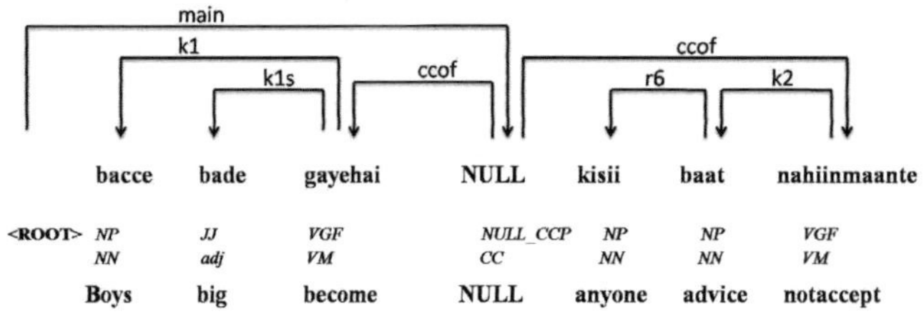

Figure 5: Conjunction ellipses (verbs).

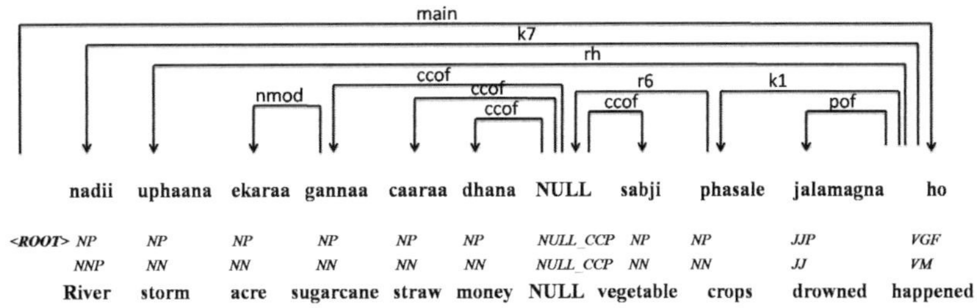

Figure 6: Conjunctuon ellipses (nouns).

'Miss Russia stood second and Miss Lebanan was third'

The third type of empty category is *Forward Gapping (Figure 3), example 3*, which is similar to the second type but with the clause with the missing verb occurring after the conjunct rather than before. The reason for a separate class for forward gapping is explained in the next section.

(3) divaalii ke dina jua Kele magara
'Diwali' 'GEN' 'day' 'gamble' 'play' 'but'
NULL gar me yaa hotala me
'NULL' 'home' 'in' 'or' 'hotel' 'in'

'Played gamble on Diwali day but was it at home or hotel'

The fourth type of empty category is due to *Finite verb ellipses (Figure4), example 4*, where the main verb for a sentence is missing.

(4) saath me vahii phevareta khadaa pyaaja
'along' 'in' 'that' 'favorite' 'raw' 'onion'
NULL.
NULL

'Along with this, the same favorite semi-cooked onion'

The fifth type of empty category is *Conjunction ellipses (Verbs), example 5 (Figure 5)*.

(5) bacce bare ho-ga-ye-hai NULL
'children' 'big' 'become' 'NULL'
kisii ki baat nahiin maante
'anyone' 'gen' 'advice' 'not' 'accept'

'The children have grown big (and) do not listen to anyone'

The sixth type of empty category is the *Conjunction ellipses (for nouns), example 6* (Figure 6).

(6) yamunaa nadii me uphaana se
'Yamuna' 'river' 'in' 'storm' 'INST'
sekado ekara gannaa, caaraa,
'thousands' 'acre' 'sugarcane' 'straw'
dhana, NULL sabjii kii phasale
'money' 'NULL' 'vegetable' 'GEN' 'crops'
jala-magna ho-gai-hai .
'drowned' 'happened'

'Because of the storm in the Yamuna river, thousand acres of sugarcane, straw, money, vegetable crops got submerged'

3 Empty categories recovery Algorithm

Given the limited amount of data available (only 159 sentences with at least one empty category in them out of 2973 sentences in the Hindi treebank, Table 12), we follow a rule based approach rather than using ML to recover the empty catogories discussed in the previous section. Interestingly, a rule-based approach was followed by R Campbell, (2004) that recovered empty categories in English resulting in better performance than previous empirical approaches. This work can be extended for ML once more data becomes available.

The techniques that are used for recovering empty categories in the Penn treebank (Collins, 1997; Johnson, 2002;) might not be suitable since the Penn treebank has all the empty categories as leaf nodes in the tree unlike the Hindi dependency treebank where

for each sentence in the input data
    try in *Empty Subject*
    try in *Forward Gapping*
    try in *Finite Verb ellipses*
for each tree in CBHP parse output
    try in *Backward Gapping*
    try in *Forward Gapping*
    try in *Finite Verb ellipses*
    try in *Conjunction ellipses (for Verbs)*

Table 3: Empty categories Recovery Algorithm.

the empty categories are always internal nodes in the dependency trees (Figure 2).

In this section we describe an algorithm which recovers empty categories given an input sentence. Our method makes use of both the lexical cues as well as the output of the Constraint Based Hybrid Parser (CBHP). Table 3 presents the recovery algorithm which first runs on the input sentence and then on the output of the CBHP.

3.1 Empty Subject

Framing rule 1 requires the formation of a set *(CueSet)* based on our analysis discussed in the previous section. It contains all the linguistic cues (lexical items such as *gaurtalab* 'noticeable', *maloom* 'known', etc). We then scan the input sentence searching for the cue and insert an empty category (NULL_NP)[5] if the cue is found. Table 4 illustates the process where we search for 'CueSet *he ki*' or 'CueSet *ho ki*' phrases. In Table 4, W+1 represents word next to W, W+2 represents word next to W+1.

3.2 Backward Gapping

To handle backward gapping cases, we take the intermediate parse output from CBHP [6] for the whole data. The reason behind choosing CBHP lies in its rule based approach. CBHP fails (or rather gives a visibly different parse) for sentences with missing verbs. And when it fails to find a verb, CBHP

[5] We insert a token 'NULL' with NULL_NP as CPOS

[6] CBHP is a two-stage parser. In the 1st stage it parses intra-clausal relations and inter-clausal relations in the 2nd stage. The 1st stage parse is an intermediate parse.

for each word W in the Sentence
if W ϵ *CueSet*
  if W+1 & W+2 = *he or ho & ki*
    Insert NULL with PRP as POS,
NULL_NP as CPOS

Table 4: Rule for identifying Empty Subject.

for each node N in tree T
  if head of N = ϕ
    insert N in unattached_subtrees[]
for each node X in unattached_subtrees[]
  while POS(X) is not VG
    traverse in the array of unattached_subtrees
    if $\exists$ a conjunct, then **recovery**=1
  if recovery = 1
    insert NULL, with VM as POS,
NULL_VG as CPOS
  Head of NULL = ϕ

Table 5: Rule for identifying Backward Gapping using CBHP.

gives unattached subtrees[7] (Figure 7, 8, 9 illustrates the unattached subtrees where the parser is unable to find a relation between the heads of each unattached subtree). Similarly whenever the parser expects a conjunction and the conjunction is absent in the sentence, CBHP again gives the unattached subtrees.

We analyze these unattached sub-trees to see whether there is a possibility for empty category. The array, in Table 5 represents all the nodes having no heads. POS represents part of speech and CPOS represents chunk part of speech and ϕ represents empty set.

3.3 Forward gapping

The main reason for handling the forward gapping as a separate case rather than considering it along with backward gapping is the prototypical SOV word-order of Hindi, i.e. the verb occurs after subject and object in a clause or sentence. We take the intermediate parse output from the CBHP for the whole data and when ever a verb is absent in a clause occurring immediately after a conjunct, we search for a VG af-

[7] CBHP gives fully connected trees in both the stages. We have modified the parser so that it gives unattached subtrees when it fails.

for each node N in tree T
  if head of N = ϕ
    insert N in unattached_subtrees[]
for each node X in unattached_subtrees[]
  if !$\exists$ a verb between two conjuncts
    if those conjuncts belongs to conjunct_set
      insert insert NULL with VM as POS,
NULL_VG as CPOS

Table 6: Rule for identifying Forward Gapping using CBHP.

for each word W in the sentence S
  if W ϵ CueSet_FG
    insert NULL with NULL_VG as POS
and CPOS
  if W = Conjunct
    if POS(W-1) = VG
      if !$\exists$ a VG in S-W
      insert NULL with VM as POS,
NULL_VG as CPOS

Table 7: Rule for identifying Forward Gapping .

ter the conjunct and insert an empty category if the VG is absent (an example of such cases can be seen in Figure 7). This procedure is given in Table 6. In addition, we use the lexical cues (such as *ya nahii* 'or not', *ya* 'or') for recovering certain types of empty categories. *CueSet_FG* is the set that contains the lexical cues and *conjunct_set* contains lexical cues like (*ki* and *ya*). This procedure is shown in Table 7.

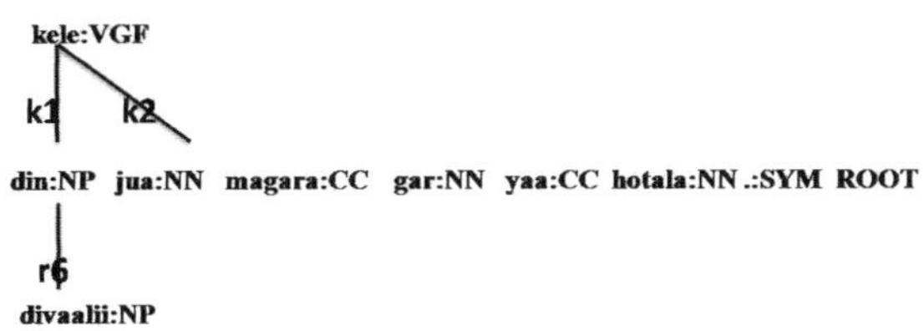

Figure 7: Unattached sub trees in CBHP parse output of an input sentence (forward gapping).

3.4 Finite Verb ellipses

In the cases where there is no VG at all in the sentence, we insert a NULL VG before the EOS (End-Of-Sentence) in the input sentence. For this case, finite verb ellipses can be recovered directly from

if !$\exists$ a VG in S-W
  insert NULL with VM as POS,
NULL_VG as CPOS

Table 8: Rule for identifying Finite Verb ellipses in sentence.

for each node N in tree T
  if head of N = ϕ
    insert N in unattached_subtrees[]
if !$\exists$ a verb in unattached_subtrees[]
    if those conjuncts belongs to conjunct_set
      insert insert NULL with VM as POS,
NULL_VG as CPOS

Table 9: Rule for identifying Finite Verb ellipses using CBHP.

the input sentence using the rule in Table 8 .Also, in a sentence with a VG, we use CBHP to ascertain if this VG is the root of the sentence. If its not, we insert an additional NULL_VG. This algorithm will correctly recover VG in the sentence but the position can be different from the gold input at times not because the recovery algorithm is wrong, but there is no strict rule that says the exact position of empty category in this case of finite verb ellipse and annotators might choose to insert an empty category at any position. For example, in Figure 8, we can insert an empty category either after first NP sub tree or second or the third etc, all these possibilities are accepted syntactically. For simplicity purposes, we insert the empty category just before the EOS. This procedure is shown in Table 9.

3.5 Conjunction ellipses (for verbs)

We again use the intermediate parsed output of CBHP for this type. Whenever there is a missing conjunction between the two finite clauses, the clausal sub trees are disconnected from each other as shown in Figure 9. Hence the rule that should be applied is to insert a NULL_CCP between two sub trees with VG heads and insert NULL CCP immediately after the first verb in the input sentence. Table 10 shows this procedure.

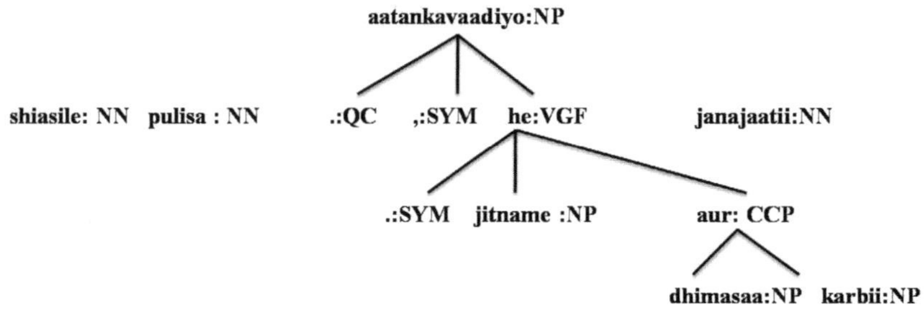

Figure 8: Unattached Subtrees (Finite verb ellipses).

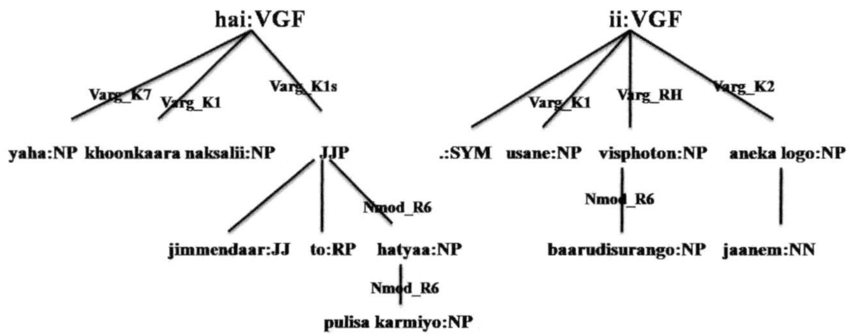

Figure 9: Unattached Subtrees in the case of conjunction ellipses.

for each node N in tree T
  if head of N = ϕ
    insert N in unattached_subtrees[]
for each node X in unattached_subtrees[]
  if X and X+1 are VG's
    insert insert NULL with CC as POS, NULL_CCP as CPOS

Table 10: Rule for identifying Finite Verb ellipses using CBHP.

Type of empty categories	Inst-ances	Prec-ision	Recall
Empty subject	69	89.8	89.8
Backward gapping	29	77.7	48.3
Forward gapping	21	88.8	72.7
Finite verb ellipses	18	78.5	61.1
Conjunction ellipses (verbs)	20	88.2	75
Conjunction ellipses (nouns)	12	0	0
Total	169	91.4	69.8

Table 11: Recovery of empty categories in Hindi treebank.

4 Results and Discussion

We have presented two sets of results, the overall empty categories detection along with the accuracies of individual types of empty categories in Table 11 and Table 12.

The results in Table 12 show that the precision in recovering many empty categories is close to 90%. A high precision value of 89.8 for recovery of Empty subject type is due to the strong lexical cues that were found during our analysis. CBHP parse output proved helpful in most of the remaining types. Few cases such as backward gapping and conjunction ellipses (for nouns) are very difficult to handle. We see that although CBHP helps in the recovery process by providing unattached subtrees in many instances, there are cases such as those of backward gapping and nominal conjunction ellipses where it does not help. It is not difficult to see why this is so. The presence of the 2nd verb in the case of backward gapping fools CBHP into treating it as the main verb of a normal finite clause. In such a case, the

Type of empty categories	Inst-ances	Prec-ision	Recall
NULL_NP tokens	69	89.8	89.8
NULL_VG tokens	68	82	60.2
NULL_CCP tokens	32	88.2	46.8
Total	159	91.4	69.8

Table 12: Empty categories in Hindi Tree bank

parser ends up producing a fully formed tree (which of course is a wrong analysis) that is of no use for us.

Similar problem is faced while handling conjunction ellipses (for nouns). Here as in the previous case, CBHP is fooled into treating two coordinating nominals as independent nouns. We note here that both the cases are in fact notoriously difficult to automatically detect because of the presence (or absence) of any robust linguistic pattern.

These results show that our system can be used to supplement the annotators effort during treebanking. We plan to use our system during the ongoing Hindi treebanking to ascertain it effect. As mentioned earlier, automatic detection of empty categories/nodes will prove to be indis pensable for parsing a sentence. We also intend to see the effect of our system during the task of parsing.

5 Conclusion

In this paper we presented an empty category recovery algorithm by analyzing the empty categories in the Hindi treebank. This, we noticed, uses lexical cues and parsed output of a constraint based parser. The results show that our system performs considerably high (90%) for many types of empty categories. Few types, on the other hand, such as backward gapping and nominal coordinating conjunctions were very difficult to handle. Our approach and analysis will be useful in automatic insertion of empty nodes during dependency annotation. It will also benefit data-driven/statistical approaches either as a post-processing tool or in recovering empty categories by helping in feature selection for various machine learning techniques.

Acknowledgments

We would like to thank Prof. Rajeev Sangal for providing valuable inputs throughout the work.

References

R. Begum, S. Husain, A. Dhwaj, D. Sharma, L. Bai, and R. Sangal. Dependency annotation scheme for Indian languages. 2008. In proceedings of Third International Joint Conference on Natural Language Processing (IJCNLP), Hyderabad, India

A. Bharati, S. Husain, D. Misra, and R. Sangal. Two stage constraint based hybrid approach to free word order language dependency parsing. 2009a. In Proceedings of the 11th International Conference on Parsing Technologies (IWPT). Paris.

A. Bharati, D. Sharma, S. Husain, L. Bai, R. Begam, and R. Sangal. Anncorra: Treebanks for indian languages, guidelines for annotating hindi treebank. 2009b. http://ltrc.iiit.ac.in/MachineTrans/research/tb/DS-guidelines/DS-guidelines-ver2-28-05-09.pdf

A. Bhatia, R. Bhatt, B. Narasimhan, M. Palmer, O. Rambow, D. Sharma, M. Tepper, A. Vaidya, and F. Xia. Empty Categories in a Hindi Treebank. 2010. In the Proceedings of the 7th International Conference on Language Resources and Evaluation (LREC).

R. Campbell. Using linguistic principles to recover empty categories. 2004. In Proceedings of the 42nd Annual Meeting of the Association for Computational Linguistics

A. Chanev. Portability of dependency parsing algorithms–an application for Italian. 2005. In Proc. of the fourth workshop on Treebanks and Linguistic Theories (TLT). Citeseer.

M. Collins. Three generative, lexicalised models for statistical parsing. 1997. In Proceedings of the 35th Annual Meeting of the Association for Computational Linguistics and Eighth Conference of the European Chapter of the Association for Computational Linguistics.

P. Dienes and A. Dubey. Antecedent recovery: Experiments with a trace tagger. 2003a. In Proceedings of the 2003 conference on Empirical methods in natural language processing.

P. Dienes and A. Dubey. Deep syntactic processing by combining shallow methods. 2003b. In Proceedings of the 41st Annual Meeting on Association for Computational Linguistics-Volume 1.

D. Higgins. A machine-learning approach to the identification of WH gaps. 2003. In Proceedings of the tenth conference on European chapter of the Association for Computational Linguistics-Volume 2.

X. Fei, O. Rambow, R. Bhatt, M. Palmer, and D. Sharma. Towards a multi-representational treebank. 2008. Proc. of the 7th Int'lWorkshop on Treebanks and Linguistic Theories (TLT-7)

M. Johnson. A simple pattern-matching algorithm for recovering empty nodes and their antecedents. 2002. In Proceedings of the 40th Annual Meeting on Association for Computational Linguistics.

M. Marcus, M. Marcinkiewicz, and B. Santorini. Building a large annotated corpus of English: The Penn Treebank. 1993. Computational linguistics.

R. McDonald, F. Pereira, K. Ribarov, and J. Hajič. Non-projective dependency parsing using spanning tree algorithms. 2005. In Proceedings of the conference on Human Language Technology and Empirical Methods in Natural Language Processing.

J. Nivre. An efficient algorithm for projective dependency parsing. 2003. In Proceedings of the 8th International Workshop on Parsing Technologies (IWPT).

M. Palmer, R. Bhatt, B. Narasimhan, O. Rambow, D. Sharma, and F. Xia. Hindi Syntax: Annotating Dependency, Lexical Predicate-Argument Structure, and Phrase Structure. 2009. In The 7th International Conference on Natural Language Processing.

Y. Yang and N. Xue. Chasing the ghost: recovering empty categories in the Chinese Treebank. 2010. In Proceedings of the 23rd International Conference on Computational Linguistics: Posters.

Annotating Events, Temporal Expressions and Relations in Italian: the It-TimeML Experience for the Ita-TimeBank

Tommaso Caselli
ILC "A.Zampolli" - CNR
Via G. Moruzzi, 1
56124 Pisa
caselli@ilc.cnt.it

Valentina Bartalesi Lenzi
CELCT
Via della Cascata 56/c
38123 Povo (TN)
bartalesi@celct.it

Rachele Sprugnoli
CELCT
Via della Cascata 56/c
38123 Povo (TN)
sprugnoli@celct.it

Emanuele Pianta
CELCT
Via della Cascata 56/c
38123 Povo (TN)
pianta@fbk.eu

Irina Prodanof
ILC "A.Zampolli" - CNR
Via G. Moruzzi, 1
56124 Pisa
prodanof@ilc.cnr.it

Abstract

This paper presents the *annotation guidelines* and *specifications* which have been developed for the creation of the Italian TimeBank, a language resource composed of two corpora manually annotated with temporal and event information. In particular, the adaptation of the TimeML scheme to Italian is described, and a special attention is given to the methodology used for the realization of the annotation specifications, which are strategic in order to create good quality annotated resources and to justify the annotated items. The reliability of the It-TimeML guidelines and specifications is evaluated on the basis of the results of the inter-coder agreement performed during the annotation of the two corpora.

1 Introduction

In recent years a renewed interest in temporal processing has spread in the NLP community, thanks to the success of the TimeML annotation scheme (Pustejovsky et al., 2003a) and to the availability of annotated resources, such as the English and French TimeBanks (Pustejovsky et al., 2003b; Bittar, 2010) and the TempEval corpora (Verhagen et al., 2010).

The ISO TC 37 / SC 4 initiative ("Terminology and other language and content resources") and the TempEval-2 contest have contributed to the development of TimeML-compliant annotation schemes in languages other than English, namely Spanish, Korean, Chinese, French and Italian. Once the corresponding corpora will be completed and made available, the NLP community will benefit from having access to different language resources with a common layer of annotation which could boost studies in multilingual temporal processing and improve the performance of complex multilingual NLP systems, such as Question-Answering and Textual Entailment.

This paper focuses on the annotation guidelines and specifications which have been developed for the creation of the Italian TimeBank (hereafter, Ita-TimeBank). The distinction between *annotation guidelines* and *annotation specifications* is of utmost importance in order to distinguish between the abstract, formal definition of an annotation scheme and the actual realization of the annotated language resource. In addition to this, documenting the annotation specification facilitates the reduplication of annotations and justify the annotated items.

The paper is organized as follows: Section 2 will describe in detail specific issues related to the temporal annotation of Italian for the two main tags of the TimeML annotation scheme,

Proceedings of the Fifth Law Workshop (LAW V), pages 143–151,
Portland, Oregon, 23-24 June 2011. ©2011 Association for Computational Linguistics

namely <EVENT> and <TIMEX3>. Section 3 will present the realization of the annotation specifications and will document them. Section 4 focuses on the evaluation of the annotation scheme on the Ita-TimeBank, formed by two corpora independently realized by applying the annotation specifications. Finally, in Section 5 conclusions and extensions to the current annotation effort will be reported.

Notice that, for clarity's sake, in this paper the examples will focus only on the tag (or attribute or link) under discussion.

2 It-TimeML: Extensions and Language Specific Issues

Applying an annotation scheme to a language other than the one for which it was initially developed, requires a careful study of the language specific issues related to the linguistic phenomena taken into account (Im et al., 2009; Bittar, 2008).

TimeML focuses on *Events* (i.e. actions, states, and processes - <EVENT> tag), *Temporal Expressions* (i.e. durations, calendar dates, times of day and sets of time - <TIMEX3> tag), *Signals* (e.g. temporal prepositions and subordinators - <SIGNAL> tag) and various kind of *dependencies between Events and/or Temporal Expressions* (i.e. temporal, aspectual and subordination relations - <TLINK>, <ALINK> and <SLINK> tags respectively).

An ISO language-independent specification of TimeML is under development but it is still in the *enquiry stage*[1]. For this reason, in the following subsections we will mostly compare the Italian annotation guidelines with the latest version of the English annotation guidelines (TimeML Working group, 2010), focusing on the two main tags, i.e <EVENT> and <TIMEX3>, in Italian.

2.1 The <EVENT> tag

The <EVENT> tag is used to mark-up instances of eventualities (Bach, 1986). This category comprises all types of actions (punctual or durative) and states as well. With respect to previous annotations schemes (Katz and Arosio, 2001, Filatova and Hovy, 2001, Setzer and Gaizauskas, 2001 among other), TimeML allows for annotating as Events not only verbs but also nouns, adjectives and prepositional phrases.

In the adaptation to Italian, two annotation principles adopted for English, that is an orientation towards surface linguistic phenomena and the notion of minimal chunk for the tag extent, have been preserved without major modifications. The main differences with respect to the English version rely i.) in the attribute list; and ii.) in the attributes values.

In Italian 12 core attributes apply with respect to the 10 attributes in English. The newly introduced attributes are MOOD and VFORM which capture key distinctions of the Tense-Mood-Aspect (TMA) system of the Italian language. These two attributes are common to other languages, such as Spanish, Catalan, French and Korean.

The MOOD attribute captures the contrastive grammatical expression of different modalities of presentation of an Event when realized by a verb. Annotating this attribute is important since grammatical modality has an impact on the identification of temporal and subordinating relations, and on the assessment of veridicity/factivity values. Mood in Italian is expressed as part of the verb morphology and not by means of modal auxiliary verbs as in English (e.g. through the auxiliary "would"),. Thus, the solution to deal with this phenomenon adopted for English TimeML (where the main verb is annotated with the attribute MODALITY="would", see below) is not applicable in Italian unless relevant information is lost. The values of the MOOD attribute, as listed below, have been adapted to Italian and extended with respect to those proposed in the ISO-TimeML specification:

- NONE: it is used as the default value and corresponds to the Indicative mood:
  (1.) Le forze dell'ordine hanno <EVENT … mood="NONE"> schierato </EVENT> 3.000 agenti. [The police has deployed 3,000 agents.]

[1] http://www.iso.org/iso/iso_catalogue/catalogue_tc/catalogue_detail.htm?csnumber=37331

- CONDITIONAL: it signals the conditional mood which is used to speak of an Event whose realization is dependent on a certain condition, or to signal the future-in-the-past:
(2.) <EVENT ... mood="COND"> Mangerei </EVENT> del pesce. [I would eat fish.]

- SUBJUNCTIVE: it has several uses in independent clauses and is required for certain types of dependent clauses.
(3.) Voglio che tu te ne <EVENT … mood="SUBJUNCTIVE">vada</EVENT> [I want you to go.]

- IMPERATIVE: it is used to express direct commands or requests, to signal a prohibition, permission or any other kind of exhortation.

The attribute VFORM is responsible for distinguishing between non-finite and finite forms of verbal Events. Its values are:

- NONE: it is the default value and signals finite verb forms:
(4.) Le forze dell'ordine hanno <EVENT … vForm="NONE">schierato</EVENT> 3.000 agenti. [The police has deployed 3,000 agents.]

- INFINITIVE: for infinitive verb forms:
(5.) Non è possibile <EVENT … vForm="INFINITIVE">viaggiare</EVENT>. [It's not possible to travel.]

- GERUND: for gerundive verb forms:
(6.) Ha evitato l'incidente <EVENT … vForm="GERUND"> andando </EVENT> piano. [Driving slowly, he avoided the incident.]

- PARTICIPLE: for participle verb forms:
(7.) <EVENT … vForm="PARTICIPLE"> Vista </EVENT> Maria, se ne andò. [Having seen Maria, he left.]

As for attribute values, the most important changes introduced for Italian in comparison with the English TimeML, are related to the ASPECT and MODALITY attributes.

The ASPECT attribute captures standard distinctions in the grammatical category of aspect or Event viewpoint (Smith, 1991). In English TimeML it has the following values: i.) PROGRESSIVE; ii.) PERFECTIVE; iii.) PERFECTIVE_PROGRESSIVE, or iv.) NONE. The main differences with respect to the English guidelines concern the following points:

i.) the absence of the value PERFECTIVE_PROGRESSIVE and

ii.) the presence of the value IMPERFECTIVE, which is part of the ISO TimeML current definition.

These differences are due to language specific phenomena related to the expression of the grammatical aspect in Italian and English and to the application of the TimeML surface oriented annotation philosophy. In particular, the assignment of the aspectual values is strictly determined by the verb surface forms. For instance, in English the verb form "is teaching" requires the PROGRESSIVE value. On the other hand, the Italian counterpart of "is teaching" can be realized in two ways: either by means of the simple present (*insegna* [s/he teaches]) or by means of a specific verbal periphrasis (*sta insegnando* [s/he is teaching]). In order to distinguish between these two verb forms, and to account also for other typical Romance languages tense forms, such as the Italian *Imperfetto*, the use of the additional IMPERFECTIVE value is necessary. Thus, *insegna* [s/he teaches], as well as the Imperfetto *insegnava* [s/he was teaching] are annotated as IMPERFECTIVE, whereas *sta insegnando* [s/he is teaching] is annotated as PROGRESSIVE. On the other hand, the absence of the PERFECTIVE_PROGRESSIVE value, used for English tense forms of the kind "he has been teaching", is due to the lack of Italian verb surface forms which may require its use.

In English, modal verbs are not annotated as Events and the MODALITY attribute is associated to the main verb (the value of the attribute is the token corresponding to the modal verb). Unlike English modals, Italian modal verbs, such as *potere* [can/could; may/might], *volere* [want; will/would] and *dovere* [must/have to; ought to; shall/should], are to be considered similar to other lexical verbs in that it is possible to assign them values for tense and aspect. Consequently, each instance of Italian modal verbs will be annotated with the tag <EVENT>. The value of the MODALITY attribute is the lemma of the verb (e.g. *dovere*).

A further language specific aspect concerns the annotation of verbal periphrases, that is special constructions with at least two verbs (and sometimes other words) that behave as a group like a single verb would. In Italian, it is possible to identify different instances of verbal periphrases, namely:

- aspectual periphrases (example 8 below), which encode progressive or habitual aspect;
- modal periphrases (example 9), which encode modality not realized by proper modal verbs;
- phasal periphrases (example 10), which encode information on a particular phase in the description of an Event.

Following Bertinetto (1991), in the last two cases, i.e. modal periphrases and phasal periphrases, both verbal elements involved should be annotated, while in the case of the aspectual periphrasis only the main verb (verb head) has to be marked; e.g.:

(8.) Maria stava <EVENT … ASPECT="PROGRESSIVE"> mangiando. [Maria was eating]

(9.) Il compito di matematica <EVENT ... MODALITY="ANDARE"> va </EVENT> <EVENT ... > svolto </EVENT> per domani. [Maths exercises must be done for tomorrow]

(10.) I contestatori hanno <EVENT ... CLASS="ASPECTUAL"> iniziato </EVENT> a <EVENT> lanciare </EVENT> pietre. [Demonstrators started to throw stones.]

Similarly to what proposed for English, in presence of multi-tokens realization of Events, two main annotation strategies have been followed:

- in case the multi-token Event expression corresponds to an instance of a collocation or of an idiomatic expression, then only the head (verbal, nominal or other) of the expression is marked up;
- in case the multi-token Event is realized by light verb expressions, then two separate <EVENT> tags are to be created both for the verb and the nominal/prepositional complement.

2.2 The <TIMEX3> tag

The TIMEX3 tag relies on and is as much compliant as possible with the TIDES TIMEX2 annotation. The Italian adaptation of this annotation scheme is presented in Magnini et al. (2006). The only difference concerns the annotation of articulated prepositions which are annotated as signals, while in the TIMEX2 specifications they are considered as part of the textual realization of Temporal Expressions:

(11a.) <TIMEX2 …> nel 2011 </TIMEX2> [in 2011]

(11b.) <SIGNAL …> nel </SIGNAL> <TIMEX3…>2011</TIMEX3> [in 2011]

On the other hand, with respect to the TIMEX3 annotation of other languages such as English, we decided to follow the TIMEX2 specification by annotating many adjectives as Temporal Expressions (e.g. *recente* [recent], *ex* [former]) and including modifiers like *che rimane* in *l'anno che rimane* [the remaining year] into the extent of the TIMEX3 tag since it is essential for the normalization of temporal expressions.

3 From Annotation Guidelines to Specifications

As already stated, the annotation guidelines represent an abstract, formal level of description which, in this case, is mainly based on a detailed study of the relevant linguistic levels. Once the guidelines are applied to real language data, further issues arise and need to be tackled. This section focuses on a method for developing annotation specifications. Annotation specifications are to be seen as the actual realization of the annotation guidelines. The identification and distinction of annotation guidelines from annotation specification is of major importance as it is to be conceived as a new level of Best Practice for the creation of semantically annotated Language Resources (Calzolari and Caselli, 2009).

The process of realization of the annotation specifications is strategic both to realize good quality annotated resources and to justify why certain textual items have to be annotated. As for the It-TimeML experience we will illustrate this process by making reference and reporting examples for two tags, namely for the <EVENT> and the <TLINK> tags.

As a general procedure for the development of the annotation specifications, we have taken inspiration from the DAMSL Manual (Core and Allen, 1997). Different decision trees have been created for each task. For instance, for the annotation of the <EVENT> tag, four different decision trees have been designed for each POS (i.e. nouns, verbs, adjectives and prepositional phrases) which could be involved in the realization of an Event. In particular, the most complex decision tree is that developed for noun annotation. The identification of the eventive reading of nouns has been formalized into a discrimination process of different properties: firstly superficial properties are taken into consideration, i.e. whether a morphologically related verb exists or not, and whether the noun co-occurs with special verb predicates (for instance aspectual verbs such as *iniziare* [to start] or light verbs such as *fare* [to do]); then, deeper semantic properties are analyzed, which involve other levels such as word sense disambiguation and noun classification (e.g. whether the noun is a functional or an incremental one).

Other decision trees have been improved to avoid inconsistencies in Event classification. For instance, the identification of *Reporting Events* showed to be problematic because of the vague definition adopted in the guidelines. A Reporting Event is a giving information speech act in which a communicator conveys a message to an addressee. To help annotators in deciding whether an event is a Reporting one, the annotation specifications suggest to rely on FrameNet as a starting point (Baker, et al. 1998). More specifically, an Italian lexical unit has been classified as Reporting if it is the translation equivalent of one of the lexical units assigned to the Communication frame, which has Message as a core element. Among the frames using and inherited from the Communication frame, only the ones having the Message as a core element and conveying a giving information speech act have been selected and the lexical units belonging to them have been classified as Reporting Events: e.g. *urlare* [to scream] from the Communication_noise frame, *sottolineare* [to stress] from the Convey_importance frame, *dichiarare* [to declare] from the Statement frame.

Similarly, for the identification of TLINKs, a set of decision trees has been developed to identify the conditions under which a temporal relation is to be annotated and a method to decide the value of the *reltype* attribute. For instance, the annotation of temporal relations between nominal Events and Temporal Expressions in the same sentence is allowed only when the Temporal Expression is realized either by an adjective or a prepositional phrase of the form "*di (of)* + TEMPORAL EXPRESSION" e.g.:

(12.) La <EVENT eid="e1" ... > riunione </EVENT> <SIGNAL sid="s1" ... > di </SIGNAL> <TIMEX3 tid="t1" ... > ieri </TIMEX3> [yesterday meeting]
<TLINK lid="l1" eventInstanceID="e01" relatedToTime="t01" signalID="s1" relType="IS_INCLUDED"/>

In addition, decision trees based on the idea that signals provide useful information to TLINK classification have been used to assign the *reltype* value to TLINKs holding between a duration and an Event. For example, the pattern "EVENT + *tra (in)* + DURATION" identifies the value AFTER, while the pattern "EVENT + *per (for)* + DURATION" is associated with the value MEASURE.

(13.) Il pacco <EVENT eid="e1" ... >arriverà </EVENT> <SIGNAL sid="s1" ... > tra </SIGNAL> <TIMEX3 tid="t1" ... > due giorni </TIMEX3> [the package will arrive in two days]
<TLINK lid="l1" eventInstanceID="e1" relatedToTime="t1" signalID="s1" relType="AFTER"/>

(14.) Sono stati <EVENT eid="e1" ... > sposati </EVENT> <SIGNAL sid="s1" ... > per </SIGNAL> <TIMEX3 tid="t1" ... > dieci anni

</TIMEX3> [they have been married for ten years]
<TLINK lid="l1" eventInstanceID="e1" relatedToTime="t1" signalID="s1" relType="MEASURE"/>

The advantages of this formalization are many. The impact of the annotators' subjectivity is limited, thus reducing the risk of disagreement. Moreover, trees can then be easily used either as features for the development of a automatic learner or as instructions in a rule-based automatic annotation system.

4 Evaluating Annotations

Two corpora have been developed in parallel following the It-TimeML annotation scheme, namely the CELCT corpus and the ILC corpus. Once these two corpora will be completed and released, they will form the Italian TimeBank providing the NLP community with the largest resource annotated with temporal and event information (more than 150K tokens).

In this section, the two corpora are briefly described and the results of the inter-coder agreement (Artstein and Poesio, 2008) achieved during their annotation are compared in order to evaluate the quality of the guidelines and of the resources.

The *CELCT corpus* has been created within the LiveMemories project[2] and it consists of news stories taken from the Italian Content Annotation Bank (I-CAB, Magnini et al., 2006). More than 180,000 tokens have been annotated with Temporal Expressions and more than 90,000 tokens have been annotated also with Events, Signals and Links. The Brandeis Annotation Tool[3] (BAT) has been used for the pilot annotation and for the automatic computation of the inter-coder agreement on the extent and the attributes of Temporal Expressions, Events and Signals. After the pilot annotation, the first prototype of the CELCT Annotation Tool (CAT) has been used to perform the annotation and to compute the inter-coder agreement on Links. For what concern the annotation effort, the work on Temporal Expressions, Events and Signals involved 2 annotators while 3 annotators have been engaged in the annotation of Links. The annotation started in January 2010 and required a total of 1.3 person/years. Table 1 shows the total number of annotated markables together with the results of the inter-coder agreement on tag extent performed by two annotators on a subset of the corpus of about four thousand tokens. For the annotation of Event and Signal extents, statistics include average precision and recall and Cohen' kappa, while the Dice Coefficient has been computed for the extent of Links and Temporal Expressions.

Markable	#	Agreement
TIMEX3	4,852	Dice=0.94
EVENT	17,554	K=0.93 P&R=0.94
SIGNAL	2,045	K=0.88 P&R=0.88
TLINK	3,373	Dice=0.86
SLINK	3,985	Dice=0.93
ALINK	238	Dice=0.90

Table 1: Annotated markables and results of the inter-coder agreement on tag extent[4]

Table 2 provides the value of Fleiss' kappa computed for the annotation of Temporal Expression, Event and Link attributes.

Tag and attribute	Agreement-Kappa
TIMEX3.type	1.00
TIMEX3.value	0.92
TIMEX3.mod	0.89
EVENT.aspect	0.96
EVENT.class	0.87
EVENT.modality	1.00
EVENT.mood	0.90
EVENT.polarity	1.00
EVENT.pos	1.00
EVENT.tense	0.94
EVENT.vform	0.98
TLINK.relType	0.88
SLINK.relType	0.93
ALINK.relType	1.00

Table 2: Inter-coder agreement on attributes

[2] http://www.livememories.org

[3] http://www.timeml.org/site/bat/

[4] Please note that the number of annotated Temporal Expressions is calculated on a total of 180,000 tokens, while the number of Events, Signals and Links is calculated on more than 90,000 tokens.

The *ILC corpus* is composed of 171 newspaper stories collected from the Italian Syntactic-Semantic Treebank, the PAROLE corpus and the web for a total of 68,000 tokens (40,398 tokens are freely available, the remaining are available with restrictions). The news reports were selected to be comparable in content and size to the English TimeBank and they are mainly about international and national affairs, political and financial subject. The annotation of Temporal Expressions, Event extents and Signals has been completed while the annotation of Event attributes and LINKs is a work in progress. A subset of the corpus has been used as data set in the TempEval-2 evaluation campaign organized within SemEval-2 in 2010. So far the annotation has been performed thanks to eight voluntary students under the supervision of two judges using BAT. The annotation started in March 2009 and is requiring a total of 3 person/years. Table 3 reports the total number of Temporal Expressions, Events, Signals and TLINKs together with the results of the inter-coder agreement on tag extent performed on about 30,000 tokens. To measure the agreement on tag extents, average precision and recall and Cohen' kappa have been calculated. The annotation of Temporal Links has been divided into three subtasks: the first subtask is the relation between two Temporal Expressions, the second is the relation between an Event and a Temporal Expression, the third regards the relation between two Events.

Markable		#	Agreement
TIMEX3		2,314	K=0.95 P&R= 0.95
EVENT		10,633	K=0.87 P&R= 0.86
SIGNAL		1,704	K=0.83 P&R= 0.84
TLINK	TIMEX3–TIMEX3	353	K=0.95
	EVENT–TIMEX3	512	K=0.87
	EVENT–EVENT	1,014	in progress

Table 3: Annotated markables and results of the inter-coder agreement on tag extent

The values of Fleiss' kappa computed for the assignment of attribute values are illustrated in Table 4.

Tag and attribute	Agreement – Kappa
TIMEX3.type	0.96
TIMEX3.value	0.96
TIMEX3.mod	0.97
EVENT.aspect	0.93
EVENT.class	0.82
EVENT.modality	0.92
EVENT.mood	0.89
EVENT.polarity	0.75
EVENT.pos	0.95
EVENT.tense	0.97
EVENT.vform	0.94
TLINK.relType	in progress

Table 4: Annotated TLINKs and results of the inter-coder agreement

Given the data reported in the above tables, it is possible to claim that the results of the inter-coder agreement are good and comparable beyond the different annotation method used to develop the two corpora. So far, the ILC corpus has been annotated without time constraints by several annotators with varying backgrounds in linguistics using BAT. With this web-based tool, each file has been assigned to many annotators and an adjudication phase on discrepancies has been performed by an expert judge. As required by BAT, the annotation has been divided into many annotation layers so each annotator focused only on a specific set of It-TimeML tags. On the other hand, few expert annotators have been involved in the development of the CELCT corpus interacting and negotiating common solutions to controversial annotations. With respect to BAT, the CELCT Annotation Tool is stand-alone and it does not require neither the parallel annotation of the same text, nor the decomposition of annotation tasks allowing to have flexibility in the annotation process and a unitary view of all annotation layers. These features are helpful when working with strict project deadlines.

A comparison with the inter-coder agreement achieved during the annotation of the English TimeBank 1.2 (Pustejovsky et al., 2006a), shows that the scores obtained for the CELCT and the ILC corpora are substantially higher in the following results: (i) average precision and recall on the identification of tag extent (e.g. 0.83 *vs*. 0.95 of ILC Corpus and 0.94 of CELCT Corpus for TIMEX3; 0.78 *vs*. 0.87 of ILC Corpus and 0.93 of CECLT Corpus); (ii) kappa score on Event classification (0.67 vs. 0.82 of ILC Corpus and 0.87 of the CELCT Corpus); (iii) kappa score on TLINK classification (0.77 *vs*. 0.86 of CELCT Corpus).

The similarity of the agreement results among the three resources and the improvement of the scores obtained on the CELCT and the ILC corpora with respect to the English TimeBank 1.2, can be taken as an indication of the quality and coverage of the It-TimeML annotation guidelines and specifications. Annotators showed to perform consistently demonstrating the reliability of the annotation scheme.

5 Conclusions and Future Works

This paper reports on the creation of a new semantic resource for Italian which has been developed independently but with a joint effort between two different research institutions. The Ita-TimeBank will represent a large corpus annotated with information for temporal processing which can boost the multilingual research in this field and represent a case study for the creation of semantic annotated resources.

One of the most interesting point of this work is represented by the methodology followed for the development of the corpora: in addition to the guidelines, annotation specifications have been created in order to report in detail the actual choices done during the annotation. This element should be pushed forward in the community as a new best practice for the creation of good quality semantically annotated resources.

The results obtained show the reliability of the adaptation of the annotation guidelines to Italian and of the methodology used for the creation of the resources.

Future works will concentrate in different directions, mainly due to the research interests of the two groups which have taken part to this effort but they will be coordinated.

An interesting aspect which could be investigated is the annotation of the anaphoric relations between Events. This effort could be done in a more reliable way since the primary linguistic items have been already annotated. Moreover, this should boost research in the development of annotation schemes which could be easily integrated with each other without losing descriptive and representational information for other language phenomena.

Another topic to deepen regards the definition of the appropriate argument structure in It-TimeML in order to annotate relations between entities (e.g. persons and organizations) and Events in which they are involved (Pustejovsky et al., 2006b).

As regards the distribution of the Ita-TimeBank, the resource will soon be available in an in-line format. In order to integrate the temporal annotation with other linguistic annotations, a standoff version of the Ita-TimeBank needs to be developed. When this is made available, we plan to merge the manual annotation of temporal and event information with other types of linguistic stand-off annotations (i.e. tokenization, lemma, PoS, multi-words, various kinds of named entities) which are already available for the I-CAB corpus.

In order to encourage research on systems capable of temporal inference and event-based reasoning, the Ita-TimeBank could be used as gold standard within specific evaluation campaigns as the next TempEval initiative.

Finally, the use of crowdsourcing will be explored to reduce annotation effort in terms of financial cost and time. The most difficult challenge to face will be the splitting of a complicated annotation scheme as It-TimeML into simple tasks which can be effectively performed by not expert contributors.

Acknowledgments

The development of the CELCT corpus has been supported by the LiveMemories project (Active Digital Memories of Collective Life), funded by the Autonomous Province of Trento under the Major Projects 2006 research program. We would like to thank Alessandro Marchetti, Giovanni Moretti and Marc Verhagen who collaborated with us in processing and annotating the CELCT corpus.

References

André Bittar. 2008. Annotation des informations temporelles dans des textes en français,. In Proceedings of RECITAL 2008, Avignon, France.

André Bittar. 2010. Building a TimeBank for French: A Reference Corpus Annotated According to the ISO-TimeML Standard. PhD Thesis.

Andrea Setzer and Robert Gaizauskas.2001. A Pilot Study On Annotating Temporal Relations In Text. In: Proceedings of the ACL 2001 Workshop on Temporal and Spatial Information Processing.

Bernardo Magnini, Emanuele Pianta, Christian Girardi, Matteo Negri, Lorenza Romano, Manuela Speranza, Valentina Bartalesi Lenzi and Rachele Sprugnoli. 2006. I-CAB: the Italian Content Annotation Bank. In Proceedings of LREC 2006, Genova, Italy.

Bernardo Magnini, Matteo Negri, Emanuele Pianta, Manuela Speranza, Valentina Bartalesi Lenzi, and Rachele Sprugnoli. 2006. Italian Content Annotation Bank (I-CAB): Temporal Expressions (V.2.0). Technical Report, FBK-irst.

Carlota S. Smith. 1991. The Parameter of Aspect. Kluwer, Dordrecht.

Collin F., Baker, Charles J. Fillmore, and John B. Lowe. 1998. The Berkeley FrameNet project. In: Proceedings of the COLING-ACL, pages 86-90. Montreal, Canada.

Elena Filatova and Eduard Hovy. 2001. Assigning Time-Stamps To Event-Clauses. In: Proceedings of the ACL 2001 Workshop on Temporal and Spatial Information Processing.

Emmon Bach. 1986. The algebra of events. Linguistics and Philosophy, 9, 5–16.

Graham Katz and Fabrizio Arosio. 2001. The Annotation Of Temporal Information In Natural Language Sentences. In: Proceedings of the ACL 2001 Workshop on Temporal and Spatial Information Processing.

ISO: Language Resource Management – Semantic Annotation Framework (SemAF) - Part 1: Time and Events. Secretariat KATS, August 2007. ISO Report ISO/TC37/SC4 N269 version 19 (ISO/WD 24617-1).

James Pustejovsky, Jessica Littman and Roser Saurí. 2006b. Argument Structure in TimeML. In: Graham Katz, James Pustejovsky and Frank Schilder (eds.) Dagstuhl Seminar Proceedings. Internationales Begegnungs- und Forschungszentrum (IB-FI), Schloss Dagstuhl, Germany.

James Pustejovsky, Jessica Littman, Roser Saurí, and Marc Verhagen. 2006a. TimeBank 1.2 Documentation. http://timeml.org/site/timebank/documentation-1.2.html

James Pustejovsky, José Castaño, Robert Ingria, Roser Saurí, Robert Gaizauskas, Andrea Setzer and Graham Katz. 2003a. TimeML: Robust Specification of Event and Temporal Expressions in Text. In: Proceedings of IWCS-5, Fifth International Workshop on Computational Semantics.

James Pustejovsky, Patrick Hanks, Roser, Saurì, Andrew See, Robert Gaizauskas, Andrea Setzer, Dragomir Radev, Beth Sundheim, David Day,Lisa Ferro, and Marcia Lazo. 2003b. The TIMEBANK corpus. In: Proceedings of Corpus Linguistics 2003, pages 647-656.

Marc Verhagen, Roser Saurí, Tommaso Caselli and James Pustejovsky. 2010. SemEval-2010 Task 13: TempEval-2. In: Proceedings of the 5th International Workshop on Semantic Evaluation.

Mark G. Core and James F. Allen. 1997. Coding Dialogs with the DAMSL Annotation Scheme. In: Working Notes of AAAI Fall Symposium on Communicative Action in Humans and Machines.

Nicoletta Calzolari, and Tommaso Caselli 2009. Short Report on the FLaReNet / SILT Workshop and Panel on Semantic Annotation, TR-ILC-CNR.

Pier Marco Bertinetto. 1991. Il verbo. In: R. L. and G. Salvi (eds.) Grande Grammatica Italiana di Consultazione, volume II, pages 13-161. Il Mulino.

Ron Artstein and Massimo Poesio. Inter-coder agreement for computational linguistics. Computational Linguistics, pages 555–596, 2008.

Seohyun Im, Hyunjo You, Hayun Jang, Seungho Nam, and Hyopil Shin. 2009. KTimeML: Specification of Temporal and Event Expressions in Korean Text. In: Proceedings of the 7th workshop on Asian Language Resources in conjunction with ACL-IJCNLP 2009, Suntec City, Singapore.

TimeML Working Group. 2010. TimeML Annotation Guidelines version 1.3.Manuscript, Brandeis University.

Increasing Informativeness in Temporal Annotation

James Pustejovsky
Department of Computer Science
Brandeis University MS 018
Waltham, Massachusetts, 02454 USA
jamesp@cs.brandeis.edu

Amber Stubbs
Department of Computer Science
Brandeis University MS 018
Waltham, Massachusetts, 02454 USA
astubbs@cs.brandeis.edu

Abstract

In this paper, we discuss some of the challenges of adequately applying a specification language to an annotation task, as embodied in a specific guideline. In particular, we discuss some issues with TimeML motivated by error analysis on annotated TLINKs in TimeBank. We introduce a document level information structure we call a *narrative container (NC)*, designed to increase informativeness and accuracy of temporal relation identification. The narrative container is the default interval containing the events being discussed in the text, when no explicit temporal anchor is given. By exploiting this notion in the creation of a new temporal annotation over TimeBank, we were able to reduce inconsistencies and increase informativeness when compared to existing TLINKs in TimeBank.

1 Introduction

In linguistic annotation projects, there is often a gap between what the annotation schema is designed to capture and how the guidelines are interpreted by the annotators and adjudicators given a specific corpus and task (Ide and Bunt, 2010; Ide, 2007). The difficulty in resolving these two aspects of annotation is compounded when tasks are looked at in a potentially incomplete annotation task; namely, where the guideline is following a specification to a point, but in fact human annotation is not even suggested as complete because it would be infeasible. Creating temporal links to represent the timeline of events in a document is an example of this: human annotation of every possible temporal relationship between events and times in a narrative would be an overwhelming task.

In this paper, we discuss how temporal relation annotation must be sensitive to two aspects of the task that were not mentioned in the TimeBank guideline (Pustejovsky et al., 2005): (a) sensitivity to the genre and style of the text; and (b) the interaction with discourse relations that explicitly reference the flow of the narrative in the text. We believe that making reference to both these aspects in the text during the annotation process will increase overall informativeness and accuracy of the annotation. In the present paper, we focus primarily on the first of these points, and introduce a document level information structure we call a *narrative container (NC)*.

Because of the impossibility of humans capturing every relationship, it is vital that the annotation guidelines describe an approach that will result in maximally informative temporal links without relying on standards that are too difficult to apply. With this in mind, we have been examining the TimeBank corpus (Pustejovsky et al., 2003) and the annotation guideline that created it, and have come to these realizations:

(1) • The guideline does not specify certain types of annotations that should be performed;
• The guideline forces some annotations to be performed when they should not always be.

Additionally, we have discovered some inconsistencies in the TimeBank corpus related to temporal links. Furthermore, upon examination, we have become aware of the importance of the text style and

Proceedings of the Fifth Law Workshop (LAW V), pages 152–160,
Portland, Oregon, 23-24 June 2011.

genre, and how readers interpret temporally unahchored events.

This gave rise, in examining the genres that are most frequent in TimeBank (namely news and finance), to the possibility that readers of news articles and narratives have possible default assumptions about when unanchored events take place. It seems reasonable for a reader to assume in a sentence such as: *Oneida Ltd. declared a 10% stock dividend, payable Dec. 15 to stock of record Nov. 17*, that the "declared" event took place soon before the article's Document Creation Time (DCT).

Exactly how soon before may be related to some proximate interval of time associated with both the publication time and frequency. That is, it appears that just as importantly, if not more so, than the DCT, is a related and dependent notion of the salient interval surrounding the creation time, for interpreting the events that are being reported or written about. We will call this the *Narrative Container*. There seems to be a default value for this container affected by many variables. For example, a print newspaper seems to associate in the content and style a narrative container of approximately 24 hours, or one business day. A newswire article, on the other hand, has a narrative container of 2-10 hours. Conversely, weekly and monthly publications would likely have a narrative container of a much longer duration (a week or more).

Along with the narrative container, there are two related concepts that proved useful in framing this new approach to temporal annotation. The *Narrative Scope* describes the timespan described in the document, with the left marker defined by the earliest event mentioned in the document, and the right by the event furthest in the future. The other important concept is that of *Narrative Time*. A Narrative Time is essentially the current temporal anchor for events in a document, and can change as the reader moves through the narrative.

With these as initial assumptions we did some cursory inspection of the TimeBank data to determine if there was a correlation between Narrative Container length and genre, and found it to be a compelling assumption. With that in mind, we determined that TLINK creation should be focused on relationships to the narrative container, rather than to the DCT.

Our goal is, to the extent possible, to see how we can use a container metaphor, albeit somewhat underspecified, to left-delineate the container within which unanchored events might be in relation to.

2 Identifying Temporal Relations

While low-level temporal annotation tasks such as identifying events and time expressions are relatively straightforward and can be marked up with high consistency, high-level tasks such as arranging events in a document in a temporal order have proved to be much more challenging. The temporal ordering of events in a document, for example, is accomplished by identifying all distinct event-event pairings. For a document that has n events, this requires the annotation of $\binom{n}{2}$ events pairs. Obviously, for general-purpose annotation, where all possible events are considered, the number of event pairs grows essentially quadratically to the number of events, and the task quickly becomes unmanageable.

There are, however, strategies that we can adopt to make this labeling task more tractable. First we need to distinguish the domains over which ordering relations are performed. Temporal ordering relations in text are of three kinds:

(2) a. A relation between two events;
b. A relation between two times;
c. A relation between a time and an event.

TimeML, as a formal specification of the temporal information conveyed in language, makes no distinction between these ordering types. But a human reader of a text does make a distinction, based on the discourse relations established by the author of the narrative (Miltsakaki et al., 2004; Poesio, 2004). Temporal expressions denoting the local *Narrative Container* in the text act as embedding intervals within which events occur. Within TimeML, these are event-time anchoring relations (TLINKs). Discourse relations establish how events relate to one another in the narrative, and hence should constrain temporal relations between two events. Thus, one of the most significant constraints we can impose is to take advantage of the discourse structure in the document before event-event ordering relations are identified.

Although, in principle, during an annotation a temporal relation can be specified between any two events in the text, it is worth asking what *informativeness* a given temporal relation introduces to the annotation. The informativeness of an annotation will be characterized as a function of the information contained in the individual links and their closure. We can distinguish, somewhat informally for now, two sources of informativeness in how events are temporally ordered relative to each other in a text: (a) externally and (b) internally. Consider first *external informativeness*. This is information derived from relations outside the temporal relation constraint set, e.g., as coming from explicit discourse relations between events (and hence is associated with the relations in (2a) above). For example, we will assume that, for two events, e_1 and e_2, in a text, the temporal relation between them is more informative if they are also linked through a discourse relation, e.g., a PDTB relation (Prasad et al., 2008). Making such an assumption will allow us to focus in on the temporal relations that are most valuable without having to exhaustively annotate all event pairs.

Now consider *internal informativeness*. This is information derived from the nature of the relation itself, as defined largely by the algebra of relations (Allen, 1984; Vilain et al., 1986). First, we assume that, for two events, e_1 and e_2, a temporal relation R_1 is more informative than R_2 if R_1 entails R_2. More significantly, however, as noted above, is to capitalize on the relations that inhere between events and the times that anchor them (i.e., (2c) above). Hence, we will say that, given an event, e_1 and a time t_1, a temporal relation R is more informative the more it anchors e_1 to t_1. That is, a containment relation is more informative than an ordering relation, and the smaller the container, the more informative the relation.[1]

The Document Creation Time (DCT) as designed in TimeML is introduced as a reference time, against which the mentioned events and time expressions in the document can be ordered. Consider the text fragment below.

[1]We defer discussion of the formal definition of informativeness for the present paper, as we are focusing on initial results over re-annotated data in TimeBank.

4-10-2011 *Local officials* **reported** *yesterday that a car* **exploded** *in downtown Basra.*

The TimeML annotation guideline (AG) suggests identifying relations between the DCT and textual events. Hence standard markup as in TimeBank results in the following sort of annotation:

(3) a. DCT= t_1, val=10-04-2011
b. t_2 = yesterday, val=09-04-2011
b. e_1 = report
c. e_2 = explode
d. $\text{TLINK}_1 = \text{before}(e_1, t_1)$
e. $\text{TLINK}_2 = \text{before}(e_2, t_1)$
f. $\text{TLINK}_3 = \text{includes}(t_2, e_1)$

This is a prototypical annotation fragment. Notice that by focusing on the link between events and the DCT, the annotator is forced to engage in a kind of periodic "back-and-forth" evaluation of the events in the text, relative to the DCT. While there is a container TIMEX3 that bounds e_1, there is no information given grounding the actual time of the event of interest, namely, the explosion, e_2. By following the AG literally and through no fault of their own, the annotators have missed an opportunity to provide a more informative markup; namely, the identification of the TLINK below:

(4) $\text{TLINK}_4 = \text{includes}(t_2, e_2)$

That is, the explosion occurred on the date valued for *yesterday*, i.e., "09-04-2011".

The point of this paper is to discuss the difference encountered when applying a specification given a particular guideline for annotating a body of text. The example we want to discuss is the manner in which events are linked (related) to the Document Creation Time (DCT) in TimeML. These considerations have arisen in the context of new annotation problems in different genre and domains, hoping to apply the principles of TimeML.

3 Narrative Scope

As previously mentioned, the Narrative Scope of a document is the temporal span over which the events in a document occur, as defined by the timexes in a document. While not every event in a document will necessarily occur inside the Narrative Scope (some may still occur before or after any dates that are specifically mentioned), the Narrative Scope provides a useful container for describing when events discussed most likely occurred. The narrative scope was not considered as part of the annotation task, but it did help to ground the concepts of Narrative Containers and Narrative Times.

4 Narrative Time

As a reader moves through a document, the introduction of a new TIMEX will often shift the temporal focus of the events to be anchored to this new time point (Smith, 2003). These temporal anchors are what we refer to as Narrative Times, and function in much the same way as newly introduced locations in spatial annotation.

However, consider how we can use Narrative Times to increase accuracy of the TLINKS over a document in TimeML. As mentioned above, we distinguish three types of temporal orderings in a text: time-time, event-time, and event-event. The first identifies orderings between two TIMEX3 expressions and is performed automatically. The second identifies what the local Narrative Time for an event is, i.e., how an EVENT is anchored to a TIMEX3. Event-event pairings, for the purposes of this paper, will not be discussed, though they are a vital and complex component of temporal annotation, largely involving discourse relations.

To illustrate our proposed strategy, consider the news article text shown below.

> *April 25, 2010 7:04 p.m. EDT* **-t0**
>
> **S1:** President Obama *paid*-**e1** tribute *Sunday* **-t1** to 29 workers *killed*-**e2** in an *explosion* **-e3** at a West Virginia coal mine *earlier this month*- **t2**, *saying*-**e4** they *died*-**e5** "in pursuit of the American dream."
>
> **S2:** The *blast*-**e6** at the Upper Big Branch Mine was the worst U.S. mine disaster in nearly 40 years.

There are three temporal expressions in the above text: the Document Creation time, **t0**; and two TIMEXes, **t1** and **t2**. Each of these TIMEXes functions as a Narrative Time, as they are clearly providing temporal anchors to nearby events. In this case, all the events are located within the Narrative Time appropriate to them. Hence, the number of orderings is linearly determined by the number of events in the document, since each is identified with a single Narrative Time. Knowing the narrative time associated with each event will allow us to perform limited temporal ordering between events that are associated with different narrative times, which, as mentioned above, is significantly more informative than if events were only given partial orderings to the DCT or to each other.

5 Narrative Containers

So far we have examined sentences that contain specific temporal anchors for the events discussed. Consider, however, the following sentences from article wsj_1031.tml in TimeBank:

> 10-26-1989
> 1 Philip Morris Cos., New York, *adopted* a defense measure *designed* to *make* a hostile *takeover* prohibitively expensive.
>
> 2 The giant foods, tobacco and brewing company *said* it will *issue* common-share purchase rights to shareholders of *record* Nov. 8.

Aside from the DCT, the only TIMEX in these two sentences is Nov. 8, which is only anchoring *issue* and *record*. The other events in the sentences can only be connected to the DCT, and presumably only in a 'before' or 'after' TLINK—in the absence of other information, any reader would assume from the past tenses of *adopted* and *said* that these events occurred before the article was published, and that any events associated with the future (*make, takeover*) are intended to happen after the DCT.

However most readers, knowing that the Wall Street Journal is published daily, will likely assume that any event mentioned which is not specifically associated with a date, occurred within a certain time frame—it would be extremely unusual for a newspaper to use the construction presented above if the events actually occurred, for example, a year or even a week prior to the publication date. We call this assumed window the Narrative Container, as it provides left and right boundaries for when unan-

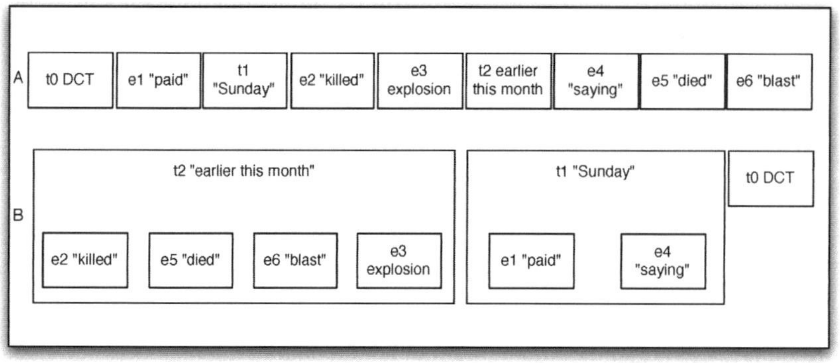

Figure 1: A: Times and events as appearing in the text; B: events grouped into their appropriate Narrative Times.

chored events most likely occurred, where in previous TimeML annotations these events would usually be given one-sided relationships to the DCT. In most cases, the right boundary of the Narrative Container is the DCT. The left boundary, however, requires other factors about the article to be taken into account before it can be given a value. The primary factor is how frequently the source of the document is published, but other aspects of the article may also determine the Narrative Container size.

5.1 Style, Genre, Channel, and Anchors

In order to determine what factors might influence the interpretation of the size of a Narrative Container, we asked an undergraduate researcher to categorize each of the articles in TimeBank according to the following characteristics (Lee, 2001; Biber, 2009).

(5) • Channel: is the document written or spoken?
• Production circumstances: how was the document distributed? broadcast, newswire, daily publication;
• Style: what format was used to present the information?
• Presence of a temporal anchor: Whether an article contained a Narrative Time in the first sentence of the document.

In general, we felt that the production circumstances would be the most relevant in determining the duration of the Narrative Container. The distributions of the different categories in TimeBank are shown in Table 1. There is a 100% overlap between the "broadcast" and "spoken" subcategories—all of those articles are word-for-word transcripts of television news reports. The "style" category proved the most difficult to define—the 'quiz' article is a broadcast transcript of a geography question asked during the evening news, while the 'biography' articles are overviews of people's lives. The editorials include a letter to the editor of the Wall Street Journal and an editorial column from the New York Times.

Category	number	percent
Production Circ.		
broadcast	25	13.7%
daily paper	140	76.5%
newswire	18	9.8%
Channel		
spoken	25	13.7%
written	158	86.3%
Style		
biography	2	1.1%
editorial	2	1.1%
finance	135	73.8%
news	43	23.5%
quiz	1	0.5%
Temporal Anchor		
no	138	75.4%
yes	45	24.6%

Table 1: Distributions of categories in TimeBank

6 Preliminary Studies

In order to assess the validity of our theories on Narrative Containers, Time, and Scope, we asked three undergraduate researchers to re-annotate TimeBank using the Narrative Container theory as a guide.

Each annotator evaluated all of the events in TimeBank by identifying the temporal constraint that anchored the event. If the annotators felt that the event was not specifically anchored, they could place it within the Narrative Container for the document, or they could give the event a simple "before" or "after" value related to the Narrative Container or Document Creation Time. We also asked them to assign start and end times to the Narrative Container for each document.

The annotation here was not intended to be as complete as the TimeBank annotation task, or even the TempEval tasks—rather, the goal was to determine if the Narrative Container theory could be applied in a way that resulted in an increase in informativeness, and whether the annotators could work with the idea of a Narrative Container. Because these annotations are not comprehensive in their scope, the analysis provided here is somewhat preliminary, but we believe it is clear that the use of a Narrative Container in temporal annotations is both informative and intuitive.

6.1 Narrative container agreement

Each annotator was asked to assign a value to the narrative container of each document. They were given limited directions as to what the size of an NC might be: only some suggestions regarding possible correlations between type and frequency of publication and size of the narrative container. For example, it was suggested that a news broadcast might have a narrative container of only a few hours, a daily newspaper would have one of a day (or one that extended to the previous business day), and a newswire article would have a narrative container that extended back 24 hours from the time of publication.

All the annotators agreed that an NC would not extend forward beyond the document creation time (DCT), and that in most cases the NC would end at the DCT. Because the annotators gave their data on the size of the NC in free text (for example, an annotator would say "1 day" to indicate that the NC for an article began the day before the article was published) the comparison of the narrative containers was performed manually by one of the authors to determine if the annotators agreed on the size of the NC.

Agreement was determined using a fairly strict matching criterion—if the narrative containers given were clearly referring to the same interval they were interpreted to be the same. If, however, there was ambiguity about the date or one annotator indicated a smaller time period than another, then they were judged to be different. A common example of ambiguity was related to newspaper articles that were written on Mondays—annotators could not always determine if the events described occurred the day before, or on the previous business day For evaluation purposes, the ambiguous cases were given "maybe" values, but were not included in analysis that relied on the NCs being the same.

Overall, using the strict agreement metric all the annotators agreed on the size of the narrative container in 95 out of 183 articles—slightly over 50% of the time. However, the annotators only completely disagreed on 6 of the 183 articles—in all other cases there was some level of agreement between pairs of annotators.

6.2 NCs and Document Classifications

We compared Narrative Container agreements against the categories outlined above: style, channel, production circumstances, and temporal anchorings in order to determine if any of those attributes lent themselves to agreement about the size of the Narrative Container. We disregarded the biography, quiz, and editorial classifications as those categories were too small to provide useful data.

For the most part, no one category stood out as lending itself to accuracy—newswire had the highest levels of agreement at 72%, while daily papers came in at 58%. Written channels had 60% agreement, and the finance style had 59%. Articles with temporal anchors in the beginning of the document were actually slightly less likely to have agreement on the Narrative Container than those that didn't—48% and 53%, respectively.

While the higher disagreement levels over Narrative Container size in the presence of a temporal anchor seems counter-intuitive, it stems from a simple cause: if the temporal anchor overlapped with the expected narrative container but was not exactly the same size, sometimes one annotator would use that anchor as the Narrative Container, while the others would not. This sometimes also happened with a Narrative Time that was not at the start of the document or sometimes even the Narrative Scope would be used as the Narrative Container. While in some articles it is the case that a Narrative Time anchors more events than the Narrative Container,

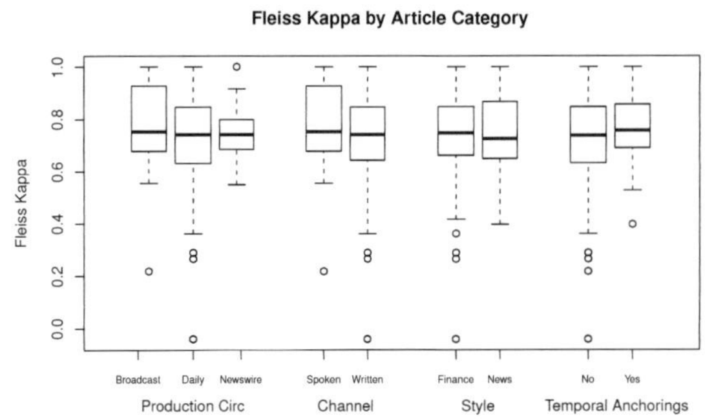

Figure 2: Distributions of Fleiss Kappa scores over TimeBank categories

that does not make that Narrative Time the Narrative Container for the document—the Narrative Container is always the interval during which an unanchored event would be assumed to have taken place. This point of confusion can easily be clarified in the guidelines.

Spoken/broadcast articles had the lowest agreement on Narrative Container size, with none of those articles having complete agreement between annotators. This was largely caused by our annotators not agreeing on how much time those categories would encompass by default–two felt that the narrative containers for broadcast news would extend to only a few hours before going on air, and the other felt that, like a daily paper, the entire previous day would be included when dealing with unanchored times.

As for the question of how large a Narrative Container should be for broadcast articles, the size of all Narrative Containers will need to be studied more in depth in order to determine how widely they can be applied— it is possible that in general, the actual size is less important than the simple concept of the Narrative Container.

6.3 Agreement over event anchors

The annotators were asked to read each article in TimeBank and "create links from each event to the nearest timex or to the DNC." They were asked specifically to not link an event to another event, only to find the time that would be used to anchor each event in a timeline. The annotators were also asked to use only three relationship types: before, after, and is_included (which also stood in for "overlap"). This was done in order to keep the annotation as simple as possible: we wanted to see if the narrative container was a useful tool in temporal annotation, not produce a full gold standard corpus.

This differs from the TimeML annotation guidelines, which suggested only that "A TLINK has to be created each time a temporal relationship holding between events or an event and a time needs to be annotated." (Saurí et al., 2006) Examples given were for sentences such as "John drove to Boston on Monday"—cases where an event was specifically related to a time or another event. However, because such examples were relatively rare, and temporal relationships are not always so clearly expressed, this annotation method resulted in a corpus that was not optimally informative. TimeML also uses a fuller set of temporal relations.

The NC annotations, on the other hand, are much richer in terms of informativeness. Annotators most often linked to the NC, often with an "is_included" relationship (as in: e1 is_included NC). In fact, roughly 50% of the events were linked to the narrative container and had "is_included" as the relationship type. In previous TimeML annotations, most of those events would have been annotated as simply occurring before or overlapping with the document creation time, which is a significantly less informative association. Clearly the narrative container was an intuitive concept for the annotators, and one that was relevant to their annotations.

6.3.1 Inter-annotator agreement

We used Fleiss' kappa (Fleiss, 1971) to obtain values for agreement between the three annotators: first, we compared the number of times they agreed what the temporal anchor for an event should be, then we compared whether those links that matched had the same relation type. Data analysis was done in R with the irr package (R Team, 2009; Gamer et al., 2010).

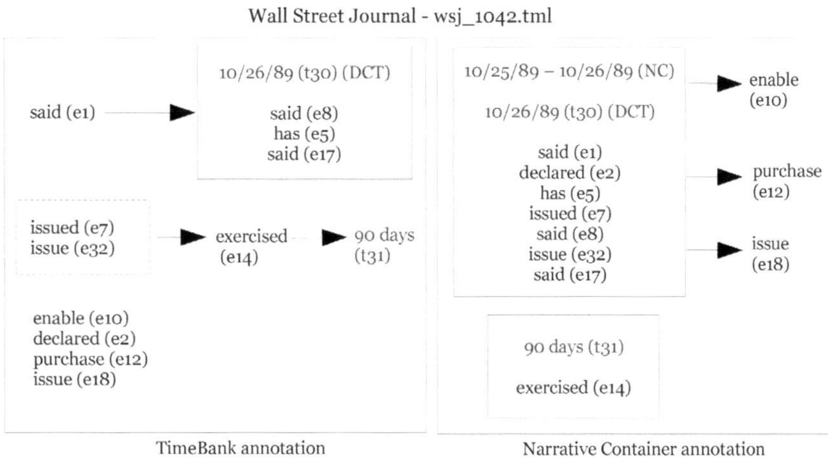

Figure 3: Visual depictions of the TLINK annotations in TimeBank and with the Narrative Container annotations. Solid lines indicate events and times in the box have IS_INCLUDED relationships with the timex at the top, and dotted lines indicate events that were given IDENTITY relationships

When looking at the kappa scores for the temporal anchor, it should be noted that these scores do not always accurately reflect the level of agreement between annotators. Because of the lack of variability, Fleiss' Kappa will interpret any article where an annotator only linked events to the NC received negative agreement scores. These values have been left in the tables as data points, but it should be noted that these annotations are entirely valid—some articles in TimeBank contain no temporal information other than the document creation time (and by extension, the narrative container), making it only natural for the annotators to annotate events only in relation to the narrative container. The average Fleiss' Kappa scores for the temporal anchors was .74, with a maximum of 1 and a minimum of -.04.

6.4 Informativeness in NC Annotation

As we previously described, Narrative Containers are theoretically more informative than Document Creation Times when trying to place unanchored events on a timeline. In practice, they are as informative as we anticipated: compare the visualizations of TLINK annotations between TimeBank and the NC links in Figure 3. These were created from the file wsj_1042.tml, one that had complete agreement between annotators about both the size of the NC (one day before the DCT through the DCT) and all the temporal anchors and temporal relations.

Clearly, the NC task has resulted in a more informative annotation–all the events have at least one constraint, and most have both left and right constraints.

7 Conclusions and Future Work

Narrative Containers, Narrative Times, and Narrative Scopes are important tools for temporal annotation tasks. The analysis provided here clearly shows that annotating with an NC increases informativeness, and that the concept is sufficiently intuitive for it to not add confusion to the already complicated task of temporal annotation. However, the work in this area is far from complete. In the future we intend to study where the left boundary of the NC should be placed for different genres and publication frequencies. Another annotation task must be performed, requiring a more comprehensive TLINK creation guideline, using both event-time and event-event links. Finally, the use of all three concepts for automated annotation tasks should be examined, as they may prove as useful to machines as they are to humans.

Acknowledgements

This work has been supported by NSF grant #0753069 to Co-PI James Pustejovsky. Many thanks to Chiara Graf, Zac Pustejovsky, and Virginia Partridge for their help creating the annotations, and to BJ Harshfield for his R expertise. We would also like to acknowledge Aravind Joshi, Nianwen Xue, and Marc Verhagen for useful input.

References

James Allen. 1984. Towards a general theory of action and time. *Arificial Intelligence*, 23:123–154.

Douglas Biber. 2009. *Register, Genre, and Style*.

J. L. Fleiss. 1971. Measuring nominal scale agreement among many raters. *Psychological Bulletin*, 76(5):378–382.

Matthias Gamer, Jim Lemon, and Ian Fellows Puspendra Singh ¡puspendra.pusp22@gmail.com¿, 2010. *irr: Various Coefficients of Interrater Reliability and Agreement*. R package version 0.83.

Nancy Ide and Harry Bunt. 2010. Anatomy of annotation schemes: Mappings to graf. In *In Proceedings 4th Linguistic Annotation Workshop (LAW IV)*.

Nancy Ide. 2007. Annotation science: From theory to practice and use: Data structures for linguistics resources and applications. In *In Proceedings of the Bienniel GLDV Conference*.

David Lee. 2001. Genres, registers, text types, domains, and styles: Clarifying the concepts and navigating a path through the bnc jungle. *Language Learning & Technology*, 5(3.3):37–72.

Eleni Miltsakaki, Rashmi Prasad, Aravind Joshi, and Bonnie Webber. 2004. The penn discourse treebank. In *In Proceedings of LREC 2004*.

Massimo Poesio. 2004. Discourse annotation and semantic annotation in the gnome corpus. In *In Proceedings of the ACL Workshop on Discourse Annotation*.

Rashmi Prasad, Nikhil Dinesh, Alan Lee, Eleni Miltsakaki, Livio Robaldo, Aravind Joshi, and Bonnie Webber. 2008. The penn discourse treebank 2.0. In *In Proceedings of the 6th International Conference on Language Resources and Evaluation (LREC 2008)*.

James Pustejovsky, Patrick Hanks, Roser Saurì, Andrew See, Robert Gaizauskas, Andrea Setzer, Dragomir Radev, Beth Sundheim, David Day, Lisa Ferro, and Marcia Lazo. 2003. The timebank corpus. In Dawn Archer, Paul Rayson, Andrew Wilson, and Tony McEnery, editors, *Proceedings of the Corpus Linguistics 2003 conference*, pages 647–656, Lancaster University. UCREL.

James Pustejovsky, Robert Knippen, Jessica Littman, and Roser Saurí. 2005. Temporal and event information in natural language text. *Language Resources and Evaluation*, 39:123–164, May.

R Team, 2009. *R: A Language and Environment for Statistical Computing*. R Foundation for Statistical Computing, Vienna, Austria. ISBN 3-900051-07-0.

Roser Saurí, Jessica Littman, Bob Knippen, Robert Gaizauskas, Andrea Setzer, and James Pustejovsky, 2006. *TimeML Annotation Guidelines*, version 1.2.1 edition, January.

Carlota Smith. 2003. *Modes of Discourse*. Cambridge University Press, Cambridge, UK.

Marc Vilain, Henry Kautz, and Peter Beek. 1986. Constraint propagation algorithms for temporal reasoning. In *Readings in Qualitative Reasoning about Physical Systems*, pages 377–382. Morgan Kaufmann.

Discourse-constrained Temporal Annotation

Yuping Zhou
Brandeis University
Waltham, MA 02452
yzhou@brandeis.edu

Nianwen Xue
Brandeis University
Waltham, MA 02452
xuen@brandeis.edu

Abstract

We describe an experiment on a temporal ordering task in this paper. We show that by selecting event pairs based on discourse structure and by modifying the pre-existent temporal classification scheme to fit the data better, we significantly improve inter-annotator agreement, as well as broaden the coverage of the task. We also present analysis of the current temporal classification scheme and propose ways to improve it in future work.

1 Introduction

Event-based temporal inference is a fundamental natural language technology aimed at determining the temporal anchoring and relative temporal ordering between events in text. It supports a wide range of natural language applications such as Information Extraction (Ji, 2010), Question Answering (Harabagiu and Bejan, 2005; Harabagiu and Bejan, 2006) and Text Summarization (Lin and Hovy, 2001; Barzilay et al., 2002). Creating consistently annotated domain-independent data sufficient to train automatic systems has been the bottleneck. While low-level temporal annotation tasks such as identifying events and time expressions are relatively straightforward and can be done with high consistency, high-level tasks necessary to eventually arrange events in a document in a temporal order have proved to be much more challenging.

Among these high-level tasks, the task of annotating the temporal relation between main events stands out as probably the most challenging. This task was the only task in the TempEval campaigns (Verhagen et al., 2009; Verhagen et al., 2010) to deal with inter-sentential temporal relations, and also the only one to directly tackle event ordering. The idea is that events covered in an article are scattered in different sentences, with some, presumably important ones, expressed as predicates in prominent positions of a sentence (i.e. the "main event" of the sentence). By relating main events from different sentences of an article temporally, one could get something of a chain of important events from the article.

This task, in both previously reported attempts, one for English (Verhagen et al., 2009) and the other for Chinese (Xue and Zhou, 2010), has the lowest inter-annotator agreement (at 65%) among all tasks focusing on annotating temporal relations. Verhagen et al. (2009) attribute the difficulty, shared by all tasks annotating temporal relations, mainly to two factors: rampant temporal vagueness in natural language and the fact that annotators are not allowed to skip hard-to-classify cases.

Xue and Zhou (2010) take a closer look at this task specifically. They report that part of the difficulty comes from "wrong" main events (in the sense that they are not main events in the *intended* sense) being selected in the preparation step. This step is a separate task upstream of the temporal relation task. The "wrong" main events produced in this step become part of event pairs whose temporal relation it makes no sense to annotate, and often is hard-to-classify. The reason "wrong" main events get selected is because the selection is based on syntactic criteria. In fact, these syntactic criteria produce results so counter-intuitive that this seemingly simple

Proceedings of the Fifth Law Workshop (LAW V), pages 161–169,
Portland, Oregon, 23-24 June 2011. ©2011 Association for Computational Linguistics

preparation task only achieves 74% inter-annotator agreement.

Another part of the difficulty comes from mechanical pairing of main events for temporal relation annotation. Simply pairing up main events from adjacent sentences oversimplifies the structure within an article and is prone to produce hard-to-classify cases for temporal relation annotation. Both causes point to the need for a deeper level of text analysis to inform temporal annotation. For this, Xue and Zhou (2010) suggest introduction of discourse structure as annotated in the Penn Discourse Treebank (PDTB) into temporal relation annotation.

So the previous two reports, taken together, seem to suggest that the reason this task is especially challenging is because the difficulty associated with temporal vagueness in natural language, which is shared by all tasks dealing with temporal relation, is compounded by the problem of having to annotate far-fetched pairs that should not be annotated, which is unique for the only task dealing with inter-sentential temporal relations. These two problems are the foci of our experiment done on Chinese data.

The paper is organized as follows: In Section 2, we describe the annotation scheme; in Section 3, we describe the annotation procedure; in Section 4 we report and discuss the experiment results. And finally we conclude the paper.

2 Annotation Scheme

As stated in the introduction, there are two problems to be addressed in our experiment. The first problem is that "wrong" main events get identified and main events that do not bear any relation are paired up for temporal annotation. To address this problem, we follow the suggestion by Xue and Zhou (2010), namely using a PDTB-style discourse structure to pick out and pair up main events. We believe that adopting a discourse-constrained approach to temporal annotation will not only improve annotation consistency but also increase the *Informativeness Value* of the annotated data, under the assumption that temporal relations that accord with the discourse structure are more valuable in conveying the overall information of a document. Since there is no Chinese data annotated with PDTB-style discourse structure available, we have to develop our own. The scheme for this step is described in Section 2.1.

The second problem is that there is too much temporal vagueness in natural language with respect to the temporal classification scheme. Since we cannot change the way natural language works, we try to model the classification scheme after the data it is supposed to classify. The scheme for the temporal annotation is covered in Sections 2.2 and 2.3.

2.1 Discourse-constrained selection of main events and their pairs

2.1.1 Discourse annotation scheme

The PDTB adopts a lexically grounded approach to discourse relation annotation (Prasad et al., 2008). Based on discourse connectives like "*since*", "*and*", and "*however*", discourse relation is treated as a predicate taking two *abstract objects* (AO's) (such as events, states, and propositions) as arguments. For example, in the sentence below, "*since*" is the lexical anchor of the relation between Arg1 and Arg2 (example from Prasad et al. (2007)).

(1) Since [$_{Arg2}$ McDonald' s menu prices rose this year], [$_{Arg1}$ the actual decline may have been more].

This notion is generalized to cover discourse relations that do not have a lexical anchor, i.e. implicit discourse relations. For example, in the two-sentence sequence below, although no discourse connective is present, a discourse relation similar to the one in (1) is present between Arg1 and Arg2 (example from Prasad et al. (2007)).

(2) [$_{Arg1}$ Some have raised their cash positions to record levels]. [$_{Arg2}$ High cash positions help buffer a fund when the market falls].

Based on this insight, we have fashioned a scheme tailored to linguistic characteristics of Chinese text. The linguistic characteristics of Chinese text relevant to discussion here can be illustrated with the following sentence.

(3) 据悉 , [$_{AO1}$ 东莞 海关
according to reports , Dongguan Customs
共 接受$_{e1}$ 企业 合同 备案
in total accept company contract record
八千四百多 份] , [$_{AO2}$ 比 试点 前
8400 plus CL , compare pilot before

略 有$_{e2}$ 上升] , [$_{AO3}$企业
slight EXIST increase , company
反应$_{e3}$ 良好] , [$_{AO4}$普遍
respond/response well/good , generally
表示$_{e4}$ 接受] 。
acknowledge accept/acceptance

"According to reports, [$_{AO1}$ Dongguan District Customs accepted$_{e1}$ more than 8400 records of company contracts], [$_{AO2}$ (showing$_{e2}$) a slight increase from before the pilot]. [$_{AO3}$ Companies responded$_{e3}$ well], [$_{AO4}$ generally acknowledging$_{e4}$ acceptance]."

One feature is that it is customary to have complex ideas packed into one sentence in Chinese. The sentence above reports on how a pilot program worked in Dongguan City. Because all that is said is about the pilot program, it is perfectly natural to include it all in a single sentence in Chinese. Intuitively though, there are two different aspects of how the pilot program worked: the number of records and the response from the affected companies. To report the same facts in English, it is probably more natural to break them down into two sentences, but in Chinese, *not only are they merely separated by comma, but also there is no connective relating them.*

Another feature is that grammatical relation between comma-separated chunks within a sentence is not always clear. In the above sentence, for instance, although the grammatical relations between AO1 and AO2, and between AO3 and AO4 are clear in the English translation (i.e. the first in each pair is the main clause and the second an adjunct), it is not at all clear in the original. This is the result of several characteristics of Chinese, for example, there is no inflectional clues on the verb to indicate its grammatical function in the sentence.

Based on these features of Chinese text[1], we have decided to use punctuation as the main potential indicator for discourse relations: the annotator is asked to judge, at every instance of comma, period, colon and semi-colon, if it is an indicator for discourse relation; if both chunks separated by the punctuation are projections of a predicate, then there is a discourse relation between them. Applying this scheme to the sentence in (3), we have four abstract objects as marked up in the example.

[1] A more detailed justification for this scheme is presented in Zhou and Xue (2011).

To determine the exact text span of each argument of a relation, we adopt the *Minimality Principle* formulated in Prasad et al. (2007): only as many clauses and/or sentences should be included in an argument selection as are minimally required and sufficient for the interpretation of the relation. Applying this principle to the sentence in (3), we can delimit the three sets of discourse relations as follows: AO1–AO2, (AO1,AO2)–(AO3,AO4), and AO3–AO4.

2.1.2 Selection and pairing-up of main events

Selection of main events is done on the level of the *simplex* abstract object, with one main event per simplex AO. The main event corresponds to the predicate heading the simplex AO. In (3), there are four simplex AO's, AO1-4 (which further form two *complex* AO's, (AO1,AO2) and (AO3,AO4)). The anchors for the four main events are the underlined verbs labeled as "*e1-4*".

Pairing up the main events is done on the level of discourse relation. In the case of a relation only involving simplex AO's, the main events of the two AO's pair up; in the case of a relation involving complex AO's, the discourse relation is distributed among the simplex AO's to form main event pairs. For example, with the discourse relation (AO1,AO2)–(AO3,AO4), four pairs of main events are formed: *e1–e3*, *e1–e4*, *e2–e3*, and *e2–e4*. This gets tedious fast as the number of simplex AO's in a complex AO increases; in this experiment, the annotator relies on her discretion in such cases. This problem should be addressed in a more elegant way in the future.

It is worth noting that in addition to picking out right main events and event pairs for temporal annotation, this scheme also broadens the coverage of the task. In the old scheme based on syntactic criteria, there is a stipulation: one main event per sentence. Because the new discourse-constrained scheme is tailored to the characteristics of Chinese text, it is able to expose more main events (in the intended sense) to temporal annotation.

2.2 Classification scheme for temporal relation annotation

By modifying the six-value scheme used in TempEval (containing *before, overlap, after, before-or-overlap, overlap-or-after* and *vague*), our classification scheme has seven values in it: *before, overlap, after, **not-before**, **not-after**, **groupie**,* and ***irrelevant***.

2.2.1 The values "*not-before*" and "*not-after*"

The values "*not-before*" and "*not-after*" are equivalent to "*overlap-or-after*" and "*before-or-overlap*" in the TempEval scheme. The reason we made this seemingly vacuous change is because we found that the old values were used for two different purposes by annotators. In addition to their intended use, i.e. to capture indeterminacy between the two simplex values, they were also used to label a specific case of "*overlap*". An example of such misuse of the value "*before-or-overlap*" is presented below:

(4) 一九九六 年 ， [$_{e1}$ 产生] 了 第一 位
1996 year , generate ASP first CL
本地 华人 法官 ， 到 目前 ，
local Chinese judge , until at present ,
已 有 近 二十 位 本地 华人 [$_{e2}$
already EXIST close 20 CL local Chinese
担任] 司法 官员 。
hold the post judicial official .

"The first local ethnic Chinese judge [$_{e1}$ assumed] the office in 1996; up until now, there have been close to 20 ethnic Chinese locals [$_{e2}$ holding] the posts of judicial officials."

The reason for such use is probably because it represents two alternative ways of looking at the temporal relation between the two events : either *e1* is *before* the later bulk of *e2* or *e1 overlaps* the beginning tip of *e2*. To avoid such mis-uses, we made the above change.

2.2.2 The value "*groupie*"

This value is set up for two events whose temporal relation to each other is unclear, but are known to happen within the same temporal range. For example, the temporal relation between the events represented by the underlined verbs should be classified as "*groupie*".

(5) 今 昨 两 天 ， 香港 特区
today yesterday two day , Hong Kong SAR
全国政协 委员 还 [$_{e1}$ 视察] 了 宁波
CPPCC member also inspect ASP Ningbo
开发区 、 宁波 西田信 染织
development district , Ningbo Xitianxin Textile
有限公司 ， [$_{e2}$ 游览] 了 天一阁 、
Ltd. , tour ASP Tianyi Pavilion ,
蒋氏 祖居 。
Chiang ancestral home .

"Yesterday and today, CPPCC members from Hong Kong SAR also [$_{e1}$ visited] Ningbo Development District and Ningbo Xitianxin Textile Ltd., and [$_{e2}$ toured] Tianyi Pavilion and the ancestral home of Chiang Kai-shek."

In this example, the common range shared by the two events is expressed in the form of a time expression, "今昨两天" ("yesterday and today"), but it does not have to be the case. It can be in the form of another event (e.g., "工程建设过程中" ("during the process of project construction")), or another entity with a time stamp (e.g., "八五期间" ("in the Eighth Five-year Plan period")).

It should be noted that the linguistic phenomenon captured by this value can occur in a situation where the internal temporal relation between two events can be classified with another value. So ideally, this value should be set up as a feature parallel to the existent classification scheme. But due to technical restrictions imposed on our experiment, we grouped it with all the others and instructed the annotators to use it only when none of the five more specific values applies.

2.2.3 The value "*irrelevant*"

We substituted this value for the old one "*vague*" because it is too vague. Anything that cannot fit into the classification scheme would be labeled "*vague*", but in fact, some cases are temporally relevant and probably should be characterized in the classification scheme. Case in point are those we now label "*groupie*".

This change reflects our guiding principle for designing the classification scheme. If the relation between two events is temporally relevant, we should try to characterize it in some way; if too many relations are temporally relevant but too vague to fit into the classification scheme (comfortably), then the adequacy of the scheme is questionable.

2.3 An additional specification: which event?

In addition to the classification scheme, it is also necessary to specify which event should be considered for temporal annotation. This question has never been clearly addressed, probably because it seems self-evident: the event in question is the one expressed by the event anchor (usually a verb). This intuitive answer actually accounts for some too-vague-to-classify cases. In some cases, the event that is easily annotated (and should be the one being annotated in our opinion) is not the event expressed by the verb, as is the case in (6).

(6) 在 吸收 外商 投资 方面 ,
PREP absorb foreign business invest aspect ,
中国 现 已 成为 世界 上 利用
China now already become world POSTP utilize
外资 最多 的 发展中 国家。
foreign fund most DE developing country.

"With regard to attracting foreign business investments, China has now become the developing country that utilizes the most foreign funds in the world."

This sentence is taken from an article summarizing China's economic progress during the "Eighth Five-Year Plan" period (from 1991 to 1995). The anchor for the main event of the sentence is clearly "成为" ("become"), but should the event it represents, the process of China becoming the developing country that utilizes the most foreign funds, be considered for the temporal relation annotation? It is both counter-intuitive and impractical.

Intuitively, the sentence is a statement of the *current* state with regard to attracting foreign business investments, not of the process leading up to that state. If we were to consider the process of "becoming" in relation to other events temporally, we would have to ask, *when are the starting and ending points of this process?* How does one decide when it is not made clear in the article? One could conceivably go as far back as to when China did not use one cent of foreign funds. Should it be restricted to the "Eighth Five-Year Plan" period since it is the target period of the whole article? But why use the five-year period, when there are more specific, syntactically explicit aspectual/temporal modifiers in the sentence, i.e. "现已" ("now already"), to restrict it? To make use of these in-sentence aspectual/temporal modifiers, we have to go with our intuition that the event is the current state of China with regard to utilizing foreign investments, i.e. the temporal location of the event is *at present*.

So the event that should be considered for temporal annotation is not the one represented by the event anchor itself, but rather the one *described by the whole clause/sentence headed by the event anchor*. This allows all sorts of temporal clues in the same clause/sentence to help decide the temporal location of the event, hence makes the annotation task easier in many cases.

3 Annotation procedure

The annotation process consists of two separate stages, with a different annotation procedure in place for each. The first stage involves only one annotator, and it deals with picking out pairs of event anchors based on the discourse relation as described in Section 2.1. The output of this stage defines the targets for the next stage of annotation: temporal relation annotation. Temporal relation annotation is a two-phase process, including double-blind annotation by two annotators and then adjudication by a judge.

With this procedure in place, the results we report in Section 4 are all from the second stage. Two annotators go through ten weeks of training, which includes annotating 10 files each week, submitting them to adjudication, and then attending a training session at the end of each week. In the training session, the judge discusses with the annotators her adjudication notes from the previous week, as well as specific questions the annotators raise.

The data set consists of 100 files taken from the Chinese Treebank (Xue et al., 2005). The source of these files is Xinhua newswire. The annotation is carried out within the confines of the Brandeis Annotation Tool (BAT)[2] (Verhagen, 2010).

4 Evaluation and discussion

Table 1 reports the inter-annotator agreement of temporal annotation, both between the two annotators (A and B) and between each annotator and the judge (J), over a training period of ten weeks. Each week, 10 files are assigned, averaging about 315 event pairs for annotation.

Table 1 shows that annotators have taken up the temporal annotation scheme fairly quickly, reaching 75% agreement within three weeks. After several

[2] http://timeml.org/site/bat-versions/bat-redesign

Week	No. of tokens	f(A, B)	f(A, J)	f(B, J)
1	310	0.4806		
2	352	0.6278		
3	308	0.7532		
4	243	0.7737		
5	286	0.8007	0.8601	0.8566
6	299	0.7659	0.8662	0.8896
7	296	0.7973	0.8784	0.8784
8	323	0.7988	0.8978	0.8793
9	358	0.8212	0.9106	0.8966
10	378	0.8439	0.9365	0.8995

Table 1: Inter-annotator agreement over 10 weeks of training.

weeks of consolidation and fine-tuning, the agreement slowly reaches the lower 80% towards the end of the 10-week training period. This level of agreement is a substantial improvement over the previously reported results, at 65%, for both English and Chinese data (Verhagen et al., 2009; Xue and Zhou, 2010). This indicates that the general direction of our experiment is on the right track.

Table 2 below is the confusion matrix based on the annotation data from the final 4 weeks:

	a	b	o	na	nb	g	i
a	148	3	19	0	1	0	1
b	0	344	29	1	0	0	7
o	14	10	1354	3	3	2	82
na	0	0	3	3	0	0	0
nb	0	0	1	0	1	0	0
g	2	1	9	0	0	13	1
i	3	7	67	0	0	1	572

Table 2: Confusion matrix on annotation from Weeks 7-10: *a=after; b=before; o=overlap; na=not-after; nb=not-before; g=groupie; i=irrelevant.*

The matrix is fairly clean except when the value "*overlap*" is concerned. This value really stands out in more than one way. It is the most nebulous one in the whole scheme, prone to be confused with all six other values. In particular, it is most likely to be confused with the value "*irrelevant*". It is also the most used value among all seven values, covering roughly half of the tokens. We will discuss this value in more detail in Section 4.2 below.

The value "*groupie*" may also seem troublesome if we look at mis-classification as a percentage of its total occurrences, however, it may not be as bad as it seems. As pointed out in Section 2.2.2, despite the fact that the linguistic phenomenon this value captures can, and does, co-occur with temporal relations represented by other values, we had to set it up as an opposing value to the rest due to technical restrictions. If/when this value is set up as a stand-alone feature to capture the linguistic phenomenon fully, the percentage of mis-classification should drop significantly because the number of total occurrences will increase dramatically.

The overall distribution of values shown in Table 2 is very skewed. At one end of the distribution spectrum is the value *"overlap"*, covering half of the data; at the other end are the values "*not-before*" and "*not-after*", covering less than 0.3% of the token combined. It raises the question if such a classification scheme is well-designed to produce data useful for machine learning.

To shed light on what is behind the numbers and to uncover trends that numbers do not show, we also take a closer look at the annotation data. Three issues stand out.

4.1 Event anchor

In our current scheme, effort is made to pick out the predicate from a clause as the event anchor for temporal annotation. Our experiment suggests maybe this step should be skipped since it, in practice, undermines a specification of the scheme. The specification is that the event to be considered for temporal annotation is the one being described by *the whole clause*, but the practice of displaying a mere word to the annotator in effect instructs the annotator to concentrate on *the word* itself, rather than the clause. Despite repeated reminder during training sessions, the suggestive power of the display still sometimes gets the upper hand. (7) presents such an example concerning *e1* and *e2*.

(7) 在 此 期间 ， 西非 维和
PREP this period , West Africa peacekeeping
部队 曾 [$_{e1}$ 出动] 战斗机 轰炸 叛军
force once dispatch fighter jet bomb rebel
阵地 ， [$_{e2}$ 炸死] 叛军 约 ５０余
position , bomb-dead rebel about 50 plus

人。
CL

"During this period, West African Peacekeeping Force [$_{e1}$ dispatched] fighter jets and bombed rebel positions, [$_{e2}$ killing] about 50 rebel troops."

One annotator classified the relation as "*before*", obviously thinking of the event of dispatching fighter jets as *e1*; had he considered the event of dispatching fighter jets *and* bombing the rebel positions, the event being described by the clause, the value would have easily been "*overlap*".

Since displaying the single-word event anchor sometimes leads annotators astray, this step probably should be skipped. Doing so also simplifies the annotation process.

4.2 The value "*overlap*"

As pointed out above, the value "*overlap*" is quite a troubling character in the classification scheme: it is both the most-used and probably the least well-defined. Annotation data show that when it is confused with "*after*", "*before*", "*not-after*", and "*not-before*", it usually involves a perceptually punctual event ("pp-event" henceforth) and a perceptually lasting event ("pl-event" henceforth), and the issue is whether the pp-event coincides with one of the temporal edges of the pl-event. If it does, then the value is "*overlap*"; otherwise, it is "*after*"/"*before*". And on top of it is the factor of how sure one is of the issue: if one is sure, either way, the value is "*overlap*"/"*after*"/"*before*"; otherwise, it is "*not-after*"/"*not-before*". Below is an example on which the two annotators disagree as to whether the relation between *e1* and *e2* should be classified as "*before*" or "*overlap*".

(8) 此外 , 巴西 女子 国家队 在
in addition , Brazil woman national team PREP
南美 足球赛 上 , [$_{e1}$ 横扫]
S. America soccer match POSTP , sweep
千军 如 卷 席 , [$_{e2}$ 登上] 了
thousand-troop like roll mat , ascend ASP
冠军 宝座 。
champion throne .

"In addition, in the South America Cup, Brazilian Women's national team totally [$_{e1}$ annihilated] all their opponents and [$_{e2}$ ascended] the throne of champion."

In this example, *e2* is the pp-event and *e1* is the pl-event. Depending on when one thinks *e2* happened, either as soon as the last match ended or at the later medal ceremony, (and if the former, whether there is temporal overlap between *e1* and *e2*), it is classified as either "*before*" or "*overlap*; and if one is unsure, it can be classified as "*not-after*".

Such cases again raise the same question as the drastically uneven distribution of values shown in Table 2: *Does the current classification scheme slice the temporal pie the right way?* Let us make a poster child out of "*overlap*": it seems to both impose too stringent a condition and not make enough distinction. It imposes too stringent a condition on those cases like (8) to which whether there is temporal overlap seems beside the point. At the same time, it does not make enough distinction for cases like (4), in which an event does share one edge of another event temporally: once such cases are classified as "*overlap*", the specific information regarding the edge is lost. Such information could be very useful in temporal inference. Since it is infeasible to annotate the temporal relation between all events in an article, temporal inference is needed to expand the scope of temporal annotation. For example, if it is known from annotation that *e1* is before *e2* and *e2* is before *e3*, then it can be inferred *e1* is before *e3*. In the case of "*overlap*", whenever it is one of the premises, no inference can be made, but if the "edge" information is supplied, some inferences are possible.

To make finer-grained distinctions in the classification scheme runs counter to the conventional wisdom that a coarser-grained scheme would do a better job handling vagueness. But our experiment has proven the conventional wisdom wrong: our seven-value system achieved much higher agreement than the old six-value system. So the key is not *fewer*, but *better*, distinctions, "better" in the sense that they characterize the data in a more intuitive and insightful way. Temporal relation in natural language is "too" vague only when we judge it against a system of temporal logic, in fact, we think the right word to describe temporal relation in natural language is "*flexible*": it is as precise as the situation calls for. To characterize the flexibility better, for starters, "*overlap*" needs to be restructured for reasons put forth above, and "*not-before*" and "*not-*

after" should be discarded since they obviously do not carry weight.

4.3 Objective vs. subjective temporal reference

A major contributor to uncertainty and disagreement in annotation is subjective temporal reference. Subjective temporal reference is made based on the author's perspective of the temporal axis, for example, "今天" ("today"), "目前" ("at present), and "过去" ("past"). In this group, references with a fixed span do not constitute a problem once the point of utterance is determined (e.g. literal use of "*today*", "*this month*"); it is those with an elastic temporal span that cause disagreement. For example, *"at present"* can have a span of a second, or several minutes, or a couple of hours, or even years depending on the context. When an event modified with this type of temporal expression is paired with another event modified with direct reference to a point/span on the temporal axis (i.e. with an objective reference), annotation becomes tricky. The event pair *e1-e2* in the two-sentence sequence below is such an example.

(9) 过去 , 在 长江 上 建 大桥
past , PREP Yangtze River POSTP build bridge
是 件 国家大事 , 现今 几乎 [$_{e1}$
be CL national affair , nowadays almost
成为] 平常事。 一九九二年, 江苏
become common scene. 1992-year, Jiangsu
扬中县 农民 [$_{e2}$ 集资]
Yangzhong County farmer raise funds
建成 了 扬中 长江 大桥 , 而
build-finish ASP Yangzhong Yangtze Bridge , and
湖北 的 赤壁 长江 大桥 总 投资
Hubei DE Chibi Yangtze Bridge total invest
三亿多 元 , 全部 靠 民间
300 million plus Yuan , all depend private
集资 建成 。
raise funds build-finish .

"In the past, building a bridge on Yangtze River was a national affair, nowadays it almost [$_{e1}$becomes] a common scene. In 1992, farmers in Yangzhong County, Jiangsu Province [$_{e2}$raised] funds and completed Yangzhong Yangtze Bridge, while Chibi Yangtze Bridge in Hubei Province cost more than 300 million Yuan, all from private fund-raising."

This is taken from a piece written in 1997. In the context, it is clear that the contrast is between the situation before the opening-up of China and the situation about 20 years later. So it is reasonable to assume that the year 1992 falls inside the span of what the author considered *nowadays*; at the same time, it seems also reasonable to assume a narrow interpretation of "现今" ("nowadays") that does not include the year 1992 in the span. These two interpretations would result in "*overlap*" and "*after*" respectively, and actually did so in our experiment.

There are also extreme cases in which objective and subjective temporal references come in direct conflict. For example,

(10) 当 记者 [$_{e1}$ 问及] 中 俄
while reporter ask about China Russia
关系 的 现状 和 合作 前景
relationship DE status and cooperation prospect
时 , 江泽民 主席 [$_{e2}$ 说] , ...
when , Jiang Zemin President say , ...

"When a reporter [$_{e1}$ asked] about the status of China-Russia relationship and the prospects for cooperation, President Jiang Zemin [$_{e2}$ said], ..."

The relation between *e1* and *e2* is *before* based on objective reference, but *overlap* according to the subjective reference, indicated by "当..时" ("when"). This problem should be factored in when a new classification scheme is designed.

5 Conclusions

In this paper, we have described an experiment that focuses on two aspects of the task of annotating temporal relation of main events: annotation target selection and a better-fitting temporal classification scheme. Experiment results show that selecting main event pairs based on discourse structure and modeling the classification scheme after the data improves inter-annotator agreement dramatically. Results also show weakness of the current temporal classification scheme. For that, we propose a restructuring along the lines of what this experiment has proven working: making more intuitive and insightful distinctions that characterize the data better. This direction can be taken to improve other high-level temporal annotation tasks that have been plagued by the same "vagueness" problem.

Acknowledgments

This work is supported by the National Science Foundation via Grant No. 0855184 entitled "Building a community resource for temporal inference in Chinese". All views expressed in this paper are those of the authors and do not necessarily represent the view of the National Science Foundation.

References

Regina Barzilay, Noemie Elhadad, and Kathleen McKeown. 2002. Inferring strategies for sentence ordering in multidocument news summarization. *Journal of Artificial Intelligence Research*, 17:35–55.

Sanda Harabagiu and Cosmin Adrian Bejan. 2005. Question Answering Based on Temporal Inference. In *Proceedings of the AAAI-2005 Workshop on Inference for Textual Question Answering*, Pittsburgh, Pennsylvania.

Sanda Harabagiu and Cosmin Adrian Bejan. 2006. An Answer Bank for Temporal Inference. In *Proceedings of LREC 2006*, Genoa, Italy.

Heng Ji. 2010. Challenges from information extraction to information fusion. In *Proceedings of COLING 2010*, pages 507–515, Beijing, China, August.

Chin-Yew Lin and Eduard Hovy. 2001. Neats: A multidocument summarizer. In *Proceedings of the Document Understanding Workshop*.

Rashmi Prasad, Eleni Miltsakaki, Nikhil Dinesh, Alan Lee, Aravind Joshi, Livio Robaldo, and Bonnie Webber, 2007. *The Penn Discourse Treebank 2.0 Annotation Manual*. The PDTB Research Group, December.

Rashmi Prasad, Nikhil Dinesh, Alan Lee, Eleni Miltsakaki, Livio Robaldo, Aravind Joshi, and Bonnie Webber. 2008. The Penn Discourse Treebank 2.0. In *Proceedings of the 6th International Conference on Language Resources and Evaluation (LREC 2008)*.

Marc Verhagen, Robert Gaizauskas, Frank Schilder, Mark Hepple, Jessica Moszkowicz, and James Pustejovsky. 2009. The TempEval Challenge: Identifying Temporal Relation in Text. *Language Resources and Evaluation*, 43(1):161–179.

Marc Verhagen, Roser Sauri, Tommaso Caselli, and James Pustejovsky. 2010. Semeval-2010 task 13: Tempeval-2. In *Proceedings of the 5th International Workshop on Semantic Evaluation*, pages 57–62, Uppsala, Sweden, July. Association for Computational Linguistics.

Marc Verhagen. 2010. The Brandeis Annotation Tool. In *Language Resources and Evaluation Conference, LREC 2010*, pages 3638–3643, Malta.

Nianwen Xue and Yuping Zhou. 2010. Applying Syntactic, Semantic and Discourse Constraints to Chinese Temporal Annotation. In *Proceedings of COLING 2010*, pages 1363–1372, Beijing, China, August.

Nianwen Xue, Fei Xia, Fu dong Chiou, and Martha Palmer. 2005. The Penn Chinese TreeBank: Phrase Structure Annotation of a Large Corpus. *Natural Language Engineering*, 11(2):207–238.

Yuping Zhou and Nianwen Xue. 2011. A PDTB-inspired Discourse Annotation Scheme for Chinese. Submitted to EMNLP 2011.

Author Index